# The Aff Photo 2 Instant Professional

The world's most user-friendly English-language guide to the powerful image processing software for photography professionals, covering photo editing, illustrations, and much more!

--For both Mac and Windows--

The copyrights for the Affinity_designer images used in this volume belong to Serif(Europe)_Ltd.
For any other photos used in this book, copyright information is noted individually.
Serif is a registered trademark of Serif(Europe)_Ltd.
Affinity is a register trademark of Serif(Europe)_Ltd.
"Illustrator" and "Photoshop" are registered trademarks of Adobe Systems Incorporated in the U.S. and other countries.

Photo shown on cover © Xavi

## Using this Book Efficiently

Affinity_Photo is a highly effective piece of software for processing digital photographs. Still, no software is useful unless you know how to use it. This book uses a tutorial format to explain the multiple, complex features of this software on an easy-to-understand presentation. The easiest and fastest way to master a piece of software, whether the user is a beginner or a professional, is to learn as you go along.

For this reason the book begins with a quick tutorial (Chapter 2). Professionals can get the gist of the software through this Chapter. Starting with Chapter 3, the book uses a Tutorial format for each chapter. This format allows even bare beginners to learn to do professional-quality work simply by following the specific examples noted here. Also the book is set up such that users can search for tool names in the Table of Contents to refer back and re-read a section at any time.

We recommend that first-time users of a paint-style software study in the following order: image processing such as merging photos, re-touching, effects, adjustment, image appearance, seatings, text design work, etc.

The second half of this book offers detailed explanations of current digital photo technologies that conventional photographers may find challenging, including raw data images, 32-bit HDR editing, tone mapping, panorama, and more. Packed with information, we are pleased that this volume will be beneficial for everyone from beginners to professionals.

The authors have been granted permission to use the photographs contained in this volume through the Creative Commons Website. Copyright holders are listed below and at the end of the book. Secondary use of this volume is prohibited.

# Index

**Chapter 1: Overview of Affinity_Photo** ............ 9
1_1: The Affinity_Photo Operating Environment ............ 10
**Chapter 2: Quick Tour and Tutorial** ............ 12
2_1: Start the Affinity_Photo Quick Tour ............ 13
2_2: Move Object/Shrink or Enlarge/Edit/Rotate ............ 32
2_3: Quit Affinity_Photo and Save ............ 53
Chapter 3: Learning to Basics of Afffinity Photo ............ 54
3_1: Opening a New Document ............ 55
3_2: Open file/Open PDF ............ 59
3_3: Open from Clipboard ............ 60
3_4: Enlarge or Shrink an Open Document/Pan ............ 61
**Chapter 4: Affinity Photo Structure and Interface** ............ 62
4_1: Interface Structure Group ............ 63
4_2: Explore the Menu Bar ............ 64
4_3: About Affinity Photo Personas ............ 66
4_4: Photo Persona ............ 67
4_5: Liquify Persona ............ 73
4_6: Develop Persona ............ 74
4_7: Tone Mapping Persona ............ 77
4_8: Export Persona ............ 78
**Chapter 5: Overview of the Photo Persona** ............ 79
5_1: Create a Unique Visual Image with Photo Persona ............ 80
5_2: New document settings ............ 81
5_3: Insert Photo in Document ............ 82
5_4: Use the Transform Panel to Change Object Size ............ 83
5_5: Layers ............ 84
5_6: Zoom Tool ............ 85
5_7: Use Navigator to Shrink or Enlarge ............ 86
5_8: Rasterize an Object (Layer) ............ 87
5_9: Use the Selection Brush Tool to Select Part of an Image ............ 88
5_10: Make your Selection Using Quick Mask Mode ............ 90

| | |
|---|---|
| 5_11: Saving and Importing Selections | 93 |
| 5_13: Create a Selection for the Outline | 94 |
| 5_12: Use Invert Pixel Selection to reverse your selection | 94 |
| 5_14: Copying and Pasting | 96 |
| 5_15: Rectangular/Elliptical/Column/Row Marquee Tool: Understanding the Differences | 97 |
| 5_16: Blending Layers | 100 |
| 5_17: Using the Filter | 104 |
| 5_18: Grouping and Ungrouping Layers | 105 |
| 5_19: Merging Layers | 106 |
| 5_20: Crop Image | 107 |
| 5_21: Flatten All Layers | 108 |
| 5_22: Use Flood Select Tool to Select | 109 |
| 5_23: Using the Flood Fill Tool to fill in large areas with color | 110 |
| 5_24: Using the Gradient Tool to create gradation | 112 |
| 5_25: Understanding How the Paint Brush Tool Works | 117 |
| 5_26: Use the Color Replacement Brush Tool to change the color of the flower from red to blue | 125 |
| 5_27: Pixel Tool | 127 |
| 5_28: The Paint Mixer Brush Tool: it's just like a real paint brush! | 129 |
| 5_29: Use the Erase Brush Tool to delete an image | 131 |
| 5_30: Use the Background Erase Brush to create a transparent background | 132 |
| 5_31: Use the Flood Erase Tool to turn the background transparent with a single click | 132 |
| 5_32: Use the Color Picker Tool to instantly pick up the image color | 133 |
| 5_33: Use the Dodge Brush Tool to lighten any part of your image. | 134 |
| 5_34: Use the Burn Brush Tool to darken part or parts of your mage | 135 |
| 5_35: Use the Sponge Brush Tool to boost image saturation | 136 |
| 5_36: Use the Clone Brush to copy a part or parts of an image and stamp it | 137 |
| 5_37: Use the Undo Brush Tool to render painted areas semitransparent | 139 |
| 5_38: Use the Smudge Brush Tool to blend color as if smudging with your finger | 140 |
| 5_39: Use the Blur Brush Tool to blur part or parts of an image | 141 |
| 5_40: Use the Sharpen Brush Tool | 142 |
| 5_41: Use the Median Brush Tool to eliminate noise for part or parts of an image | 143 |
| 5_42: Be a master at cropping! | 144 |

5_43: Difference Between a JPEG File Opened with File>Open and File>Place  146

5_44: Alter Object Using Place Command after Rasterize  149

## Chapter 6: Using the Retouch Tools   152

6_1: Using the Retouch Tools  153

6_2: Use the Healing Bush to Clone Sheep  155

6_3: Use the Patch Tool to Remove Problem Areas  158

6_4: Use the Blemish Removal Too to Erase Minor Imperfections  159

6_5: Use the Inpainting Brush Tool to erase any unneeded areas of a photo  160

6_6: Use the Red Eye Removal Tool to Correct Red Eye  162

6_7: Use the Mesh Warp Tool to Create an Abstract Look  163

6_8: Use the Perspective Tool (Single Plane) to Correct Tilt  167

6_9: Use the Perspective Tool (Dual Plane) to Correct from a Two-Point Perspective  170

## Chapter 7: Using the Liquefy Persona   174

7_1: Using the Liquefy Persona  175

7_2: Using the Liquefy Persona Masking Tool (Liquify Freeze Tool)  176

7_3: Use the Liquefy Push Forward Tool to enlarge the face portion only  177

7_4: Use the Liquefy Push Left Too to Transform Object  178

7_5: Use the Liquefy Twirl To to Rotate Clockwise  179

7_6: Use the Liquefy Pinch Tool for a Face Close-Up  179

7_7: Use the Liquefy Punch Tool for a Concave Effect  180

7_8: Use the Liquefy Turbulence Tool to Fragment Photo  180

7_9: Liquefy Mesh Clone Tool  181

7_10: Use the Liquefy Turbulence Tool to Correct Distortion  182

## Chapter 8: Using the Drawing Tools (Vector Data)   183

8_1: Using the Pen Tool  184

8_2: Using the Node Tool  185

8_3: Use the Pen Tool to Draw a Curved Line  186

8_4: Use the Node Tool to Connect Curved Lines  187

8_5: Working with Pressure Levels in Line Drawing  188

8_6: The Rectangular Tool: Draw Lines and Fill  191

8_7: Draw an Ellipse with the Ellipse Tool  194

8_8: UUse the Ellipse Tool to Draw a Donut, Fan, etc.  195

| | |
|---|---|
| 8_9: Rounded Rectangle Tool: Color settings for lines and the screen | 196 |
| 8_10: Changing the Shape with the Rounded Rectangle Tool | 197 |
| 8_11: Draw a triangle with the Triangle Tool | 198 |
| 8_12: Drawing with the Diamond Tool | 199 |
| 8_13: Use the Trapezoid Tool to draw | 200 |
| 8_14: Using the Double Star Tool to Draw | 201 |
| 8_15: Draw a polygon with the Polygon Tool | 202 |
| 8_16: Draw a variety of stars with the Star Tool | 204 |
| 8_17: Using the Square Star Tool to Draw | 206 |
| 8_19: Using the Donut Tool to Draw | 210 |
| 8_20: Use the Cloud Tool to Draw | 211 |
| 8_21: Using the Pie Tool to Draw | 212 |
| 8_22: Using the Segment Tool | 214 |
| 8_23: Use the Crescent Tool to Draw | 216 |
| 8_24: Use the Cog Tool to Draw | 218 |
| 8_25: Use the Callout Rounded Rectangle Tool to Draw Balloons | 220 |
| 8_26: Use the Callout Ellipse Tool to Draw a Balloon | 222 |
| 8_27: Use the Tear Tool to Draw | 224 |
| 8_28: Use the Heart Tool to Draw | 226 |
| 8_29: Line up Multiple Figures | 227 |
| 8_30: Create a Composite Object | 230 |
| 8_31: Change the figure to curve | 232 |
| 8_32: Duplicate and Object | 237 |
| **Chapter 9: Using the Text Tool** | **241** |
| 9_1: Inputting text | 242 |
| 9_2: Using the Artistic Text Tool to input text | 244 |
| 9_3: Use the Frame Text Tool to input the main text | 245 |
| 9_4: Beautiful framing: the Tracking feature | 246 |
| 9_5: Leading Override between lines | 247 |
| 9_6: Vertical Scale/Horizontal Scale | 249 |

## Chapter 9: Using the Text Tool 250
9_7: Change Text Color 251
9_8: TText Kerning and Outlining 252
## Chapter 10: Effects 257
10_1: Using Filters 258
10_2: Creating an Effect for an Object 265
## Chapter 11: The Three Primary Colors/Adjusting Color 273
11_1: The Three Primary Colors 274
11_2: Adjusting Color 275
11_3: The Three Primary Colors (RGB) 289
11_4: Create a Channel Mixer Color Circle 290
11_5: Use the Color Channel to Change Car Color from Red to Yellow 297
## Chapter 12: Data Export Formats/Configuration/Alignment/Record Macro 303
12_1: Export in Different Format 304
12_2: Place Object on Screen 305
12_3: Object (layer) Alignment 306
12_4: Record a Macro 307
12_5: Exporting with Batch Jobs/Batch Processing of Raw Data 310
## Chapter 13: Raw Data Processing 311
13_1: Opening Raw Data Images 312
13_2: The Develop Assistant Feature 313
13_3: Use the Split Display for Raw Data Processing 313
13_4: Adjust Raw Data Exposure 314
13_5: Check Clipping 315
13_6: Adjust Enhance/White Balance/Shadows & Highlights 316
13_7: Develop Persona Overlays Feature 317
13_8: Lens Panel 318
13_9: Details Panel 318
13_10: Other Panels 318
13_11: Synchronize Settings in Display Mode 319

**Chapter 14: 32bitHDR editing/Tone mapping/32bitOpenEXR**    320

14_1: Creating a 32-bit HDR formatted image    321

14_2: Use Tone Mapping on a High Dynamic Range Image (HDR)    323

14_3: 32-bit OpenEXR Import/Export    325

**Chapter 15: Image Stacking/Focus Merge/Panorama/Equirectangular Projection**    326

15_1: Imaging Stacking Feature    327

15_2: Use Focus Merge to create focused images both near and far    329

15_3: Creating a Panorama Photo    330

15_4: Equirectangular (Panorama) Live Projection Mapping    333

15_5: Edit Live Projection    334

**Chapter 16: Create a Slice/Compatible Formats and Export/Configuration**    337

16_1: Create a 32-Bit HDR Formatted Image    338

16_2: Create a Slice and Export    341

16_3: Affinity Photo Export Format    342

16_4: Importing to Affinity Photo    347

# Chapter 1: Overview of Affinity_Photo

Chapter 1: Overview of Affinity_Photo

Affinity_Photo is a professional-grade photo editing software. An all-around player, it accommodates a wide variety of formats ranging from Bitmap data to vector data. Bitmap data, a data format that recreates images using colored dots, is suitable for showcasing complex tones such as in photographs. The vector data format, which involves re-creation of images using mathematical calculations including coordinates and the lines that connect them, is ideal for use in figures and diagrams.

Affinity_Photo reads virtually all digital Paint software formats including illustrator data (.ai), Photoshop, PNG, PDF, RAW, and more. It is also write-compatible for a number of applications, as described in subsequent chapters.

### 1_1: The Affinity_Photo Operating Environment

First, ensure that your system meets the following requirements:
Mac: OSXL Lion (10.12.0) or later, 64-bit processor, 2GB or greater of RAM, 601 MB or greater of hard disk space, a display of 1224X768 or higher resolution, compatibility with MacOS Sierra (10.12.0)

Windows: Windows 7/8/10 or later, 64-bit processor, 2GB or greater of RAM, 624 MB or greater of hard disk space, and a display of 1224X768 or higher resolution

Note that photos shown are current Web pages as of the time this was written.

Chapter 1: Overview of Affinity_Photo

## The first step: Install Affinity_Photo

Go to the Website and download the software:
https://affinity.serif.com/

Hit **Menu**, followed by **Affinity Photo**, **Mac Version** or **Windows Version** to purchase. Follow the instructions provided and install on your PC.

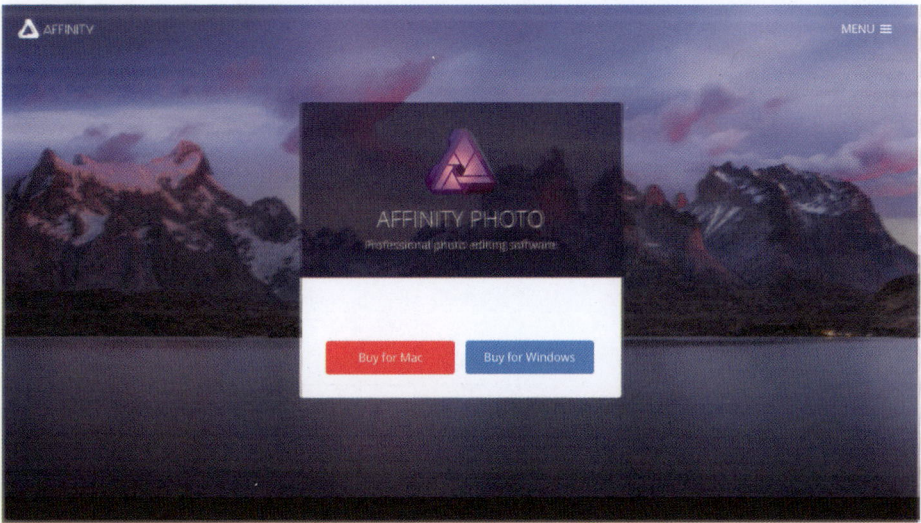

Note that photos shown are current Web pages as of the time this was written.

"Serif" ia a registered trademark of Serif (Europe) Ltd.
"Affinity" is a registered tradmark of Serif (Europe) Ltd.
"Apple," "App Store," "iPhone," and "iPad" are registered trademarks or service logs of Apple Inc.
"Adobe" and Photoshop" are trademarks or registered tradmarks of Adobe Systems Incorporated in the U.S. and other countries.

# Chapter 2: Quick Tour and Tutorial

Chapter 2: Quick Tour and Tutorial

## 2_1: Start the Affinity_Photo Quick Tour

The best way to quickly and easily understand key Affinity_Photo operations, features, etc., is to take the Quick Tour noted in this chapter. If you have used digital painting software before, you should be able to utilize this software for your work almost immediately. For those new to digital painting software, we recommend that you first take the Quick Tour to get a general understanding of operations, and then proceed to the fine points of Affinity_Photo starting with the next Chapter. Let's get started!

**Click on the Affinity_Photo icon to launch.**

Once you have clicked on the Affinity_Photo icon, you will see the following screen. This is the Affinity_Photo workspace. Hit **Exit** when you see **the Future Work screen**.

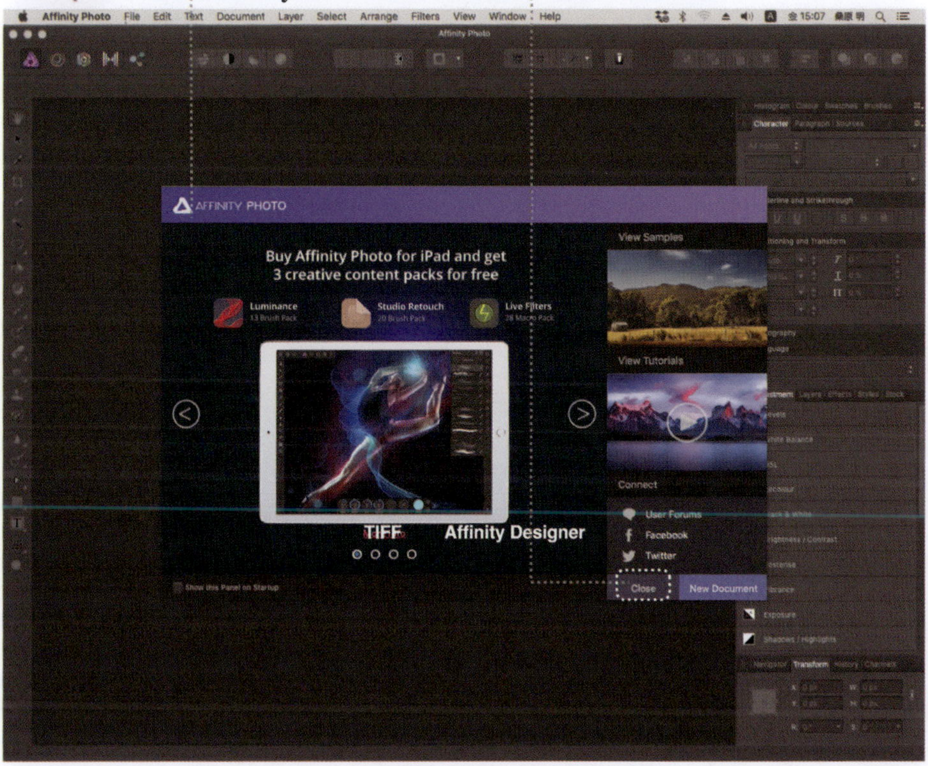

13

Chapter 2: Quick Tour and Tutorial

Click on **File** on the Menu Bar to show the Dropdown Menu. Then click **New**.

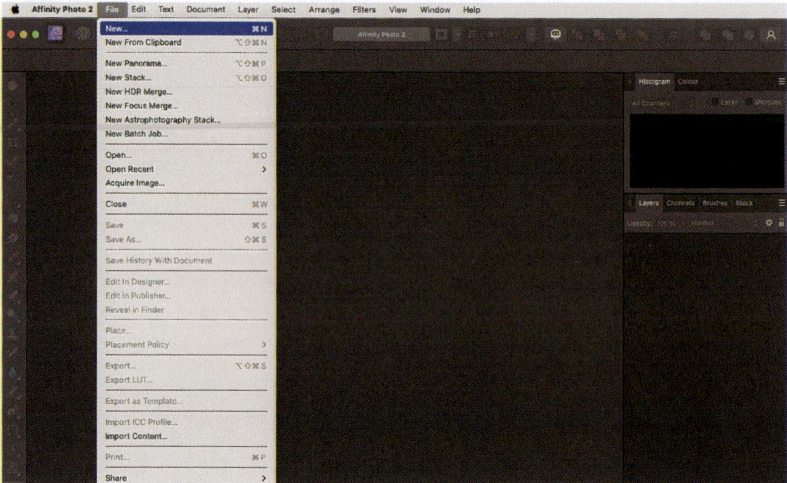

The Document Settings screen appears. Details will follow, but for the moment we recommend memorizing the names of the larger headings. Settings including the following can be adjusted from the top:
**Type**, Page Preset, Document Units, Color Format, Color Profile, Page Width, Page Height, DPI, Margins, etc. For learning purposes, however, use the Default settings and press **Crate**.

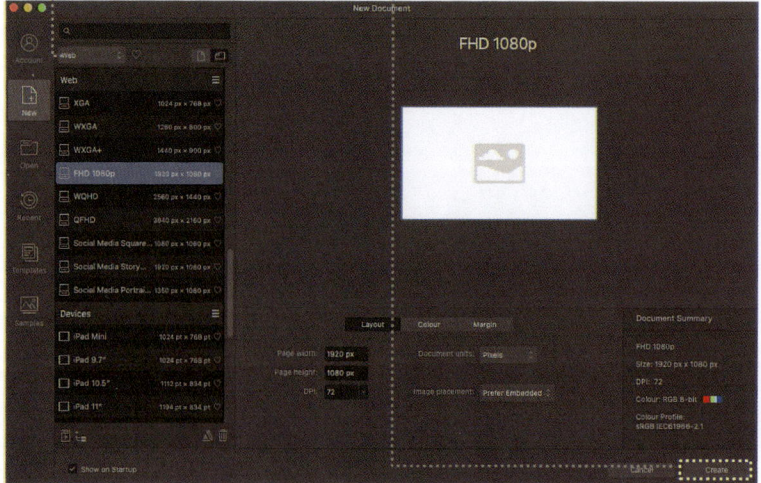

14

Chapter 2: Quick Tour and Tutorial

This is the workspace layout of Affinity_Photo. At the top is **the Menu Bar**, underneath followed by **the Persona Tool Bar**, which features **Photo Persona, Liquify Persona, Develop Persona, Tone Mapping Persona** and **Export Persona**. Next to the bar is the editing icon used for the set of tools. Find **the Context Tool** underneath this bar.

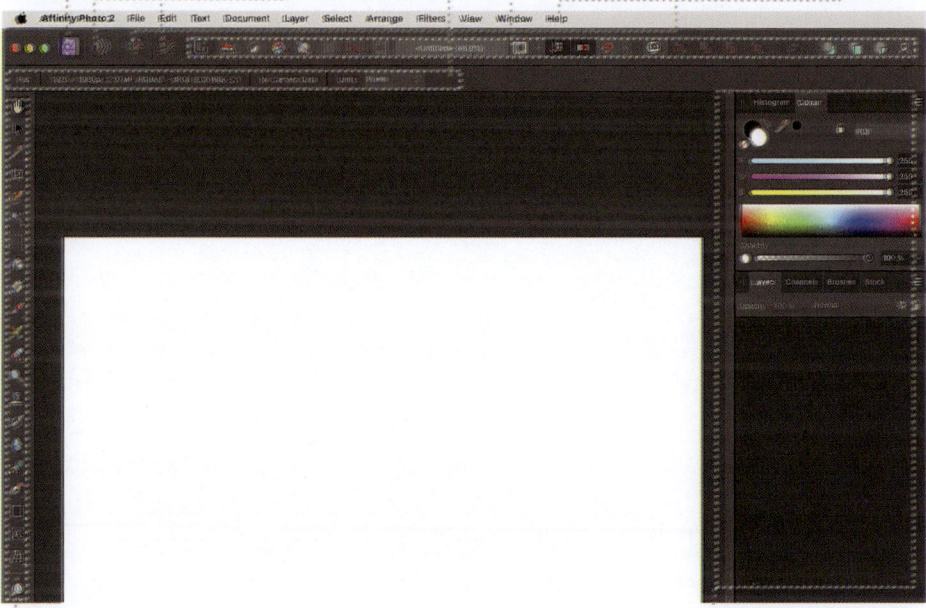

**The Tool Panel** is the series of vertically postioned icons on the left. When you select any of the tools, the Context Tool Bar buttons at the top change features to accomodate the individual tool. On the right is **the Studio Panel**. Settings on this panel can be adjusted visually for color, layers, and more.

Once you have viewed the Workspace Layout, close Affinity_Photo. Click **Affinity_Photo** and **Quit** to end your session.

Chapter 2: Quick Tour and Tutorial

**Affinity_Photo is compatible with various file formats.**

Affinity_Photo is capable of opening files in various digital painting software files formats, including Illustrator and Photoshop. Now let's try opening Affinity_Photo using a different order of operations than last time. If you have a file (e.g **a JPEG photo**) in one of the file formats listed below on your PC, drag it to the top of the Affinity_Photo icon.

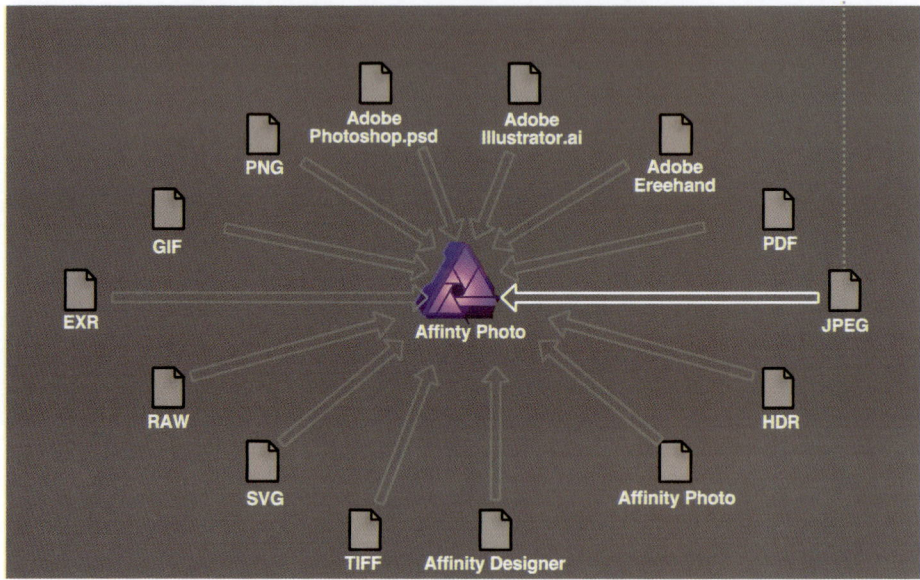

If you don't have a photo appropriate for learning purposes, you may use the following JPEG on the author's site Launch your Internet browser and enter the correct address in the URL line.

**http://goo.gl/poq163**
Click on the image and save under a new name.

Note: Note: The above address utilizes Google url shortener.

Chapter 2: Quick Tour and Tutorial

## Using Affinity_Photo Tools

Were you able to open the file (either your own file or the JPEG on the author's site)? For example, When you first open the JPEG file, you may notice that you are **unable to edit the Image/Object**. This is because the image first needs to be unlocked. Click on **the Lock/Unlock icon** on the **Layer Tab** to the right (Lock/Unlock) to unlock. You may now edit the Image/Object.

As noted below, the X has is now **a circle** (o). Make sure that **the Lock icon has disappeared**, and proceed with the following steps.

17

Chapter 2: Quick Tour and Tutorial

First, let's check to make sure that we can edit the Image/Object. Click on **the Move Tool**, and drag **the left point** to the right. Note that the object width has shrunk. By maneuvering **the eight points**, we can control Object size, rotation, etc.

Once you have checked your work, go back to your original. Use Command/Control*+Z or hit **Menu Bar**, **Edit**, **Undo**. Note that at this point your photo is not horizontally level. Affinity_Photo features tools that can fix this problem easily. Locate the **Crop Tool** on the left-hand Tool Panel and click on it.

Note: "Command" for Mac, "Control" for Windows.

18

## Chapter 2: Quick Tour and Tutorial

Click on the Crop Tool to change the **Context Tool Bar**. This is the selected Tool Settings Menu. Click on the **Straighten** button to straighten the Object. Click to **the left** on the Horizon and drag to the **the right-hand Horizon**.

Correct sloping. **Using the mouse, move the cursor upward.**

Chapter 2: Quick Tour and Tutorial

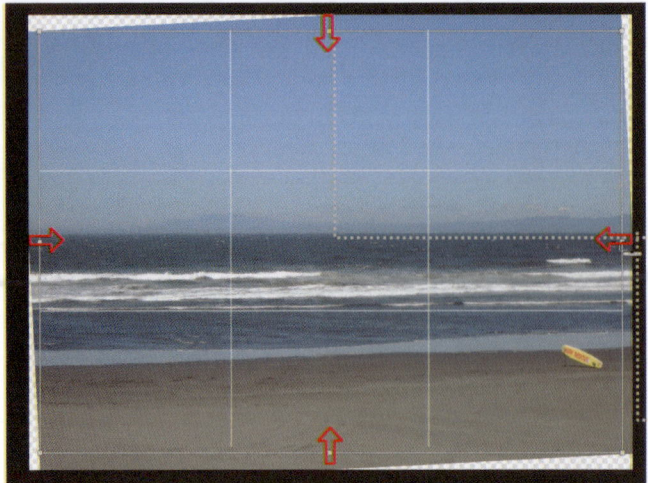

Note that the the tilt has been corrected, there is now unwanted space in the upper and lower as well as left and right margins. Let's crop to fix it. Note **the arrows** in the center of the top-bottom and right-left margins. Grab **the arrows** and drag toward the inside.

Double-click on the Object to check on your cropping.
Note that this is just one small example of Affinity_Photo's vast array of features. At this point, you should have a sense of how easy the software is to use.

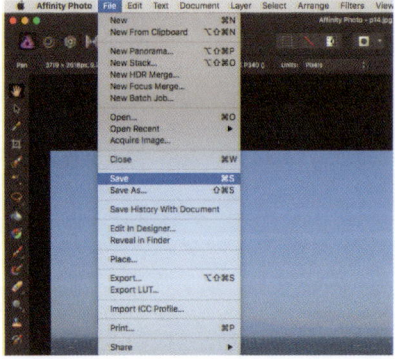

Let's now save the file. Click on File and **Save** to open the dialog box below. Hit **Save As** and give the file a new name. Click **Quit** to conclude your session.

20

Chapter 2: Quick Tour and Tutorial

## Photo Editing

This volume was designed entirely with Affinity_Photo, from cover to cover. Now let's get to the editing of the cover photo. To give this a try, first you need a photo. The author downloaded free photographs from the Creative Commons link: http://creativecommons.org
Creative Commons is operated based on a truly admirable philosophy. Provided that the rules noted on the site are observed, it can be utilized by virtually anyone. For this reason it is highly recommended by the author.

Launch your Internet browser and type in the URL noted below.
**http://goo.gl/8K3rSR**
This photo is edited as follows to devise the cover design.

Note: The above address utilizes Google url shortener. If the link is broken, search the Creative Commons (http://creativecommons.org) site.

# Chapter 2: Quick Tour and Tutorial

Do you have your photo ready to work with? Click on the Affinity Photo icon to launch. Close the Future Work and other screens. Click **File** and **Open** to begin working. When the folder appears, select your photo. Does it look like the screen below? Click on **Studio**, followed by **Layers** and the Lock icon. If the image is locked, hit **the Lock icon** to unlock.

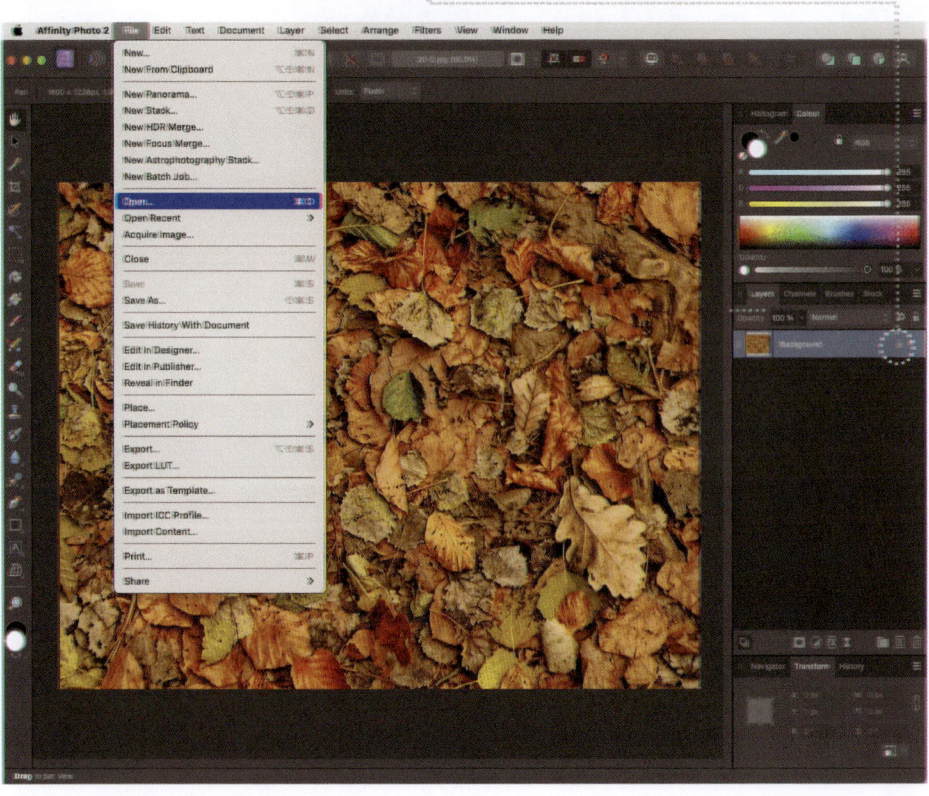

## Select Painting Area

To edit pixel data (format where image is displayed as dots), use the Select Tool. Determine any limitations on the painting area of the image, and use the array of tools as desired, e.g. fill in with color, copy, devise a mask for the layers, delete, etc. The Select Tools are shown in broken lines in the selected areas.

Let's now give the Select Tools a try. Find **the Selection Brush Tool** on the Tool Panel to the left. Click on it, and then click **Add** to add **Mode** to Context Menu, click on the **Width flyout button** and select **25 px**. **Drag any of the leaves.**

When you **drag** one of the leaves, note how the tool automatically selects the contour of the leaf. See how smart the Selection Brush Tool is! Let's continue.

Still, even smart tools make mistakes! To correct any spilling over in your selections, click **Mode** on **Context Tool**, followed by **Subtract**. Then drag from **the outside of your selection**.

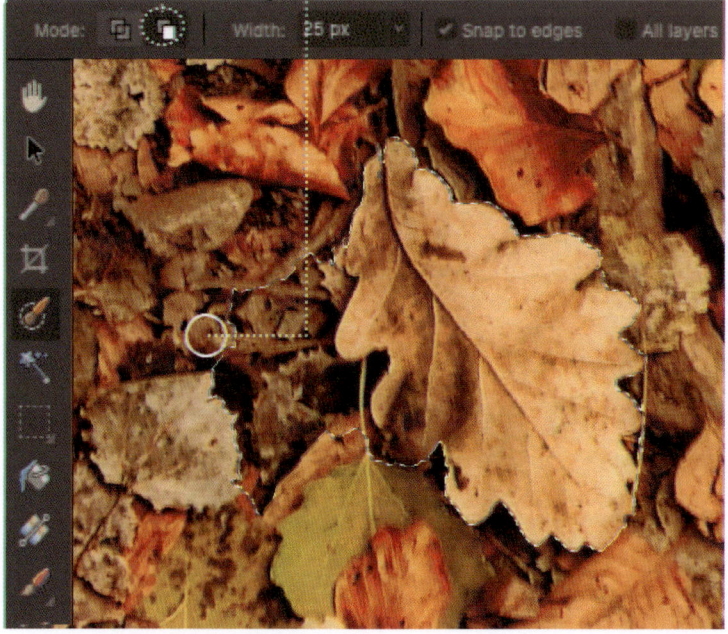

Chapter 2: Quick Tour and Tutorial

How does it look? You've now successfully selected the leaf. Use the Select Tool to switch as you wish between **Add** and **Subtract** modes to create your selection as you wish.

Next, continue to select more leaves, one at a time.

25

## Tone correction (adjustment)

Affinity_Photo offers an array of color correction and adjustment features. Once you have selected a number of fallen leaves, Click **Studio** followed by the **Adjustments** tab to show Menu options. Then select **Recolor**. When the **Recolor** settings panel appears, note that the selected leaves have turned red in color. This is because the Default value is set at red.

Next, move the slider to the point where **the blue tone is nearly purple**. Slide **Saturation** to 90%, and click **the Add Preset button**.

Chapter 2: Quick Tour and Tutorial

Once you are satisfied with the recoloring, delete your selection. Click **Menu Bar** and **Select**, followed by **Deselect**. This feature is useful if you unintentionally erase your selection: simply follow these steps to re-select.

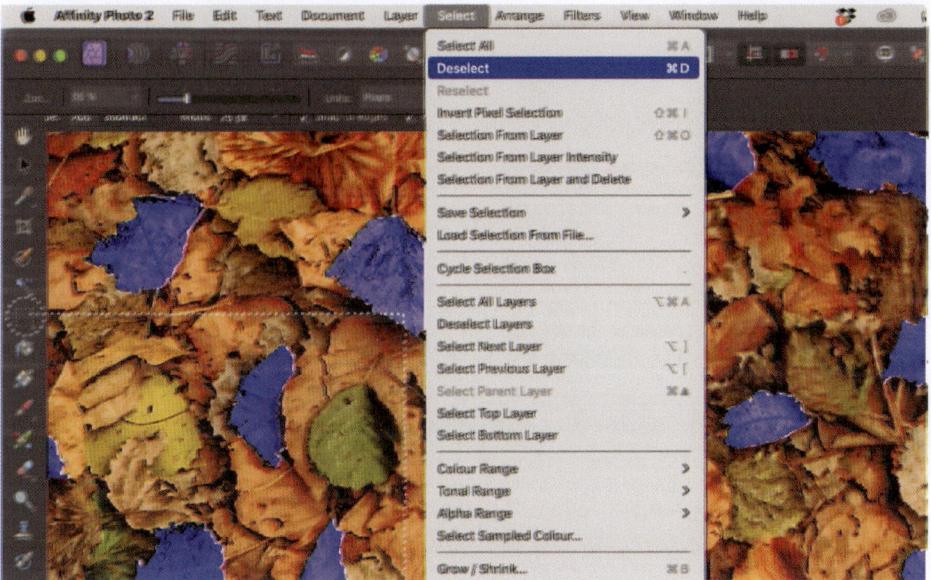

Additionally, you may use **the Marquee Tool** by clicking outside of your selection to delete it. If you accidentally delete your selection, use Command + Z for Mac and Control + Z for Windows to restore it.

27

Chapter 2: Quick Tour and Tutorial

As above, use **the Selection Brush Tool** to select a different leaf.

Once you have selected another leaf, try changing colors by hitting **Studio**, **Adjustment**, and **Channel Mixer.** Computer screen image colors recreate all colors with the three primary colors of Red, Green, and Blue. Next, let's try controlling **the Red output channel** to change colors. On the Channel Mixer settings panel, select "Red" as the Output channel Slide the output-adjust **red slider** from 100% to the left, all the way to 0%. Note that the color is now **green**. Since the red element in the yellow is now at zero, the color changes to green. Details on the Channel Mixer will be provided subsequently chapters.

Chapter 2: Quick Tour and Tutorial

Close the Color Channel panel to delete your selection. In a difference with the above example, here we did not click the Combine Button. Looking at **the Layer Panel**, the layers we worked on in the Color Channel are now active. Because the layers have not yet been combined, they can still be changed at this point. Still, to prevent any mistakes in operation, right-click on the layer and click **Merge Selected** to create a single layer as in the example above.

Next, select a leaf for which the color has not yet been changed. Now let's try HSL, which stands for Hue, Saturation, and Luminosity (HSL). Click on **Adjustment**, followed by **HSL**. Slide **Hue shift** to 121.1°, Saturation and Luminosity to 0%, **Opacity** to 75%, and Blend mode to **Soft Light**. Then click the **Merge** button to Deselect.

29

Chapter 2: Quick Tour and Tutorial

Lastly, adjust overall white balance. Click **Adjustment** followed by **White Balance**. On the White Balance settings panel, slide the bar to **the right, to around 20%**, to add a slight yellow hue to the image.

On the Layer Panel, click on **Merge Selected**. This completes the color correction process.

Chapter 2: Quick Tour and Tutorial

Next, we'll learn more specifics about the Move Tool, We'll conclude our work for this section here. Click **Menu Bar**, **Affinity Photo 2**, and **Quit** to name your file and save it.

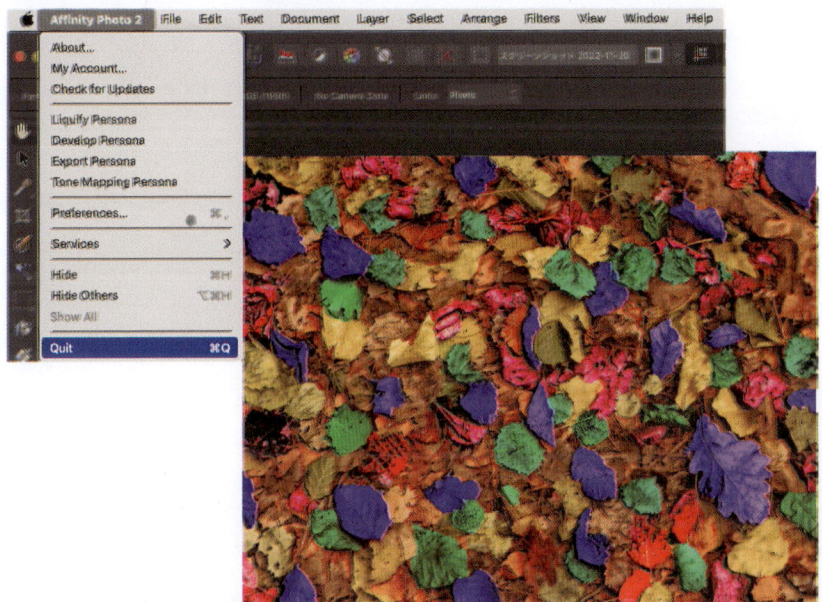

Once you have saved it, double-click on the file and open it. Click **Menu Bar**, **File**, **Save As**, and give it a different name. The reason for this is that we will be trying out a number of new features and then reverting to the original. If you are unable to get back to your original, you have the option to begin again with a previously saved file.

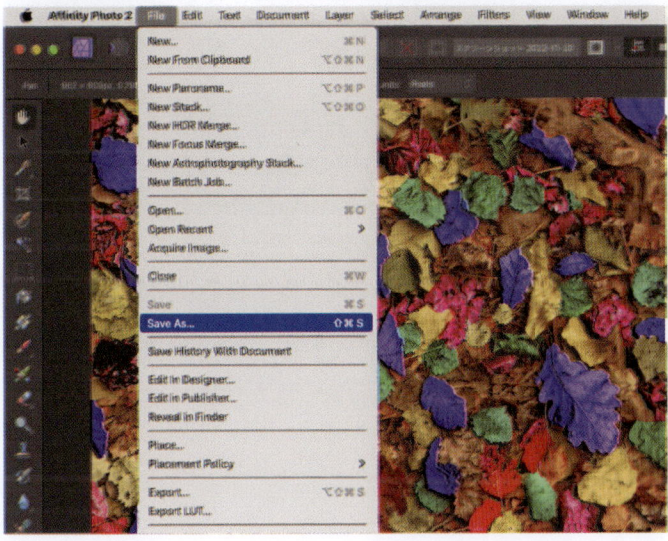

31

Chapter 2: Quick Tour and Tutorial

## 2_2: Move Object/Shrink or Enlarge/Edit/Rotate

Often we want to expand or rotate a photo to give it a different look. For this purpose, the Move Tool is a very convenient option. Since this tool is used quite frequently, let's now try a quick review. Click on **Move Tool** on the Tool Panel, and click on the Object (photo) to display eight points as well as the anchor point. Grasp **the corner point** at the top left and drag downward diagonally.

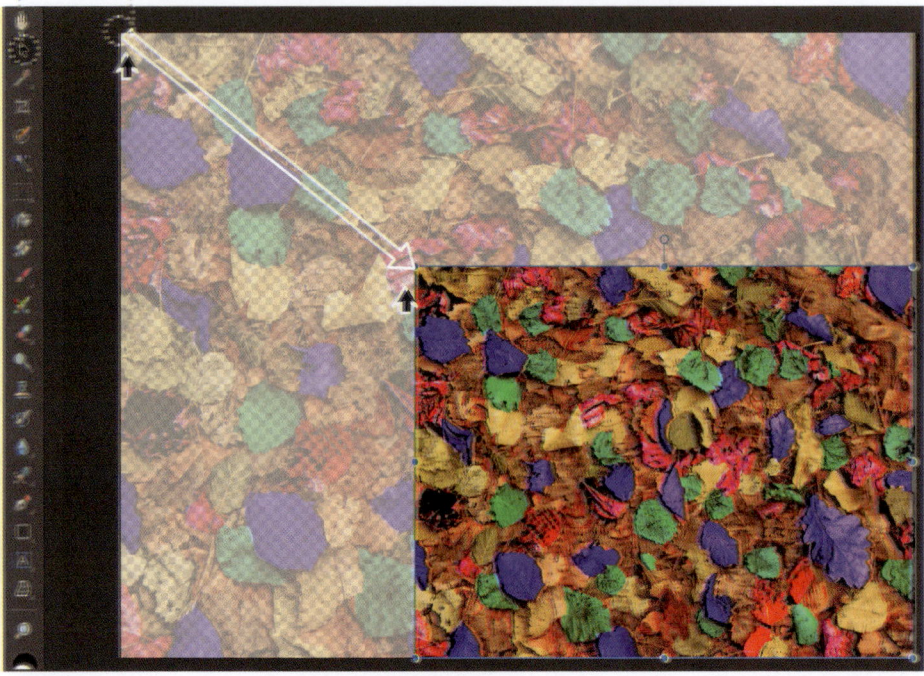

Were you able to shrink the object? **Move Tool** can be used to Select, Move, Expand, Shrink, Rotate, or Draw Diagonally. Incidentally, when you want to shrink more than one object equally in both the horizontal and vertical directions, drag holding down the Shift button.

Chapter 2: Quick Tour and Tutorial

Once you have shrunk the Object, then try to move it. Click on **the desired point on the Object** and drag to the center. The key here is to make sure that **the eight points and the anchor point** are showing. Mouse-over a point or next to it to show **the arrow**. The arrow provides us with some hints on how to shrink and enlarge, tilt, alter, or rotate.

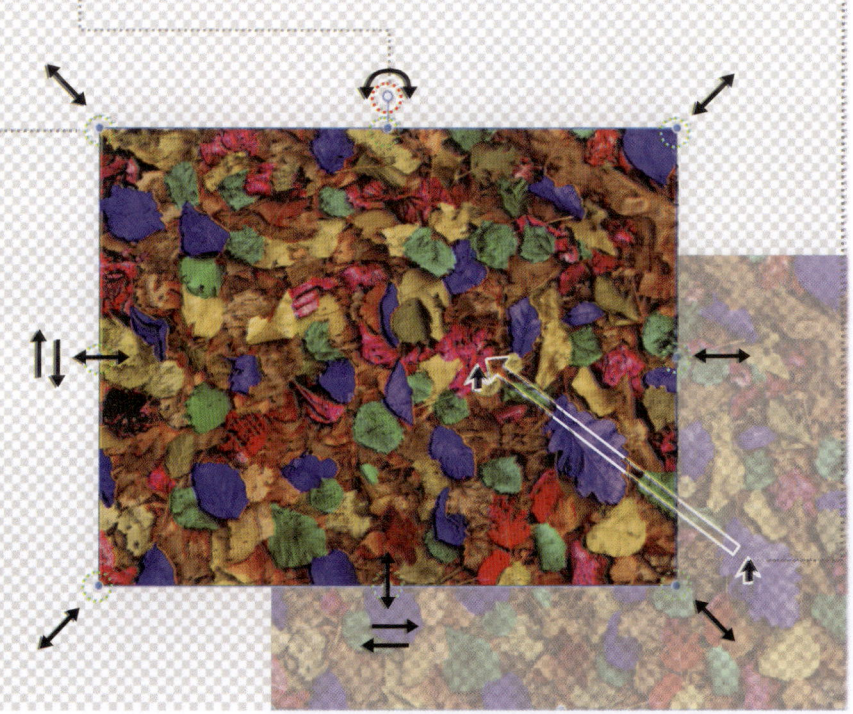

33

Chapter 2: Quick Tour and Tutorial

A pair of arrows are displayed when the mouse is placed over **a point**. Grab it and drag to the left to shrink from right to left while keeping the margins the same. Restore using Command/Control + Z.

Let's try the Rotate function. To rotate, bring the tool close to **the angle point**. You will see the arrow icon. Then drag to rotate. Restore using Command/Control + Z.

Chapter 2: Quick Tour and Tutorial

Bringing the Move tool near **the point**, you will notice a pair of arrows in the direction of the margins. Drag the point upward. Note the tilt.

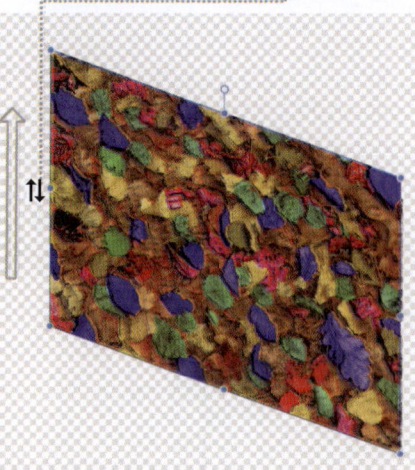

Bring the Move Tool underneath **the point**, you will see a pair of arrows to the right and left. Drag to tilt to the horizontal diagonal. The Move tool is a multi-purpose tool used for everything from object selection to editing objects. Best of all, since it can be easily manipulated with a little intuition, it is extremely easy to use.

Next, use Command/Control +Z to restore the original image, as follows.

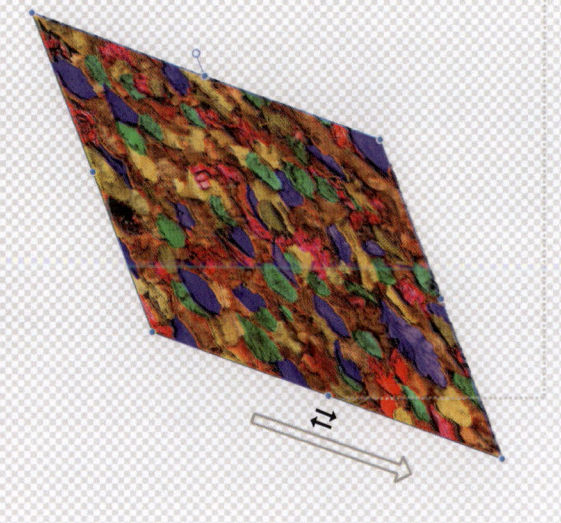

Chapter 2: Quick Tour and Tutorial

Once you are accustomed to using the Move Tool, take the following steps. Here we are going to create a cover page. To vertically adjust the size of the cover, we change the canvas size. Hit Menu>Document>**Resize Canvas.**

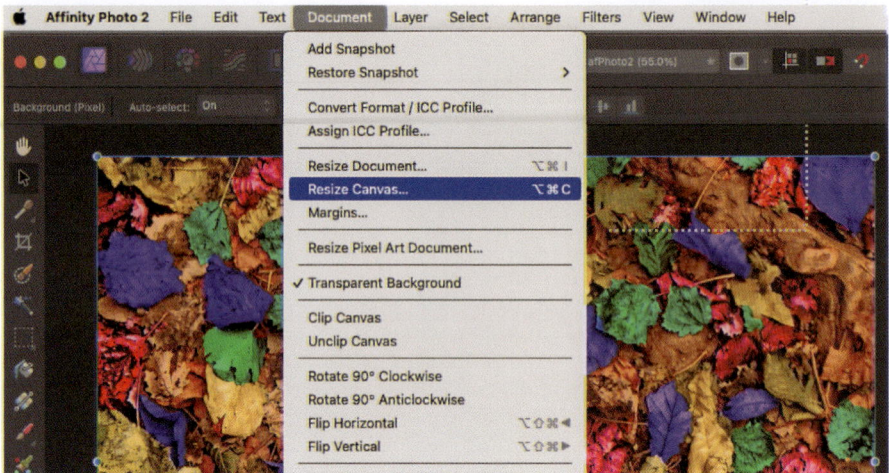

Note that the Size Panel has dropped down. When you see **the Lock symbol**, click on it to unlock. Enter **Size**: 1360 px, 1772 px and click on the **Resize** button.

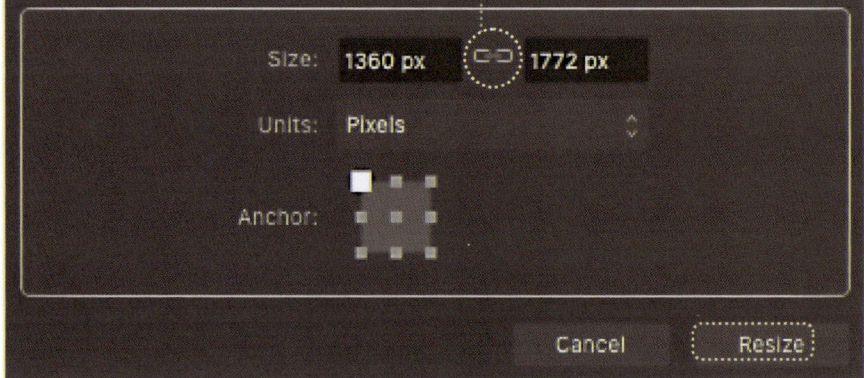

Chapter 2: Quick Tour and Tutorial

Note that the canvas is now vertical. Next, let's expand the object so that it fits the screen, and trim it. Switch to the Move Tool, grab **the corner points at the bottom left**, and drag diagonally to the left. Enlarge the object, considering the composition, so that it protrudes slightly from the edges. Incidentally, the grey checkered pattern represents the transparent portion of the image.

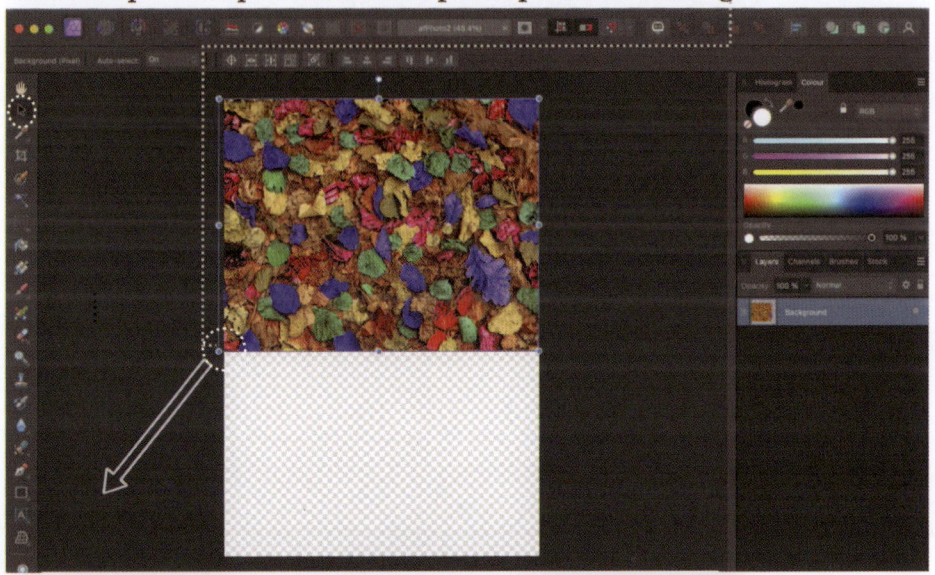

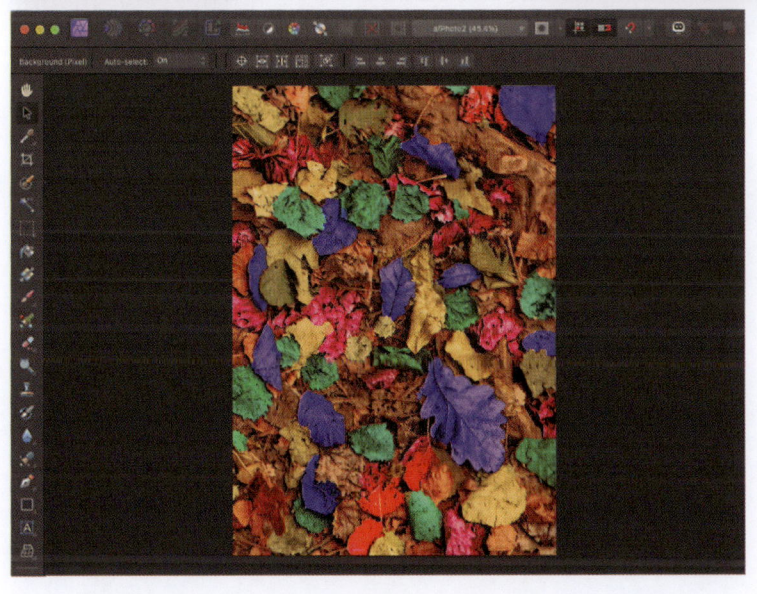

Chapter 2: Quick Tour and Tutorial

Next, position **the Rectangular Marquee Tool** in the lower half of the picture. Holding down the Shift button, choose your Selection and **drag to create a square**.

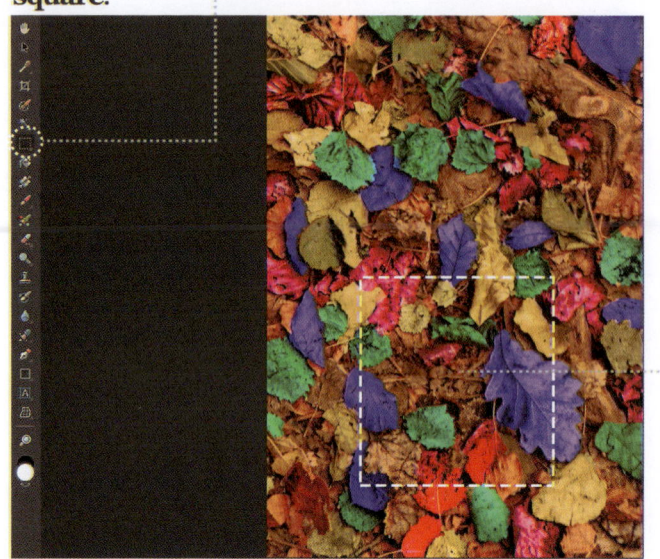

Change your selection to Black and White. Click on Studio>Adjustment>**Black & White** to open the Settings panel. **Your selection should now be monotone**. Keep the default settings for now. Click on the Object to close the Settings panel. It should now be in monotone.

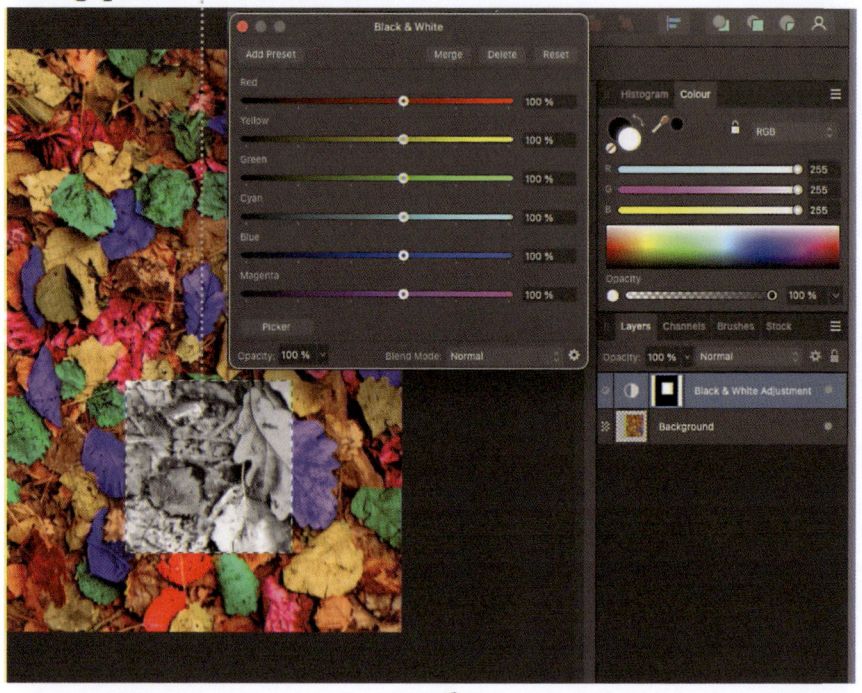

# Chapter 2: Quick Tour and Tutorial

The monotone is fine as it is, but it might be somewhat bright, which means that it may lack modulation.

Next, click Studio>Adjustment>**Brightness/Contrast**. Use the Slider to adjust Brightness to **-53%** and Contrast to **13%**.

Chapter 2: Quick Tour and Tutorial

Once you have three layers (Studio>Layers), click on all the layers to **activate**. Click on **the Group Layers icon** to group the layers.

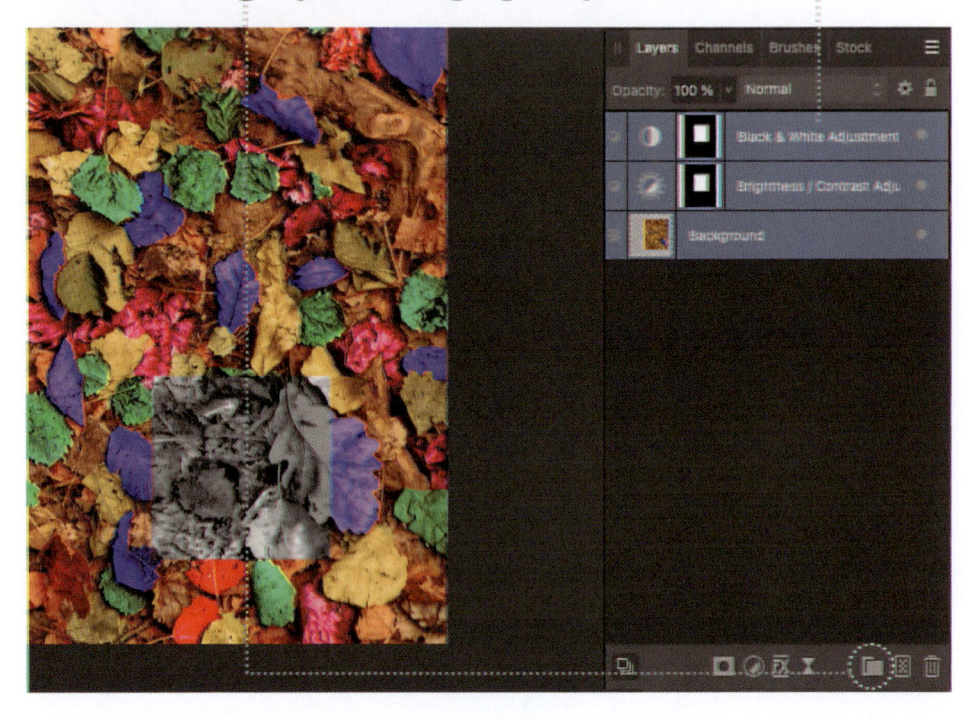

## Draw Figure

Next, let's draw a figure. Affinity_Photo is compatible not only with Bitmap data used in photo editing, but also the vector data used in figures. As noted above, vector data is a data format capable of re-creating images using numeric calculations to generate coordinates and the lines connecting them. Now let's take a moment to draw a figure. Open the Tool Panel and select the Ellipse Tool. This tool can instantly create a variety of shapes. Note that **the Flyout button** is located next to the Ellipse Tool. Click on it to show other tool icons. This time, Select **the Ellipse Tool**. Using the Shift button, **drag the monotone area from left to right to create a circle**. Release the Shift button to draw an elliptical instead.

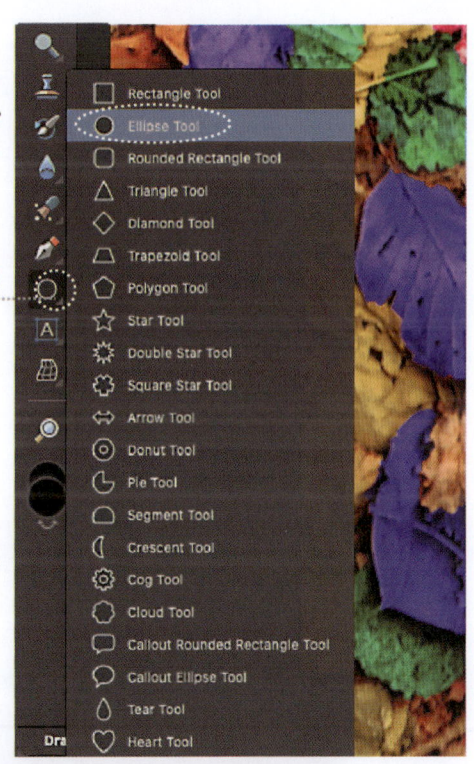

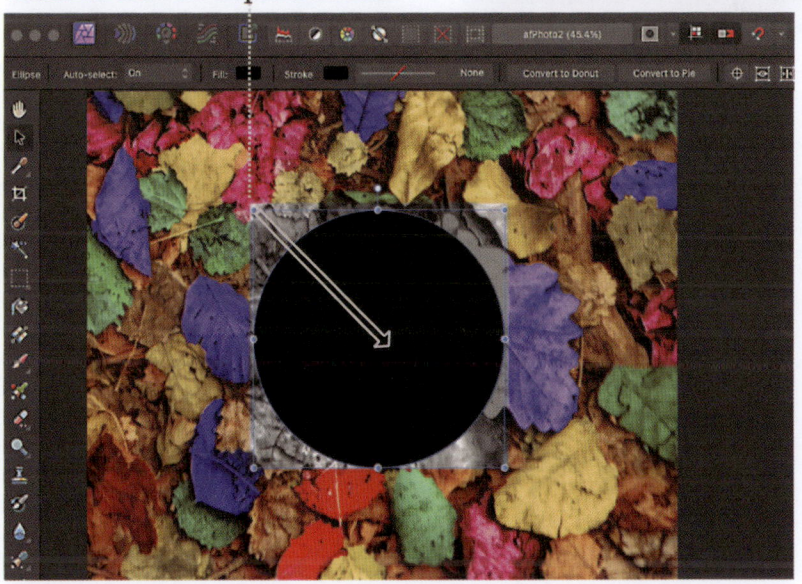

Chapter 2: Quick Tour and Tutorial

Once you have drawn a circle, then change it to a donut shape. It's easy! Click on the Context Tool Bar>**Convert to Donut**. Note that the Tool Bar display now reads **Hole Radius**. Click on the **Flyout button** and move the Slide Bar to 80%. Adjust the width of the circle by grabbing **the red dots**.

Next, click on Too Bar >**Gradient**. Using the Gradient Tool, click on the Context Tool Bar>Type>**Linear**. Click on **the point** inside the Donut and drag down to the right. Note the change to grey gradation.

## Chapter 2: Quick Tour and Tutorial

## Change Color

Change the color of the Gradation. Change the Context Menu Type to **Linear** and click on **the Color Box**. Click on **Gradient** in the Dropdown menu. If there is no Gradient option in the Dropdown menu, click on the donut shape and switch the tool to Gradient. Click on **the circle (o)** to the left to activate it. Click on the **color button** to show the Color Wheel. If it does not appear, click on **the HSL Color Wheel**. Click on **the blue portion of the circle**, and then on the triangle at **the top** to switch the color on the left to blue.

Chapter 2: Quick Tour and Tutorial

Change the Gradation at the right. Click on **the circle (o) to the right**, and note that it is now slightly bigger. This indicates that it is active. Click on **the color button**, on the red part of the Color Wheel, and then on the triangle at **the top**.

How does it look?
The gradation color is now blue instead of red.

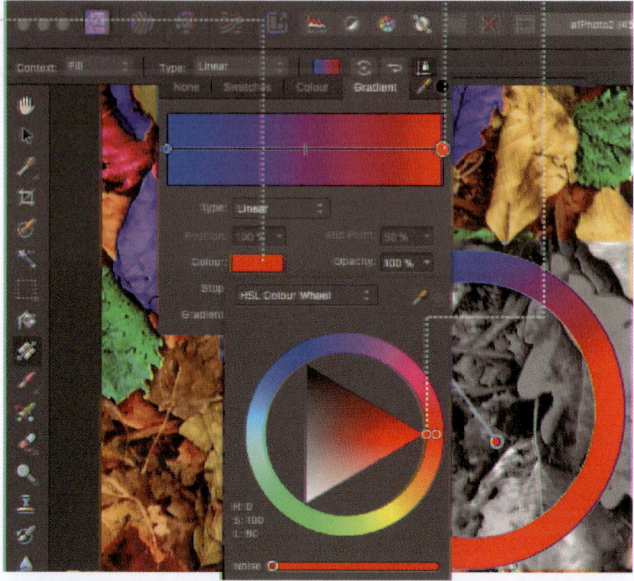

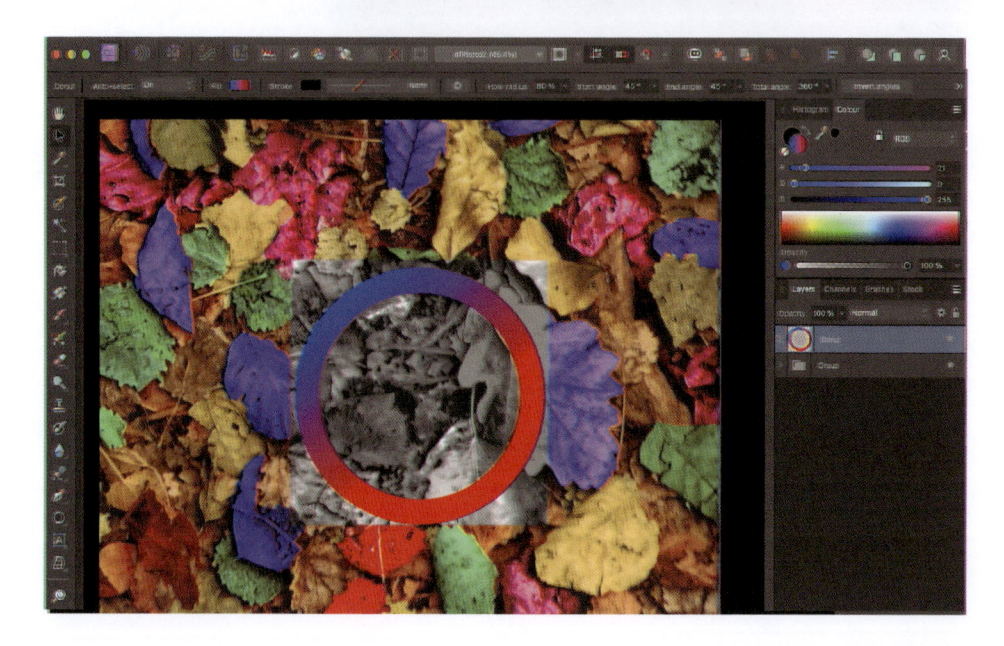

Chapter 2: Quick Tour and Tutorial

Draw a triangle inside the donut. Click on **the Flyout button** next to the Elliptical Tool. Select **the Triangle tool** from amongst the tools shown. Use the Context Tool > **Fill**>Blue, and indicate **None** for the boundary. To accurately fit to the inside of the circle, use the Move Tool to Enlarge, Shrink, Rotate, etc.

Once the blue triangle is Active, switch to **the Gradient Tool** and **drag from the top left to the bottom right**. The Gradation is created by the initial and concluding clicks. Ignore any color discrepancies for now. Colors can be changed on the next page.

45

Chapter 2: Quick Tour and Tutorial

Change the Gradation Color of the triangle to finish Once you see that the Context Menu has changed to Gradation, click on Gradient > and **the circle (o) to the left.** The color should now be green.

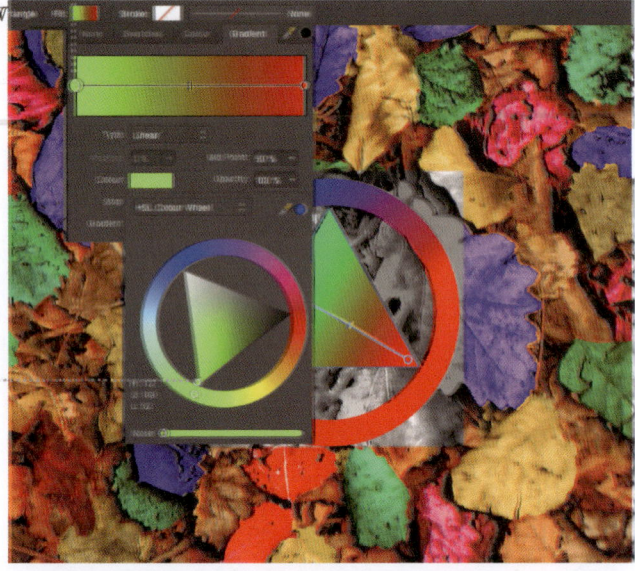

Similarly, click **the circle (o) to the right.** Then click on the Color button, followed by the blue portion of the Color Wheel. Then click on the triangle at the top to blue.

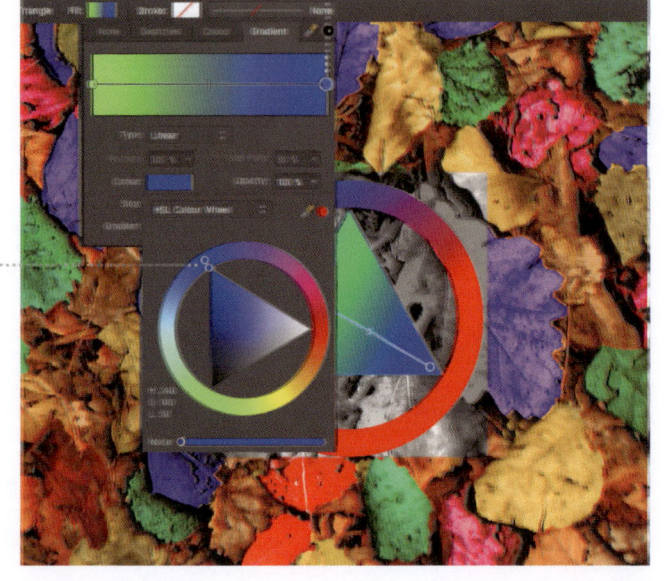

46

Chapter 2: Quick Tour and Tutorial

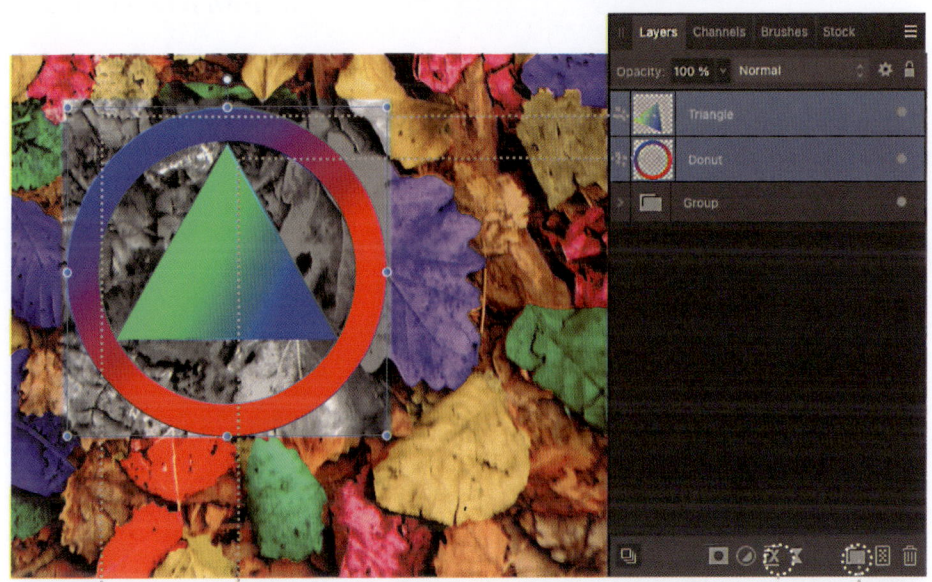

Now let's try adding effect to the picture. To do this, we group the layers, activating **the triangle and circle** layers. Click on **the Folder icon** above to activate. Once the layers are grouped, click on Studio>**Layer Effects**, followed by **Bevel/Emboss** in the dropdown menu.

Under Type, select **Emboss**, 3.1 px. Use default for the other settings. How does the Emboss effect look?

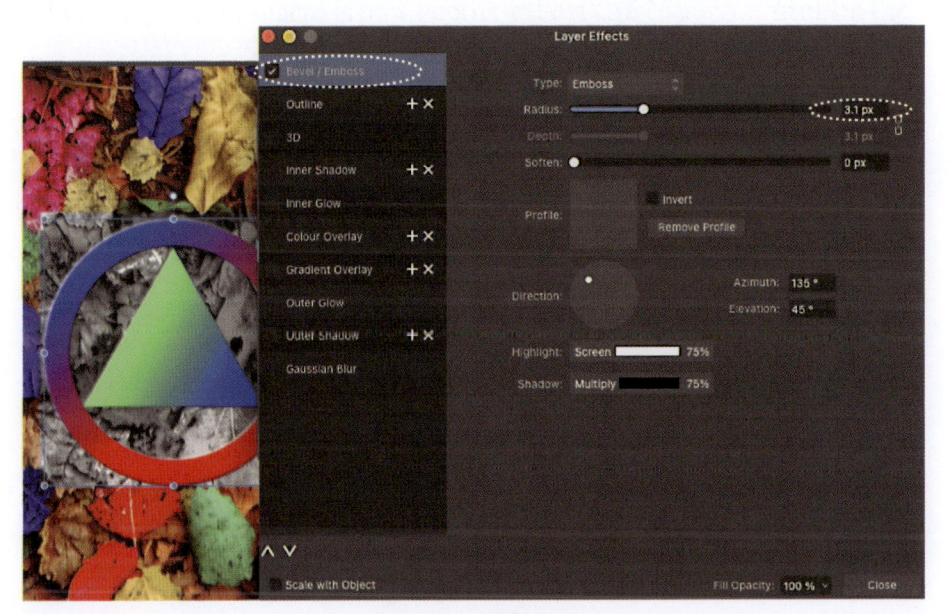

47

Let's now apply Shadow. If you don't see the Effects screen, click on **Outer Shadow**. Slide **Opacity** to 60%, **Radius** to 9.9 px, and **Offset** to 16.9 px. The numbers can be random. When you are finished, click on the Close button.

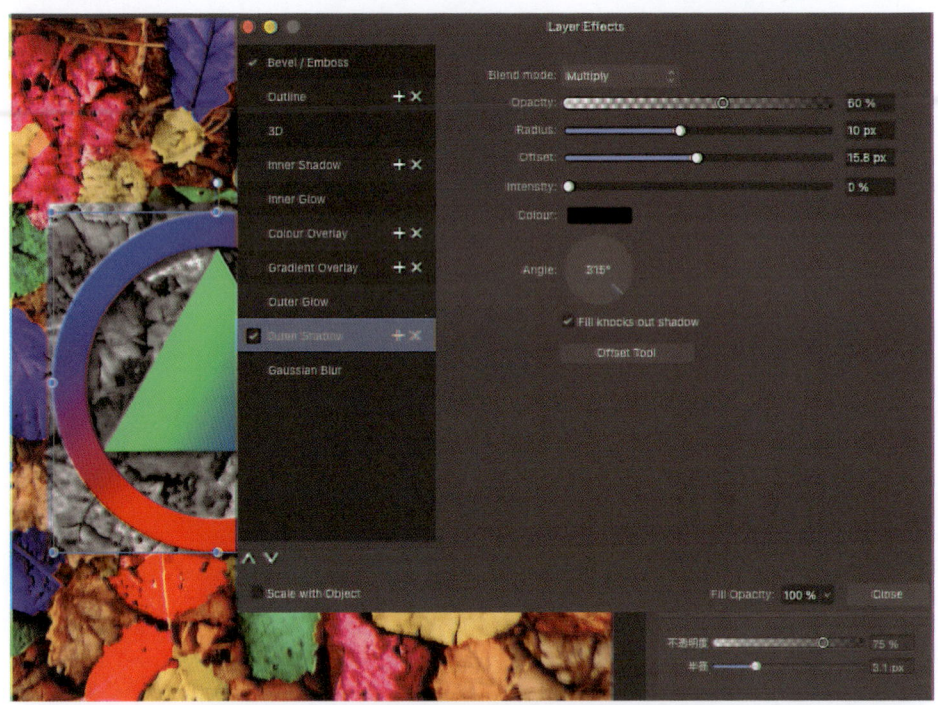

You've now completed the graphic proportion. To enlarge, hold down **the Zoom Tool** > Option/Alt, and click to Shrink in order to view the entire image.

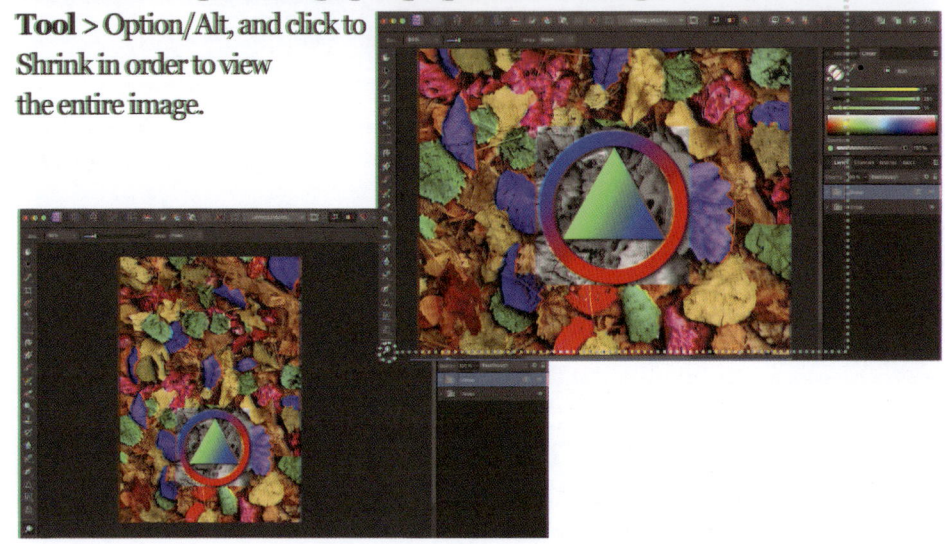

48

Chapter 2: Quick Tour and Tutorial

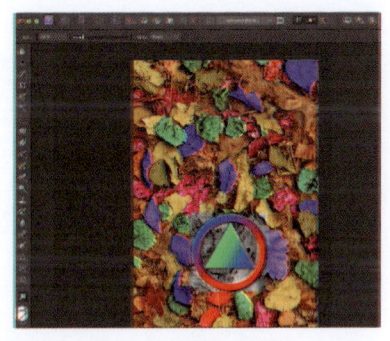

Next, we enter the title for the Cover page. To make sure the characters are displayed clearly, paint the top half of the screen. Click on the Tool Panel > click on the Graphics Tool **Flyout button** > **Rectangle tool**.

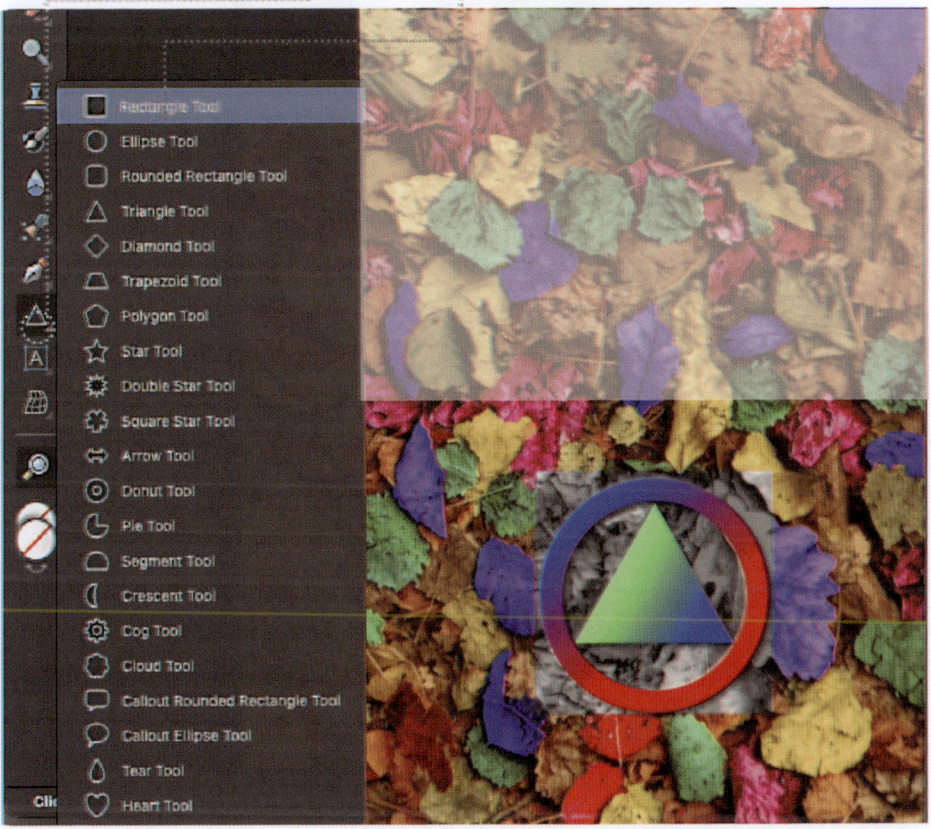

49

## Chapter 2: Quick Tour and Tutorial

Next, click on the Context Tool > **Fill Color button**. Select Color Type > colour>**HSL Color Wheel** . Then click on Green on the Circle. Click on **the bottom middle second of the Triangle**, then under Boundary click on **None** and drag diagonally from the top left to the bottom. Mouse up on **the midpoint of the Object on the right side**.

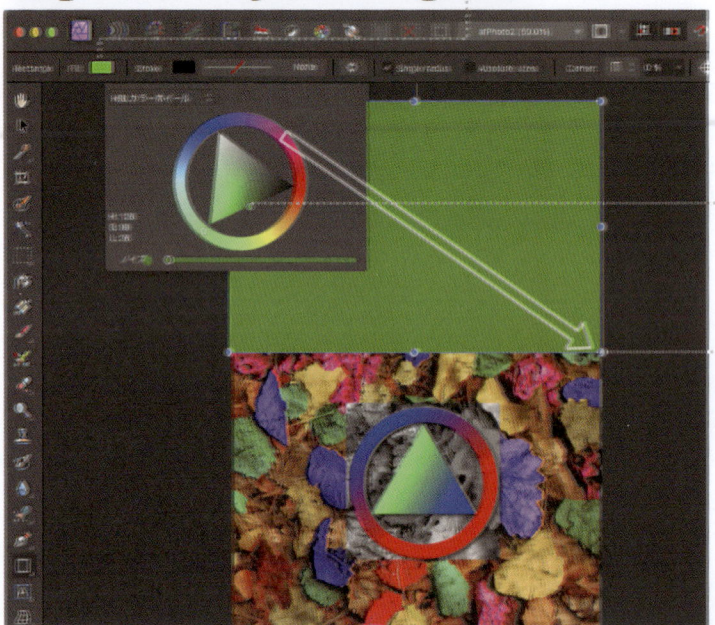

Note that the Object now has a green layer over it. Here, Multiply the Color (clear color ink) to incorporate the under-layer (photo). **Multiply** the Color Style and set **Opacity** to 75%.

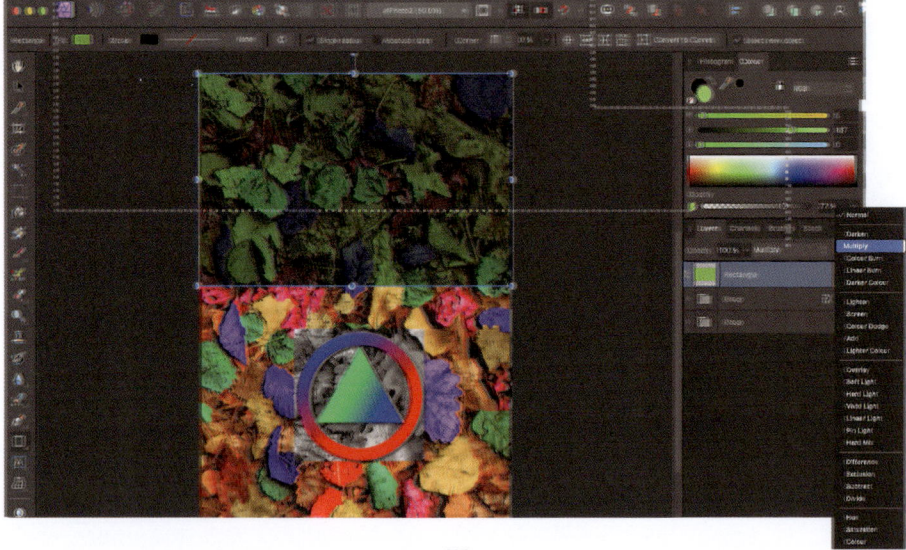

## Insert Text

Insert the text. Affinity_Photo has two kinds of text tools. Click on the Text Tool **Flyout button** to open the Artistic Text Tool and Frame Text Tool select screens. **The Artistic Text tool** is ideal for creating single-line logo text. Meanwhile, **the Frame Text Tool** is useful for body copy text. Since we are creating a title here, we select the Artistic Text Tool.

Open the Context Tool Bar > **Font**: Helvetica, set **Size:** 54 pt, **Style:** Bold, and **Color:** White

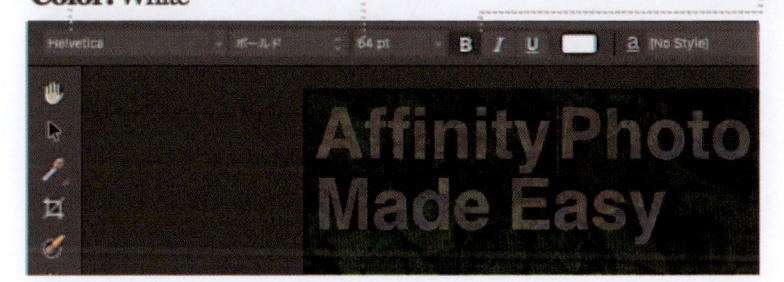

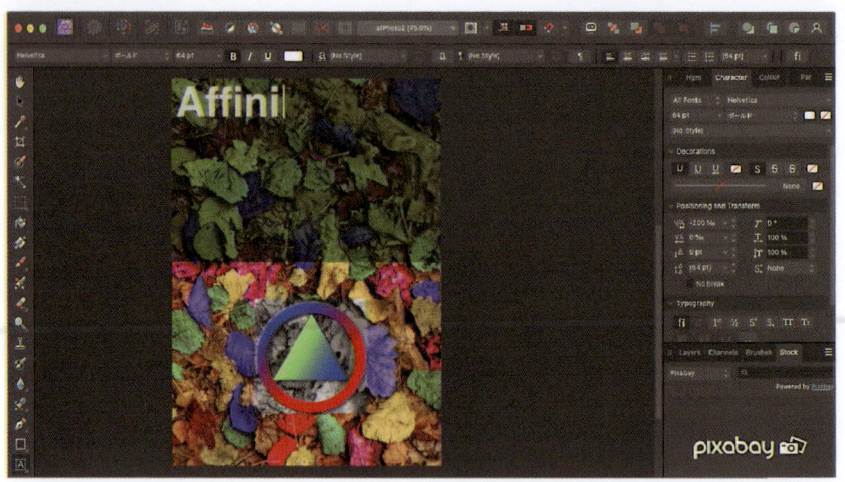

On the top left screen, type in **Affinity Photo Made Easy**. Using the mouse, move the cursor upwardYou may find that there is not much space between characters. Click on Text Tool between **Y and P**, and click on Window > Text > Character > **Character** Panel > **Kerning** and set to -200. Note that the space between the characters shrinks. Underneath is the Tracking feature, which shrinks the space between characters on all lines. Adjust the spacing as appropriate to arrange the characters. Check on the layers tocreate a dedicated character layer. To blend the characters with the base, select **Opacity**: 75%. You're done!

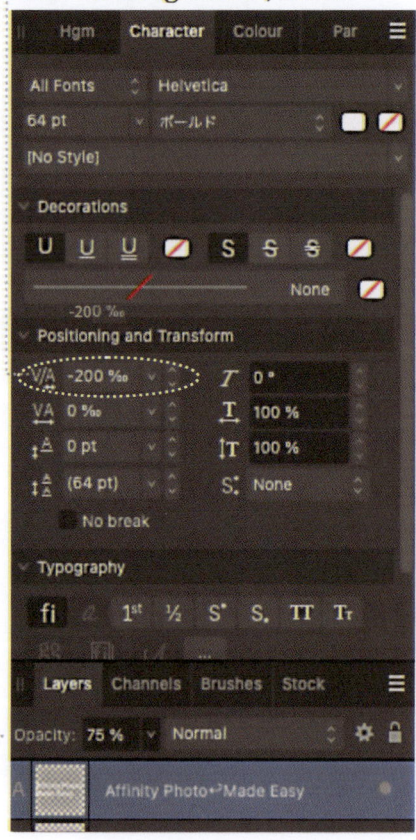

Chapter 2: Quick Tour and Tutorial

## 2_3: Quit Affinity_Photo and Save

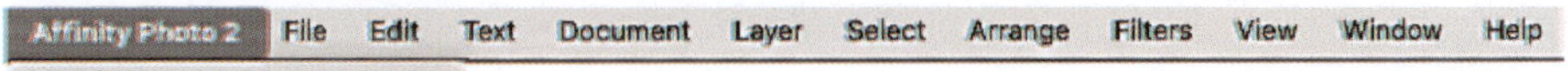

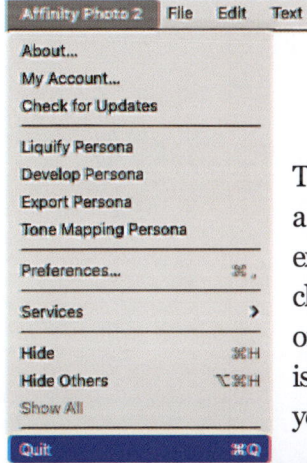

This concludes the Quick Tour. Affinity Photo boasts a great many more features. In the next Chapter, we explain in detail how to use each of them. Let's now close Affinity Photo. On the Menu Bar at the top, click on Affinity Photo 2>Quit. Dialog to be saved in the file is shown here. Give it any name you like and Save ( your file namm.afphoto).

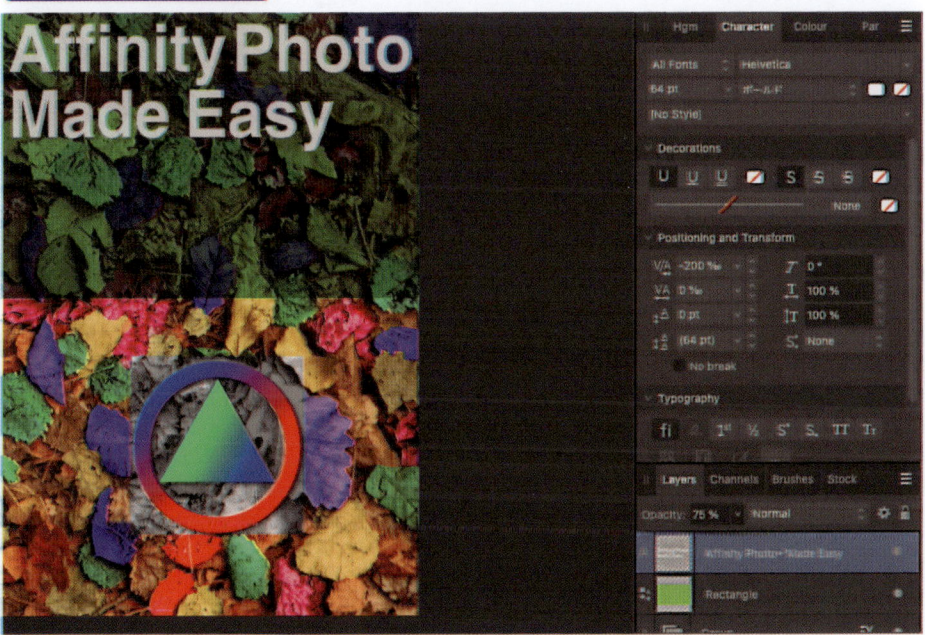

# Chapter 3: Learning to basics of Affinity Photo

Chapter 3: Learning the basics of Affinity Photo

Once you have completed the Quick Tour, the next step is to learn the wide variety of features offered by Affinity Photo. The Quick tour is designed for people who have prior experience with photo editing software. For those using this type of software for the first time, we recommend that you begin with Chapter 3. Let's now open a document with Affinity Photo.

### 3_1: Opening a New Document

Click on the Affinity Photo icon, then click Menu Bar>File>**New**. You can also open **Document Settings** with Command/Control+N*. First, choose your document settings.

## Chapter 3: Learning the basics of Affinity Photo

The **Type** noted on the line below indicates the type of document. Select the Print, Photo, Web, and Devices settings here. Next, click on the lower right at **Page Preset**. If you selected **Print** under **Type**, you will then see Print Size (A). If you Select **Photo**, option B will appear. For Web, (C) is be shown, and for **Devices**, (D) is indicated. **Customize** can be specified for other options.

A: Print size

B: Photo size

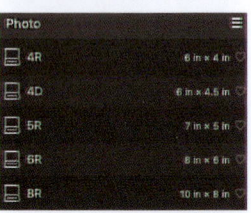

Typeface

C: Website size

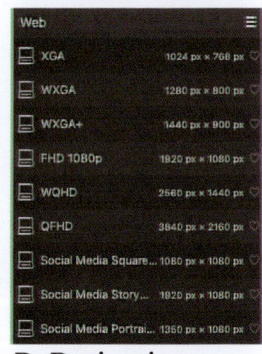

D: Device size

# Chapter 3: Learning the basics of Affinity Photo

Next we proceed to **Document Units**. Here we select the number of pixels, meter, etc., under Page Preset at the top. **Click on the right** to open (A).

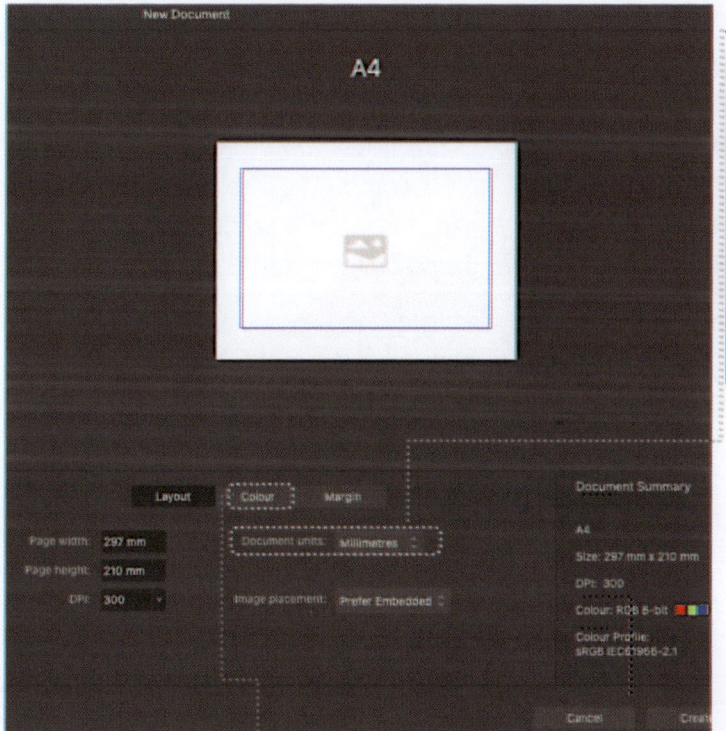

A: Document Unit

Next, choose your **Color Format** settings including CMYK for printing materials, RGB for PCs, etc. Click on the Drop Menu (B) at right. The more advanced feature is the **Color Profile** just below. Select the Type on the top to display the recommended settings, but leave them as they are for the moment.

B: Color Format

C: Color Profile

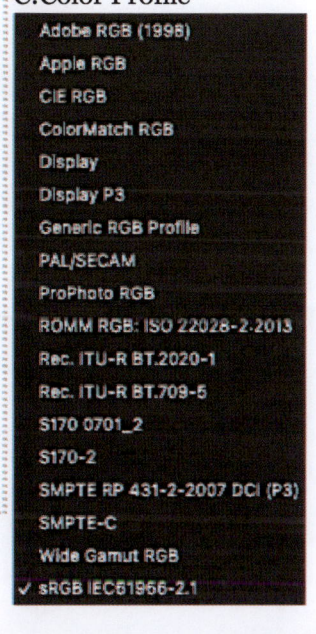

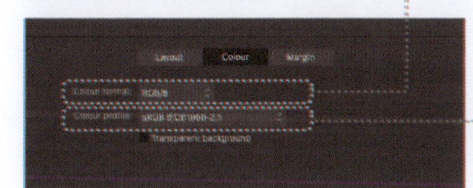

Next, to render the background **transparent**, place a Check mark in the Transparent setting. Under **Dimensions**, enter the page width, page height, and DPI (resolution or dots per inch). Use the Default settings. Place a Check mark next to the **Portrait** heading to render the document vertical, or remove the Check mark to create a horizontal document.

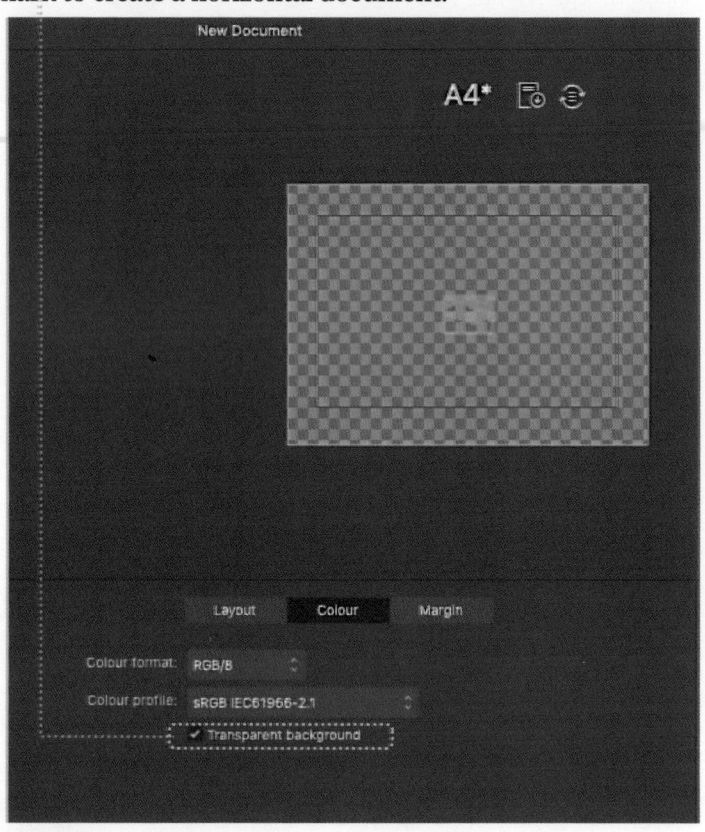

Lastly we **Include Margins**.

Put in a Check mark here to implement page settings. Set left, right, top, and bottom margins to show the blue guidelines (note that these are not printed). In general, the Default settings are acceptable. Click on the button below under Printer and Margins to input Printer values.

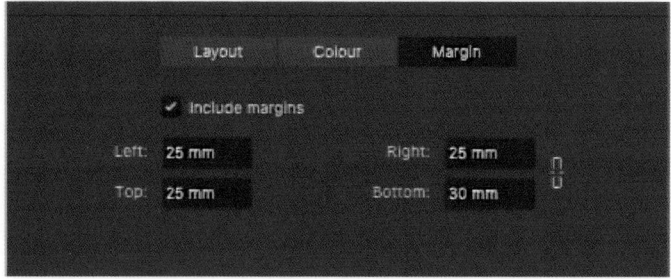

### 3_2: Open file/Open PDF

To open an existing file, click Menu Bar>File>**Open**. Click on the desired file to select it from the files shown to open your document.

If you selected a PDF file, you will see **the PDF option dialog box**. Here you may choose to download all pages or a specified page, implement settings such as resolution and text, switch fonts, and more.

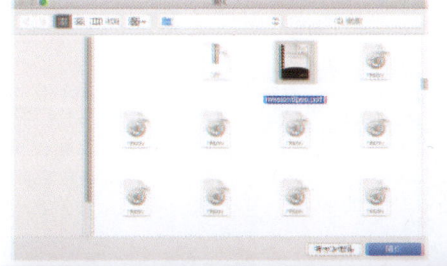

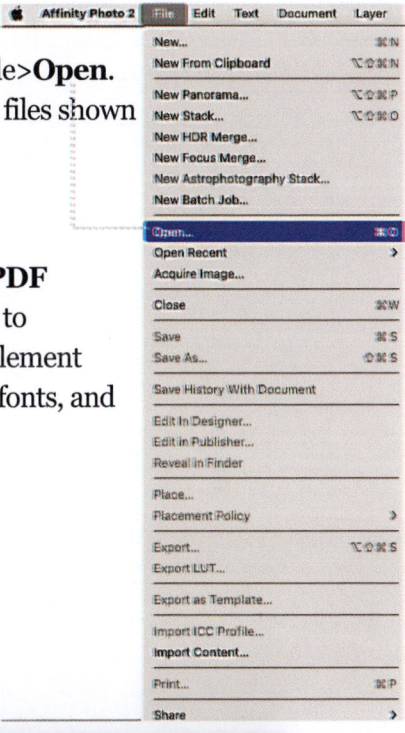

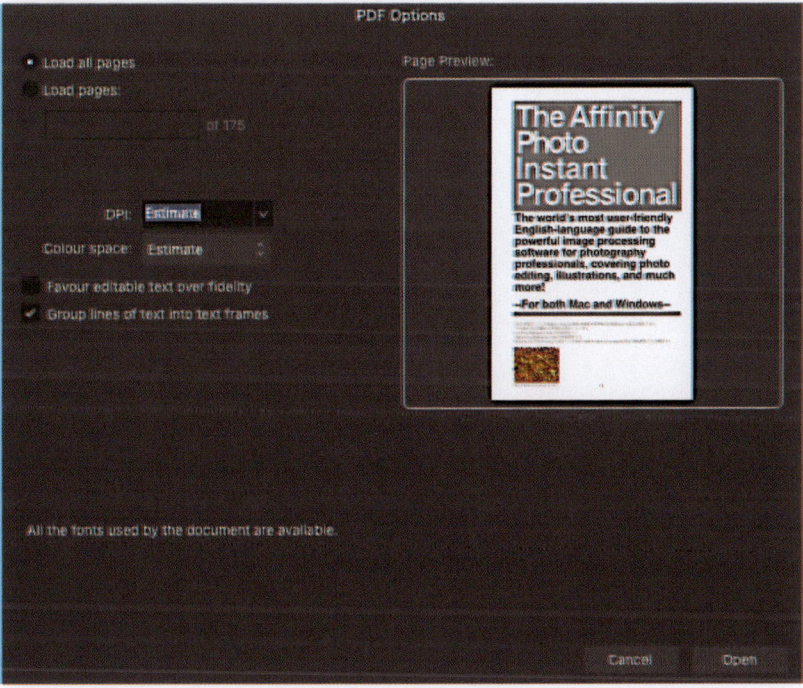

Chapter 3: Learning the basics of Affinity Photo

## 3_3: Open from Clipboard

Documents from other applications compatible with Affinity_Photo can be accessed directly with the clipboard (copy document) and opened as a new document. For example, open a PNG document using Control/Command+C and copy.

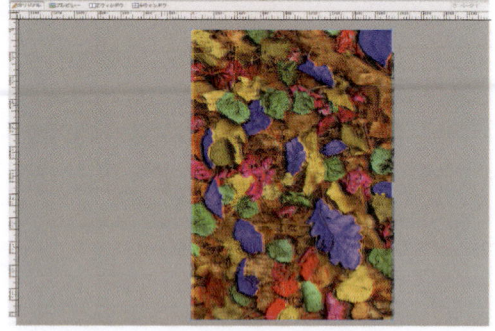

Next, launch Affinity_Photo, and click File>**New From Clipboard**

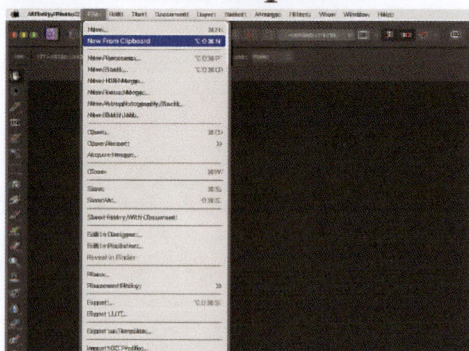

Continue working .

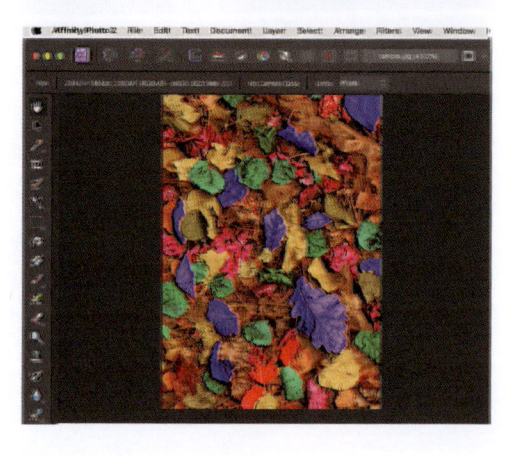

60

Chapter 3: Learning the basics of Affinity Photo

## 3_4: Enlarge or Shrink an Open Document/Pan

I'd like to introduce two very useful tools that we'll be using frequently from this point onward: the Zoom Tool and the View Tool.

Let's try shrinking the document. On the Tool Panel, select the **Zoom Tool**. Hold down the Option key and Click. Note how it has shrunk.

Next, click on the **View Tool** at the very top of the Tool Panel and drag the Object. It should now have moved. In this way, use the View Tool to move objects in your work space.

Next, click Tool Panel and select Zoom Tool. Then hold down the Option key and click to enlarge.

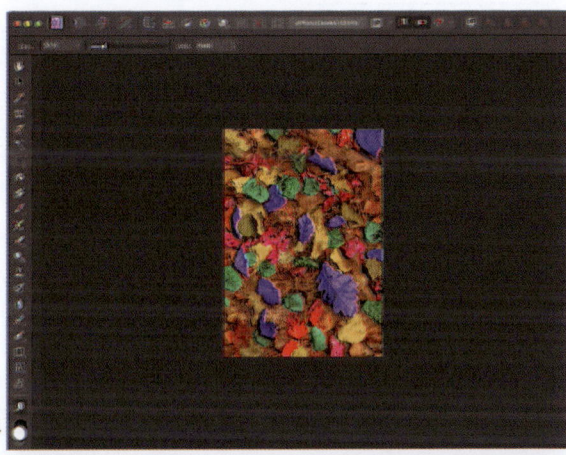

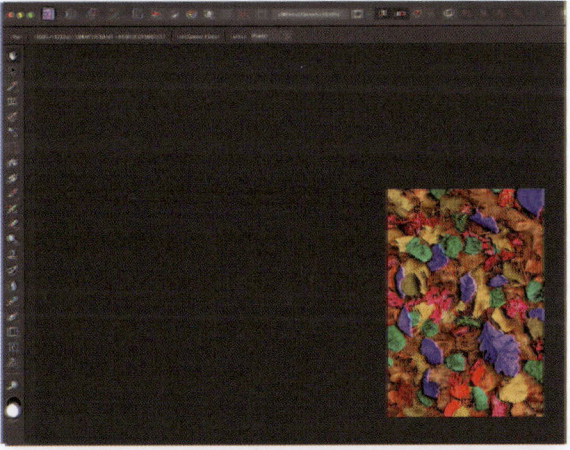

61

# Chapter 4: Affinity Photo Structure and Interface

Chapter 4: Affinity Photo Structure and Interface

In this Chapter we will learn all about the Affinity Photo Interface. If you prefer, you can skip this Chapter and proceed to the next. Subsequent chapters will detail the features of individual tools. In this Chapter, our goal is to gain a solid preliminary understanding of the interface, naming, role, etc. of each individual tool.

## 4_1: Interface Structure Group

Affinity Photo can be grouped into the following five categories: Persona Tool Bar, Context Tool Bar, Tool Panel, and Studio.

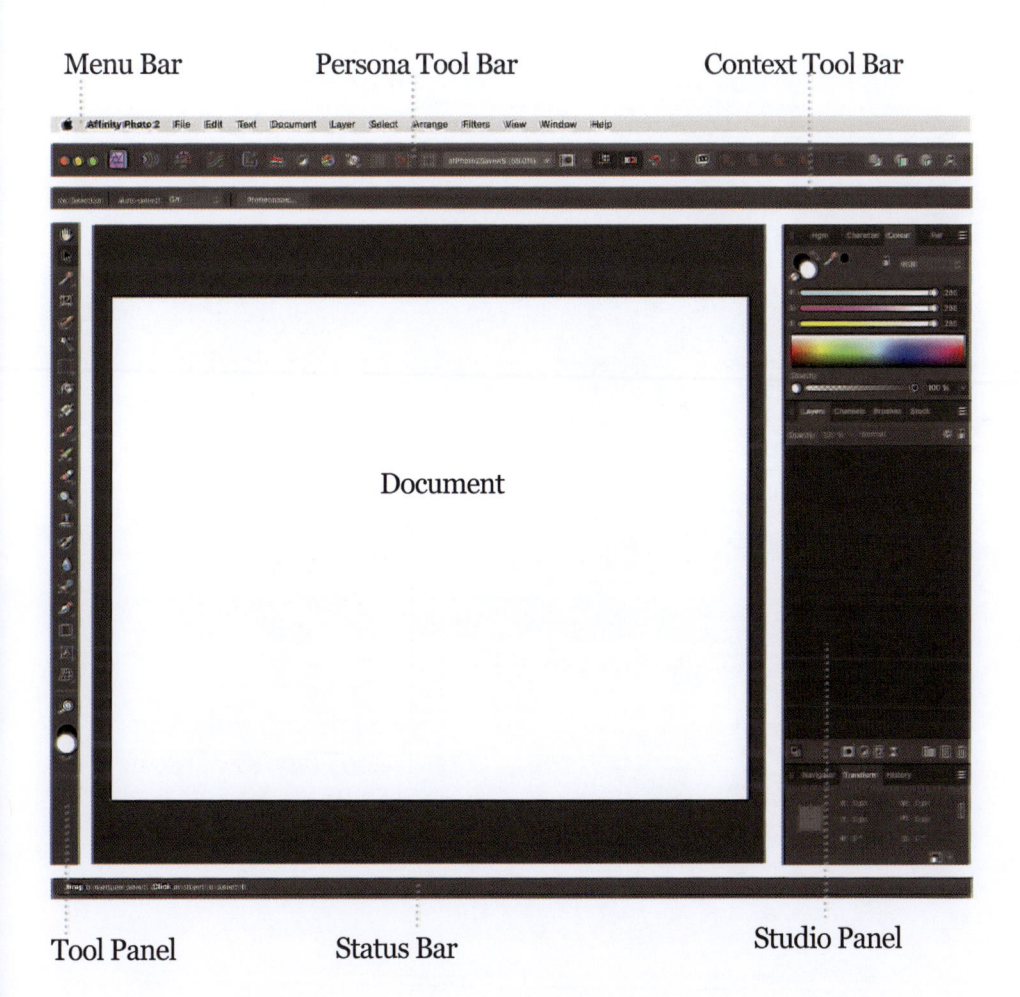

Menu Bar   Persona Tool Bar   Context Tool Bar

Document

Tool Panel   Status Bar   Studio Panel

## Chapter 4: Affinity Photo Structure and Interface

### 4_2: Explore the Menu Bar

The Menu Bar contains all Affinity Photo commands. The command that you are currently working with is displayed—to enable quick access.

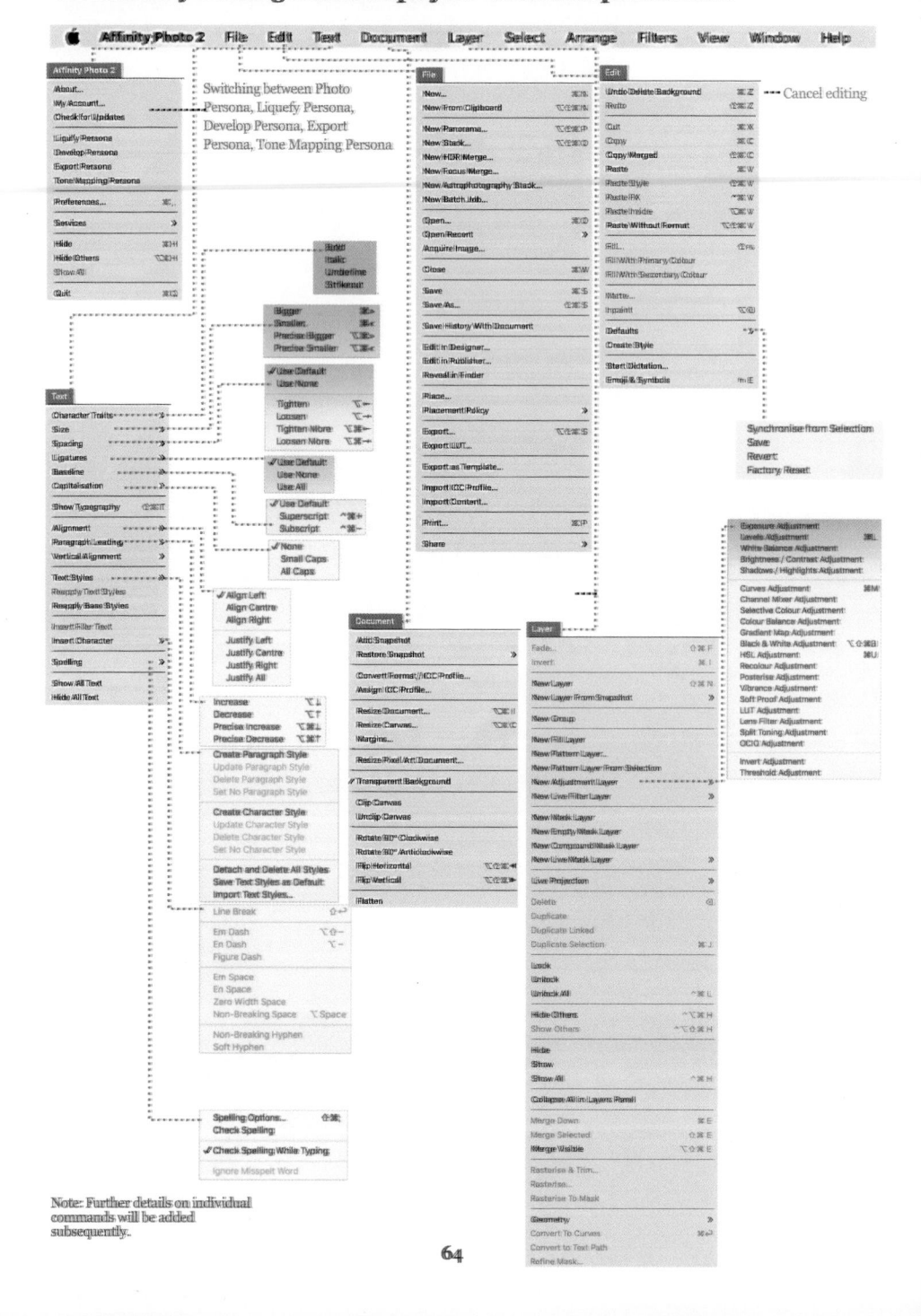

Note: Further details on individual commands will be added subsequently.

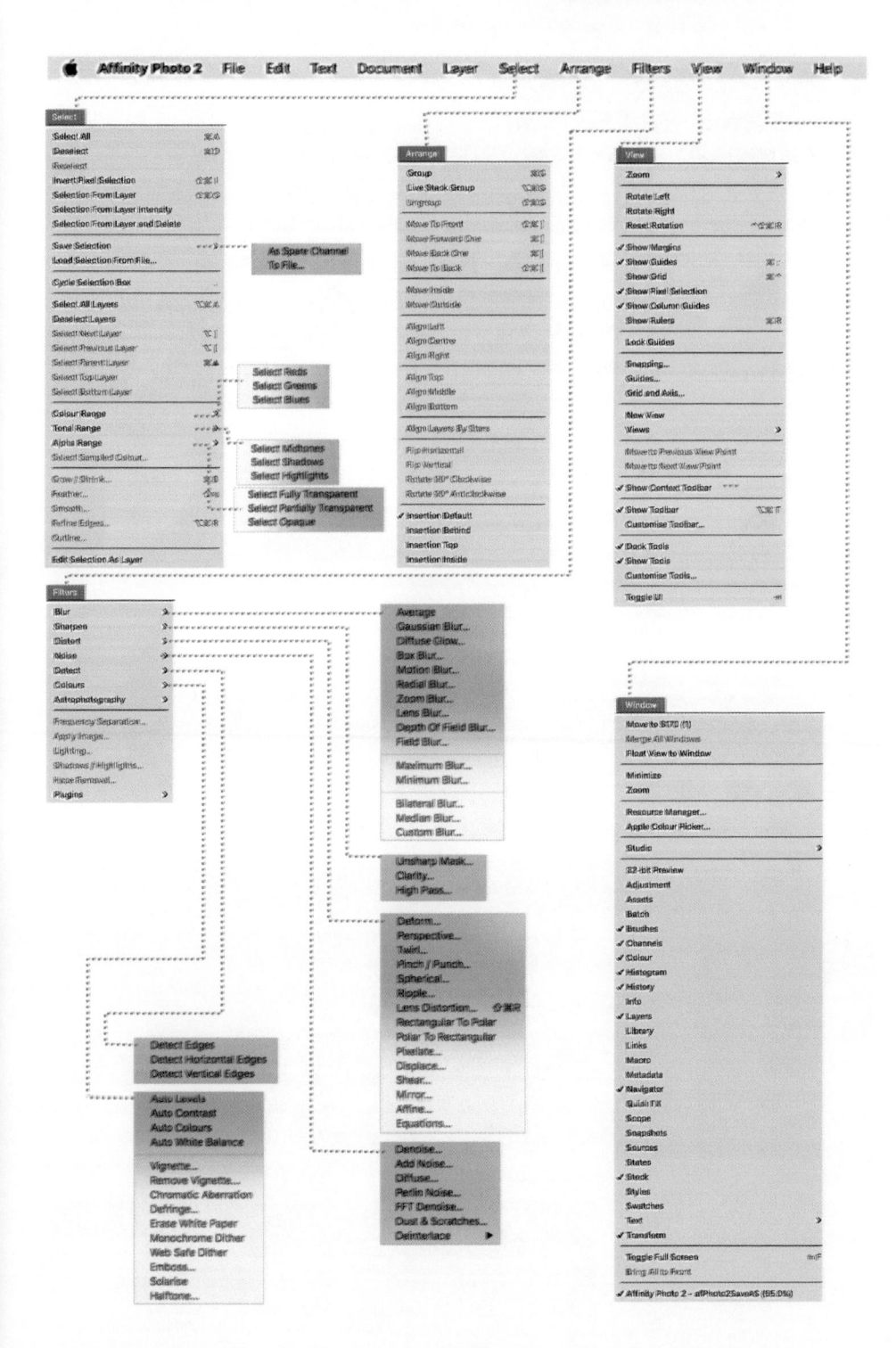

# Chapter 4: Affinity Photo Structure and Interface

**Menu bar:** Affinity Photo 2 | File | Edit | Text | Document | Layer | Select | Arrange | Filters | View | Window | Help

## Select
- Select All ⌘A
- Deselect ⌘D
- Reselect
- Invert Pixel Selection ⇧⌘I
- Selection From Layer
- Selection From Layer Intensity
- Selection From Layer and Delete
- Save Selection ▸
  - As Spare Channel
  - To File...
- Load Selection From File...
- Cycle Selection Box
- Select All Layers ⌥⌘A
- Deselect Layers
- Select Next Layer ⌥]
- Select Previous Layer ⌥[
- Select Parent Layer ⌘↑
- Select Top Layer
- Select Bottom Layer
- Colour Range ▸
  - Select Reds
  - Select Greens
  - Select Blues
- Tonal Range ▸
- Alpha Range ▸
  - Select Midtones
  - Select Shadows
  - Select Highlights
- Select Sampled Colour...
- Grow / Shrink... ⇧D
- Feather... ⌥⌘F
  - Select Fully Transparent
  - Select Partially Transparent
  - Select Opaque
- Smooth...
- Refine Edges... ⌥⌘R
- Outline...
- Edit Selection As Layer

## Arrange
- Group ⌘G
- Live Stack Group ⌃⌘G
- Ungroup ⇧⌘G
- Move To Front ⇧⌘]
- Move Forward One ⌘]
- Move Back One ⌘[
- Move To Back ⇧⌘[
- Move Inside
- Move Outside
- Align Left
- Align Centre
- Align Right
- Align Top
- Align Middle
- Align Bottom
- Align Layers By Size
- Flip Horizontal
- Flip Vertical
- Rotate 90° Clockwise
- Rotate 90° Anticlockwise
- ✓ Insertion Default
- Insertion Behind
- Insertion Top
- Insertion Inside

## View
- Zoom ▸
- Rotate Left
- Rotate Right
- Reset Rotation ⌥⇧⌘R
- ✓ Show Margins
- ✓ Show Guides ⌘;
- Show Grid ⌘'
- ✓ Show Pixel Selection
- ✓ Show Column Guides
- Show Rulers ⌘R
- Lock Guides
- Snapping...
- Guides...
- Grid and Axis...
- New View
- Views ▸
- Move to Previous View Point
- Move to Next View Point
- ✓ Show Context Toolbar
- ✓ Show Toolbar ⌥⌘T
- Customise Toolbar...
- ✓ Dock Tools
- ✓ Show Tools
- Customise Tools...
- Toggle UI

## Filters
- Blur ▸
  - Average
  - Gaussian Blur...
  - Diffuse Glow...
  - Box Blur...
  - Motion Blur...
  - Radial Blur...
  - Zoom Blur...
  - Lens Blur...
  - Depth Of Field Blur...
  - Field Blur...
  - Maximum Blur...
  - Minimum Blur...
  - Bilateral Blur...
  - Median Blur...
  - Custom Blur...
- Sharpen ▸
  - Unsharp Mask...
  - Clarity...
  - High Pass...
- Distort ▸
  - Deform...
  - Perspective...
  - Twirl...
  - Pinch / Punch...
  - Spherical...
  - Ripple...
  - Lens Distortion... ⇧⌘R
  - Rectangular To Polar
  - Polar To Rectangular
  - Pixelate...
  - Displace...
  - Shear...
  - Mirror...
  - Affine...
  - Equations...
- Noise ▸
  - Denoise...
  - Add Noise...
  - Diffuse...
  - Perlin Noise...
  - FFT Denoise...
  - Dust & Scratches...
  - Deinterlace ▸
- Detect ▸
  - Detect Edges
  - Detect Horizontal Edges
  - Detect Vertical Edges
- Colours ▸
  - Auto Levels
  - Auto Contrast
  - Auto Colours
  - Auto White Balance
- Astrophotography ▸
- Frequency Separation...
- Apply Image...
- Lighting...
- Shadows / Highlights...
- Haze Removal...
- Plugins ▸
  - Vignette...
  - Remove Vignette...
  - Chromatic Aberration
  - Defringe...
  - Erase White Paper
  - Monochrome Dither
  - Web Safe Dither
  - Emboss...
  - Solarise...
  - Halftone...

## Window
- Move to SITD (1)
- Merge All Windows
- Float View to Window
- Minimize
- Zoom
- Resource Manager...
- Apple Colour Picker...
- Studio ▸
- 32-bit Preview
- Adjustment
- Assets
- Batch
- ✓ Brushes
- ✓ Channels
- ✓ Colour
- ✓ Histogram
- ✓ History
- Info
- ✓ Layers
- Library
- Links
- Macro
- Metadata
- ✓ Navigator
- Quick FX
- Scope
- Snapshots
- Sources
- States
- ✓ Stock
- Styles
- Swatches
- Text ▸
- ✓ Transform
- Toggle Full Screen ⌃⌘F
- Bring All to Front
- ✓ Affinity Photo 2 - afPhoto2SaveAS (85.0%)

## 4_3: About Affinity Photo Personas

Affinity Photo offers a wide variety of tools. The concept of Persona is a unique means of organizing these features. Switch tools by clicking on the icon above. The first is **Photo Persona**. Choose from tools such as Cut, Select, Brush, Retouch, Erase, or Warping. Next we have **Liquefy Persona**, which includes such tools as Retouch as well as tools for special warping. The next tool you see is **Develop Persona**, which features numerous tools for Raw image processing. With the **Tone Mapping Persona,** create an environment especially for Tone Mapping. Lastly we have the **Export Persona**, which allows the user to export slices in various file formats.

### Photo Persona

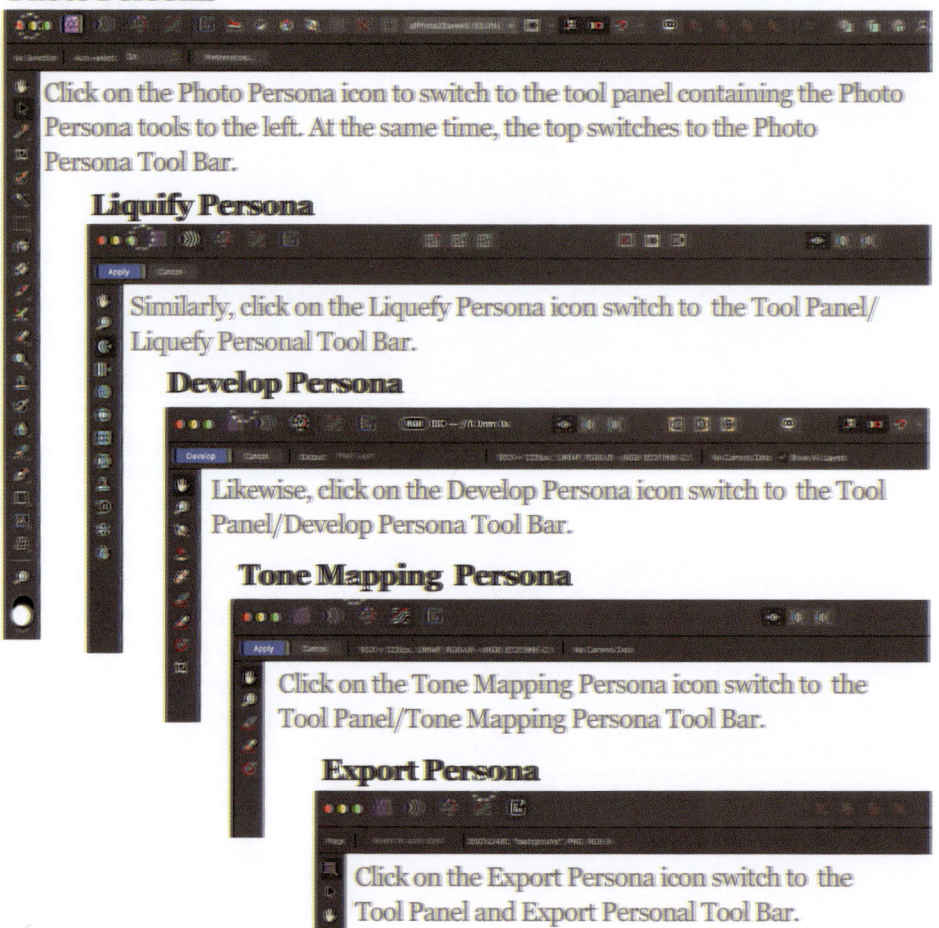

Click on the Photo Persona icon to switch to the tool panel containing the Photo Persona tools to the left. At the same time, the top switches to the Photo Persona Tool Bar.

### Liquify Persona

Similarly, click on the Liquefy Persona icon switch to the Tool Panel/Liquefy Personal Tool Bar.

### Develop Persona

Likewise, click on the Develop Persona icon switch to the Tool Panel/Develop Persona Tool Bar.

### Tone Mapping Persona

Click on the Tone Mapping Persona icon switch to the Tool Panel/Tone Mapping Persona Tool Bar.

### Export Persona

Click on the Export Persona icon switch to the Tool Panel and Export Personal Tool Bar.

# 4_4: Photo Persona

## Photo PersonaTool Bar

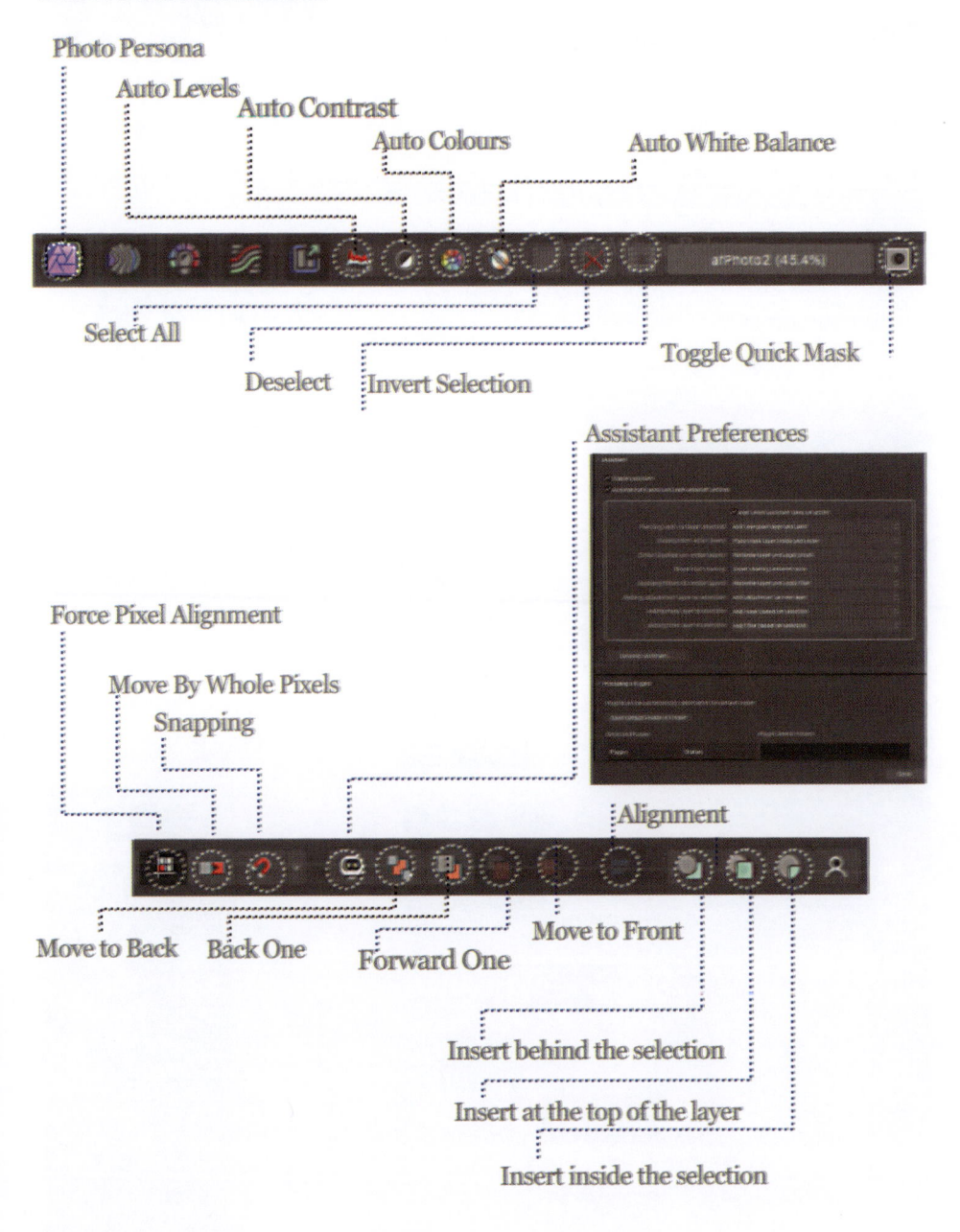

- Photo Persona
- Auto Levels
- Auto Contrast
- Auto Colours
- Auto White Balance
- Select All
- Deselect
- Invert Selection
- Toggle Quick Mask

- Assistant Preferences
- Force Pixel Alignment
- Move By Whole Pixels
- Snapping
- Alignment
- Move to Back
- Back One
- Forward One
- Move to Front
- Insert behind the selection
- Insert at the top of the layer
- Insert inside the selection

## Chapter 4: Affinity Photo Structure and Interface

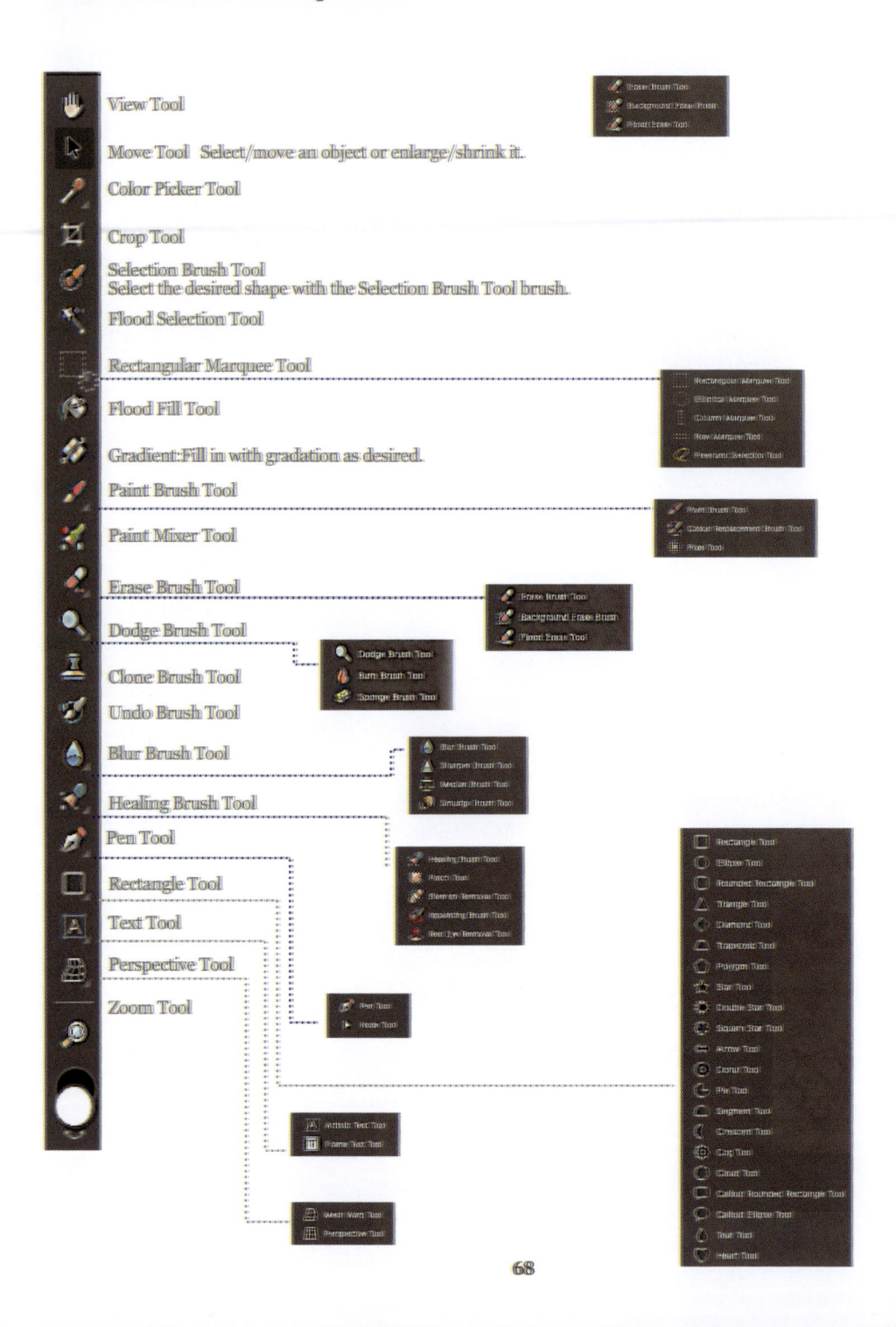

This is the Photo Persona Tool Panel. Click on the **Flyout menu icon** next to the icon to show an array of tools.

- View Tool
- Move Tool   Select/move an object or enlarge/shrink it.
- Color Picker Tool
- Crop Tool
- Selection Brush Tool
  Select the desired shape with the Selection Brush Tool brush.
- Flood Selection Tool
- Rectangular Marquee Tool
- Flood Fill Tool
- Gradient:Fill in with gradation as desired.
- Paint Brush Tool
- Paint Mixer Tool
- Erase Brush Tool
- Dodge Brush Tool
- Clone Brush Tool
- Undo Brush Tool
- Blur Brush Tool
- Healing Brush Tool
- Pen Tool
- Rectangle Tool
- Text Tool
- Perspective Tool
- Zoom Tool

68

## Photo Persona Studio Panel

This Persona frequently overlaps with other persona. Click on the individual tables to check your work.

### Histogram

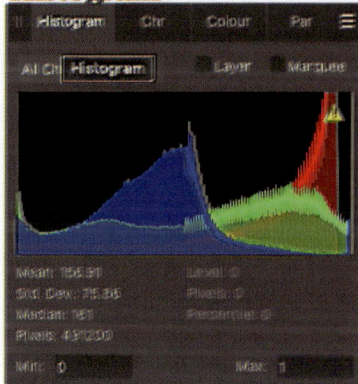

Histogram displays value distribution for the red, green, blue tones of the object as well as brightness. This tool is useful for determining whether color correction is needed, as well as for checking on clipped highlights.

All channels: Select channel
Layer: Select a layer
Marquee: Make your selection (specify boundaries).

### Colour

On the Color Panel, use the **top right icon** to choose Selector Type. Click to select Slider, Wheel, or Box. Select the Wheel at the figure to the left. **The point** above the circle is the Hue of your selected color. Use the **triangle point** to set Saturation and Luminosity. These values for H (Hue), S (Saturation), and L (Luminosity) indicate the fill colors as well as border colors. Use the Slider to set Opacity at a point on a scale from 0 to 100.

### Swatches

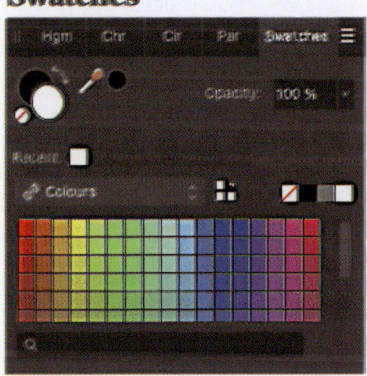

**Swatches** displays recently-used colors and other features. It also shows gray tones selectable from the Dropdown menu, Web safe colors, PANTONE® color samples, etc., enabling fast-and-easy color selection.

## Chapter 4: Affinity Photo Structure and Interface

### Brushes

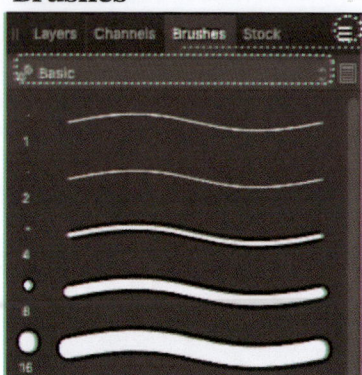

Under Brushes, **click** on the Dropdown menu to display the Brush Set that you've designed. To create your own designs, **click on the top right** to display the menu and activate a new category.

### Character

Select Font, Size, Style Color, Tracking, Vertical Scale, Horizontal Scale, Shear, Leading Override, etc.

### Adjustment

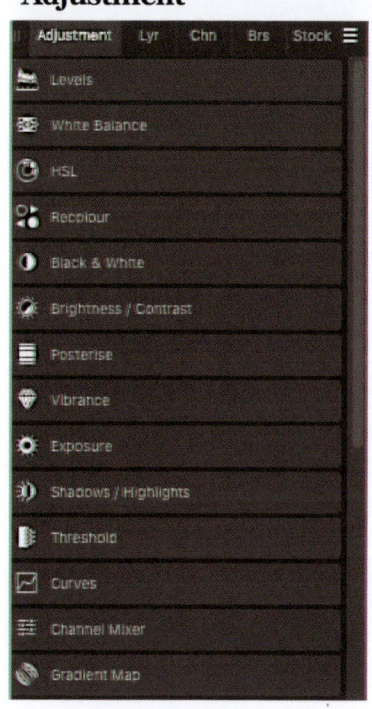

The Adjustment Panel contains a variety of setting panels for object tone correction including: Levels, White Balance, HSL correction, Recolor, Black & White, Brightness/Contrast, Posterise, Vibrance, Exposure, Shadows/Highlights, Threshold, Curves, Channel Mixer, Gradient Map, Selective Color, Color Balance, Invert, Soft Proof, LUT, Lens Filter, Split toning, and OCIO. In addition, using the Adjustment Panel, the User can create new individual layers without directly changing the object. In other words, layers can be altered or deleted subsequently. The user may also choose to use the opposite settings.

## Layers

Layers are organized and managed depending on content. By correcting specified layers only, the work can be completed with minimum effort.

**Opacity:** Layer opacity settings
**Lock/unlock:** Work cannot be edited when the file is locked.
**Display/hide:** Place a check mark to display.
**Edit All Layers:**
**Mask Layer:** Display part of the layers as you hide the remaining layers and build a mask.
**Adjustment:** Correct color
**Layer Effects:** Effect settings
**Live Filters: Display** filter menu screen
**Group Layers:** Categorize multiple layers into groups
**Add Pixel Layer:** Add a new empty pixel layer
**Remove Layer:** Delete an active layer

## Styles

Using the Styles Panel, the User can determine results and colors by defining object design. Register user customized settings. To activate customized details, select the object you designed, and click on "Add New Category" at the right top. Next, customize your style from the selections below.

## Chapter 4: Affinity Photo Structure and Interface

## Stock

From the Stock Panel, access stock photos directly from amongst Affinity Photo photos.

## Navigator

With the Navigator Panel, expand and contract documents, and use the Slider to zoom in and out.

## Transform

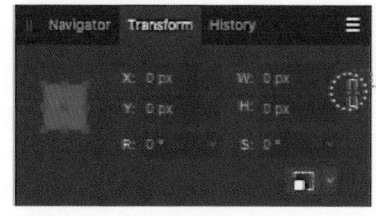

Object size (width and height), X coordinate, Y coordinate, rotate, tilt, and more. Use this **feature** to shrink or enlarge an object without changing the aspect ratio, or to change the settings so that the aspect ratio is not altered.

## History

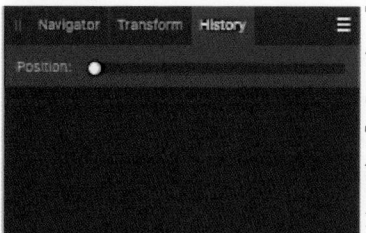

The History Panel displays work done through the present time as a list of labelled entries.
The top contains your oldest work, while the bottom is your latest work. Click on the list to revert to the original.

72

# Chapter 4: Affinity Photo Structure and Interface

## 4_5: Liquify Persona

### Liquify Persona: Tool Bar

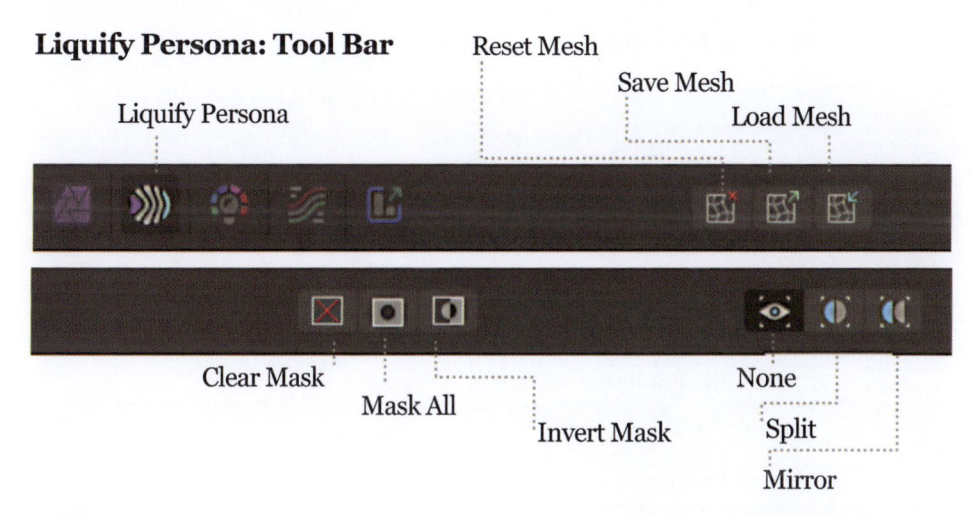

- Liquify Persona
- Reset Mesh
- Save Mesh
- Load Mesh

- Clear Mask
- Mask All
- Invert Mask
- None
- Split
- Mirror

### Liquify Persona: Left side Tool Panel

- Liquify Hand Tool
- Liquify Zoom Tool
- Liquify Push Forward Tool
- Liquify Push Left Tool
- Liquify Twirl Tool
- Liquify Pinch Tool
- Liquify Punch Tool
- Liquify Turbulence Tool
- Liquify Mesh CloneTool
- Liquify Reconstruct Tool
- Liquify Freeze Tool
- Liquify Thaw Tool

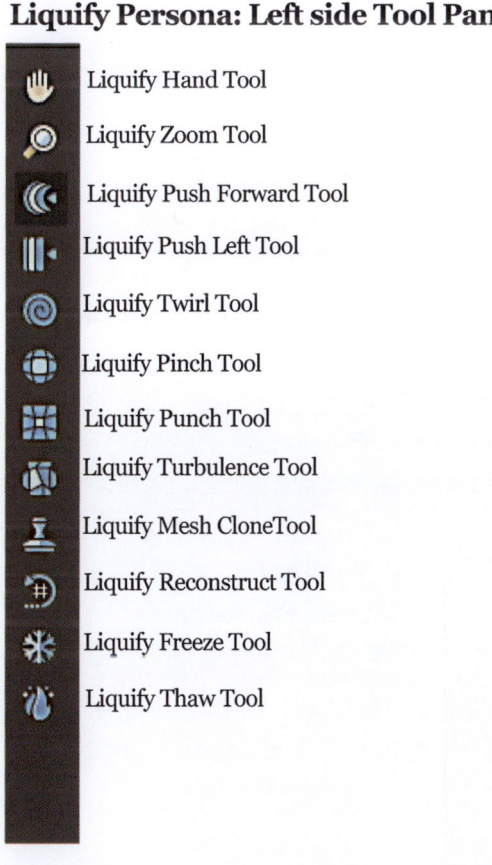

### Liquify Persona: Studio

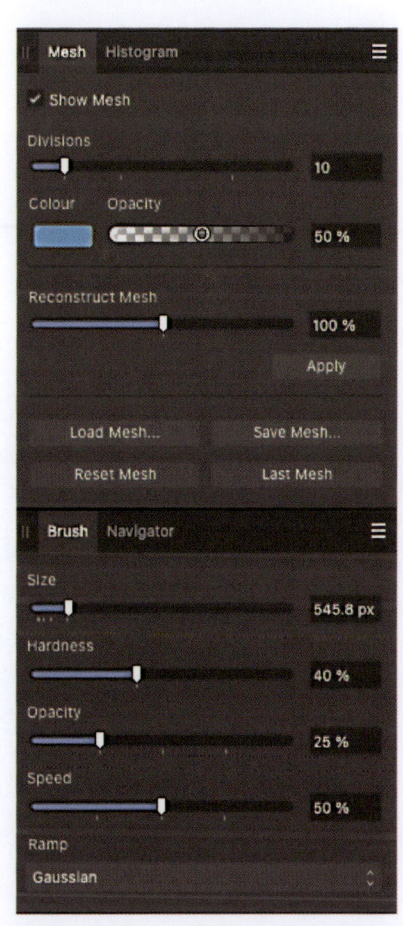

Mesh | Histogram

✓ Show Mesh

Divisions: 10
Colour / Opacity: 50 %
Reconstruct Mesh: 100 %
Apply

Load Mesh... | Save Mesh...
Reset Mesh | Last Mesh

Brush | Navigator

Size: 545.8 px
Hardness: 40 %
Opacity: 25 %
Speed: 50 %
Ramp: Gaussian

73

## 4_6: Develop Persona

### Develop Persona Tool Bar

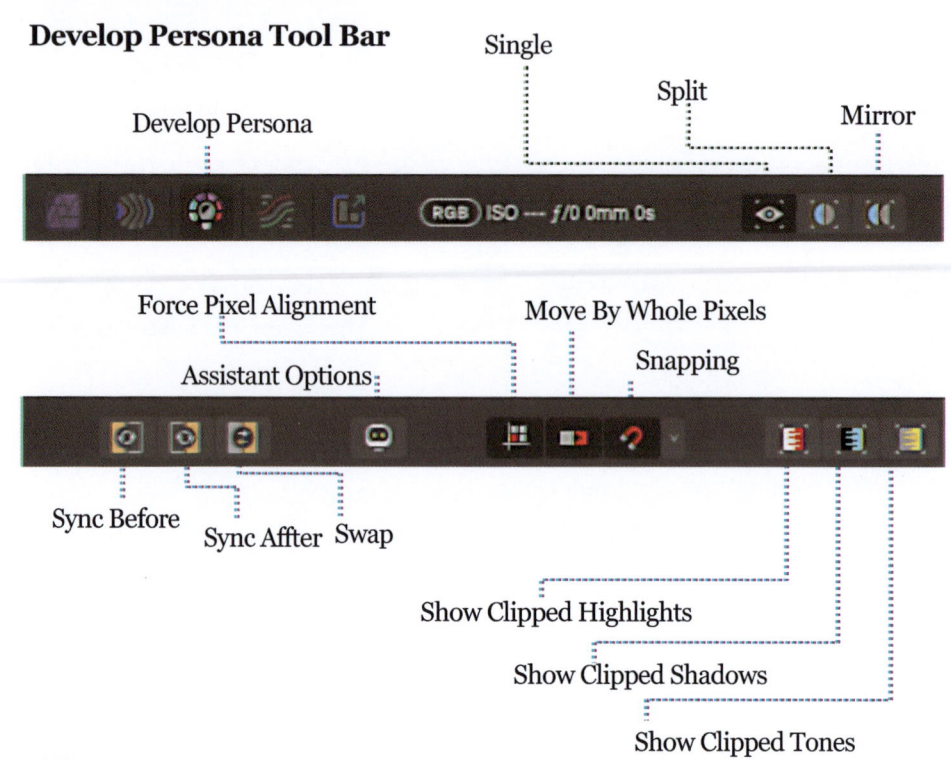

Labels: Develop Persona, Single, Split, Mirror

Labels: Force Pixel Alignment, Assistant Options, Move By Whole Pixels, Snapping, Sync Before, Sync Affter, Swap, Show Clipped Highlights, Show Clipped Shadows, Show Clipped Tones

### Develop Persona: Tool Panel on left

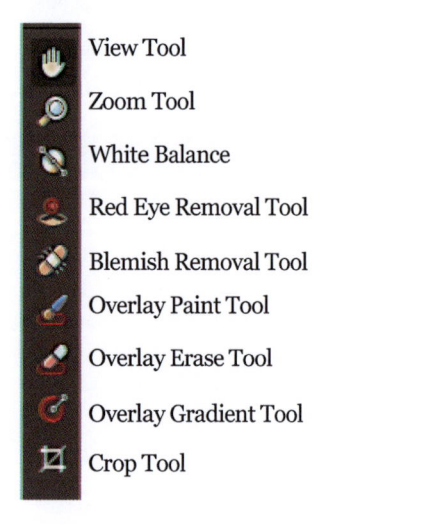

- View Tool
- Zoom Tool
- White Balance
- Red Eye Removal Tool
- Blemish Removal Tool
- Overlay Paint Tool
- Overlay Erase Tool
- Overlay Gradient Tool
- Crop Tool

### Develop Persona Studio

**Focus**

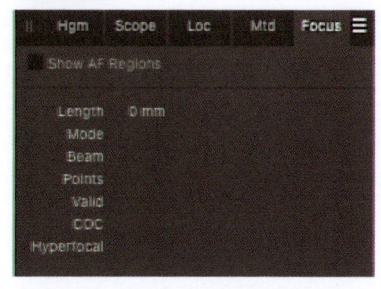

The Focus Panel indicates focus information for the time the image was taken.

## Develop Persona Studio

### Scope

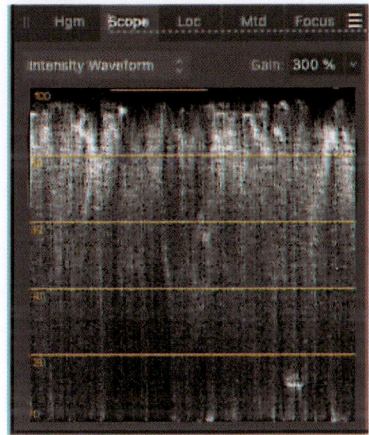

The Scope Panel displays a chart indicating brightness, distribution of color, etc. **Click here** to switch the various charts.
**Intensity Wave form**: Indicates distribution of image brightness.
**RGB Wave form**: Indicates distribution of image RGB value.
**RGB Parade**: Indicates division of RGB color composition.
**Power Spectral Density**: Indicates image frequent domain.
**Vector scope**: Displays a circular chart showing information on image color.

### Location

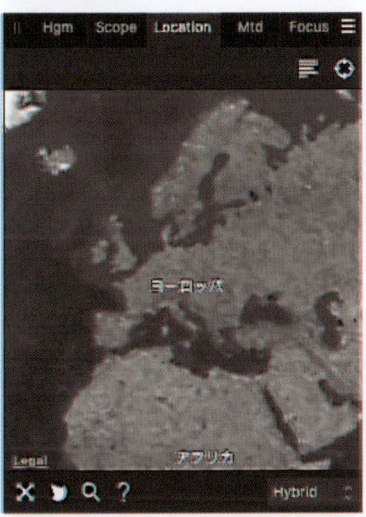

Where the location panel is shot with an embedded GPS camera, the user can confirm shooting location and implement meta data settings. Also, where a GPS lacks a camera, the user can set meta data to a manually indicated location.

Note: As of the publication of this volume, this feature is only for users of MacOSX10.9.

### Info

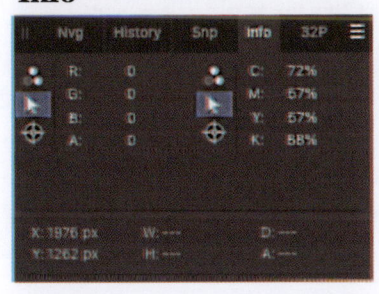

The Info Panel samples images and presents them as data.

## Basic

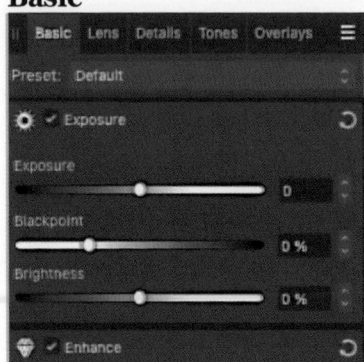

Use the Basic Panel to adjust color.
Exposure: Correct blackpoint and brightness.
Enhance: Select contrast, clarity, saturation, etc. settings for natural tone.
White Balance: Give an image a warmer or cooler feel.
Shadows & Highlights: Adjust the lightness of the shadows and highlights in your image.

## Lens

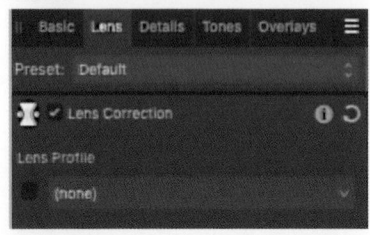

The Lens panel corrects and adjusts for Lens warping.

## Details

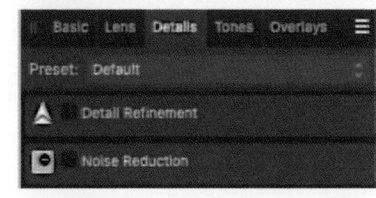

The Details Panel adjusts image edging and eliminates or adds noise.

## Tones

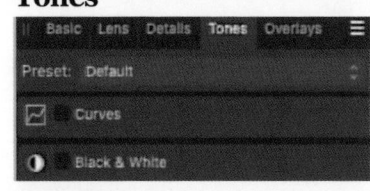

The Color Panel adjusts image tone and color values to adjust color as desired.

## Overlays

The Overlays Panel allows for processing of images using the Overlay tools at the top. Because Raw images are separated from the rest of the work, the Overlays can be deleted.

## Snapshots

The Snapshot Panel can save raw snapshots.

## 4_7: Tone Mapping Persona

### Tone Mapping Persona: Tool Bar

Tone Mapping Persona

Single  Split  Mirror

### Tone Mapping Persona: Tool Panel

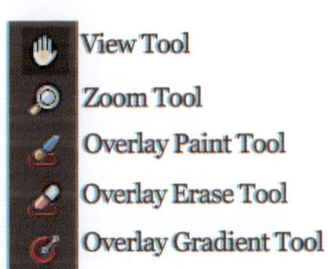

- View Tool
- Zoom Tool
- Overlay Paint Tool
- Overlay Erase Tool
- Overlay Gradient Tool

### Tone Mapping Persona: Studio

The Tone Map Panel is used to adjust Tone Compression, Local Contrast, Exposure, Black point, Brightness, etc.

### Tone Map

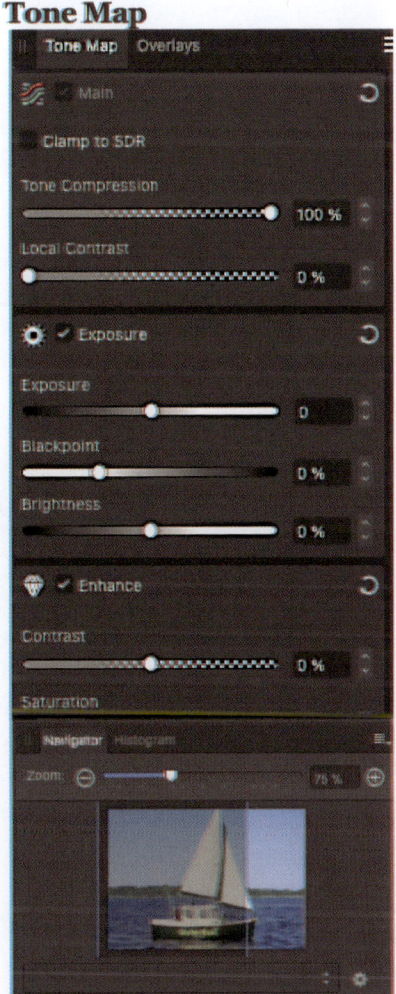

### Tone Mapping Persona: Preset screen

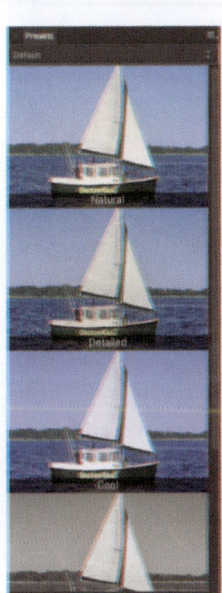

Switch to the Tone Mapping Persona to display the Preset screen to the left. You can then immediately make your selection. Save your settings using the Tone Mapping Panel.

Chapter 4: Affinity Photo Structure and Interface

## 4_8: Export Persona

### Export Persona: Tool Bar

- Export Persona
- Move to Back
- Back One
- Forward One
- Move to Front
- Alignment

### Export Persona: Tool Panel

- Slice Tool
- Slice Selection Tool
- View Tool
- Zoom Tool

### Export Persona: Studio

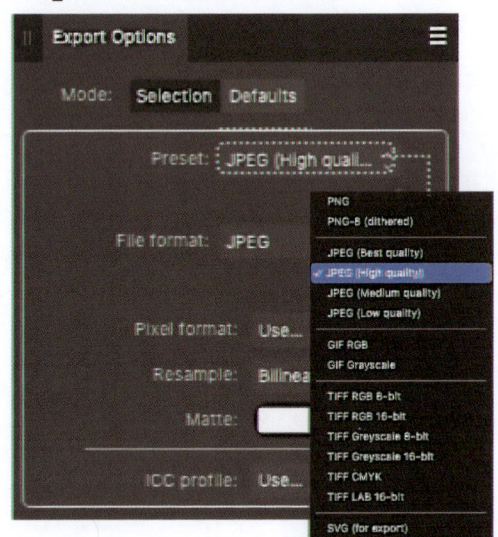

### Export Option

Once your Slice settings are complete, you can now adjust the slice property settings.
Mode/Selection/Defaults: Click on Selection to select an option other than Default Export.

Preset:
Select your settings for general file format, color mode, bit depth options, etc.
File format: Select export graphic format.
Pixel format: Select format from amongst RGB, CMYK, Greyscale, etc.
Resampler: Set sampling options.

# Chapter 5: Overview of the Photo Persona

Chapter 5: Next, we'll be learning about Photo Persona.

## 5_1: Create a Unique Visual Image with Photo Persona

In the previous chapter, we learned about the Quick Tour and Interface. Starting with this Chapter, we will provide detailed information on each tool in Tutorial format.

We first need some practice materials. Here we'll use one photo of green leaves and another of flowers. If you have something you like in your own album, feel free to use that. If you do not have any photos you can use to practice with, download a free photo from the Creative Commons link: http://creativecommons.org

Let's visit the Creative commons site to download two sample photographs. Launch your Internet browner and enter the above URL

We showed you the first one—the picture below-during the Quick Tour.
http://goo.gl/lcaqjD

©Hanna Sörensson

The second one is the photo below:
http://goo.gl/LE1Bcd

©Photography Peter101

Note: The above address utilizes Google_url_shortener.
If you experience any problems, including a broken link, search for the Creative Commons site.

Chapter 5: Next, we'll be learning about Photo Persona.

## 5_2: New document settings

Do you have a working photo ready?

Launch Affinity_Photo and Command/Control+N (or Command/Control+N) to control settings on a new file document. Once you have your visual, adjust settings as follows:

Type →**Print**

Page Present →**A4**

Document Unit →**Pixels**

Leave **Portrait** and "**Include Margins** unchecked.

Use the Default for other settings. If everything is correct, click on the **Create** button.

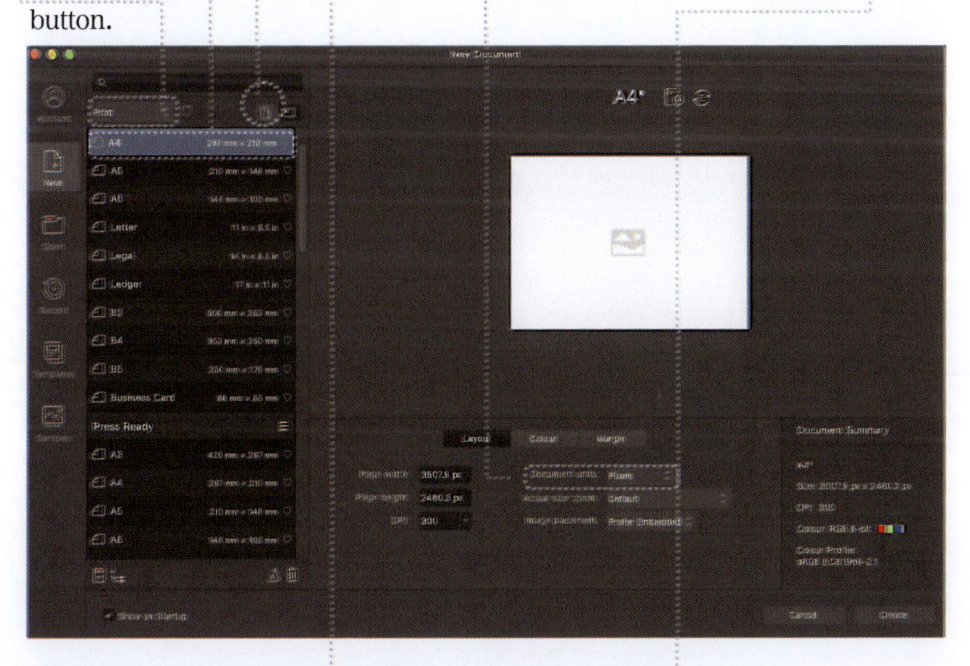

Note: "Command/Control" refers to the Command Key for Macs and the Control Key for Windows.

81

Chapter 5: Next, we'll be learning about Photo Persona...

You should now see your work space as follows. **The white area** in the middle represents an A4 size piece of paper placed horizontally. It serves as the canvas.

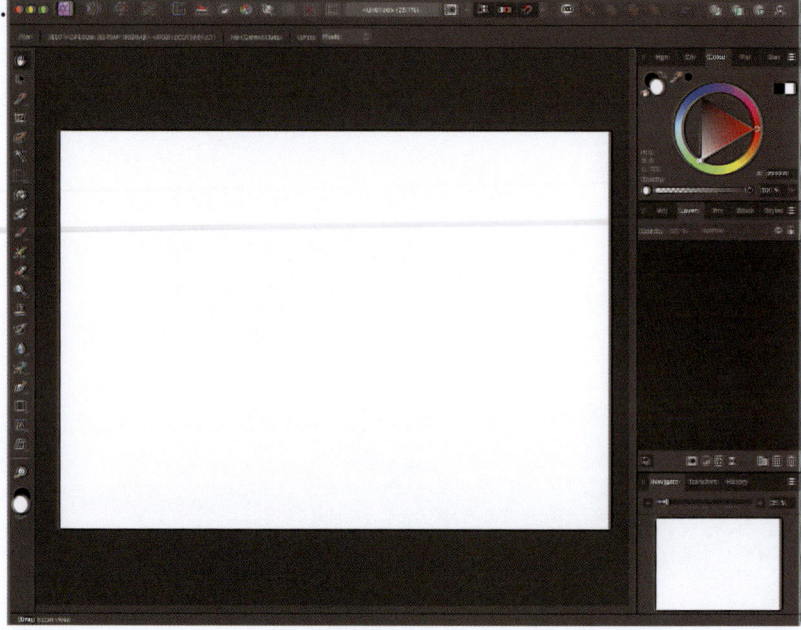

### 5_3: Insert Photo in Document

Place the photo of the leaves onto the canvas. Click on Menu Bar>File > **Place**. Then open the file saved there.

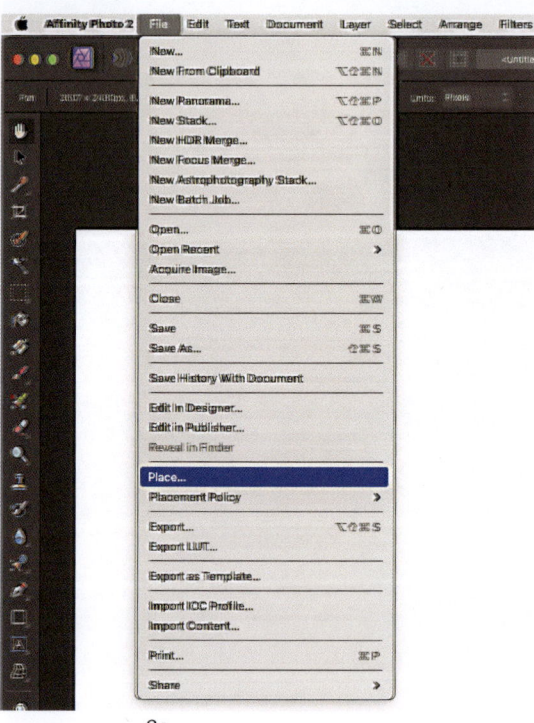

## 5_4: Use the Transform Panel to Change Object Size

The photo displays larger than the screen. Let's make it the right size to fit in the canvas. First, click on an object (photo). Have a look at **the Layers**; the blue color indicates they are active, which means they can be manipulated by the user. We recommend checking to make sure the layers are active before starting work each time. Let's now shrink the photo. Click on the **Transform tab** on the right under Studio. Clicking on **the infinity symbol (∞)**, the link will be shown as in the diagram. Changing the Width (W) value automatically sets the Height (H) in accordance with **the aspect ratio**. Set the Width (W) value to **3500** px. Once you see that the reference point is at **the top left**, set X to **0** px and Y to **0** px.

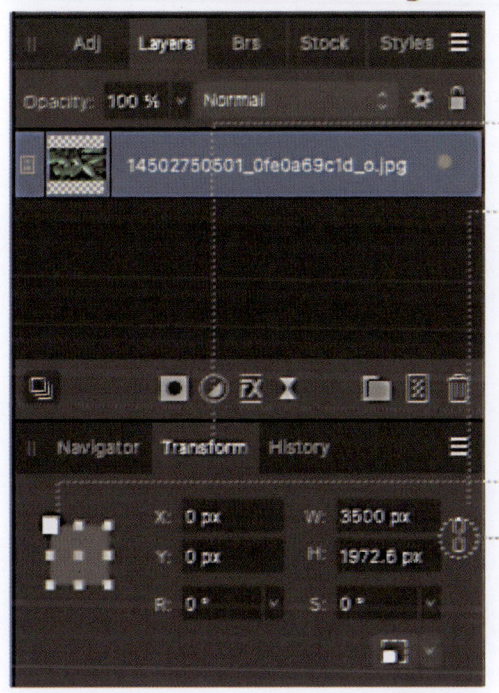

Chapter 5: Next, we'll be learning about Photo Persona

The photo now fits into an A4 size canvas. Proceed making sure the edges do not protrude. Next, insert your second photo. As above, click on Menu Bar>File>Place, and open the photo of the flower petal.

### 5_5: Layers

The photo of the leaves has now disappeared and the photo of the flowers has appeared in its place. In fact the photo of **the leaves** is underneath the photo of **the flowers**. Check Studio>**Layers**. Both photos are now embedded in the layers. Many paint software tools manage layers in this manner.

Chapter 5: Next, we'll be learning about Photo Persona.

The following is a conceptual diagram of the layers:

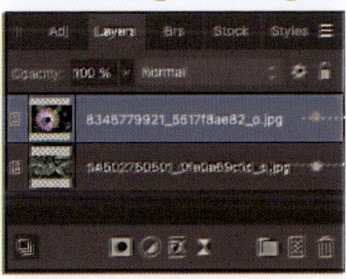

By organizing your layers, you can edit or delete specified layers at any time. Note that the layers overlap at the top and those at the bottom are no longer visible. This problem can be addressed by permeabilization or changing the order. The concept of the layer will be mentioned further later in the book as we proceed with the tutorial.

### 5_6: Zoom Tool

The second photo, of the flowers, is now also larger than the canvas. Let's check how far the edges are outside of the canvas. To switch to the Zoom tool, click on **the Zoom icon** and drag it to the center of the object. Then click on it to enlarge. Hold down the Option/Alt keys at the same time to shrink the overall image. For our purposes here, click on Option/Alt key and hold it down. Click on the object and note **the corner points** just outside of the screen. Switch to **the Move tool**. Drag on the counterpoints to maintain the size of the image to fit the screen.

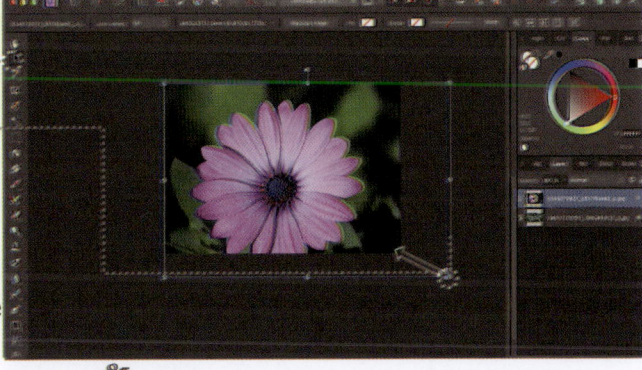

85

Chapter 5: Next, we'll be learning about Photo Persona

Your second photo, of the flowers, is now in the canvas.

## 5_7: Use Navigator to Shrink or Enlarge

Enlarge to make working on the photo easier. Instead of the Zoom Tool, here we use Navigator. Click on Studio>**Navigator**. Drag the **Zoom Slider** to get the desired size.

Chapter 5: Next, we'll be learning about Photo Persona.

## 5_8: Rasterize an Object (Layer)

First, let's rasterize this picture of flower petals. Affinity Photo utilizes both vector data, which is geared specifically for graphs, lines, etc., as well as Bitmap data, which is for vector data, photographs, etc. For this reason, when we work with an object as Bitmap data, we first rasterize vector data and then convert it to Bitmap.

Rasterizing refers to conversion to pixels; in fact we rasterized when we first inserted the flower picture. With Affinity Photo, at this point we convert Bitmap data to layered objects. There is no longer any Bitmap data. Since this chapter describes how to **clip** photos and other similar operations, the first order of business is how to rasterize layers. Click on the flower photo and go to Menu Bar>**Layer>Rasterize**.

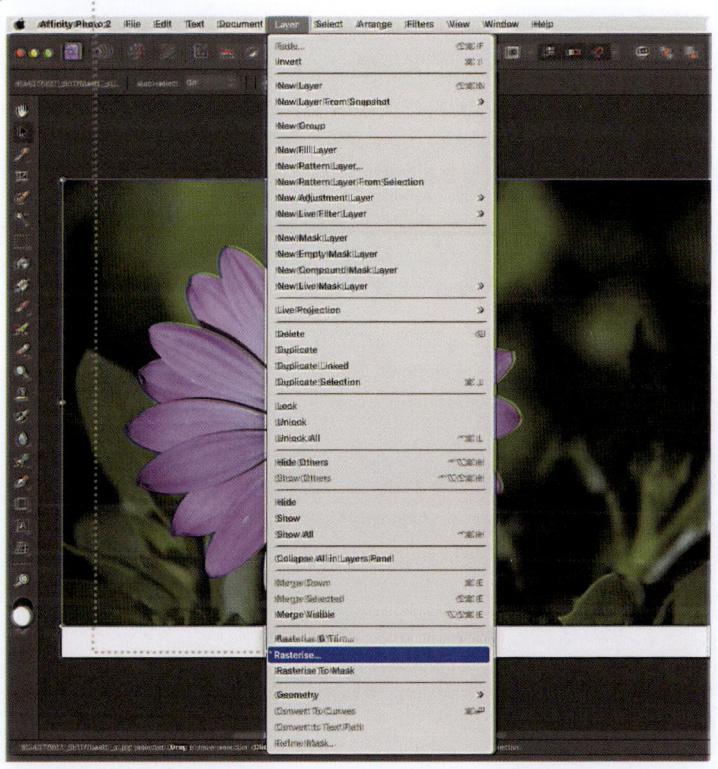

Further, as we move through Affinity Photo with the tutorial, we will show you how to rasterize.

## 5_9: Use the Selection Brush Tool to Select Part of an Image

The second photograph is of petals only. Here we make our Selection; and once we do so, we do not work outside of it. By defining the area we are working with, we perform operations such filling in the area, copying as pixels, erasing, creating a mask, etc. Affinity Photo offers a myriad of tools including:

Selection Brush Tool, Flood Select Tool, Rectangular **Marquee Tool**, Elliptical Marquee Tool, Column Marquee Tool, Row Marquee Tool, Free Hand Selection Tool, and more. The Menu Bar also has separate menu options, making for a truly wide range of useable commands.

Next, click on **the Selection Brush Tool.** Then click on the Context Tool Bar>Mode: Select **Add**, setting **Width** to 160 pixels. **Slowly drag** the background (area other than the flower petals). The area inside the dotted line is your Selection. Strange as it may seem, the Tool selects an area other than flower petals (that is, the background!), and automatically selects a pixel level comparable to the color level where your mouse is placed. It then pushes the boundaries to the edge where it detects significant contrast within the image. Continue to drag the background.

Note that part of your Selection has now crept onto the flower petals.

Click on Context Tool Bar>**Subtract**. Then drag to the outside of your Selection.

## 5_10: Make your Selection Using Quick Mask Mode

Next, let's use the Quick Mask Mode to make your selection. Use the **Deselect button** to undo your work.

Next, click on the **Toggle Quick Mask button**. Note the half red tone that can cover objects. This is the Mask feature.

Click on the **Selection Brush Tool** and change the **Width** to **100** pixels. **Drag on the background** with the Selection Brush Tool. The red mask disappears and the background is now clear.

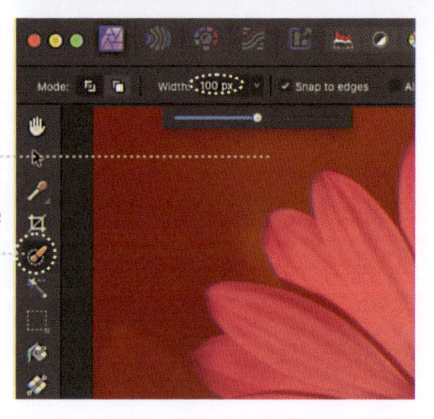

Chapter 5: Next, we'll be learning about Photo Persona.

Note that you may accidentally one of the petals when dragging the background. In Quick Mask Mode, remember that you can erase using the Erase Brush Tool.

Select Tool Panel>**Erase Brush Tool** and drag the protruding flower petals. The Erase Brush Tool is smaller to enable the user to make fine-tuned revisions. Note how you are able to **fill in the delicate flower petals**!

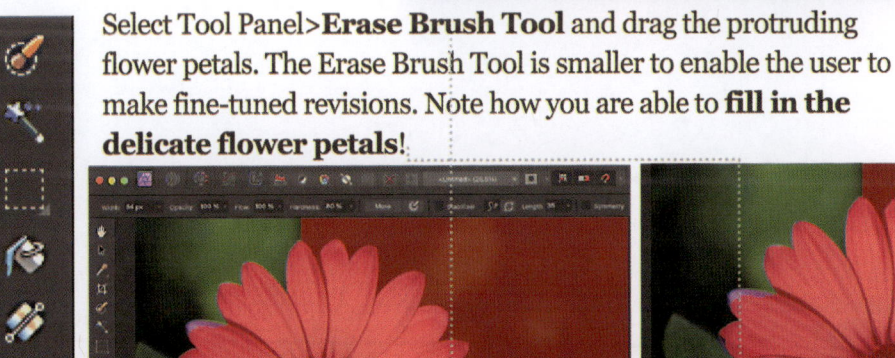

Once you have fixed any problem petals, again use the Selection Brush Tool to drag the background.

Chapter 5: Next, we'll be learning about Photo Persona.

Leaving only the flower petals, remove the background mask. Click the Persona Tool Bar>**Toggle Quick Mask button**.

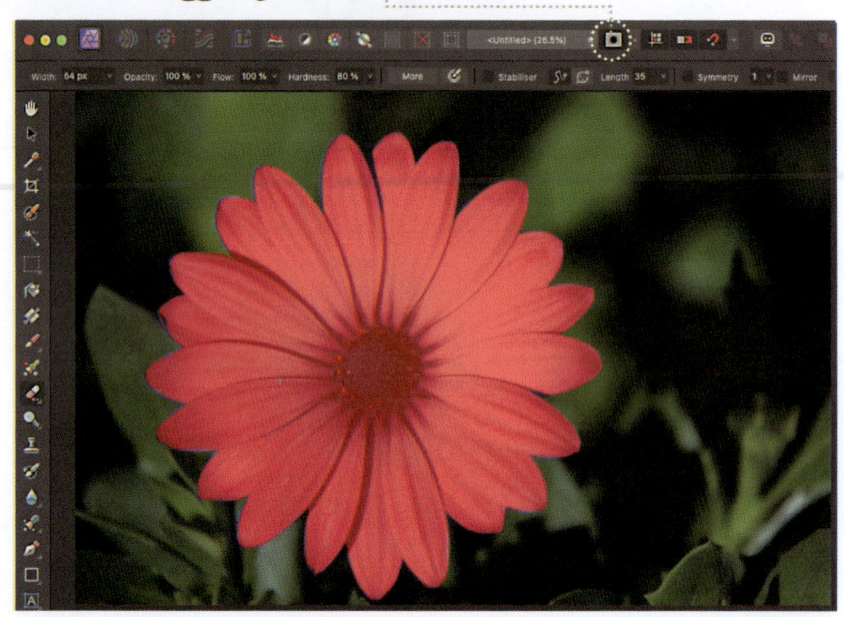

Note that the **background is selected**. The concept here is to create an area protected by the Mask feature (unselected area).

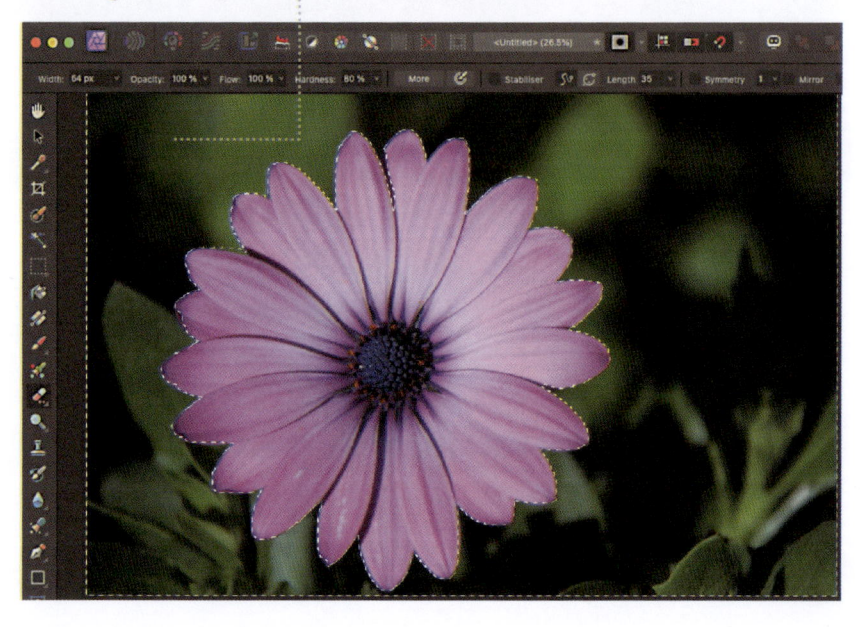

## 5_11: Saving and Importing Selections

You've decided on your Selection and you realize you might want to use it again. For this reason Affinity_Photo is equipped with a Save feature that you can use to save your Selection. Click Menu Bar>Select>**Save Selection**. There are two different ways to save it: Spare Channel and saving To File on your PC.

Firstly, click on **As Spare Channel** to proceed to Studio>Channels Pixel Selection and save. Once you have saved the file, hit Deselect. Then download the file. Click on Studio>Channels>**Spare channei and click, holding down the Ctrl key**, followed by a right click. The Dialog Box appears, at which point we click on **Load to Pixel Selection**. Note that the same Selection as before appears.

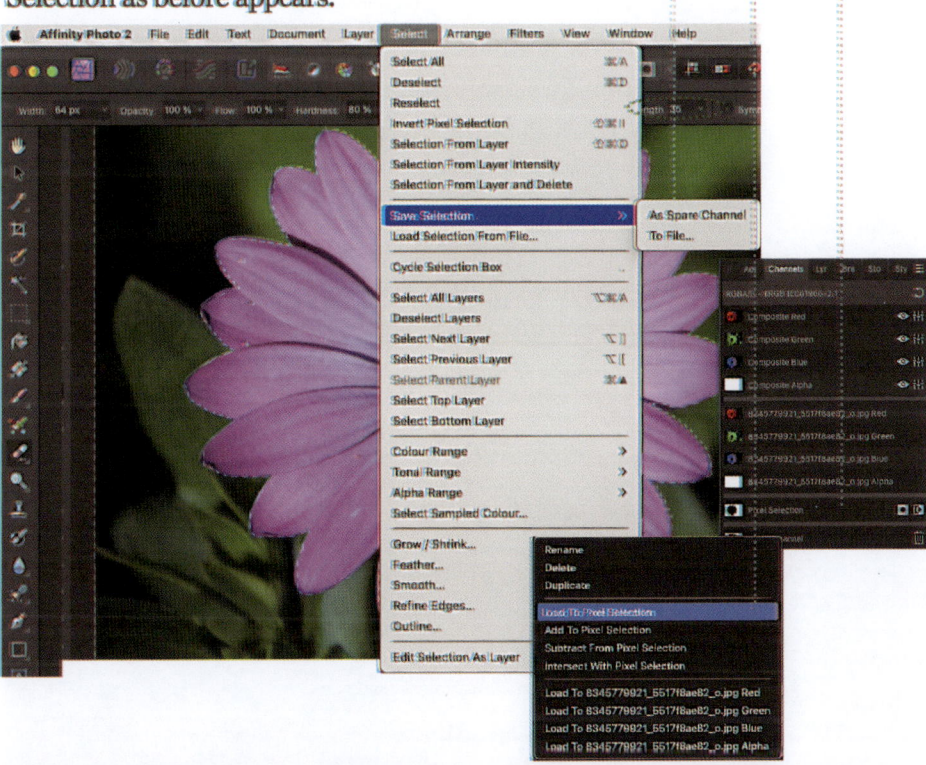

Next, let's try saving it as a file. Once your Selection is active, click on Menu Bar>Select>**Save Selection>To file**. Give it a name and save to a folder on your PC. It will be saved in the **.afselection** format. To download, click on Menu Bar>Select>**Load Selection From File** and open the **xxx.afselection** file.

## 5_12: Use Invert Pixel Selection to reverse your Selection

Until now, we have selected background, but in reality what we needed for our work was the flower petals in the photo. Click on Menu Bar>Select>**Invert Pixel Selection**. Note that only the flower petals are selected at this point.

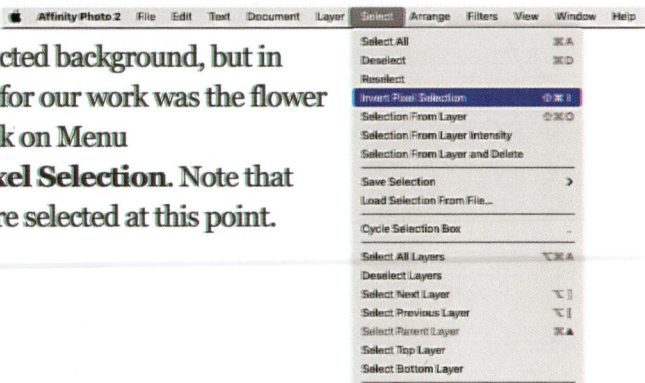

## 5_13: Create a Selection for the Outline

Since you have now selected the flower petals, we'll now take you on a little tangent: let's create an Outline for your Selection. Moving along the outside edge of your Selection, choose your Outline. Click Menu Bar>Select>**Outline**.

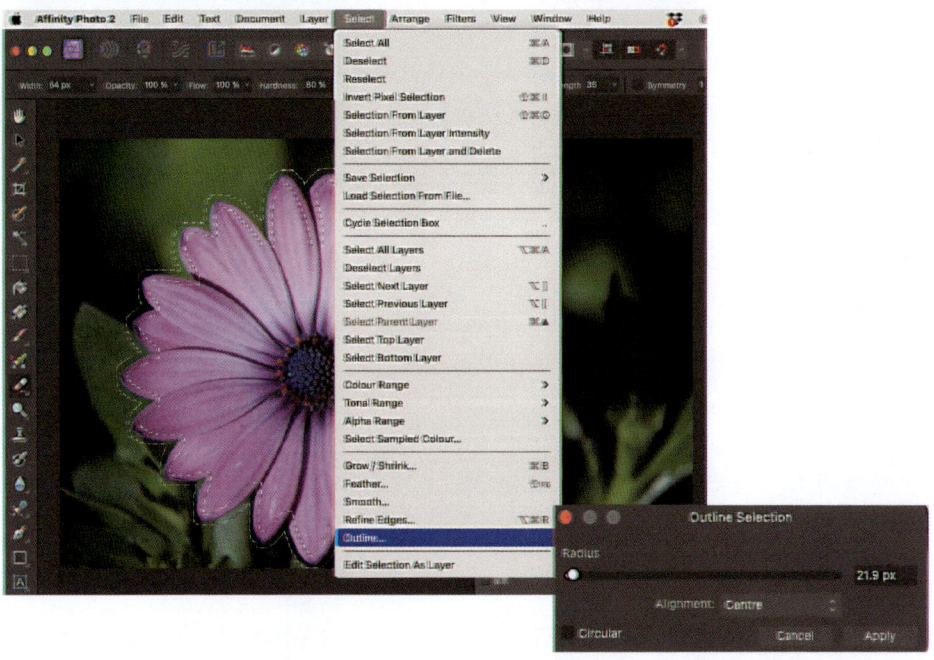

**The Dialog Box** will appear. Using the slider, set the Outline width to a radius of 18.4 px. Set Alignment to Center. Click on the delete key to view the transparent Outline width. Undo your work with Control/Command + Z.

94

Chapter 5: Next, we'll be learning about Photo Persona.

Have you restored the petals to how they looked in 5_12? Your selection should now consist of the flower petals. Making sure that each of the petals is cut out, switch to the **Move Tool**. Note how the petals have moved.

If your Selection does not move using the Move Tool, this means your photo consists of layered objects: that is they have not been converted to Bitmap data. Click on the object and hit Menu Bar>Layer>**Rasterize**

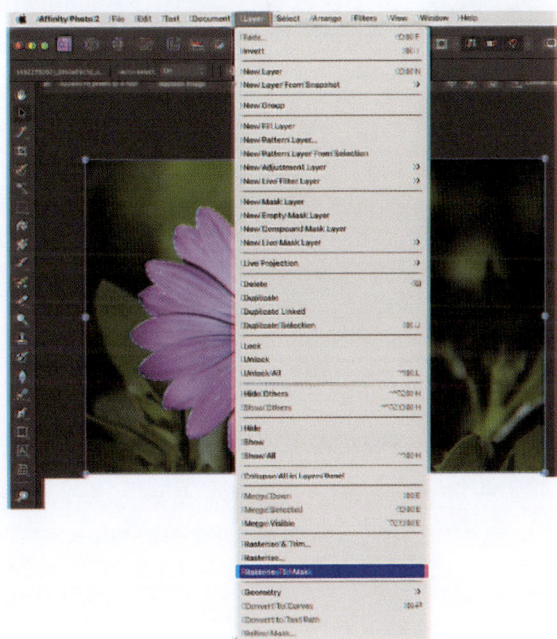

95

## 5_14: Copying and Pasting

Next, copy the flower petals. Hit Command/Control + C (Edit >**Copy**) and paste with Command/Control+V(Edit>**Paste** ). Note that there is no change in the image. Now let's have a look at the bottom layer. The latest layer you worked on—**at the top**—has only flower petals. Layers are automatically added. Note that there are now three layers.

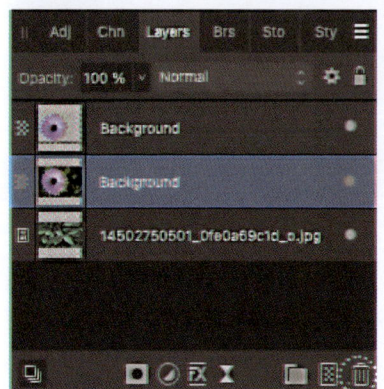

To explain in detail about the layers, at the bottom we have **the layer of the leaves** we first created. Above that is **another layer** with a photograph where the flower petals and background have been separated using the Selection tool. The layer also contains the background. **The layer at the very top** consists of copied-and-pasted flower petals only. To see it visually, un-check the box to the right of each layer.

Next, let's check each of the layers using Show and Hide. Add a check to all of them. Then delete the layer in the middle. Activate the layer in the middle and **click on Trash**. Activate the middle layer and place a check mark next to Trash.

Chapter 5: Next, we'll be learning about Photo Persona.

## 5_15: Rectangular /Elliptical/Column/Row Marquee Tool: Understanding the Differences

Switch to the Move Tool, and activate **the top layer** (flower petal layer). Then move it left and right. It's perfect if you've got only flower petals. **This** author had an area to the right that was no longer needed. We delete any such areas.

Now switch to **the Rectangular Marquee Tool**. Drag diagonally from the top to enclose the shape.

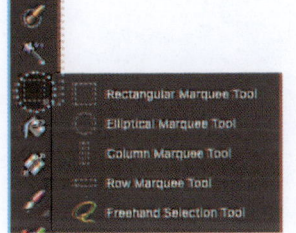

Elliptical Marquee Tool: Create an elliptical shape.

Column Marquee Tool: Create a column.

Row Marquee Tool: Create a row.

Free hand Selection Tool: Draw a figure as you wish.

97

Chapter 5: Next, we'll be learning about Photo Persona.

Once you have confirmed that the unnecessary part of the image has been deleted, let's try some other tools and review at the same time. First, go to Selection Tool Context Tool Bar Mode. You will see the New, Add, Subtract, Intersect options.

**New**: Select, **Add**: This is added to the current Selection.
**Subtract**: This is the opposite of Add. It cuts space from areas already selected.
**Intersect**: Creates a selection from areas where two Sections overlap. Let's give it a try! Choose **the Rectangular Marquee Tool**, then click Mode>**Add**. While holding down the Shift key, drag until you get a **rectangle**.

Next, switch to the **Elliptical Marquee Tool** and then click on Mode>Add. Drag diagonally until you get an **elliptical**. Click on Mode>Add, and drag as you hold down the Shift key until you arrive at a **circle shape**. Again, hit Add to create a Column and/or row. And finally, switch to the **Free Hand Selection tool** to draw your shape in a single stroke. When you come back to the point that you first clicked on, mouse-up to determine your Selection. This completes the process. More details will be provided as we move along in the Tutorial.

Chapter 5: Next, we'll be learning about Photo Persona.

Once you have finished your settings for your Selection, then Deselect. Click the Persona Tool Bar>**Deselect** and click on the icon. Hit the Menu Bar>Select>Deselect.

Next, click on **the flower petal photo** to activate. Once the layer panel turns blue, it's time to move on to the next chapter.

Chapter 5: Next, we'll be learning about Photo Persona.

## 5_16: Blending Layers

We now return to the subject of layers. Layers are blended with the pixels of the layers underneath. Here we have a number of pre-blended samples that serve as potential blend patterns. Switch to the Move Tool, grasp **the corner points** of the flower petals that we worked on earlier, and shrink.

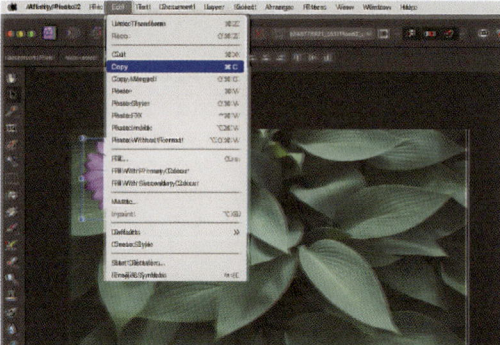

Click Menu Bar>**Edit**>**Copy**, followed by Menu Bar>**Edit**>**Paste**. Then use the **Move Tool to shift the object to the right**. Now you have added a layer to the layer panel. There should now be **two layers of flower petals**.

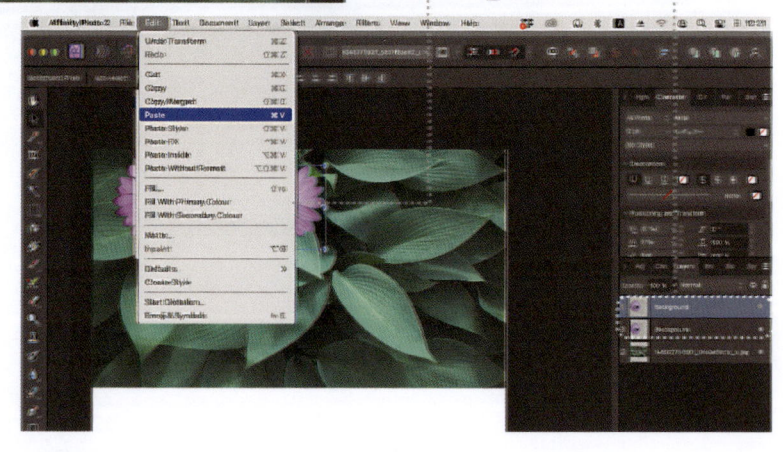

100

Chapter 5: Next, we'll be learning about Photo Persona.

Drag **the second flower petal** to the right, holding down the Option/Alt key. There are now **three flowers shown**. Remember this shortcut key, since you'll be using it often! Drag horizontally holding down the Shift key.

Next, drag the **three flower petals while holding** down the shift key. Once you have confirmed on the layer panel that the three layers are active, copy using the Command/Control+C.

Then paste using Command/Control+V. Note that three active layers have been added. Hold down the Shift button to drag downward. The Shift key can only be used to move text in a horizontal direction, perpendicularly, or diagonally at 45°.

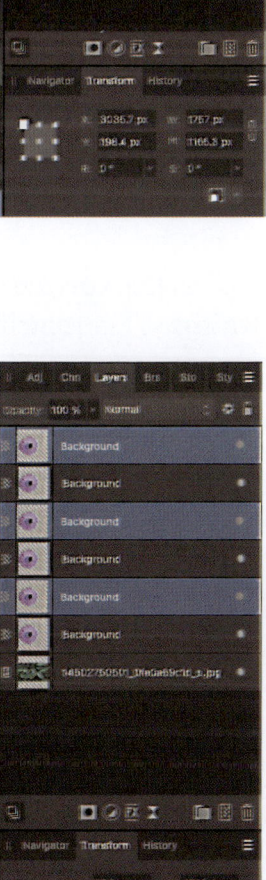

101

Chapter 5: Next, we'll be learning about Photo Persona.

We are now going to move on to the actual blending process. For the first one, we can use the default (standard) setting. Now **click on the second one**. Check to make sure that only the second layer is active. Then click on **Opacity**, and move the Slider to **75%**. The image, now semi-transparent, is blended with the photo underneath.

Click on the **Normal** button to open the Dropdown menu. Then select **Multiply**. The combination of the upper and lower layers yields a darker-tone pixel.

Chapter 5: Next, we'll be learning about Photo Persona.

Select as follows:

**Screen** for the third petal

**Hard Light** for the 4th petal

**Linear Light** for the 5th petal, and

**Difference** for the 6th petal.

103

Chapter 5: Next, we'll be learning about Photo Persona.

## 5_17: Using the Filter

Now let's save the document you are working on.
Click on Menu Bar>File>**Save**.

Next, we soften the image using a filter to render the background leaves more natural. Click on the layer of **the photo showing the leaves** (bottom of the layer panel). Then Select.

Click on **the Live Filters icon** at the bottom of the Layer Panel. Then choose **Gaussian Blur Filter** from the Dropdown Menu.

104

Chapter 5: Next, we'll be learning about Photo Persona

Slide the Live Gaussian Blur **Radius** to about 40 pixels. Note how the flower petals remain the same while the background is blurred. Click on the red dot to choose your settings.

### 5_18: Grouping and Ungrouping Layers

Since we decided to blur the photo of the background leaves, let's now group the other photos of petals (in six layers) into a single layer. Click on each of the petals as you hold the Shift button down. Once you see that the six layers are activated, click on **the Group Layers icon** to the lower right.

Chapter 5: Next, we'll be learning about Photo Persona

Let's now try moving the grouped flower petals. Note how they all move together! Grouping layers differs from merging in that the layers are not combined into one single layer—which means they can be restored to their original state at any time. Let's do that now. Click on **the grouped layers**. For Mac, hold down the Ctrl key and click. For Windows, hold down the Ctrl key and right click. Open the Dropdown Menu and click on **Ungroup**. See how we've gone back to the original? If you wish to change the appearance of the object with the layers grouped, you may choose to automatically rasterize. Remember that if you do this, however, you will not be able to Ungroup.

### 5_19: Merging Layers

Are you able to ungroup the layers? We now have six layers. Let's now try Merging. Click Menu Bar>Layer>**Merge Visible**. The merged layer has been inserted at the top.

Chapter 5: Next, we'll be learning about Photo Persona

### 5_20: Crop Image

This topic was introduced in Chapter 2. Let's now review it. Firstly, let's try using the Crop Tool. Select **Crop Tool** from the Tool Panel to display. You will then see a dotted line around the entire document. Drag each point until the gradation disappears. Then double-click.

You're done! Note how everything looks sharper without the gradation. More details on the Crop Tool will be provided in the latter half of the Chapter.

107

## 5_21: Flatten All Layers

We described the merging process in Section 5_20 above. In this case, the top layer was the one that was merged, while the bottom layers remained, in the order in which they were created. Ordinarily with Affinity_Photo, it is optimal to retain individual layers, but this time—in order to make the following process easier to understand—we will flatten the document. That is, we will take the photos (objects) used through the present time and merge them into a single layer. Under the layer will be a white A4 canvas. Click Menu Bar>Document>**Flatten.**

Let's now have a look at the Layer Panel. In contrast to multiple layers, we now have only **a single pixel layer**. As displayed when printing, the layer is now shown as bit map data.

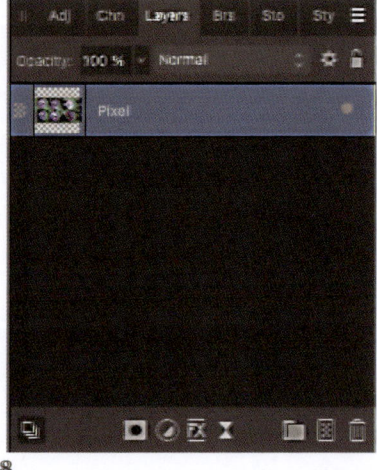

## 5_22: Use Flood Select Tool to Select

Here we have introduced a number of Affinity_Photo tools, but there are also additional selection tools that we have yet to explain. First I would like to explore the Flood Select Tool. Select a similar pixel level as when you first clicked. Set the precision level with the Tolerance settings. Let's give it a try! Choose Tool Panel>**Flood Select Tool**. Under Mode, click on **New**. Click on **the inside of the flower petals** on the flower to the far right in the top row. You should now have one flower petal selected. Click Mode>**Add**, and then click on the petal next to it. Then click on **Subtract** to eliminate more.

Switch to the **Move Tool** and move the selected petal to the left. You should see the white canvas underneath.

109

Chapter 5: Next, we'll be learning about Photo Persona

## 5_23: Using the Flood Fill Tool to fill in large areas with color

You should now have a light pink petal selected. Let's try painting this petal bright red. From the Tool Panel, click on **Flood Fill Tool**. The concept of the Flood Fill Tool—also known as the Bucket Paint Tool—is to turn over a bucket filled with paint to cover the entire floor.

Click on Studio>Color, followed by **the area** you want to fill. Then click on **the red circle**. Once you have chosen your settings, click above the flower petal selected. The selected area should now be red.

Let's now find out more about why the Flood Select Tool is also known as the Bucket Tool. De-select using Command/Ctrl+D. Click on Studio>Layer>**Add Pixel Tool**, and then select Menu Bar>Layer>New Layer. Once you have activated the newly-added layer, click on the Flood Select Tool, switch the color to purple, and then click the top of the screen. It's as if you've knocked over a bucket of paint and spread it all over!

110

Chapter 5: Next, we'll be learning about Photo Persona.

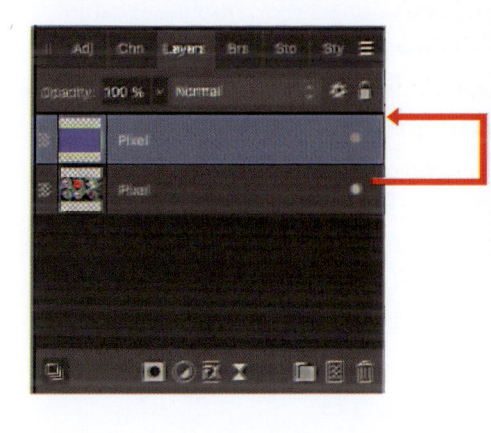

If your selection is entirely purple, the photo you're working on will be hidden. The solution is to switch the position of the top and bottom layers: that is to bring the purple fill on top to the layer below. It's easy! Drag the layer with the composite photograph on the bottom to the gap at the top of the upper purple layer. Are you able to switch them?

Note that the white traces left after moving the flower petals is **the canvas**.

Chapter 5: Next, we'll be learning about Photo Persona.

## 5_24: Using the Gradient Tool to create gradation

The Gradient Tool is located beneath the Flood Fill Tool. Working with **the purple layer** once again, drag it to the top of the layer panel to the very top. Select Tool Panel> **Gradient**, and drag **from the left** of the image all the way to the right.

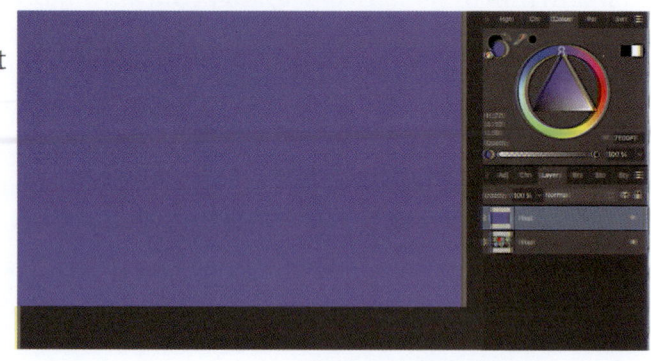

Keeping the Gradation Tool Context Tool Bar>**Type: Linear** as is, click on **the color button next** to it to display the Gradation settings panel. Let's now try some color gradation.

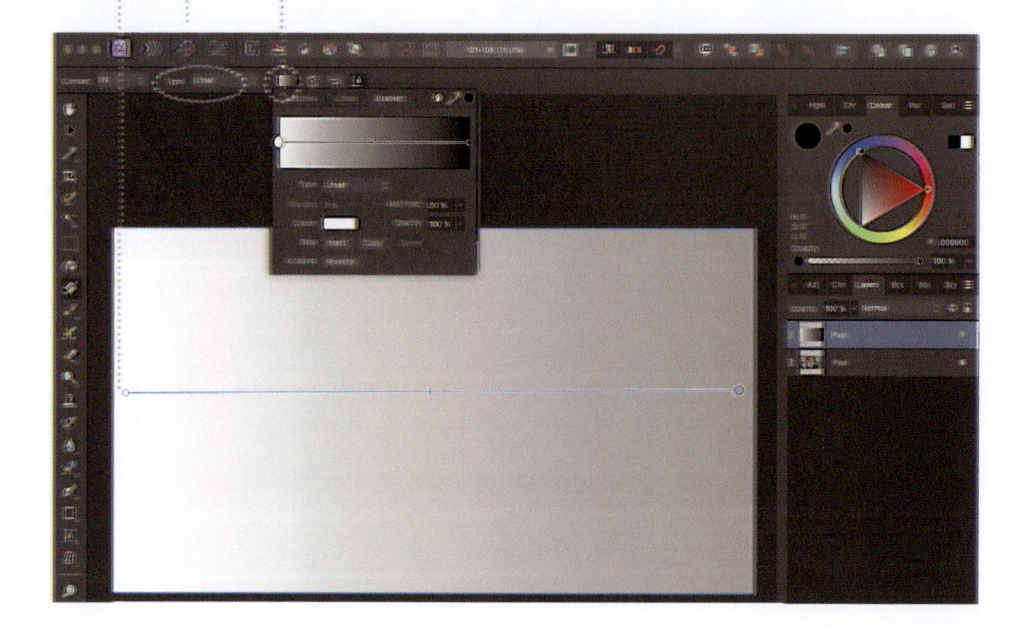

112

Chapter 5: Next, we'll be learning about Photo Persona.

Firstly, click on **the point to the left**, and then click on **the color button** on the panel. When the Color Wheel appears, **click on cyan**. The left side will turn the color cyan.

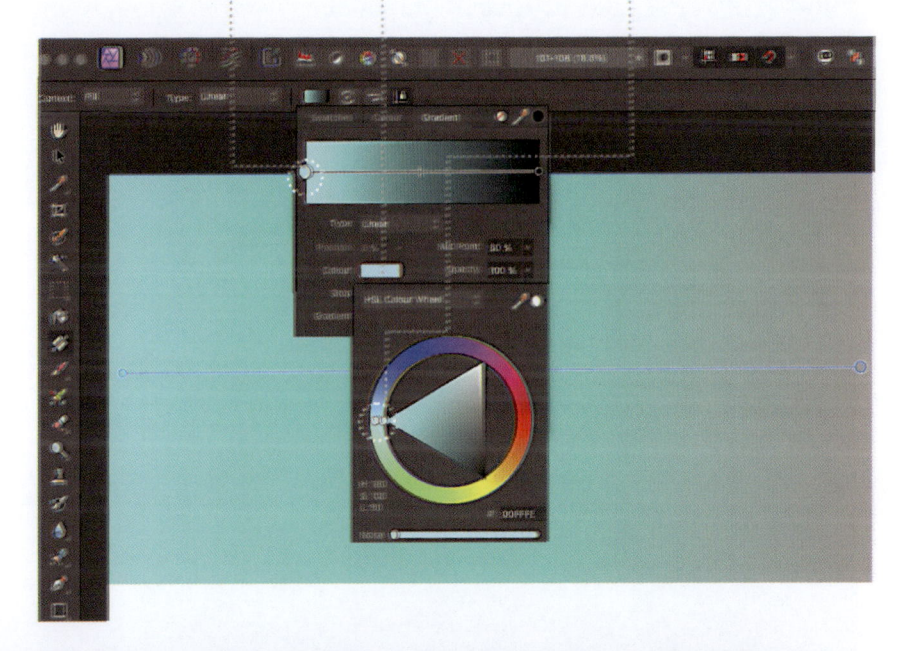

Next, click on **the point** to the right. **The color button** will now be purple.

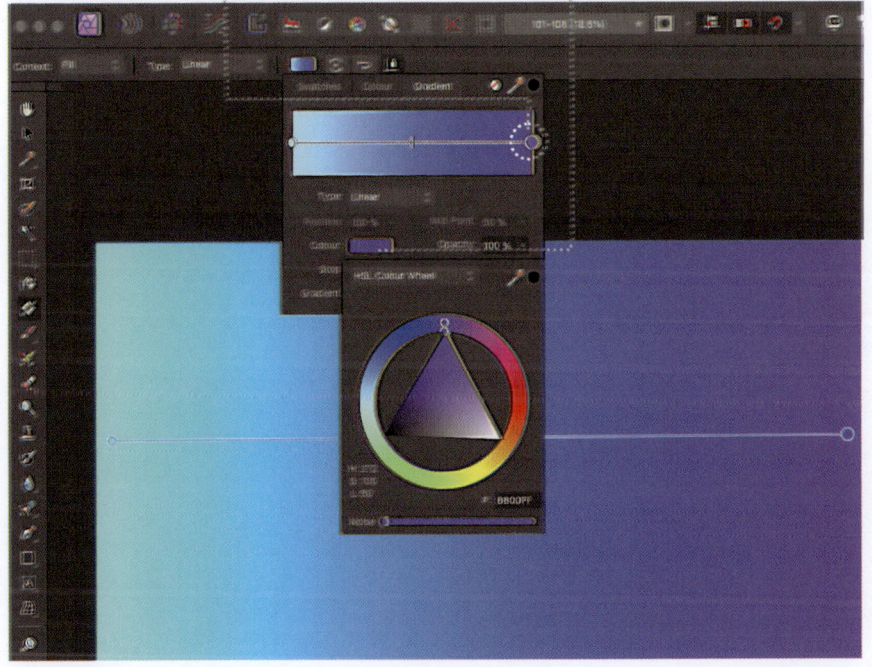

113

Chapter 5: Next, we'll be learning about Photo Persona.

Let's take a little detour! Our Gradation Tools include not only Linear Mode but also Elliptical, Radial, Conical patterns, and more. Let's have a look! Context Tool Bar>**Type: Elliptical**. As you drag from left to right, you may notice that the center of the elliptical shifts, so let's correct that. **This point** is now the center of the elliptical.

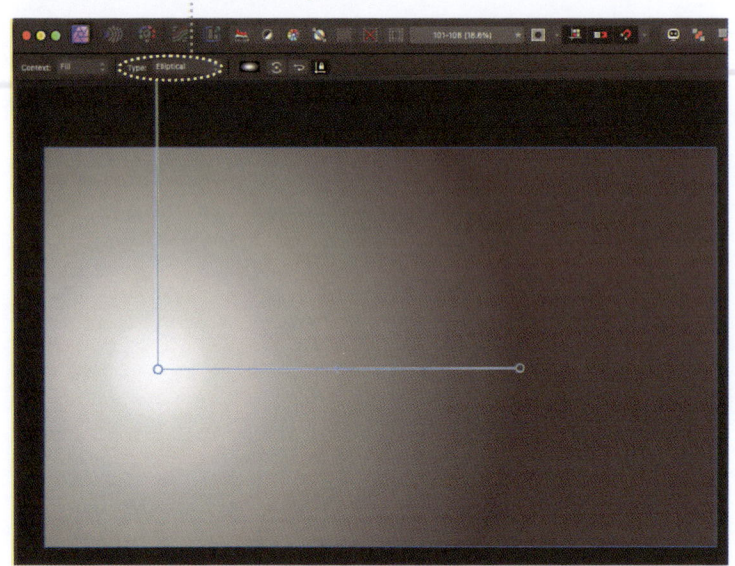

Let's now shift to the right. The point to the left also moves. The left side is now outside the circle. Again drag the point above downward. Note the gradation of the circle.

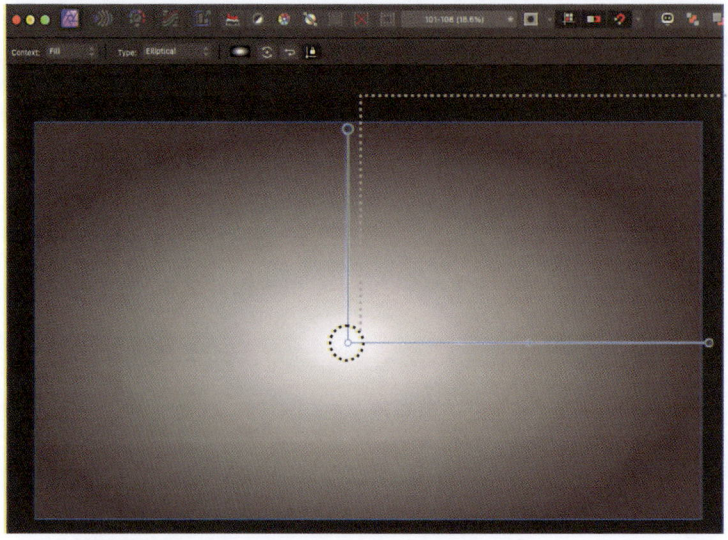

# Chapter 5: Next, we'll be learning about Photo Persona.

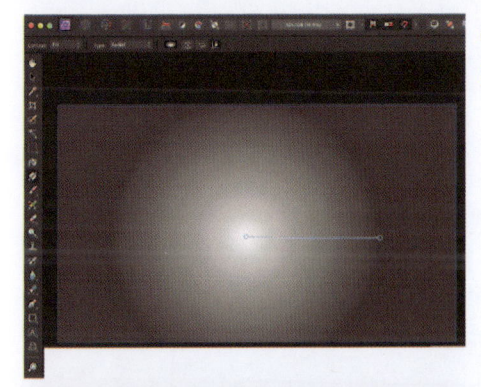

Other:
Radial Gradation

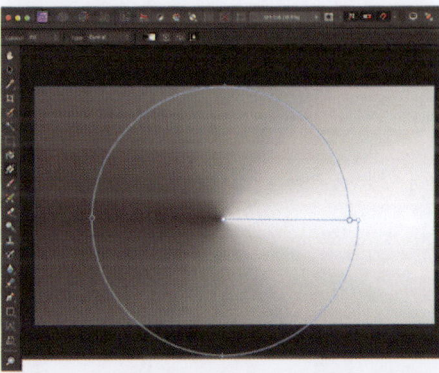

Conical Gradation

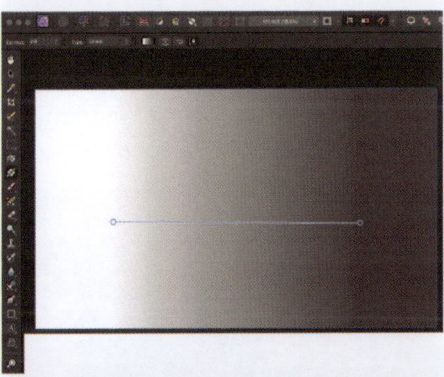

Linear Gradation

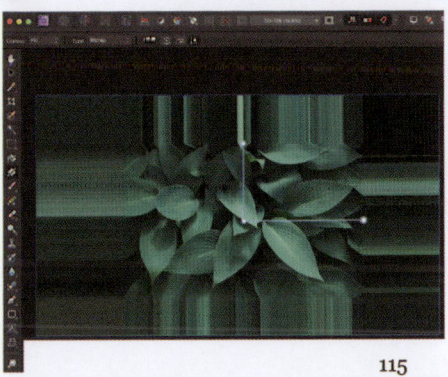

Bitmap Gradation

115

Chapter 5: Next, we'll be learning about Photo Persona.

This is the end of our detour. Let's now restore the cyan color to purple gradation.

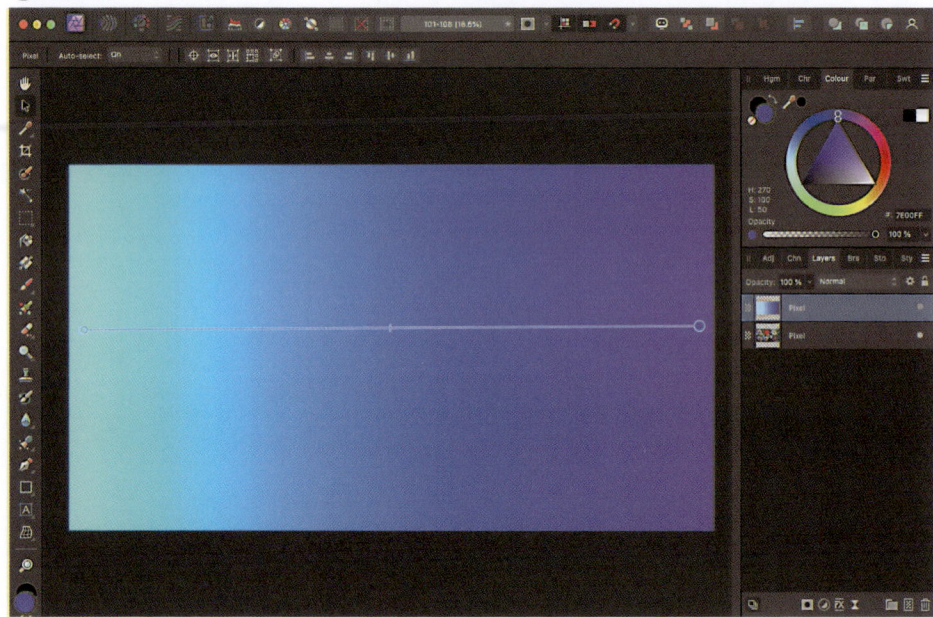

As we did earlier, we will now **switch the position of our layers**. Check to make sure your screen looks like the one below. Let's now move on to the next step.

Chapter 5: Next, we'll be learning about Photo Persona.

### 5_25: Understanding How the Paint Brush Tool Works

Do you see the Paint Brush Tool underneath the Gradation Tool? **The Paint Brush Tool** is comparable to the kind of round brush used in painting

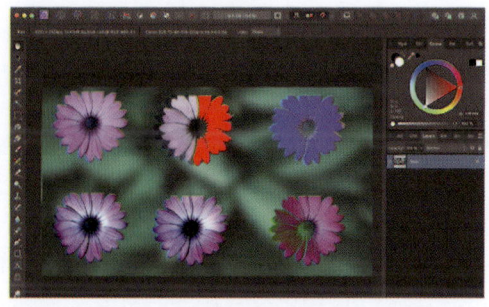

Next, click on Studio>Color to display the Color Wheel. **The circle** at the top left (background in the sample) is used to determine the color of the boundary. The circle next to it is the color setting button for the paint. Click to switch between the front and back. Here the front is active. Click on **the Paint setting buttons**. Clicking on the yellow part of the circle, note that the Paint setting button turns yellow.

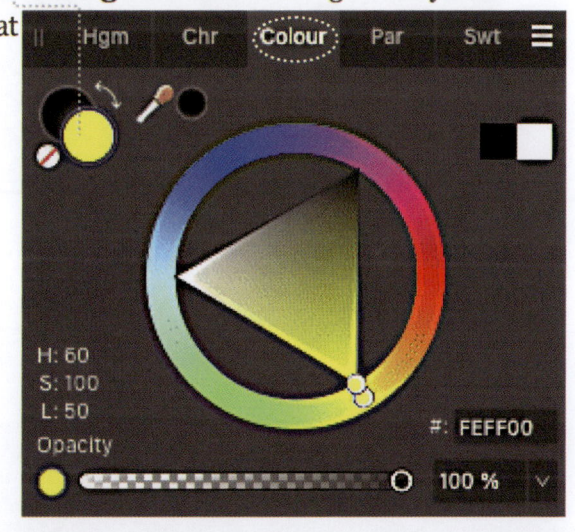

Once you have decided on the color settings, adjust the **Width** with the slider on the Context Tool Bar to 300 px. Now we're ready! **Let's draw a line** above the photo.

117

Chapter 5: Next, we'll be learning about Photo Persona.

Were you able to draw a yellow line? This should be a clear, rounded-stroke line. To better understand how this works, let's first learn about round strokes. Round strokes feature a continuous circular pattern. Click on Studio>**Brushes** to display the brush line. Any sample will work: simply click on any one of the samples to activate it (blue). **Click on** the upper right of the Brush Setting panel. Select **the General** Tab, and use the slider to set **Size** to 300px and **Spacing** to 82%. The Default settings will suffice for the other settings.

A sample will be displayed at the top. Note that the elements constituting the round brush are round. Now let's start **drawing!**

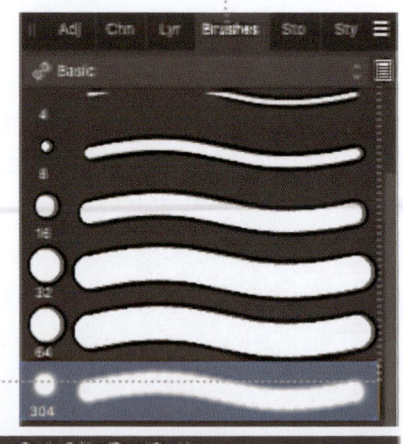

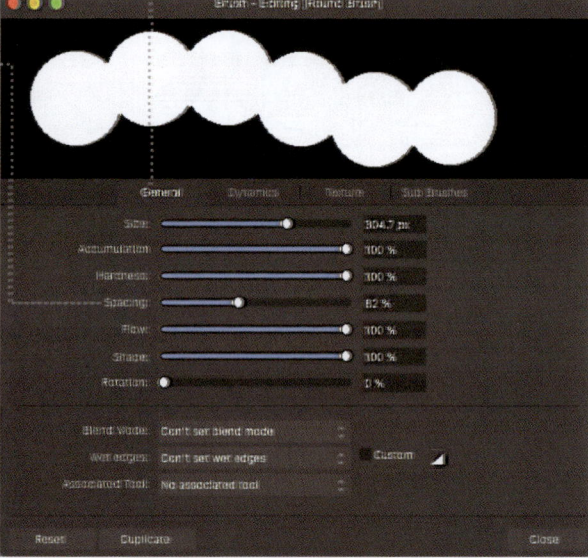

118

Chapter 5: Next, we'll be learning about Photo Persona.

Next, change the Hardness factor. Adjust the Size to 300 px, Hardness to 38%, and Spacing to 37%. The stroke now looks **very soft**, doesn't it?

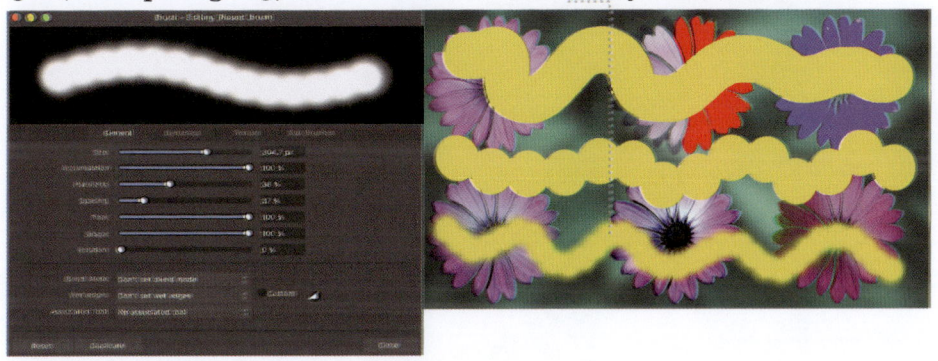

Let's now move on to Flow. Set Size to 300 px, Hardness to 38%, Spacing to 37%, and **Flow** to 50%.

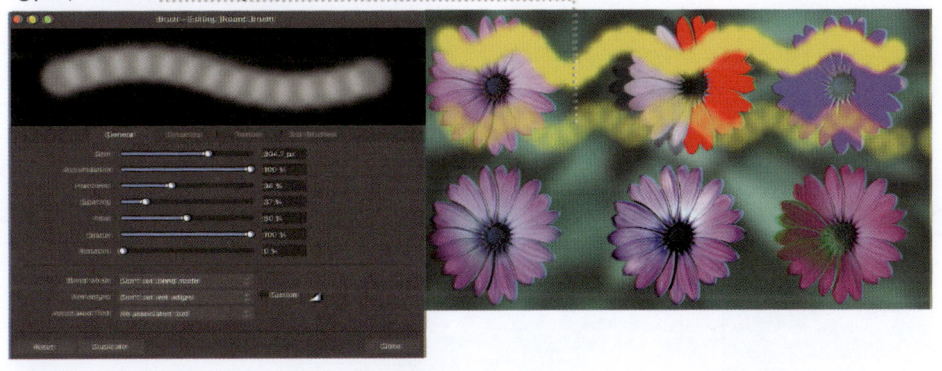

To ensure smooth brush strokes, Adjust Spacing to 10%. Note that the strokes are now **more rounded**.

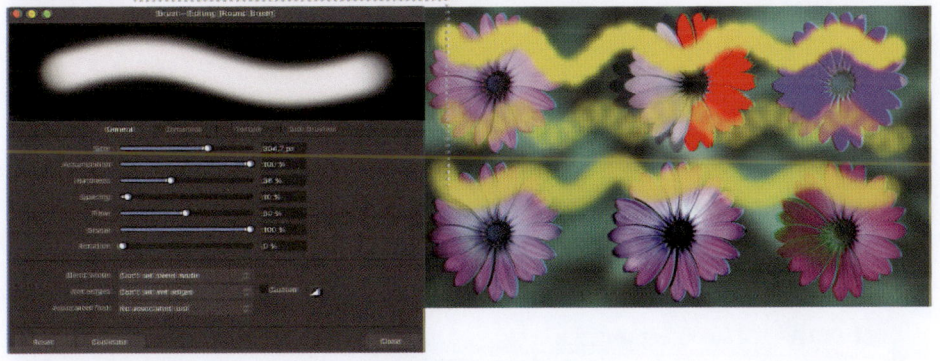

## Wet Edges

Depending on the composition of the picture, the edges may blend. Let's try our hand at this. Under the Context Tool Bar, place a check next to **Wet Edges**.

Note how well the edges have blended.

Next, select **Vivid Light** for the Blend Mode. Impacted by the background, the colors of the lines are now varied.

Now set Blend Mode to **Difference**. Note the jumbled strokes at this point.

Lastly, to fix this issue, select **Subtract** under Blend Mode. How does it look? The strokes now appear in different colors because of how Draw mode works with the background.

## Protect Alpha

Place a check next to Protect Alpha to paint without placing any color in the clear areas. This s a highly convenient feature for filling in objects. Let's give it a try. Let's first restore to our original background free of yellow lines.
Next, delete all lines drawn with the Paint Brush.

Switch to the Selection Brush Tool, drag **the purple flower petal** to the upper right, and select. Once you have made your selection, remove the paint using the Delete key. The background should now be **clear or white**, as if a hole were opened. Switch to **the Paint Brush Tool**. Click on Context Tool Bar and place a check next to **Protect Alpha**. Click on **More** and adjust Size to 300 px. Adjust Accumulation/Hardness/Flow/Shape to 100%, and **Spacing** to 1%. Yellow will suffice as the color. Begin **painting above the flowers**, and note how the white parts are not painted.

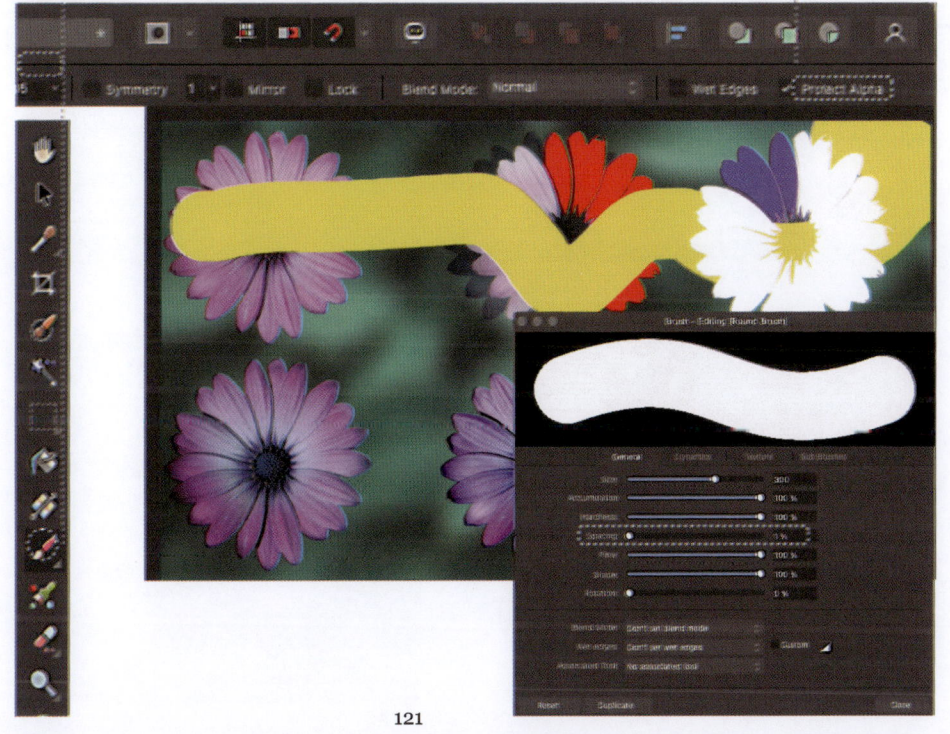

## Brushes

Besides the basic brush, Affinity_Photo also offers a wide variety of brush patterns for purposes of expression. Click on Basic under Brush Panel to see the options.

Pencils

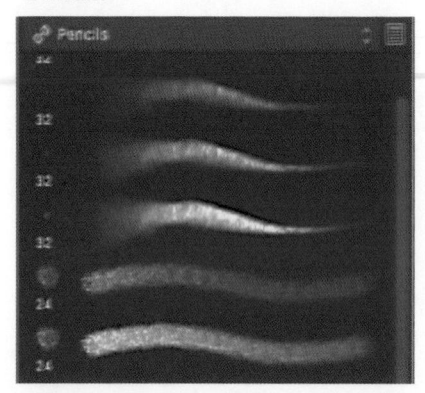

Dry Media

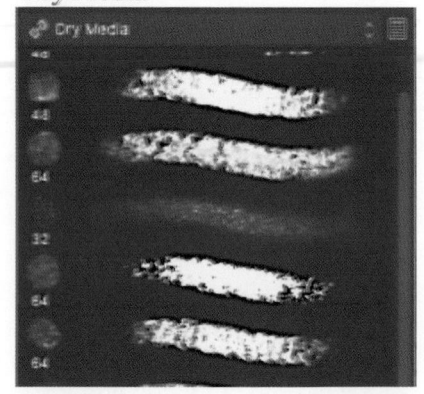

Engraving

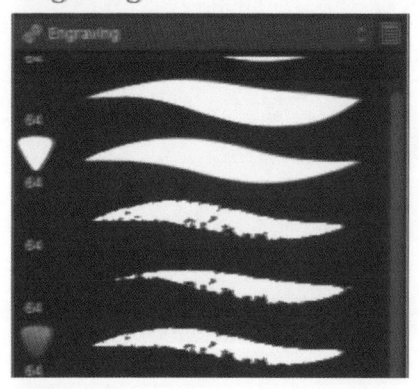

Guaches

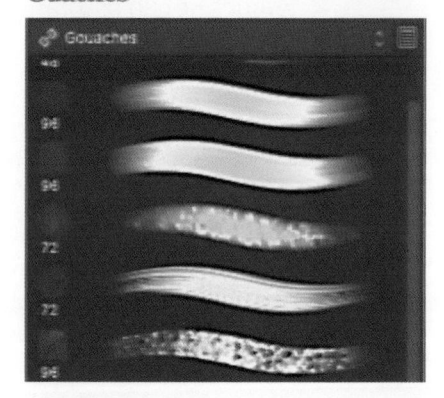

Inks

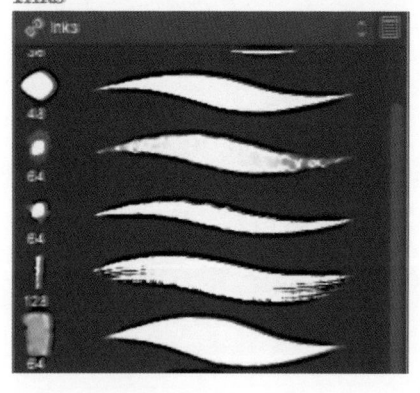

Oils

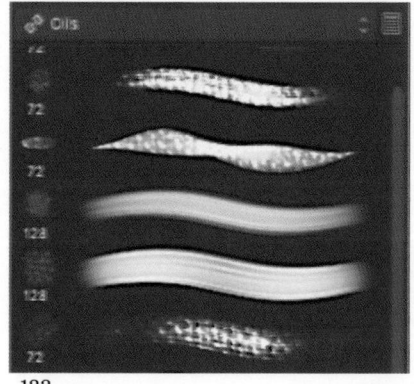

Chapter 5: Next, we'll be learning about Photo Persona.

Let's try out the Spray Pant features. Click on Studio>Brush>**Spray Paint**, select yellow for the color, and drag on the screen.

Change the color to green,

switch to another Spray Brush, change the Size, Opacity, Draw Mode, etc., and drag. You can also confirm that the Protect Alpha feature is on.

To get ready for the next step, let's first erase our work using Control/Command+Z.

Chapter 5: Next, we'll be learning about Photo Persona

## Pressure

If your device can be adjusted for pressure, click on the Context Tool Bar > **Pressure button** to control the pressure of your brush.

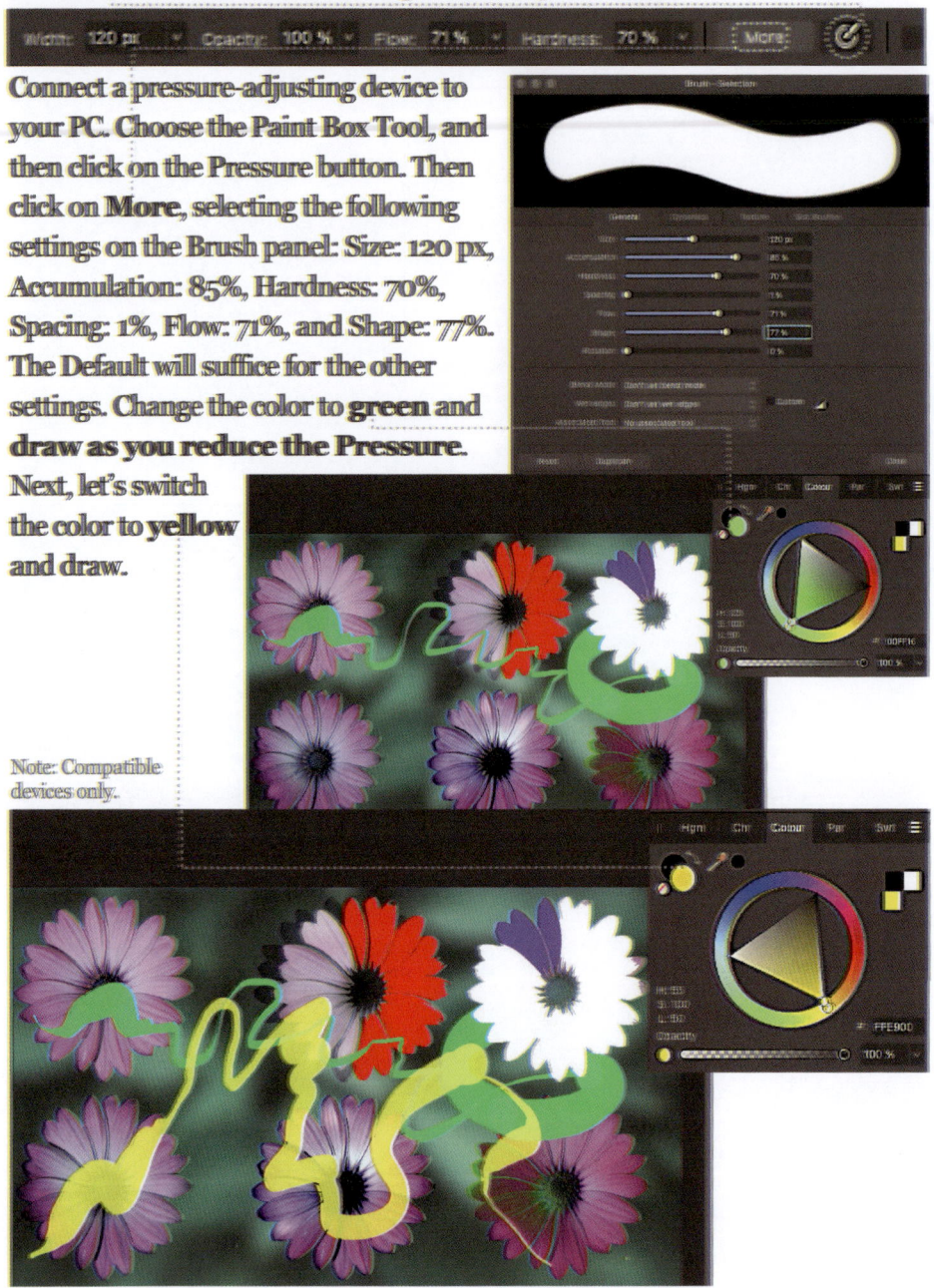

Connect a pressure-adjusting device to your PC. Choose the Paint Box Tool, and then click on the Pressure button. Then click on **More**, selecting the following settings on the Brush panel: Size: 120 px, Accumulation: 85%, Hardness: 70%, Spacing: 1%, Flow: 71%, and Shape: 77%. The Default will suffice for the other settings. Change the color to **green** and **draw as you reduce the Pressure**.

Next, let's switch the color to **yellow** and draw.

Note: Compatible devices only.

124

Chapter 5: Next, we'll be learning about Photo Persona

## 5_26: Use the Color Replacement Brush Tool to change the color of the flower from red to blue

There are times when you might want to change the color of an object, for example a red flower to a blue one. **The Color Replacement Brush Tool** is convenient for this purpose. If for some reason you can't find **the Color Replacement Brush Tool**, click on the Paint Brush Tool **fly-out button**. Were you able to locate it? Choose the Replacement Brush Tool to change the Context Tool Bar Menu. Adjust **Width** to 100px, **Opacity** to 100%, **Flow** to 100%, **Hardness** to 100%, **Tolerance** to16%, and remove the check next to **Sample continuously**. Place a check next to **Contiguous**.

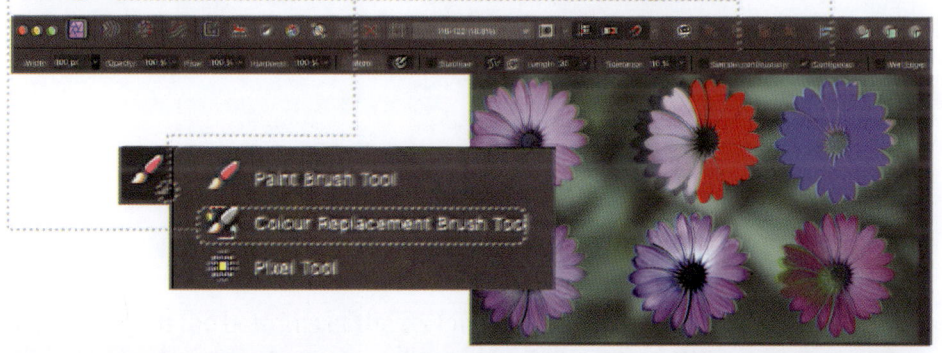

Next, select the color that you would like to change to a different color. Click on Studio>**Color**>Tab, select **No Color** for the Border, activate the Paint settings button, and select Blue. Once you have ascertained that **the flower petal layer** is active, click on the Color Replacement Brush Tool and drag. **The red petal turns blue!**

The Color Replacement Brush Tool recognizes the color you clicked first (red in this case), changing that color to a new color (blue).

125

Chapter 5: Next, we'll be learning about Photo Persona

Let's change the color in the flower photo.

Switch the color of the upper left flower petal to green and drag.

Then switch the petal on the lower right to red,

and the petal in the lower middle to blue.

*__Tolerance__—sets the range of pixels affected when a pixel is clicked. For lower tolerance settings, pixels must be very close in value to the clicked pixel. For higher tolerance settings, pixel color can vary widely from the clicked pixel.

**__Sample continuously__—if this option is off (default), the initial click position determines the reference color to be replaced. When selected, new reference colors are determined as the cursor moves.

***__Contiguous__—when selected (default), only adjacent qualifying pixels under the stroke are recolored. If this option is off, all qualifying pixels under the stroke are recolored, even if they are non-adjacent.
(From Affinity Photo Help)

Chapter 5: Next, we'll be learning about Photo Persona

## 5_27: Pixel Tool

The Pixel Tool is used to draw hard-edged lines. Click on the Brush Tool fly-out button to display the **Pixel Tool**. Select it to limit the Context Tool Bar to Pixel Tools. Adjust the settings for **Width** to 110px, **Opacity** to 100%, **Flow** to 100%, and Drawing Mode to Normal. Place a check next to Protect Alpha, and switch the color to Green. Now let's try drawing a **line** on the image.

Let's take a look at the structure of the line. Click on **More** on the Context Tool Bar. Select the **General Tab**, and adjust **Spacing to 110%**. Leave the Default settings for the rest. Have a look at the sample. Are the squares lined up? This is what a hard-edge line actually looks like. Now let's get right to drawing a line.

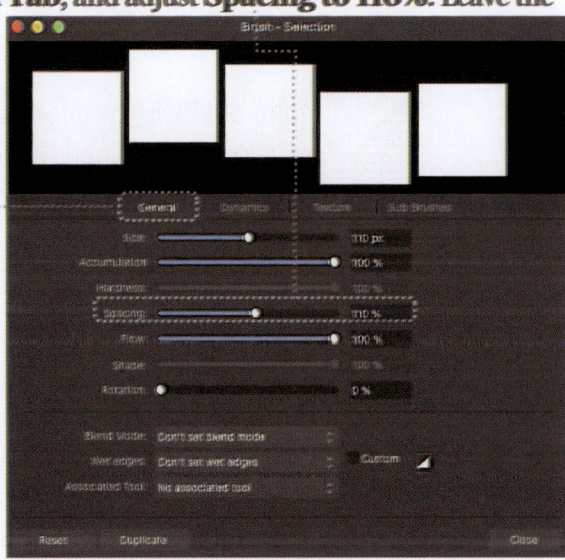

Note: The above examples are for use with Mac computers. Windows settings may differ slightly.

127

Chapter 5: Next, we'll be learning about Photo Persona

Well, how does it look? Do you see **the continuous squares**?

Now let's go back to using the tool as it was originally intended. Adjust the **Size** to 20 px, and **Spacing** to 1%. Leave other settings as default. You should now have **a hard edge line** with no anti-aliasing.

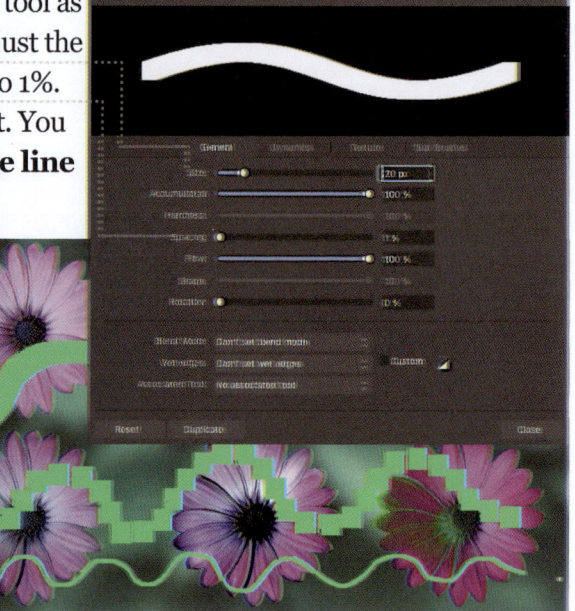

128

Chapter 5: Next, we'll be learning about Photo Persona.

### 5_28: The Paint Mixer Brush Tool: it's just like a real paint brush!

The Paint Mixer Brush Tool is a paint brush used to "paint over" fresh paint on a "not-yet-dry canvas." Let's now go back to the **Flatten** feature discussed above. If there are multiple layers (layer has not been Flattened), click on Document>Flatten. Choose the **Paint Mixer Brush Tool** on the Tool Panel, and adjust **Width** to 300px, **Flow** to 100%, and Strength to 90% on the Context Tool Bar. Select **No Color** for the Border, and activate **the Paint settings button**. Select **the Red color circle**. Drag from **the position of the white petal.** Note that the area is mixed with the color underneath.

\***Load Brush**—removes the mixed color currently on the brush and replaces it with the Color 1 swatch color set on the Color panel.

**Auto Load Brush**—when selected, each new stroke will automatically Load Brush as described above before pixels are applied to the page.

**Clean Brush**—removes the mixed color currently on the brush, leaving a brush with no initial color applied to it.
Model—selects a different color model for use with the brush. RYB is a historical subtractive color model based on red, yellow and blue as primary colors.
**(From Affinity Photo Help)**

Chapter 5: Next, we'll be learning about Photo Persona.

Next, click on **the Auto Load Brush** and start painting. **A red tone will be painted first**, followed by gradual mixing.

Let's now change the color. **Choose yellow** in the Color Circle. Note how the color yellow is mixed in. Then give it a try with **the Clean Brush**. What do you think? Do you have an idea of how the Paint Mixer Brush works now?

130

Chapter 5: Next, we'll be learning about Photo Persona.

### 5_29: Use the Erase Brush Tool to delete an image

The Erase Brush Tool is exactly what the name indicates: an eraser! Before trying it out, open your working photo. Do you remember the photo you downloaded at the beginning of this chapter? It was the second one we downloaded. Drag the JPEG photo to the Affinity_Photo icon and open it.

If you don't have it, you can download it here:
http://goo.gl/LE1Bcd
Use the Google_url_shortener for the address. If the link is broken, search Creative Commons:
http://creativecommons.org

© Photography Peter101

Click on Tool Panel>**Erase Brush Tool** Adjust Width to 90px, Opacity to 100%, Flow to 100%, and Hardness to 100%; then draw a line as if painting. Note the **light gray background**. Then Adjust Opacity to **75%**. Next, try setting Opacity to **50%**, noting **the semi-transparent look** of the image. When you're finished, undo your work to restore it to its original state and get ready for the next step.

Chapter 5: Next, we'll be learning about Photo Persona.

### 5_30: Use the Background Erase Brush to create a transparent background

The Background Erase Brush erases similar pixel colors. Click on the Erase Brush Tool fly-out button, and select **the Background Erase Brush**. On the Context Tool Bar, adjust Width to 110 px, Tolerance to 10%, and turn on Sample Continuously as well as Contiguous. Leave the rest as the Default settings. Then **drag the background**. Now you should see only the flower petals, with no background.

### 5_31: Use the Flood Erase Tool to turn the background transparent with a single click

The Flood Erase tool allows the user to erase similar color pixels with a single click. Lett's give it a try. Click on Tool Panel>Erase Brush Tool fly-out button, and select **the Flood Erase Tool**. Adjust Tolerance on the Context Tool Bar to **26%**. Then click **anywhere** on the background, which should virtually disappear at this point.

Chapter 5: Next, we'll be learning about Photo Persona.

## 5_32: Use the Color Picker Tool to instantly pick up the image color

Flood Erase Tool. We're now going back to follow the order of the Tool Panel. Here we explain **the Color Picker Tool**, which is third from the top. Also called an eyedropper tool, it picks up part of the background color with a single click.

Click on Tool Panel>**Color Picker Tool**. Under Source on the Context Tool Bar, select **Current Layer** or **Global**.

Radius can pick up 1 x1 or a wide range of values. Let's use 1x1 here. Click on **any spot**.

Click on Studio>Color Tab, noting **the purplish red tone**. This is the color that will be saved. Next, select **Flood Fill Tool** and click on **the transparent part** of the image. Note how the purplish red tone now fills the background.

Once you are done, undo to restore your work to its original state.

133

## 5_33: Use the Dodge Brush Tool to lighten any part of your image.

The Dodge Brush Tool employs the same technique as in photography to lighten part or parts of an image. Select the Tool Panel>**Dodge Brush Tool**, followed by the Context Tool Bar. Adjust width to 64 px, Opacity to 100%, Flow to 100%, Hardness to 80%, Tonal Range to Midtones, and turn on Protect Hue. **Drag on the flower petal**. Then drag on the whole petal as if painting, noting how your image should now be brighter. Mouse up one more time to lighten even more. Then drag on the same spot once again.

At 100% Opacity, mouse up three times on the flower petals.

Original

Restore your work to its original state to prepare for the next step. Display the Studio>**History** panel and position **the Slider at 0**. Make sure you are now back to your original document.

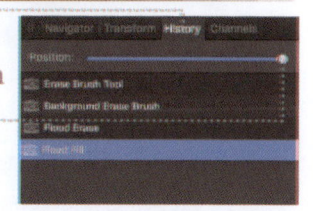

### 5_34: Use the Burn Brush Tool to darken part or parts of your mage

The Burn Brush Tool—the opposite of the Dodge Brush Tool—employs the same technique as in photography to darken part or parts of an image. Click on the Tool Panel>Dodge Brush Tool Flyout Button to display the **Burn Brush Tool icon**. Click on the Context Tool Bar and adjust Width to 64 px, Opacity to 100%, Flow to 100%, Hardness to 80%, Tonal Range to Midtones, and turn on Protect Hue. **Drag the top of the flower petals** and note how they darken. Let's now make it three levels darker. Mouse up and drag the same spot three times.

Original

At 100% opacity, mouse up three times on the flower petal and drag.

Chapter 5: Next, we'll be learning about Photo Persona.

## 5_35: Use the Sponge Brush Tool to boost image saturation

The Sponge Brush Tool is used to adjust the saturation of part or parts of an image. Then click on the Tool Panel>Burn Brush Tool>Flyout Button to display the **Sponge Brush Tool icon**. Click on the Context Tool Bar adjust width to 64 px, Opacity to 100%, Flow to 100%, Hardness to 80%, and click on **Saturate**. Drag the flower petals. Mouse up and drag the same spot three times.

Original

Drag to Saturate three times

Drag to Desaturate three times

Incidentally, note that **Vibrance** adjusts the intensity of lighter colors, and at the same time minimizes clipping of saturated pixels. **HSL Saturation** adjusts the intensity of all pixel colors while keeping clipping to a minimum.

136

Chapter 5: Next, we'll be learning about Photo Persona.

## 5_36: Use the Clone Brush to copy a part or parts of an image and stamp it

The Clone Brush Tool, also known as a **stamp tool**, is used to copy and paste parts of images. Go to the Tool Panel and select **Clone Brush Tool**. Then go to the Context Tool Bar and adjust Width to 60 px, Opacity to 100%, Flow to 100%, Hardness to 80%, and turn on **Aligned**. The Default settings are sufficient for the other settings. **First, hit the Option/Alt key and click on the flower petal** top copy. We will call this Point **A**.

Next, **click on a spot a slight distance away from the flower petal** and click (Point **B**). Then drag. This action determines the initial distance between A and B. The image positioned at Point A is copied.

137

Chapter 5: Next, we'll be learning about Photo Persona

The image at Point A is then recreated at Point B.

Now let's do the opposite: let's erase the petal. **Click on the background color holding down the Option/Alt key**. This action copies the image. We will call this Point C. Then **click on the flower petal**. We will call this Point D. Then drag. If you want to change the source pixels, place the mouse where you would like to bring in the pixels. Hold down the Option/Alt key and click.

138

Chapter 5: Next, we'll be learning about Photo Persona

## 5_37: Use the Undo Brush Tool to render painted areas semitransparent

First, use **the Paintbrush Tool** to adjust Width to 55 px, and Opacity/Flow/Hardness to 100%. Then paint red.

Now let's try the Undo Brush Tool. Click on the Tool Panel and select the **Undo Brush Tool**. On the Context Tool Bar, adjust Width to 55 px, and Opacity/Flow/Hardness to 100%. Then trace the outline of what **you have painted so far**. Note how only the parts you have painted with a brush have disappeared. You might think that Command/Control+Z is sufficient for deleting images, but remember that this Undo Brush Tool can do much more: for example it can erase erase so that the object looks transparent. Let's give it a try. Returning to the spot we painted earlier with the Paint Brush, select the Undo Brush Tool. Then go to the Context Tool Bar and adjust **Opacity** to 60%. Start drawing, and see how handy this tool is!

139

Chapter 5: Next, we'll be learning about Photo Persona

## 5_38: Use the Smudge Brush Tool to blend color as if smudging with your finger

On the Tool Panel, select **the Smudge Brush Tool**. The Smudge Brush Tool works in the same way as the idea of blending paint with you finger that hasn't quite dried yet. On the Context tool Bar, adjust Width to 310 px, Flow to 100%, and Hardness to 50%. Then rub from **the circle** to the right.

Note how the flower petals have now blended into the background. This tool is often used to blend borders on composite images.

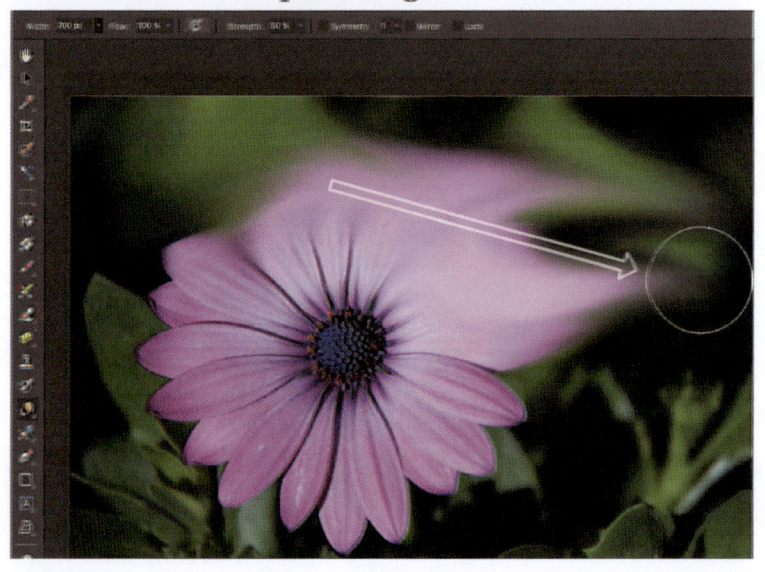

Chapter 5: Next, we'll be learning about Photo Persona

## 5_39: Use the Blur Brush Tool to blur part or parts of an image

Let's try out **the Blur Brush Tool**. On the Context Tool Bar, adjust Width to 280 px, Opacity to 100%, Flow to 100%, and Hardness to 100%. Then rub the petals a few times. Because the Blur Brush Tool works cumulatively, the more you rub, the blurrier the image becomes.

Original

A few brush strokes

141

Chapter 5: Next, we'll be learning about Photo Persona

## 5_40: Use the Sharpen Brush Tool

The Sharpen Brush Tool is used to sharpen images by boosting pixel contrast. Hit the Tool Panel and select **Sharpen Brush Tool**. Then hit the Context Tool Bar and adjust Width to 280 px, Opacity to 100%, Flow to 100%, and Hardness to 100%. Then rub the petals a few times. Because the Sharpen Brush Tool works cumulatively, the more you rub, the sharper the image becomes.

Original

A few brush strokes

Chapter 5: Next, we'll be learning about Photo Persona

**5_41: Use the Median Brush Tool to eliminate noise for part or parts of an image**

The Median Brush tool helps to minimize noise. The tool is located in the same place as the Smudge/Blur/Sharpen tools. Choose the **Median Brush Tool** and adjust Width to 280 px, Opacity to 100%, Flow to 100%, and Hardness to 100%. Then rub the flower petal a few times. Note how any noise has diminished.

Original

A few brush strokes

143

## 5_42: Be a master at cropping!

Now that we have some knowledge of image processing, it's time to learn more details about the Crop Tool, which we've already seen a number of times. You can use any photo you like for our purposes here. If you do not have an appropriate photo, you can use an image provided by this author, as follows:
Left-click on the following site:
http://goo.gl/poq163
Give the image a different name and save it.

Next, drag the image to the Affinity Photo icon and launch. If the image is locked, unlock it and click on **Crop Tool** on the Tool Panel to switch the Context Menu. On the left, click on **Apply** and Crop. Then choose **Mode** to keep the same aspect ratio, or select from various options such as **Units**, **Rotate**, **Straighten**, or **Overlay** to create an even more beautiful structure.

Click on **Overlay**. Note **None**, **Thirds Grid**, **Golden Spiral**, and **Diagonals**.
Refer to this baseline to determine photo structure.

Thirds Grid                                               Diagonals

Chapter 5: Next, we'll be learning about Photo Persona

Let's try the Golden Spiral Overly using the Golden Ratio. The Golden Ratio is a mathematical ratio found in the natural world, which is used in design, and much more. Its application results in a beautiful structure to look at. Click on **Context Tool Bar>Overlay>Golden Spiral**. The structure of the sample photo may appear unrefined at this point. Click on the Golden Spiral center, on the appropriate point in the photo. Move it so that **the center of the Spiral** is the point shown in the photo. Then adjust the other eight points and click on **Apply**.

You did it! The left side is now complete.

145

Chapter 5: Next, we'll be learning about Photo Persona.

**5_43: Note the difference between a JPEG file opened with File>Open and File>Place.**

Launch Affinity_Photo and create a new file with Command/Control (or File>**New**). On the Setting screen, select Type to Print, and Page Preset to A4. For other settings, use the Default. Your workspace should be blank.

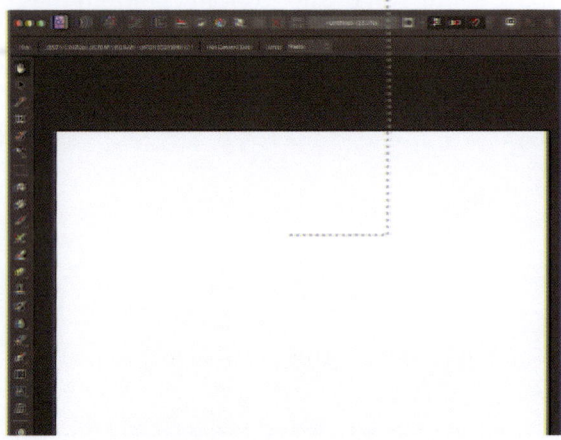

Next, click on **File > Open** to open the JPEG file noted above. In a difference with the file **opened with New Document** above, **it opens second**. If the screen is locked, unlock the layer lock and shrink the image **to one-third** the workspace. **Copy the image to the clipboard.**

146

Chapter 5: Next, we'll be learning about Photo Persona..

Then click on **the white workspace file** (first file) and **paste** to the left side of the workspace.

Next, click on **File > Place** to shrink the and place the same JPEG file in the same folder and place **it to the right of the screen**. Be careful not to make a mistake here! **The left side was put in position using Copy & Paste, while the right side photo was put here using the Place command.**

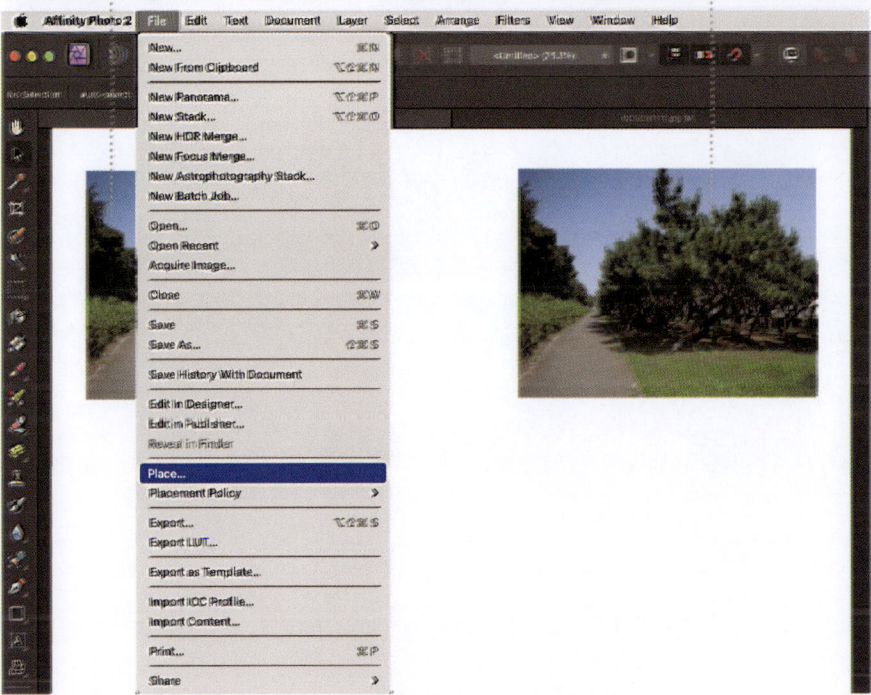

Chapter 5: Next, we'll be learning about Photo Persona

**Select half** the photo on the left using Tool Panel> **Rectangular Marquee Tool**.

Copied & Pasted JPEG

Object put here using the Place command

Once you have made your selection, try using the Delete key, and note how **half the picture disappears**.

Once you have deselected an image using Command/Control+D, use the Rectangular Marquee Tool to select half of the image, as we did in the photo on the right side. Then click on Delete.

Object put here using the Place command

Amazing, isn't it? It's all disappeared.

148

Chapter 5: Next, we'll be learning about Photo Persona

## 5_44: Alter the object put in positon using the Place command after using the Rasterize command

The layer object is now vector data, which means the layer has been completely deleted. It is important to understand that Bitmap data is a collection of dots. Because the JPEG photo on the left was opened directly, it is already comprised of Bitmap data from the beginning. For this reason, part of the photo is easily deleted using the Marquee Tool.

In contrast, when the photo on the right was put in position using the Place command, it was converted from Bitmap data to a layer object. As it is at this point, it is not Bitmap data. To process part of the photo, we first need to Rasterize. Let's give it a try! **Click on the objec**t to the right. Check that it is active and click on Layer>**Rasterize**.

In the same way, use the Rectangular Marquee Tool to **select half** the image and Delete.

Rasterized image put in position using the Place command

Note how it's **disappeared!**

Rasterized image put in position using the Place command

149

Chapter 5: Next, we'll be learning about Photo Persona

In fact images are very often put in positon using the Place command. We need to consider this. To divide an object into three parts, click on the object and activate it. Click on Layer>Rasterrise, and using the Rectangular Marquee Tool to **select 1/3 on the right**.

Switch to the Move tool, **drag your selection to the right**,

and deselect your selection using Command/Control+D. In the same way, use the Rectangular Marquee Tool to **select 1/3** and use **the Move Tool to shift to the lef**t.

You've successfully divided in into three!

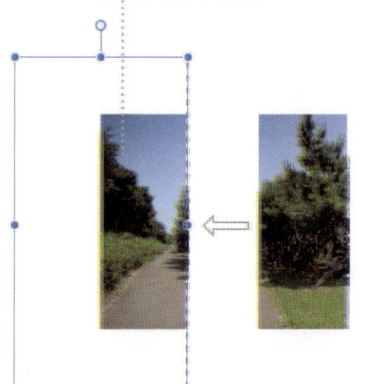

Chapter 5: Next, we'll be learning about Photo Persona.

Let's practice a little more with placed objects. Next we'll crop an image, starting from the beginning. Click on the object to activate. Then click on Layer>Rasterize, using the Rectangular Marquee Tool to select **the top part of the photo that you want to crop**.

Then select the Rectangular Marquee Tool from **the right side of the photo that you want to crop**, followed by the bottom and left. Once you have selected **all the parts of the photo that you wish to crop**, hit Delete.
Check that the cropping is complete.

Finally, deselect using the Command/Control+D command to finish.

151

# Chapter 6: Using the Retouch Tools

# Chapter 6: Using the Retouch tools

## 6_1: Using the Retouch Tools

Affinity_Photo has a set of high-performance retouch tools (Healing Brush Tool/Patch Tool/Blemish Removal Tool/Inpainting Brush Tool/Red Eye Removal Tool). Here we'll start with the Healing Brush Tool, but first we'll need something to practice on. Ideally the photo would have a number of objects, such as animals or flowers, spread over green grass. If you already have something that will work for this purpose, go ahead and use that.
If you don't have an appropriate photo, we recommend downloading a free image from the Creative Commons link:
http://creativecommons.org

Let's download a sample photo from the Creative Commons site. Launch your Internet browser and enter the following in the URL line.
http://goo.gl/yRosHV

Note: The above address uses Google url shortener. Should the link be broken, search the Creative Commons site:
http://creativecommons.org

Chapter 6: Using the Retouch tools

Once your photo is ready, drag the Affinity_Photo icon directly. Since the photo is vertical, we have cropped it to the 8 x 10 size for use in the tutorial. Choose Tool Panel>**Crop Tool.** On the Context Tool Bar, click on Mode and select **8:10**. To render the image horizontal, choose **10** in the next frame and then **8** in the next. Frame the following by **dragging**. Click inside the frame.

Good job! You're done cropping now. We will be using this picture next with other tools to practice on. Give the photo a name and **save** it. Once it is saved, click on **Save As** and give it another name. Then proceed to the next step.

## Chapter 6: Using the Retouch tools

### 6_2: Use the Healing Brush Tool to clone sheep

The Healing Brush Tool is used to copy pixels from parts of images and paste them into another location. This might be difficult to understand at first, but let's give it a try. Choose the **Healing Brush Tool** on the Tool Panel. Click on the sheep to the left, **holding down the Option/Alt key**. At this point **the Global Source** is registered. **Paint to the right** as if using a brush.

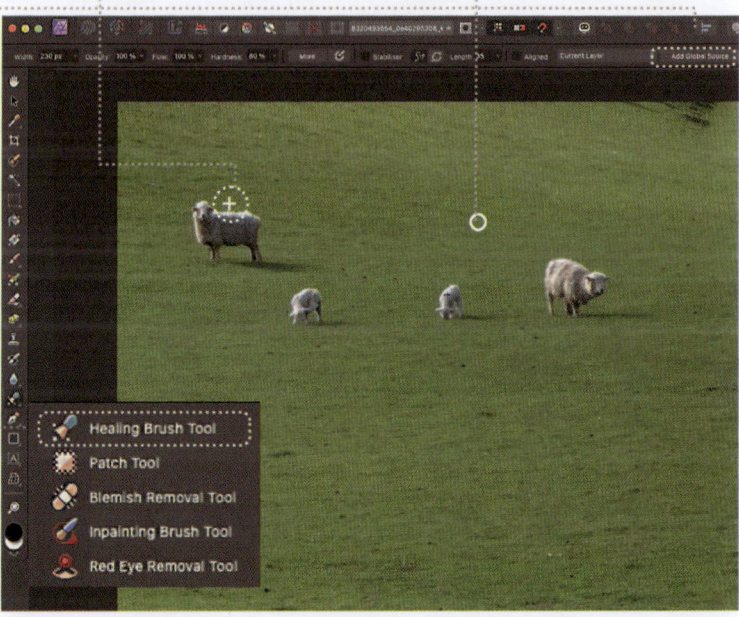

Look, we've got **another sheep!**

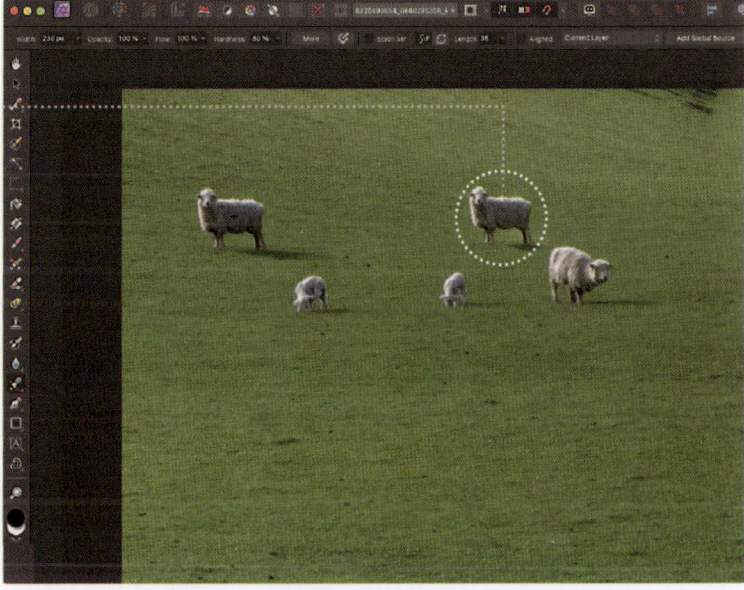

Chapter 6: Using the Retouch tools

Note how the sheep has come back. Let's add one more, and let's make it a little further away. To do that we have to make it smaller. **Click on the Scale Layout button** on the Context Tool Bar. Move the Slider to **65%**. Use the mouse to paint **area to the left.**

**The sheep, shrunk to 65%,** has now reappeared. Use techniques appropriate to your objective including Rotate, Invert, etc.

# Chapter 6: Using Using the Retouch tools

Let's add another sheep to the front right part of the paragraph. Since we are switching the source, click on the sheep at the front left, holding down the **Option/Alt key** to add a new Global Source. **Paint the left front**.

Now let's also add more lambs. Click on the **Option/Alt key** and **paint** as above. What do you think? Do you now have an idea of how to use the Healing Brush Tool? In fact the original purpose of this tool is the opposite of the above: to retouch areas that we want to hide. That is, we use it to Global Source the grassy area and paint over the sheep.

157

Chapter 6: Using the Retouch tools

## 6_3: Use the Patch Tool to hide problem areas

The Patch Tool is used to retouch areas that you want to hide. The user simply selects the area they would like to cover by free hand, and then pastes. Let's give it a try. This author didn't have an appropriate photo to work with, so I searched for one on the following Creative Commons site: http://creativecommons.org
But all of the photos were great ones, with nothing to cover at all! Since I couldn't find a photo with any imperfections, I had to create one myself! To download the photo I used, go to the following Website:http://goo.gl/VHUHnM

© Justus Blümer

Do you have a photo with some imperfections on it? If so, click on Retouch Tools on the Tool Panel and then click on Flyout>**PatchTool**. Turn on **Selection is Source** on the Context Tool Bar. Select **area of the image that is free of imperfections.**

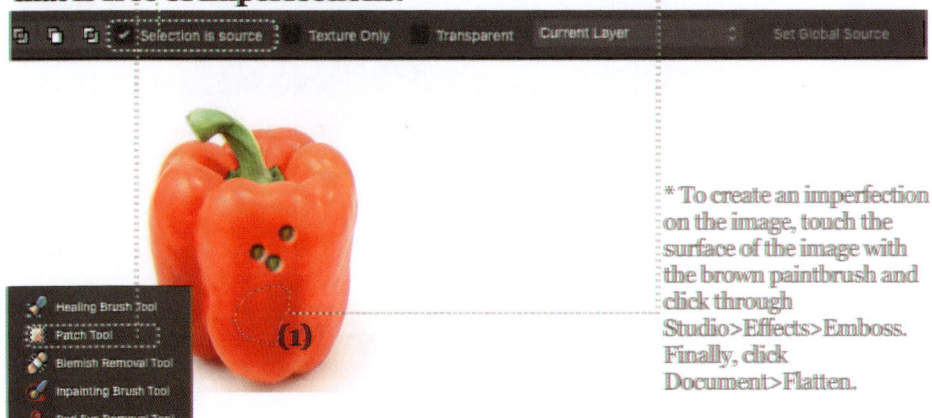

\* To create an imperfection on the image, touch the surface of the image with the brown paintbrush and click through Studio>Effects>Emboss. Finally, click Document>Flatten.

(2) Hover the mouse over the area of the imperfection.

(3) Adjust with **Rotation** and **Scale** on the Context Menu.

(4) To finish, click on Select > "Deselect."

158

Chapter 6: Using the Retouch tools

## 6_4: Use the Blemish Removal Tool to remove small imperfections

The Blemish Removal Tool can be used to hide small imperfections with a single click. Firstly, take the Publica downloaded above and add an imperfection to it. Then click on Document>"Flatten" and you're ready! Click on the Tool Panel>Retouch Panel, followed by the Flyout button, and select **the Blemish Removal Tool**. Adjust Width on the Context Tool Bar to **the size of the imperfection.**

From here it's easy! Place **the mouse over the imperfection**, click, and drag.

159

## 6_5: Use the Inpainting Brush Tool to erase any unneeded areas of a photo

Using the Inpainting Brush Tool, erase any undesired parts of an image, such as telephone poles or electrical wiring. In a very useful feature of this program, the computer automatically fills in the background. Let's give it a try! Do you remember the photo of sheep that we downloaded when we were learning about Retouch Tools? We cropped a vertical photo to make it a horizontal one.

Here I'd like to use that photo to give you some more information. Choose the Retouch tool Flyout button on the Tool Panel, and click on the **Inpainting Brush Tool**. Adjust **Width** on the Context Tool Bar to the size of any unwanted objects in the photo. Then click on Context Tool and Bar and set **Width to 50 px**.

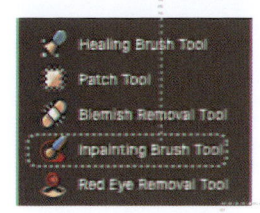

In a single action, paint over **the lamb to the front left**. When you're done painting, bring the mouse over it.

Note how **this lamb disappears** without a trace, and the grass in the background has reappeared.

Chapter 6: Using the Retouch tools

Let's paint over the sheep at the front right.

You did it! It disappeared!

Next let's paint over the sheep on the left, including its shadow.

Well, what do you think? It looks great, doesn't it?

Still, the background in particular may not come out as you'd like, depending on the subject matter.

161

Chapter 6: Using the Retouch tools

## 6_6: Use the Red Eye Removal Tool to correct red eye caused by camera flash

Red eye is a phenomenon caused by the Flash feature of the camera. Use the Red Eye Removal Tool to remove it, simply by encompassing the red eye area with your mouse. Click on Retouch on the Tool Panel, followed by the Flyout button, and select **the Red Eye Removal Tool**. Then envelop the **red area** with your mouse.

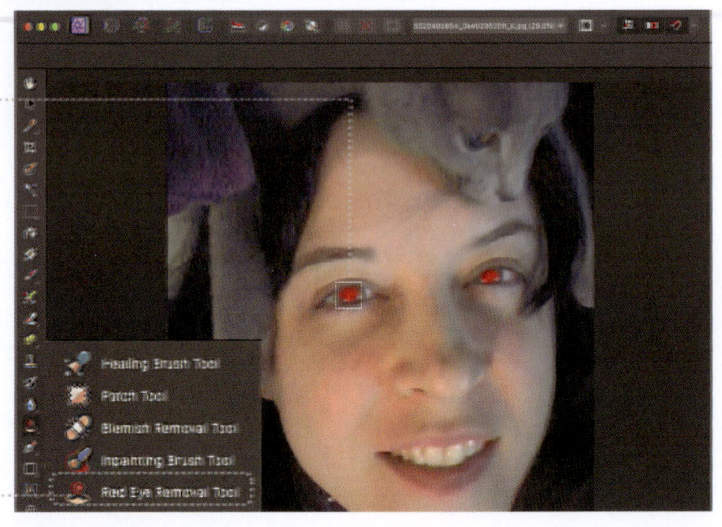

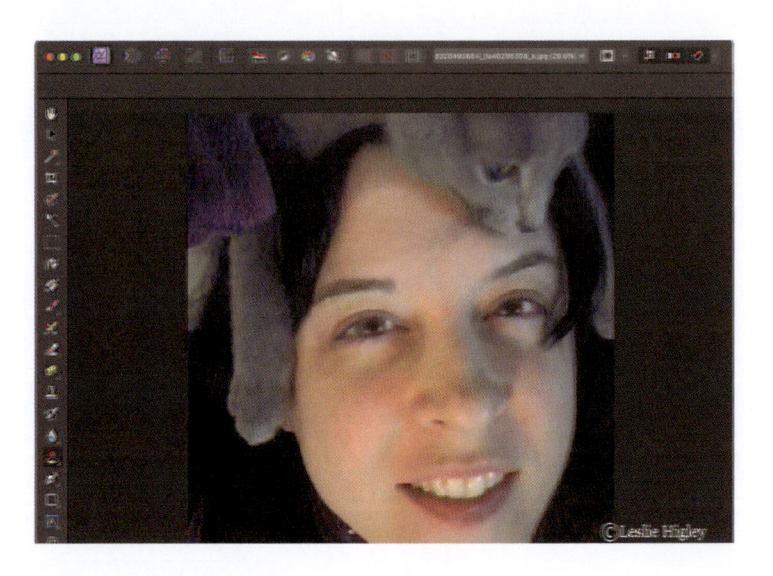

Chapter 6: Using retouch Tools

## 6_7: Use the Mesh Warp Tool to render the photo unrealistic.

The order of operations for using the tool may differ, but let's take a look at the Mesh Warp Tool, second from the bottom of the Tool Panel. This is a tool unique to Affinity_Photo! But before that, we've got some preparation to do.

Let's download a sample photo from the Creative Commons site. Launch your Internet browser and enter the following in the URL line.
http://creativecommons.org
http://goo.gl/ZnLuio

©Toshiyuki IMAI

Once you have a photo ready, drag the file directly to the Affinity_Photo icon and launch. If the document is locked, click on Studio>Layers>**Key**. It should now be active. Let's now move on to the next step.

Note: The above address uses Google url shortener. If the link is broken, search the Creative Commons site: (http://creativecommons.org)

163

Chapter 6: Using the Retouch Tools

On the Tool Panel, select **the Mesh Warp Tool**. You will now see the Context Tool Bar for the Mesh Warp Tool. Under Mode, select **Destination** to work on the grid and image concurrently. The Destination setting is more intuitive and easier to use than the Source setting, which moves only the Grid. On the Default settings,

**double-click anyplace** you want to add a Node. Nodes, Corner points, and lines are displayed. Activating the Note creates a Warp effect.

Chapter 6: Using the Retouch Tools

Shift the additional Node to the right to view the Handle. Grasp the handle to control it.

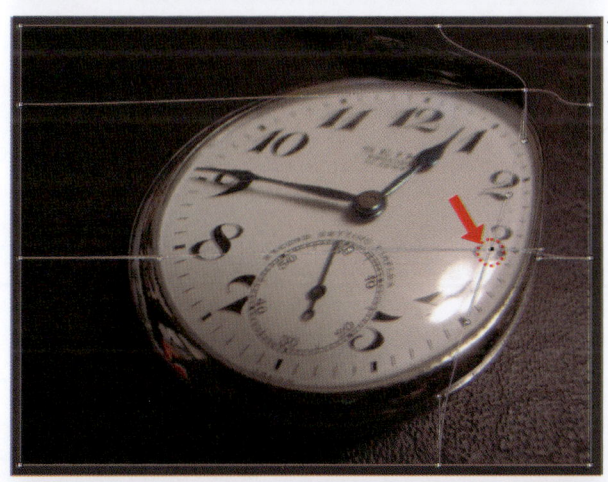

Let's now add a second node.

Shift the Node to the left, controlling with the Handle as above.

Chapter 6: Using the Retouch Tools

Thirdly, add the fourth Node. Drag the Node, controlling with the Handle as above.

If your result makes you think of Salvatore Dali's famous surrealist clock, then you've done well! To finish, click on **Apply** on the Context Tool Bar.

Chapter 6: Using the Retouch Tools

## 6_8: Use the Perspective Tool (Single plane) to correct tilt

To use the **Perspective Tool,** first click on the Fly button. But before that we do, as usual, we need a photo to practice on. Go to the Creative Commons site http://creativecommons.org
Then type in the following URL in your browser:
**http://goo.gl/8QU9VU**

Drag the downloaded file to the Affinity_Photo icon. Did it work?
Note how the building does not look as it if was taken straight on. This is an inevitable phenomenon, occurring due to the camera's angle of elevation. Specialist photographers shooting architecture use a large camera equipped with a bellows to correct the photo and make the building appear perpendicular. Here we use Affinity_Photo to correct it.
Click on the Mesh Warp Tool Flyout Button to display and select **the Perspective Tool**. The grid should be displayed on the screen.

Chapter 6: Using the Retouch Tools

Under Planes, Select **single Plan**, and under Mode, select Destination. Drag **the left-side Corner Point** horizontally to the left to shift the angle of the left side of the building to slightly more than perpendicular. When correcting the left side, the right is pulled up slightly. This is part of the correction process.

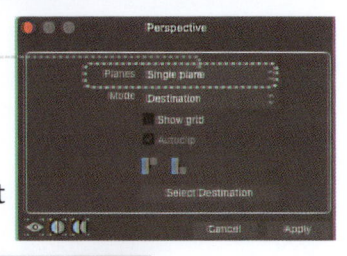

Next, **drag the right side** to the right, until the right side of the building is perpendicular to the top right of the building (not horizontal). In fact this picture tilted downward to the right, so we corrected this at the same time.

To finish, click on **the Apply button** on the Perspective setting dialog.

Before correction

After correction: you're finished!

Chapter 6: Using the Retouch Tools

## 6_9: Use the Perspective Tool (Dual Plane) to correct photos from a two-point perspective.

Next, use the Perspective tool to try out the Dual Plane features. Again, we need a photo for practice purposes. Go the Creative Commons website: http://creativecommons.org and type in the following URL:
**http://goo.gl/isQZA4**

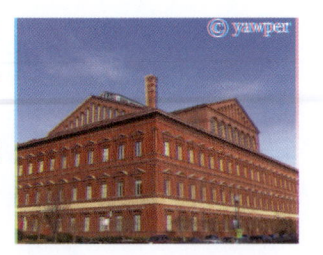

Let's now launch it. Click on the image to activate it. If it is locked, first unlock it. Click on Perspective Tool on the Tool Panel.
When the grid is displayed, set Plane to **Dual Plane** on the Perspective Settings Dialog Box.

Chapter 6: Using the Retouch Tools

Drag **the point on the upper left** to see how it affects perspective.

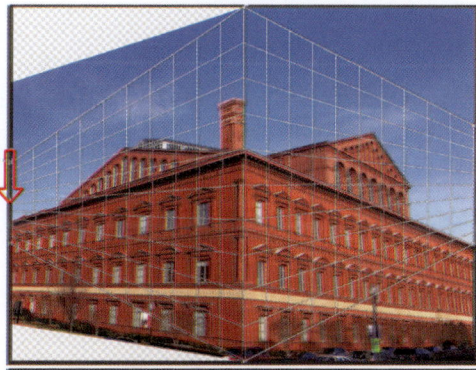

Next, drag t**he top left point** downward.

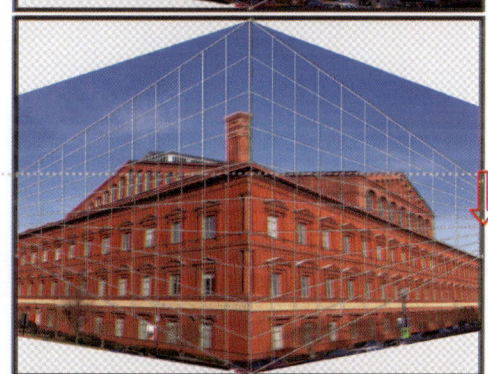

To render the bottom horizontal, drag **the lower left point** downward,

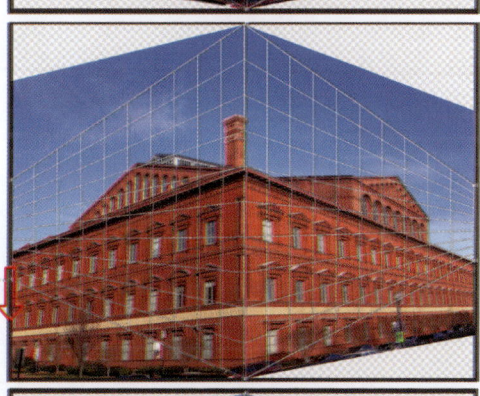

until **the lower right point** is parallel to the bottom.

Chapter 6: Using the Retouch Tools

Drag **the upper middle point** horizontally and right to left. Then click **Apply** on the Perspective Dialog Box.

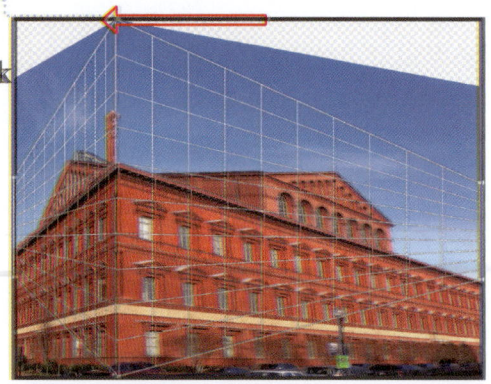

Let's crop the empty space at the top. On the Tool Panel, select **Crop Tool**, drag the top point downward, and double-click on the image.

Before correction

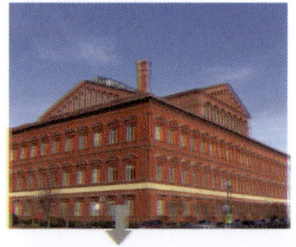

After correction: you're finished!

Chapter 6: Using the Retouch Tools

**Additional notes**: Those of you who worked with the sample photo might have noticed that the angle of the building in this photo is **not centered**; that is, the grid and the image are misaligned. You can work with it as it is, but this author decided to line up the building and grid angles. As noted above, I used the settings Perspective Tool>Dual Plane, shifting **the top center point** slightly to the left.

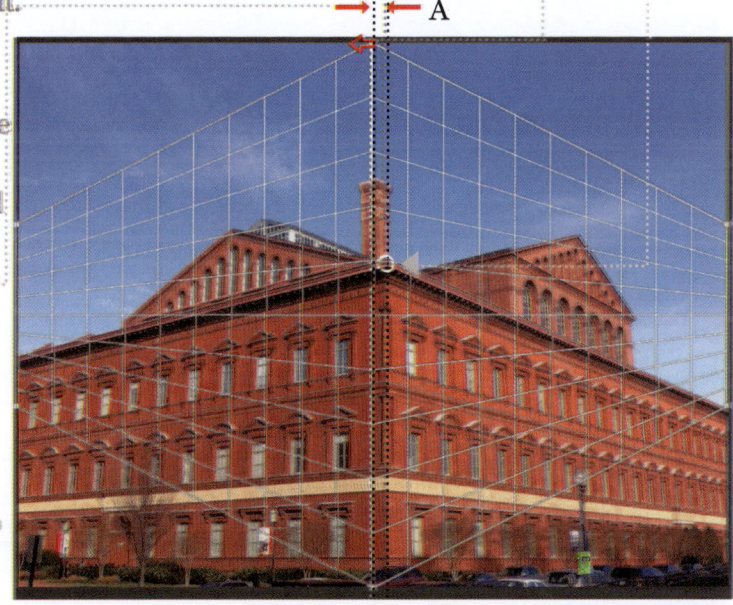

For purposes of precision, let's call the difference between the center of the grid and the edge of the building **A**. Move the center point to the left the same distance as **A** to bring the building angle to the center of the photo. Click Apply, Document > **Flatten**, and Save.

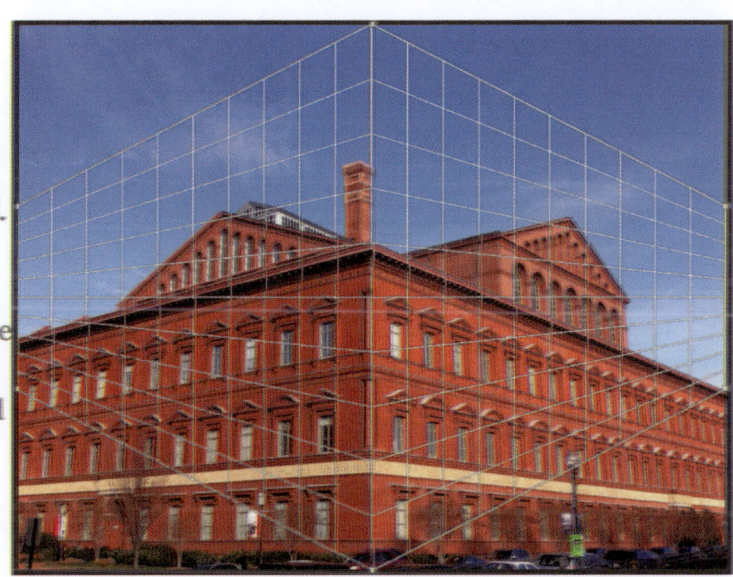

Try the Perspective Tool. Notice how the building angle and middle of the grid fit perfectly. This author used this photo as a resource.

173

# Chapter 7: Using the Liquefy Persona

# Chapter 7: Using the Liquefy Persona

## 7_1: Using the Liquefy Persona

We learned how to use the Mesh Warp Tool in the previous chapter. Affinity_Photo incorporates the Liquify Persona, a special warping feature. Let's take a break from Photo Persona for a moment and switch to Liquify Persona. There are a number of warp tools available.

**http://goo.gl/QpSTf8**

We'll need a photo to practice using Liquify Persona. You may choose to use one of your own snapshots, but if you don't have one, download your choice of mages from Creative Commons:

Visit the following URL:http://creativecommons.org

Drag the Affinity Photo icon to launch it. Click on the screen to activate. If it is locked, proceed to unlock it. Check that the layer is activated and click on **Liquify Persona**. You will then see the mesh grid. This is a standard Affinity Photo screen.

## 7_2: Using the Liquefy Persona Masking Tool (Liquify Freeze Tool)

Before using the Warp Tool, let's try masking. To protect any areas that you do not want to warp on the screen, click on the Tool Paper and use the Liquify Freeze Tool. Choose **Liquefy Freeze Tool**, select Size: **500 px**, and paint the background with the brush. The red area is the mask. This area will not be affected by the Warp Tool.

The mask should be as shown below.

## 7_3: Use the Liquefy Push Forward Tool to enlarge the face portion only

Once you have masked the target area, let's now try the Warp Tool. First click on Liquify Persona>Tool Panel>**Liquefy Push Forward Tool**. Adjust Size: to **400 px** and drag **the rabbit's face** downward. Using the Liquify Push Forward Tool, shift the pixels in the direction of your strokes.

Click on **Apply**, and compare to before —The rabbit's head will now be very large!

## 7_4: Use the Liquefy Push Left Tool to transform the object

Use the Liquefy Push Left Tool to shift pixels in the right angle direction in the stroke direction. Let's now try masking.

Select Liquefy Persona>Tool Panel>**Liquefy Push Left Tool**. Select Size: 400 px, and drag the photo from **right** to left.

Click on **Apply** to finish.

## 7_5: Use the Liquefy Twirl Tool to rotate in the clockwise direction

The Liquefy Twirl Tool creates distortion in the clockwise direction. Once you have marked the target area, Click on Liquefy Persona>Tool Panel>**Liquefy Twirl Tool**. Select Size: 700 px, click on the center, and hold. Continue to hold to intensify the effect, and holding the mouse where desired. Click "Apply" to finish.

## 7_6: Use the Liquefy Pinch Tool for a close-up of the subject's face only

Use the Liquefy Pinch Tool to produce distortion of a convex spherical surface. After using the Masking Feature, click on Liquefy Persona>Tool Panel> **Liquefy Pinch Tool**. Select Size: 700 px, click on the middle part, and hold. Continue to hold to intensify the effect, holding the mouse where desired. Click on "Apply" to finish.

Chapter 7: Using the Liquefy Persona

## 7_7: Use the Liquefy Punch Tool to create a concave effect

Use the Liquefy Punch Tool to produce distortion of a concave spherical surface. After using the Masking Feature, click on Liquify Persona>Tool Panel> **Liquefy Punch Tool**. Select Size: 700 px, click on the middle part, and hold. Continue to hold to intensify the effect, positioning the mouse where desired. Click **Apply** to finish.

## 7_8: Use the Liquefy Turbulence Tool to fragment the photo

Use the Liquefy Turbulence Tool to fragment your photo. After using the Masking Feature, click on Liquify Persona>Tool Panel> **Liquefy Turbulence Tool**. Select Size: 700 px, click on the middle part, and hold. Continue to hold to intensify the effect, positioning the mouse where desired. Click **Apply** to finish.

Chapter 7: Using the Liquefy Persona

## 7_9: Liquefy Mesh Clone Tool

The Liquefy Turbulence Tool is used to copy mesh created by the user into another location. Let's give it a try. Use the Liquefy Turbulence Tool on the previous page to create mesh. Next, select Liquify Persona>Tool Panel >**Liquefy Mesh Clone Tool**. Select Size: 700 px, hold down the Option/Alt key, and click on the appropriate spot on the screen. You've now copied the mesh!

**Click on the appropriate spot.**

Then click again to re-create the mesh. Don't click on the Apply button this time. Instead,
let's move on to
the next Chapter.

Chapter 7: Using the Liquefy Persona

## 7_10: Use the Liquify Reconstruct Tool to correct distortion

We created distortion on the previous page. The Liquify Reconstruct Tool is used to correct this distortion and restore the original. Click on Liquefy Persona>Tool Panel> **Liquefy Reconstruct Tool**. Select Size: 700 px. Click on the distorted mesh area. Then click repeatedly on **the same areas**. How does it look? The distortion has now been corrected!

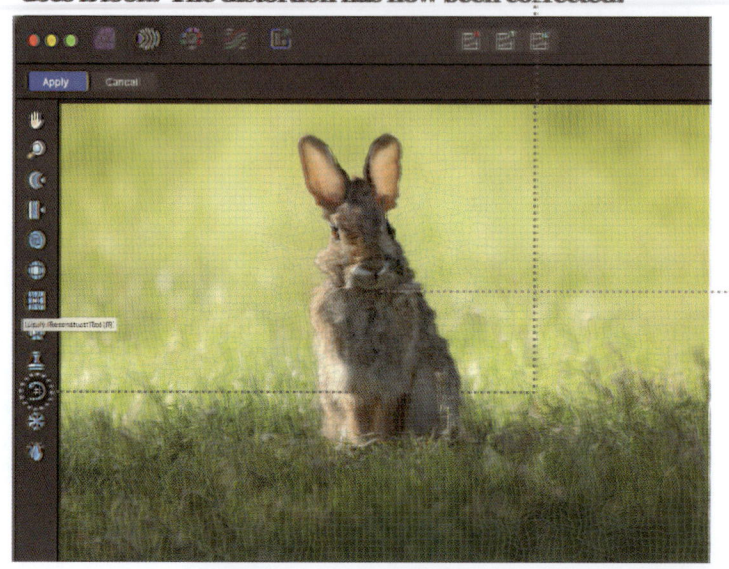

The above is an overview of Liquify Persona. Click on **the Apply button.**

182

# Chapter 8: Using the Drawing Tools (Vector Data)

Chapter 8: Using the Drawing Tools (Vector Data)

Affinity Photo can utilize not only Bitmap data but also vector data for diagrams and more. This Chapter revisits Photo Persona so that we can learn primarily about vector tools.

## 8_1: Using the Pen Tool

Let's try out the Pen Tool. This tool is located in the same place as the Node Tool: Persona>Tool Panel>Node Tool. Click on the Node Tool Flyout Button, select **Pen Tool**, click on the Context Tool Bar Border **Color Button**, and select black. Click on **the line** next to it to adjust settings for broken or solid lines as well as line thickness. Click on **the solid line** and adjust Width to three points. Then draw a straight line, clicking in the desired place. Double click where you would like to end the straight line. Single click to bring the line to the next spot clicked. Double click to complete the straight line.

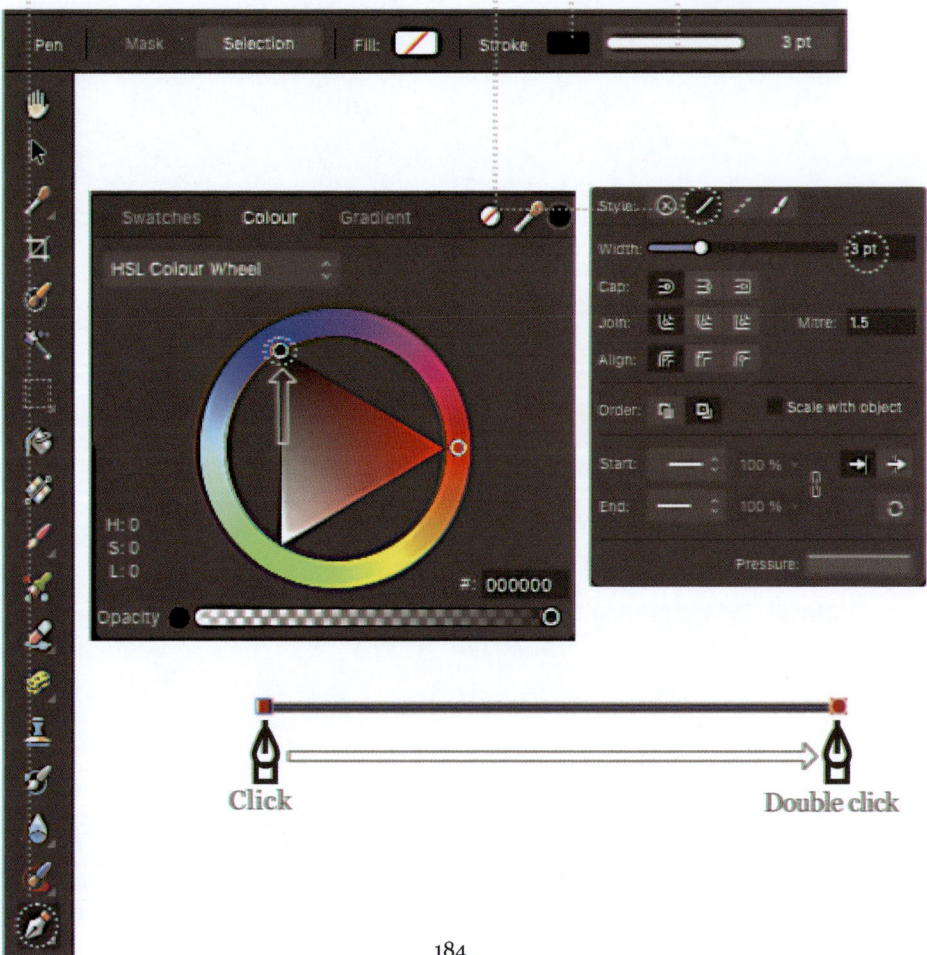

184

## 8_2: Using the Node Tool

Were you able to draw a straight line? It's easy, right? Let's make this straight line into one that bends in an acute angle. Then switch to **Node Tool.** This tool is displayed when you click on the pen tool flyout button. Choose **Sharp** on the Context tool Bar and **click on the middle** of the straight line mentioned above. Then **drag** upward. Note the right angle. Using the Node Tool, you can still convert the line afterward. The conversion features can also change straight lines to curved lines.

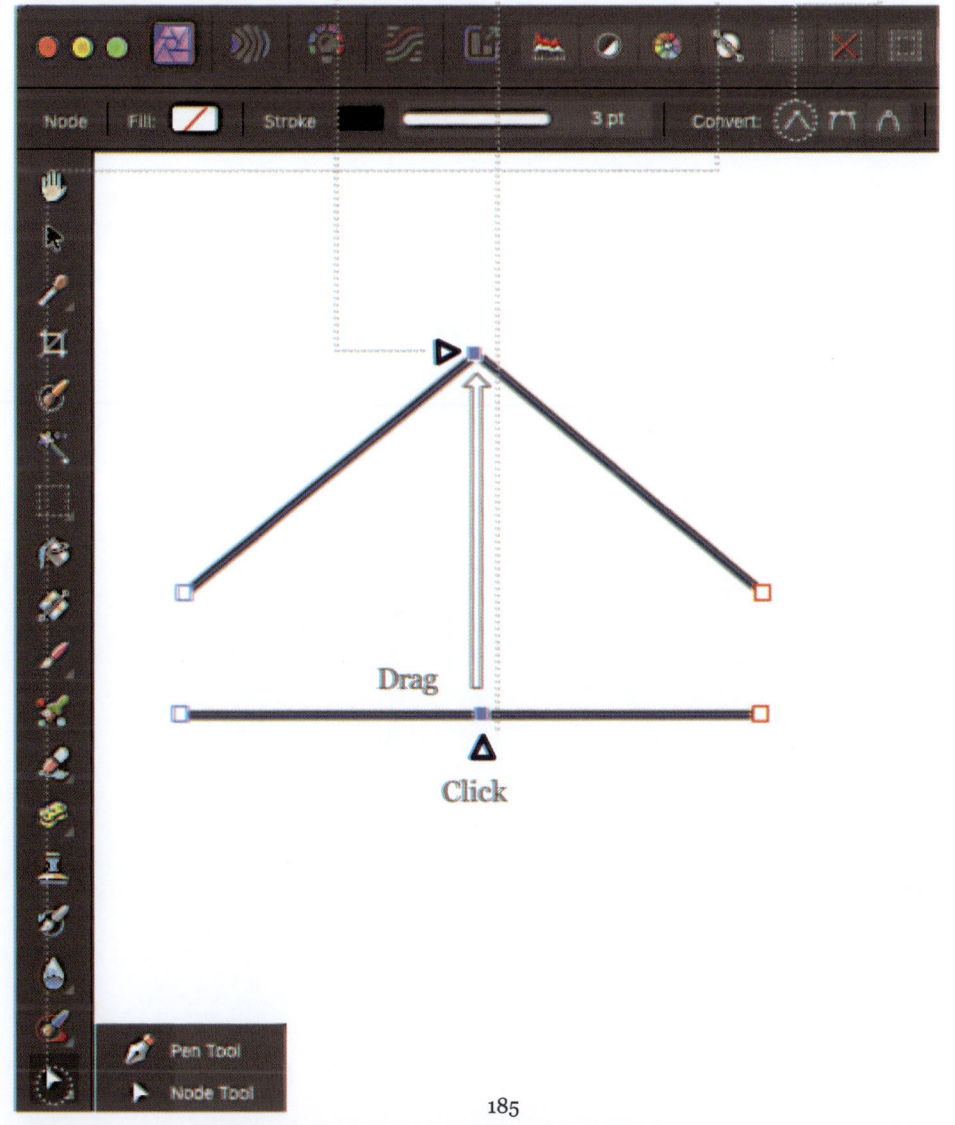

Drag

Click

Pen Tool

Node Tool

185

Chapter 8: Using the Drawing Tools (Vector Data)

## 8_3: Use the Pen Tool to draw a curved line

Next, let's try drawing a curved line. Select **Pen Tool** from the Tool Panel, check that Stroke is black, click on **the appropriate position** as with the straight line, and then click on **the area above** it. Then **drag** to the right and hover the mouse over it. **Double click** on the area to the lower right to complete a semicircular curved line. Drag on the curved line at the point where you would like it to curve. Try your hand at it!

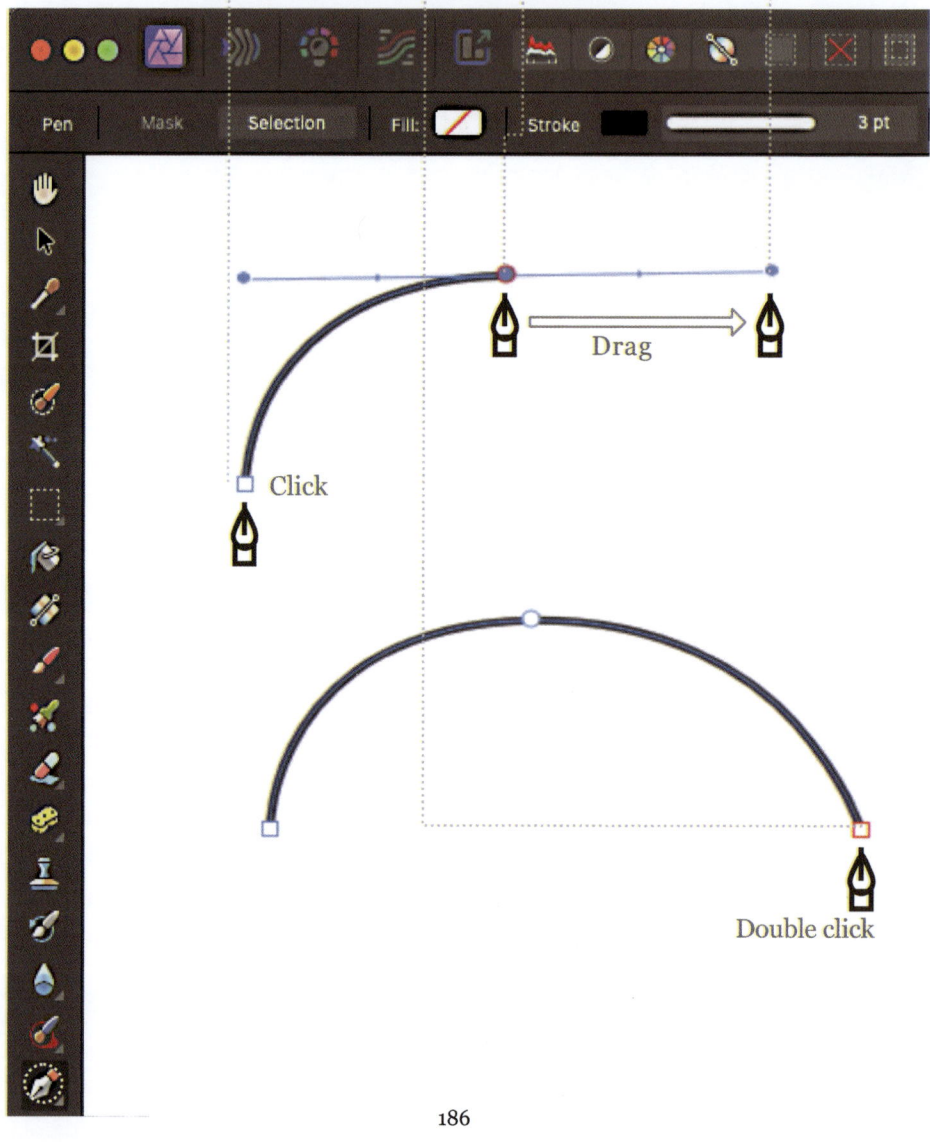

## 8_4: Convert curved lines using Node Tool

Now that you have been able to draw a straight line, let's revisit **Node Tool**. On the Context Tool Bar, click on **the Smooth icon**. Then click on **the middle part** of the curved line you drew on the previous page. **Drag** diagonally in a downward direction. Note how the curved line has now changed. The Node Tool transforms by adding corner points on the curved/straight lines as the user desires. You may also choose to drag **the existing corner points**. Add nodes to display the arms to **the left and right**. Control these arms with the mouse to make subtle changes to the curve of the line.

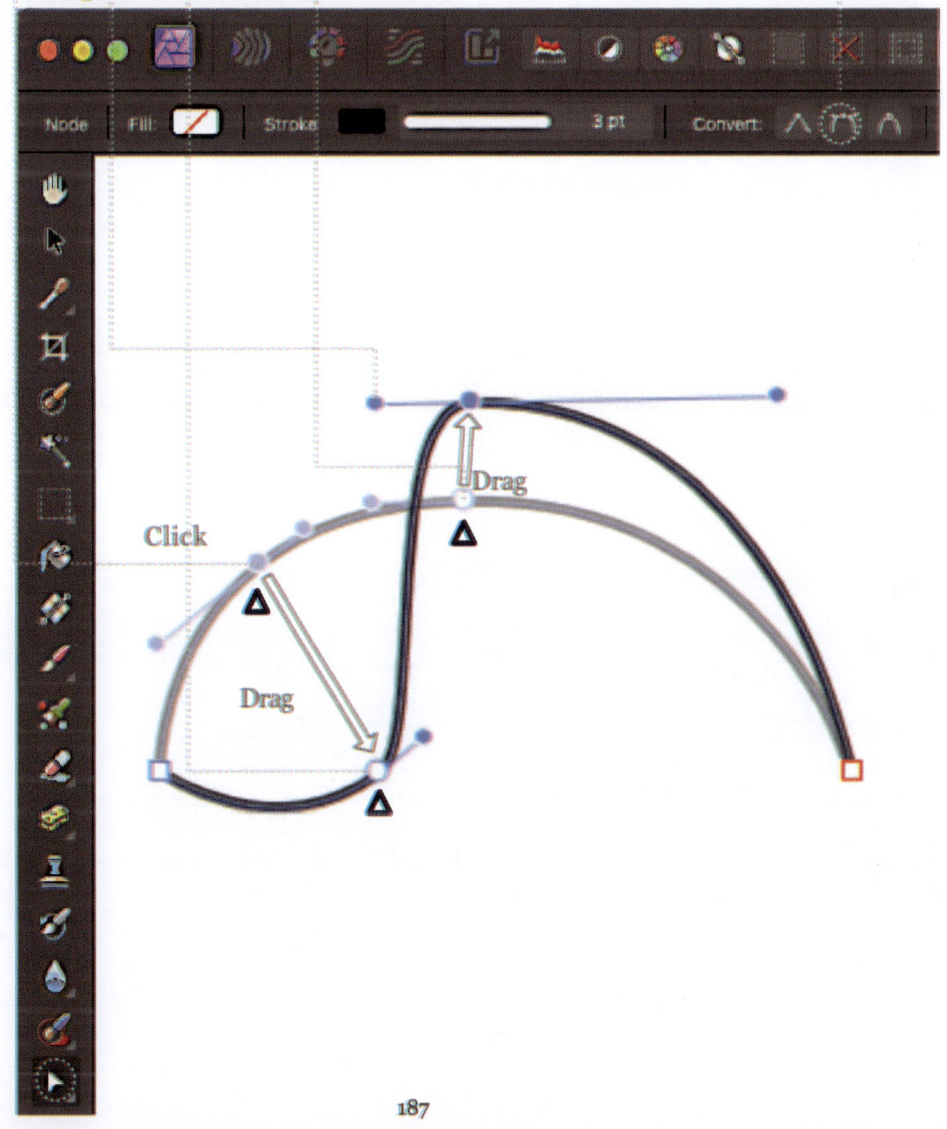

Chapter 8: Using the Drawing Tools (Vector Data)

## 8_5: Pressure levels in line drawing

Affinity_Photo allows for adjustment of pen pressure using vector tools, even without a tablet. Let's give it a try! Choose **Pen Tool**, then **None** for **Fill** on the Context Tool Bar, adjust **Stroke** to Black. Click on the **line** and adjust Style to **Straight Line**, Width to **50 pt** and **Circle** at the end of the line.

At the bottom of the screen, **click**, **drag**, **drag**, **double click**, etc., to draw curved lines.

Chapter 8: Using the Drawing Tools (Vector Data)

Once you have drawn a line of even thickness, click on **Line** on the Contract Tool Bar and open the Settings panel. Click on the **Pressure button** to display a matrix allowing for adjustment of thickness. Note the points to the right and left.

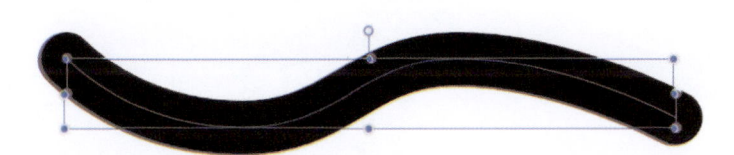

Grab onto the points and drag to the bottom center. Check to make sure the line is now thinner. Once you have dragged down to the center, the line should be half as thick.

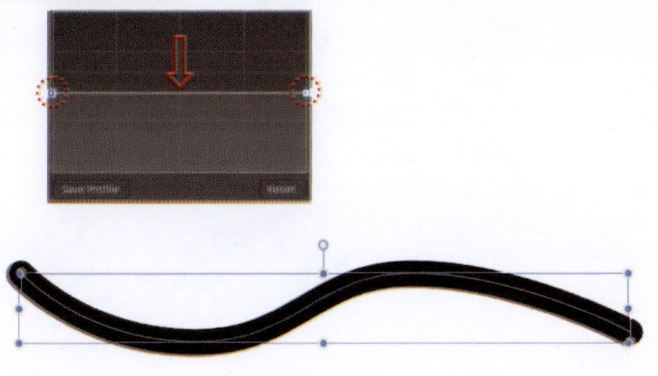

Chapter 8: Using the Drawing Tools (Vector Data)

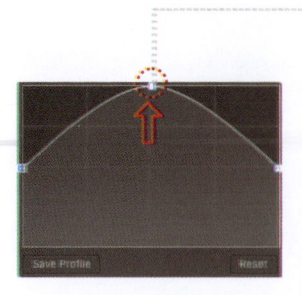

Next, change the thickness of the previous page (50%) to 100%. Click on **the line in the center** of the matrix, and drag upward in a mountain-shaped curve. Check on the line you have drawn. It should be thin, thicker, and then thin.

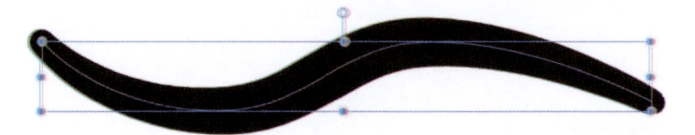

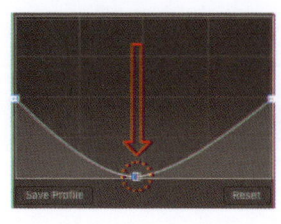

Next, do the opposite and drag downward. Note how the curve is now in the shape of a valley instead of a mountain. What do you think? It should be thick, thin, and then thick again—all even without a pen tablet! You can also add pressure to your lines.

Chapter 8: Using the Drawing Tools (Vector Data)

## 8_6: Understanding the Rectangle Tool: drawing lines and filling

Let's give **the Rectangle Tool** a try. This tool is for drawing squares. Use it to fill in and also to draw borders at the same time. Click on the flyout button for the tools we've been learning to daily the diagram tool icons. Next, click on the Context Tool Bar, **Fill**, and Color Button to display the Color Wheel Dialog Box. If you do not see the Color Circle noted below, select **Color** on the tab. **Click on the Blue** part of the Color Circle, and click on Stroke on the Context Tool Bar with the blue point at the **top** of the triangle. Then click on **the Red** part of the Color Circle in the same manner.

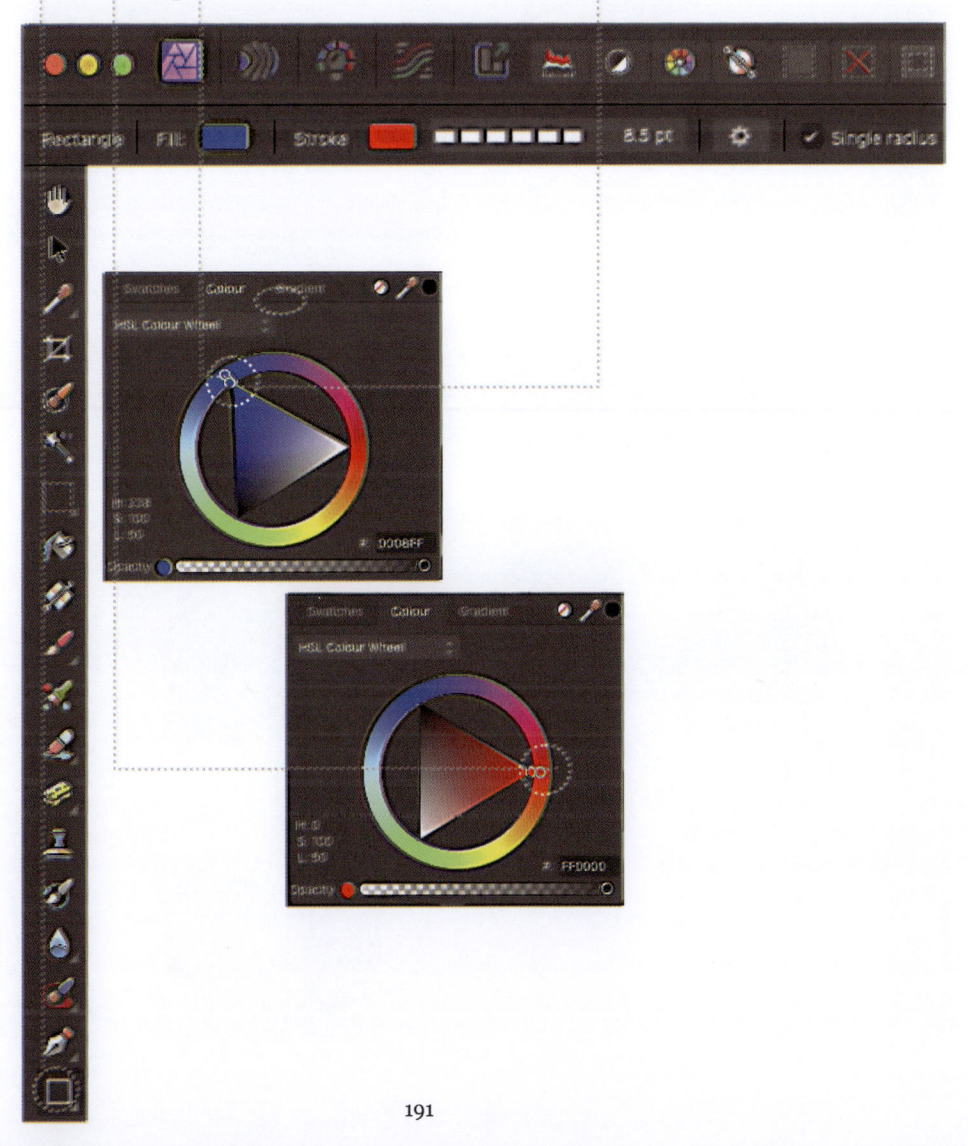

Chapter 8: Using the Drawing Tools (Vector Data)

Next, drag diagonally in appropriate position to draw a square. Holding your selection, click on the Context Tool Bar line. Once the **Line** Setting dialog box appears, locate **Dash Line Style**, adjust Width to 8.5 pt, adjust Cap all the way to the right, and adjust Dash to "1__1.5__0__0." Does it now look like Figure A? Check that there is now a line down the center of the solid Blue area. Next, click on the **center** of the setting dialog. The dotted line should now be inside the solid, as in Figure B. Then again click on **the far right**; the dotted line should now be on the outside, as in Figure C.

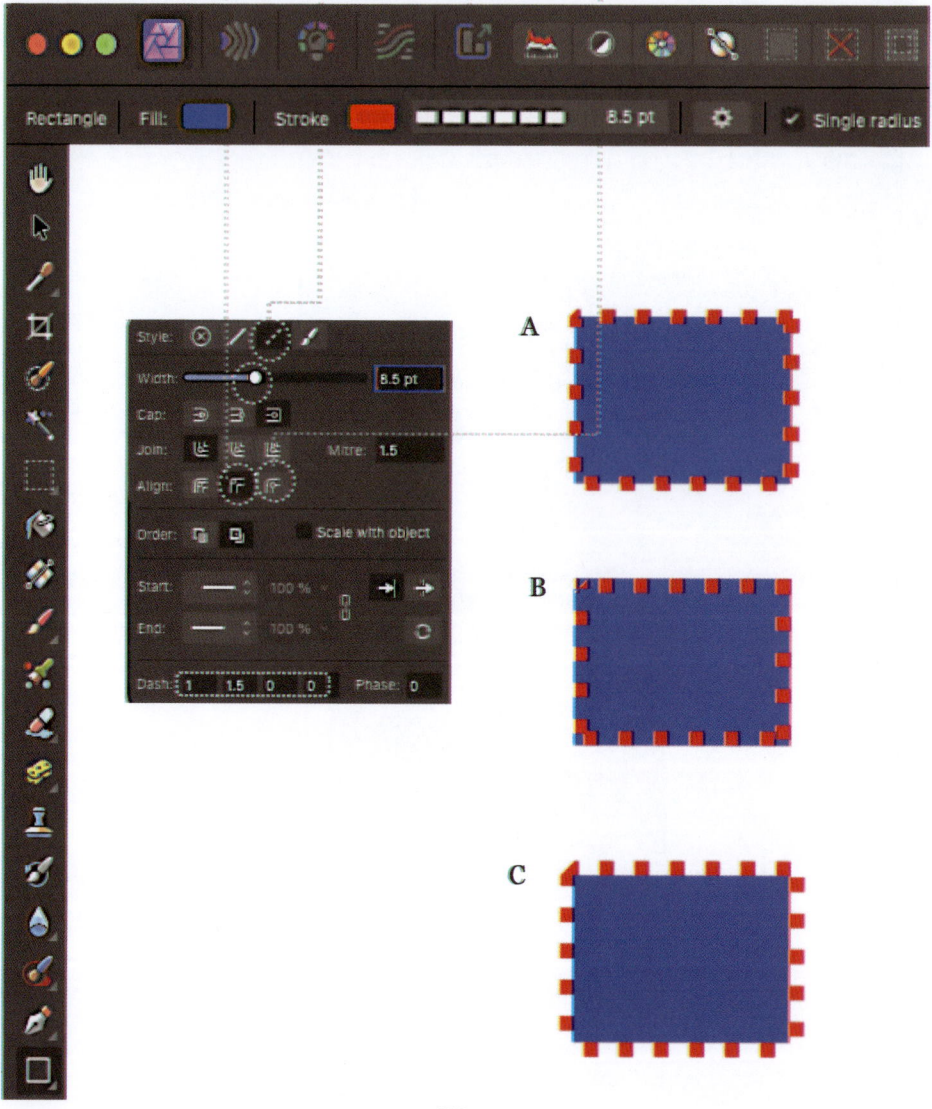

192

# Chapter 8: Using the Drawing Tools (Vector Data)

Let's discuss the concept of the dotted line some more. To view the line settings panel, click on the Line button on the Context tool Bar. See the four lines to fill in at the bottom, under Dash. On the first line, enter the size of the first dash. On the next line, enter margin size. Enter "0" for the third dash to create a dotted line with a specified amount of space between characters. We've already done this on the previous page. Note that if you input a value other than "0" for the third and fourth values, you create a complex dotted line pattern. Let's give this a try.

**Dash** is set to: 0.5_3_3_6. Do you now see dashed lines as in the Figure?

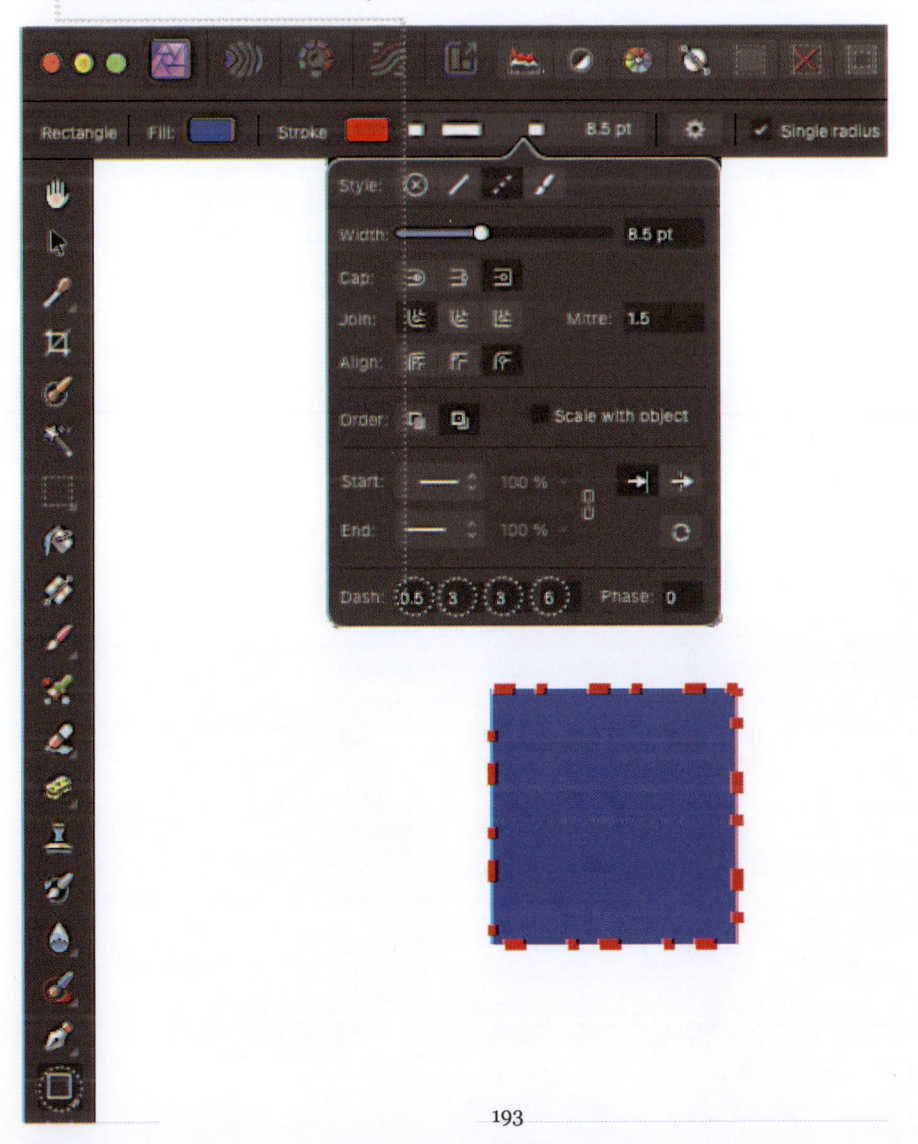

## 8_7: Draw an ellipse with the Ellipse Tool

Let's now give the Ellipse Tool a try. Click the Tool Panel Shape icon flyout button to show the Ellipse icon. **Click on Ellipse**, check that the Context Tool Bar is set to elliptical. Set the Fill Color Button to blue, **click on Line under Stroke** and Settings Dialog Style to **None.** From the appropriate point on the screen, hold down the Shift key and drag diagonally to draw a perfect circle. By not holding down the Shift key, the tool draws an elliptical instead.

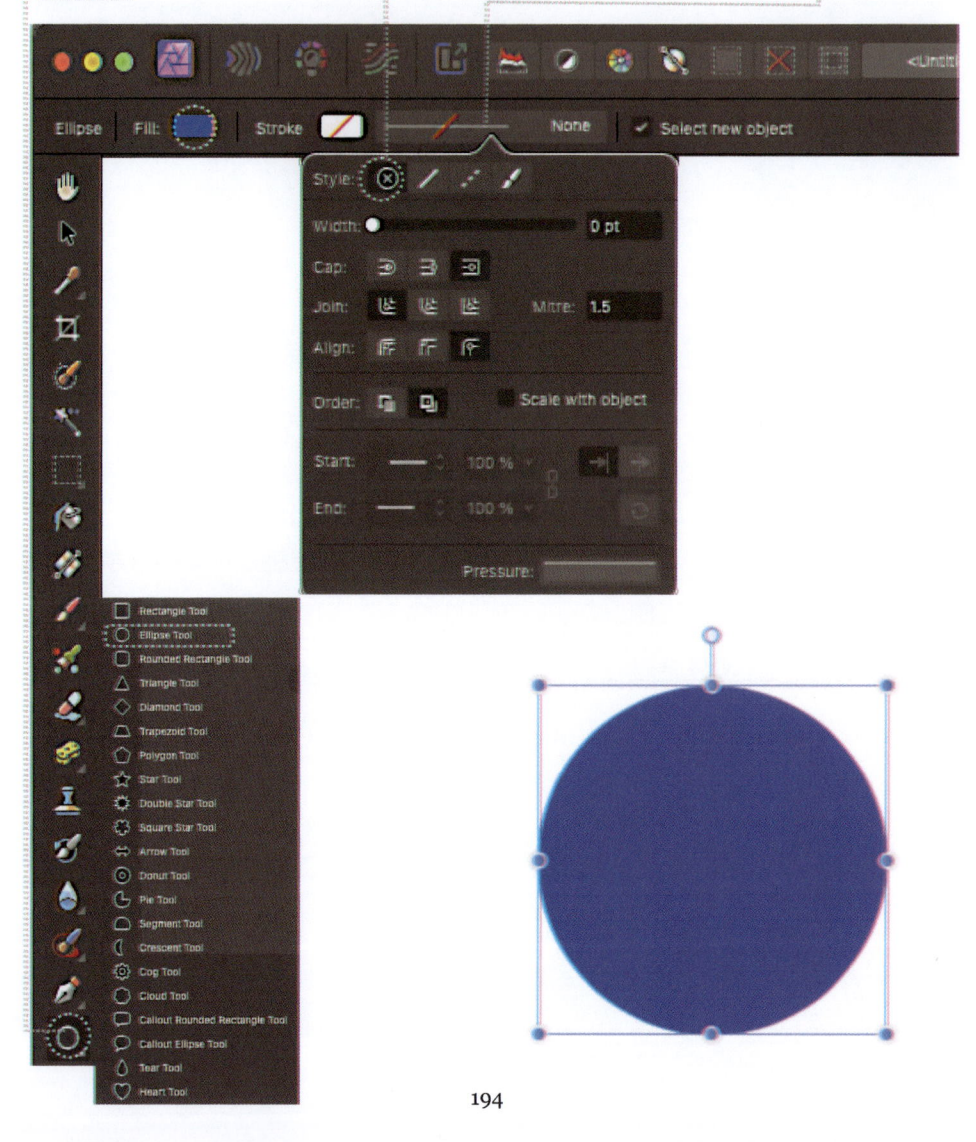

Chapter 8: Using the Drawing Tools (Vector Data)

## 8_8: Using the Ellipse Tool, draw a donut, fan, etc.

Were you able to draw a circle? The shape can be changed instantly to a donut shape. This is Affinity_Photo...and it's easy! Click on **Convert to Donut** on the Context Tool Bar. If you are unable to locate the **Convert to Donut** feature, click on the circle you drew, and activate to display **Convert to Donut**. Were you able to draw a donut?

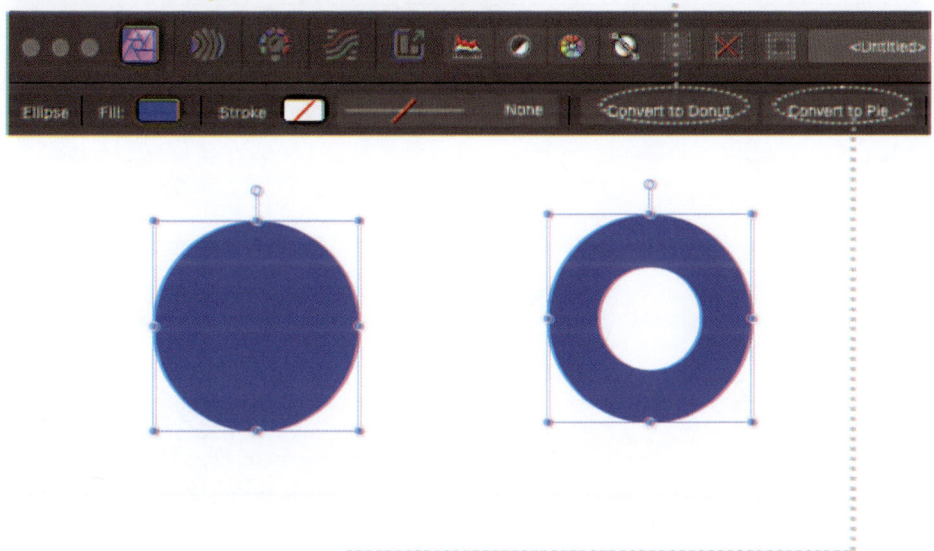

Have you noted the **Convert to Pie** button? Let's give this one a try, too. Click on "Convert to Pie" to switch to the Context Tool Bar. Adjust the Start angle to **23°** and the End angle to**158°**. Well, how does it look? Were you able to draw a fan?

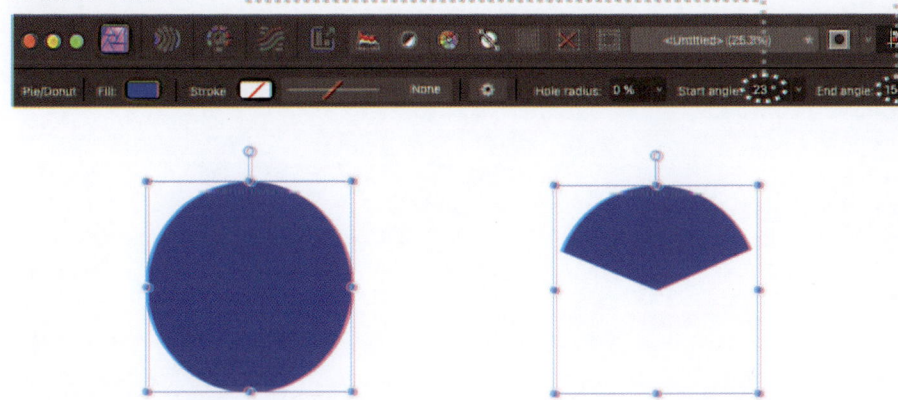

195

Chapter 8: Using the Drawing Tools (Vector Data)

## 8_9: Rounded Rectangle Tool: Color settings for lines and the screen

Next, let's draw a square with rounded corners. Click on **the Rounded Rectangle** Tool on the Control Panel Shape Tool. Hold down the Shift key and drag. Once the outline appears, control it from the Color Settings panel on the right side of the screen.

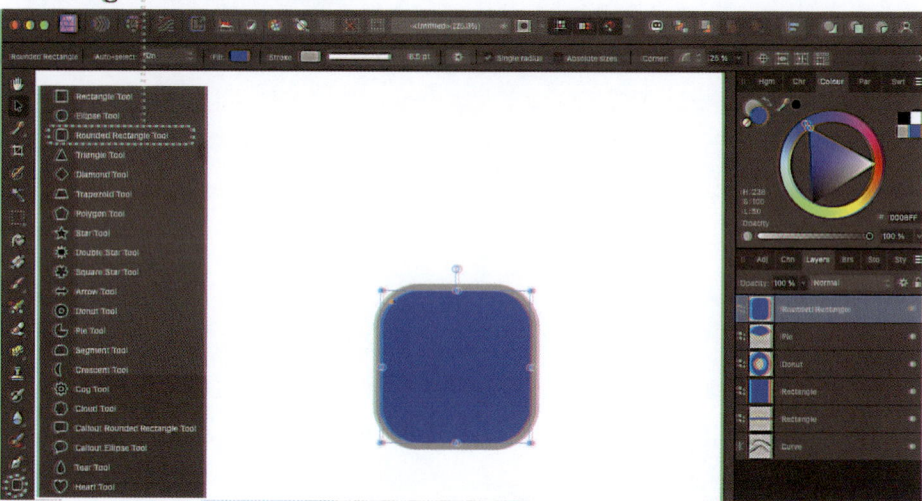

To recap, once the outline appears on your screen, click on **the Outline Settings button** and then click on **the little mark** just below to remove the outline. Let's now focus on the color settings. Click on the rounded-corner shape to activate it. Then click on **the Color Fill settings button** to activate it as well. Click on the outer edge **coloring** to show the appropriate primary color. Drag the **small circle** to the place where you want it inside the triangle to change the color intensity. Then drag on the circle. The top to the right of the triangle should be white, while the top of the lower left should be black. Change **Opacity** with the slider, for our purposes to 100%. Do you now have a rounded-corner square as to the left?

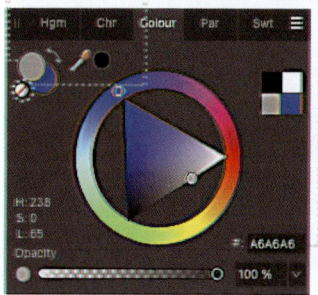

Chapter 8: Using the Drawing Tools (Vector Data)

**8_10: Changing the Shape with the Rounded Rectangle Tool**
You should now have a blue square with rounded corners. Leave the tool as it is and make the rounded corners smaller. Note **the red circle**. If the red circle does not appear, click on the Rounded Rectangle Tool, and drag **the red circle** to the outer edge. The diameter should be smaller as in the figure to the right. Next, let's switch to **the Move Tool**. This Tool is used to move or shrink/enlarge shapes.

Click on the figure to show the points that we work with. Drag **corner A** to the lower left to shrink it. Then drag the center of **side B** left and right to adjust the width of the figure. Likewise, drag the center of **side C** on the bottom up and down to adjust the height. Move **Point D** of the square, which you have now shrunk, left and right to rotate the figure.

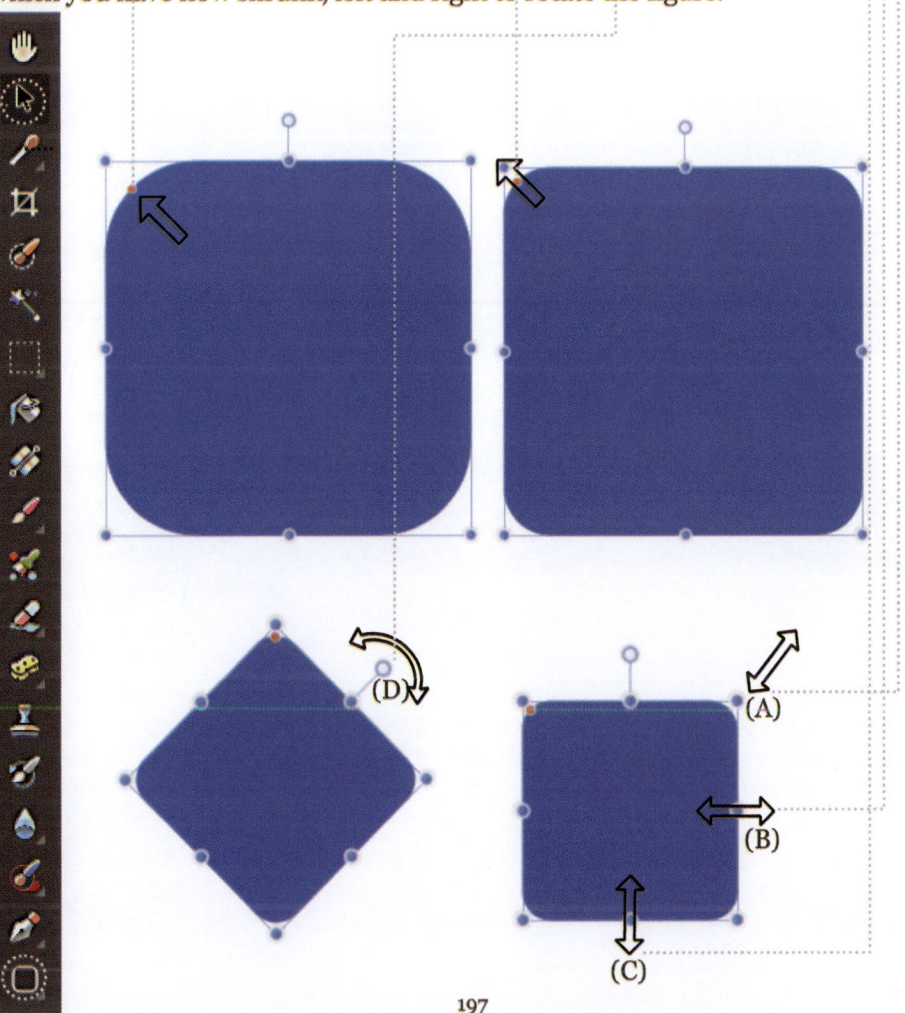

# Chapter 8: Using the Drawing Tools (Vector Data)

## 8_11: Draw a triangle with the Triangle Tool

We've now gone over squares, ellipticals, and rounded-corner squares, but Affinity_Photo actually has a lot more tools than that! Let's give them all a try, one at a time. Choose **Triangle Tool** on the Tool Panel. Choose the color blue and **None** for **Stroke**, and then drag to the appropriate position.

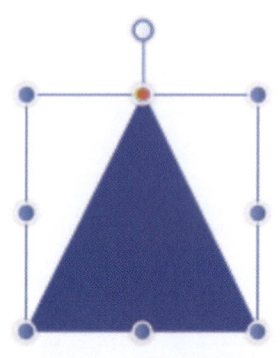

Were you able to draw an isosceles triangle? Note the red circle at the top. Click on **Top point** of the Context Tool Bar to reveal the Slider. Then move **the slider** to the left. How does it look? The bottom is the same but the top has moved. Next, slide to the right. You can also grab onto the red circle directly and slide it to the left and right.

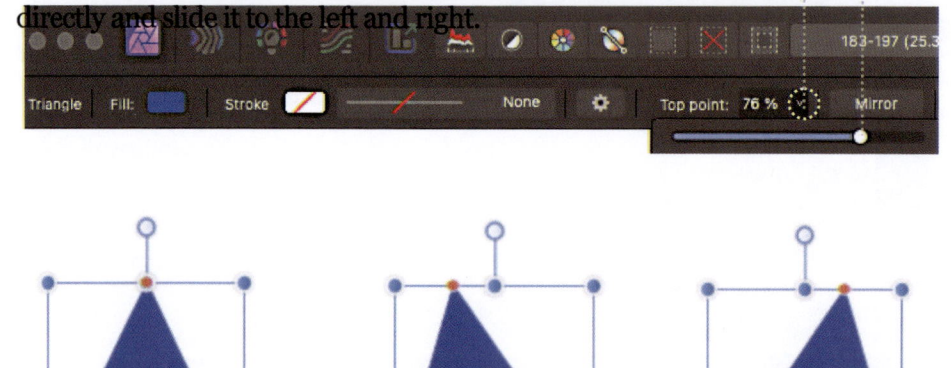

198

Chapter 8: Using the Drawing Tools (Vector Data)

**8_12: Drawing with the Diamond Tool**

Next, let's try the Diamond Tool. Select **the Diamond Tool**, hold down the Shift key, and drag to draw a rhombus. Note **the red color** at the top to the left. Next, click on the **midpoint** of the Context Tool Bar to display **the Slider**. Slide to the left to create Figure A and to the right to create Figure B. You can also pick up the red circle directly and slide.

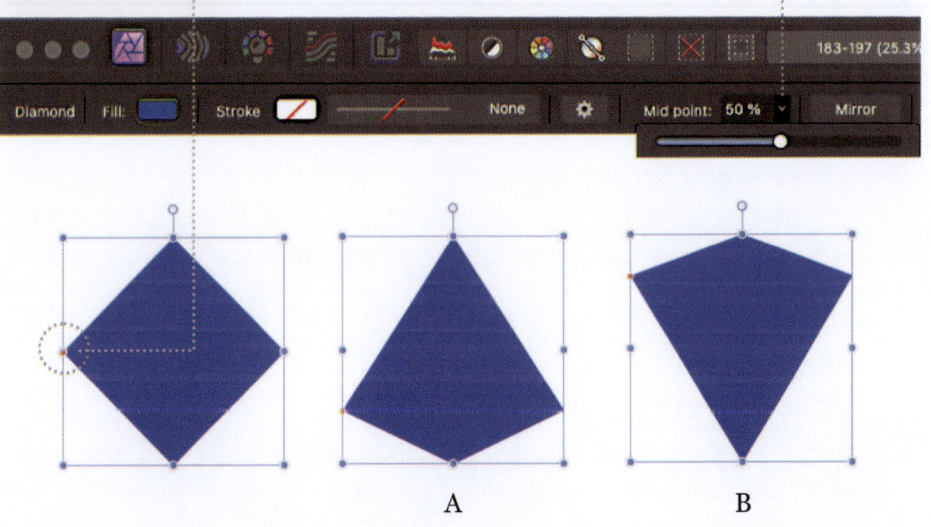

A

B

Chapter 8: Using the Drawing Tools (Vector Data)

## 8_13: Use the Trapezoid Tool to draw

Next we have **the Trapezoid Tool**. Drag for the default trapezoid. The settings should be: **Left point**:25%, **Right point**:75%. Click on the Flyout Button to display the Slider Handle. Move to the right and left.

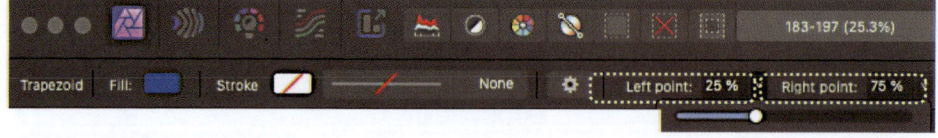

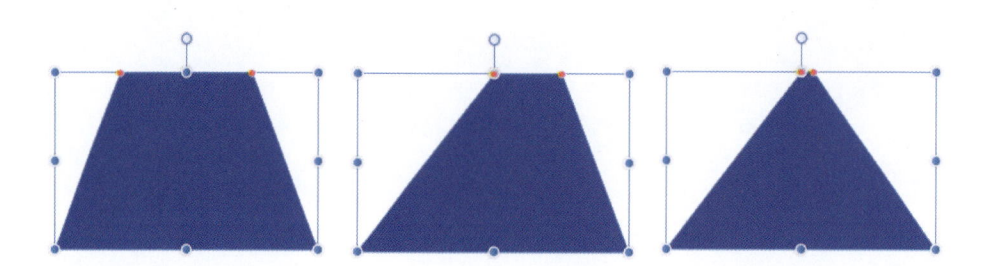

Chapter 8: Using the Drawing Tools (Vector Data)

## 8_14: Using the Double Star Tool to Draw

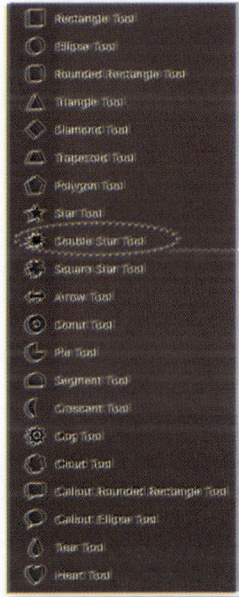

Select the **Double Star Tool**. The Context Tool Bar should now display the Double Star settings. Depending on the line, choose Blue for the Fill color. For Stroke, adjust settings to "None." Hold down the Shift key in the desired spot and drag.

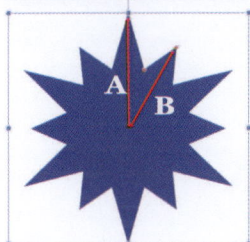

This is the default double-star shape. Have a look at the Context Tool Bar. The **Inner Radius** should display as xx%. This value is the percentage of the inner star radius (B) in relation to the outer star radius (A).

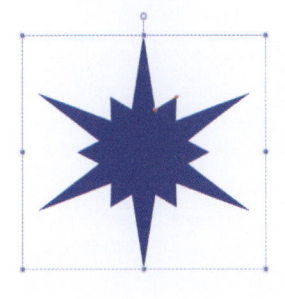

Note the **Point radius** next to this feature. Click on **the Flyout button** and adjust the Slider to 67%. It should now look like the sample.

Chapter 8: Using the Drawing Tools (Vector Data)

## 8_15: Draw a polygon with the Polygon Tool

Next comes the **the Polygon tool**. The Default setting is the Pentagon. Pick up the tool and hold down the Shift key. Were you able to locate the red points? This tool is also capable of various patterns. Look at the Context Tool Bar for categories such as Sides, Curve, Smooth points, etc. We'll explore what they do on the next page.

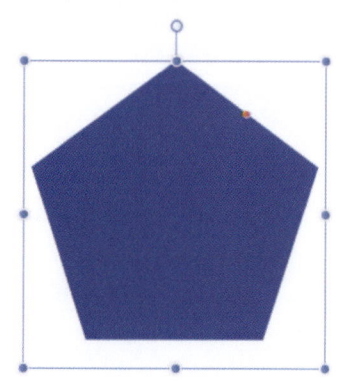

# Chapter 8: Using the Drawing Tools (Vector Data)

This is an example of the default pentagon shape that we drew on the previous page.

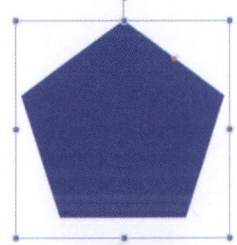

The shape now has six sides, creating a hexagon.

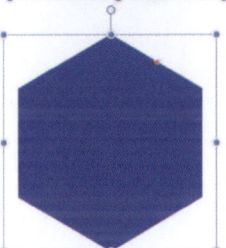

We added four more sides for a total of **ten** to make a decagon.

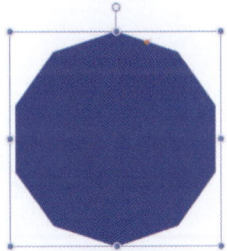

At this point, we showcase the amazing capabilities of Affinity_Photo as we draw an inner curve on the side. Slide to the negative zone, and adjust to **-84%**.

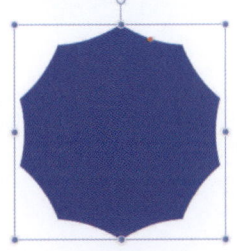

The curve is **100%** in the figure to the right. We now have a circle.

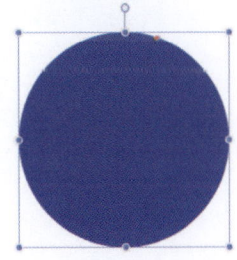

203

## 8_16: Draw a variety of stars with the Star Tool

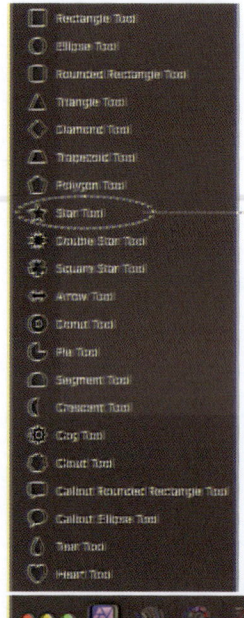

Select the **Star Tool**. The Context Tool Bar should now display the Star settings. Depending on the line, choose Blue for the Fill color. For Stroke, hit adjust settings to **None**. Hold down the Shift key in the desired spot **and drag**.

# Chapter 8: Using the Drawing Tools (Vector Data)

This is an example of the Default star shown on the previous page. Have a look at **Points** on the Context Tool Bar. It should say **5**.

**The Flyout button** is next to the 5. Click and change Points to **10** using the slider. It should now look like the sample on the right.

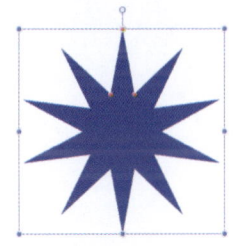

Now adjust the **Inner Radius** settings. Use the slider to select 16%.

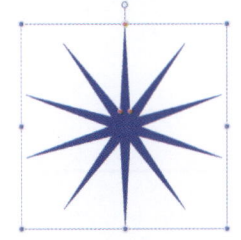

Next, adjust the Inner Radius to **80%**.

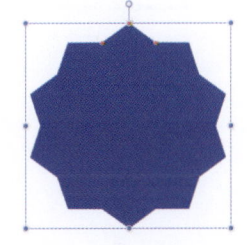

You can also create a curve on the inside of the circle. Click on the Inner Circle Flyout Button and adjust **Inner Circle** to 51%.

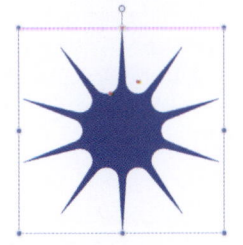

# Chapter 8: Using the Drawing Tools (Vector Data)

## 8_17: Using the Square Star Tool to Draw

Select the **Square Star Tool**. The Context Tool Bar should now display the Square Star settings. Depending on the line, choose Blue for the Fill color. For Stroke, hit adjust settings to **None**. Hold down the Shift key in the desired spot and drag.

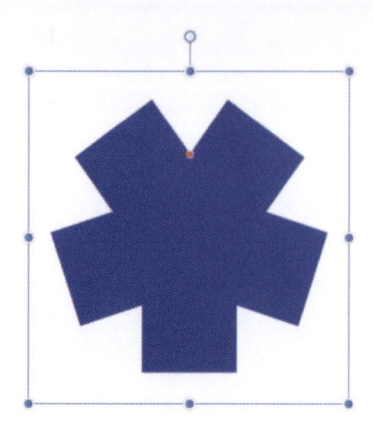

Chapter 8: Using the Drawing Tools (Vector Data)

This is an example of the default right-angle triangle star that we drew on the previous page. Check Sides on the Menu Bar to make sure it reads **5**.

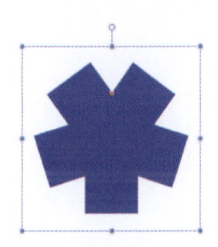

Click on the Sides **Flyout Button** and adjust the Slider to **12**. Does your star now have 12 right-angle sides?

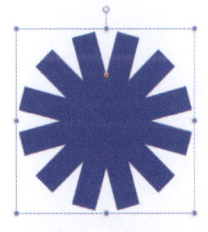

Adjust **Cutout** to 31%. It should now look like the sample to the right.

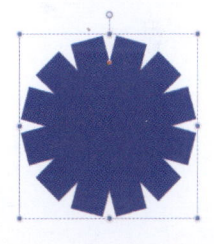

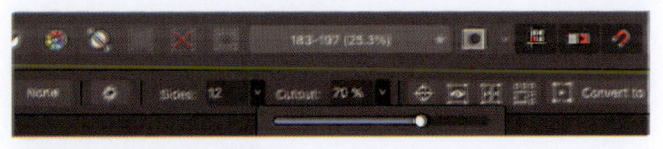

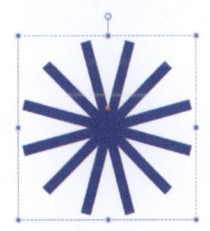

Adjust Cutout to **79%**.

207

## 8_18: Using the Arrow Tool to Draw

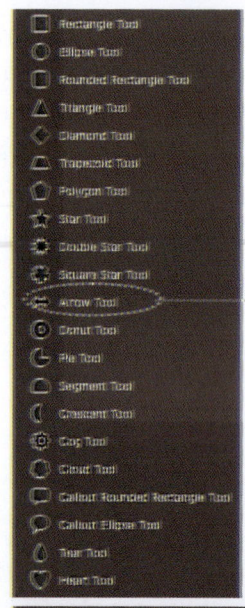

Select the **Arrow Tool**. The Context Tool Bar should now display the Arrow Star settings. Depending on the line, choose Blue for the Fill color. For Stroke, hit adjust settings to **None**. Hold down the Shift key in the desired spot and drag.

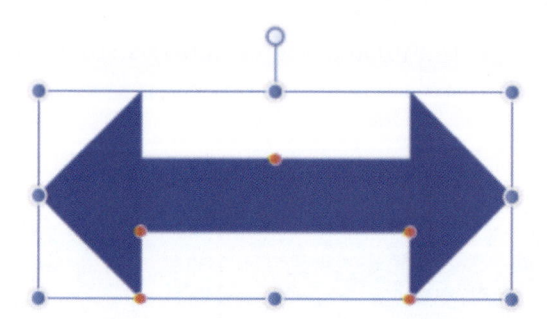

## Chapter 8: Using the Drawing Tools (Vector Data)

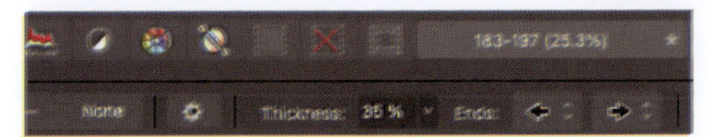

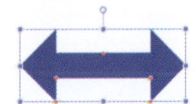

This is an example of the default Arrow Tool on the previous page.

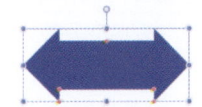

Use the Slider to adjust **Thickness** to 66%. The shaft of the arrow should be thicker at this point.

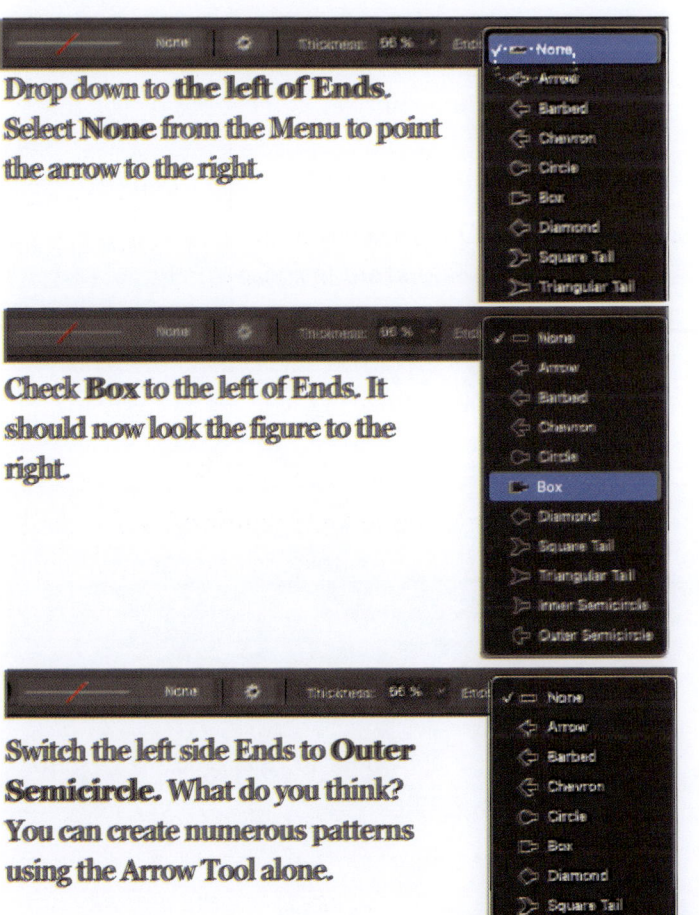

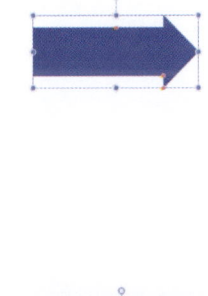

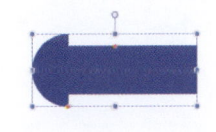

Drop down to **the left of Ends**. Select **None** from the Menu to point the arrow to the right.

Check **Box** to the left of Ends. It should now look the figure to the right.

Switch the left side Ends to **Outer Semicircle.** What do you think? You can create numerous patterns using the Arrow Tool alone.

209

Chapter 8: Using the Drawing Tools (Vector Data)

## 8_19: Using the Donut Tool to Draw

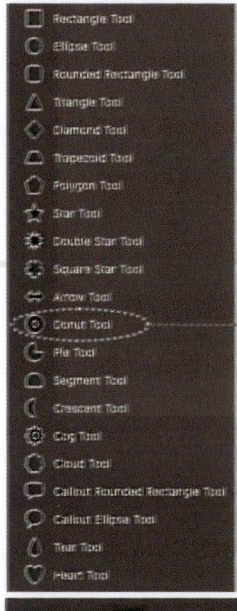

Select the **Donut Tool**. On the Context Tool Bar, choose Blue for the Fill color. For Stroke, hit adjust settings to **None**. Hold down the Shift key in the desired spot and drag.

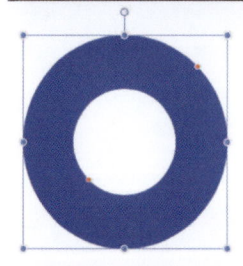

This is the Default donut shape. Check the Context Tool Bar. **Hole Radius** should be adjusted at 50%. This value shows the percentage of the inner radius to the outer radius.

Adjust the Hole Radius Slider to **14%.** Your work should now look like the sample.

210

Chapter 8: Using the Drawing Tools (Vector Data)

## 8_20: Use the Cloud Tool to Draw

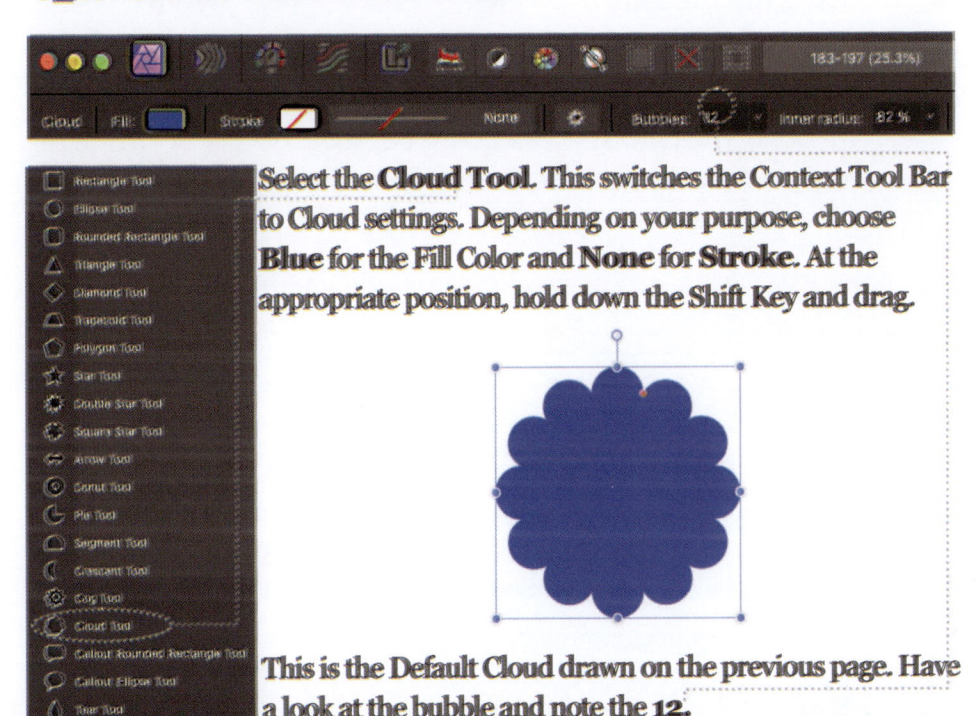

Select the **Cloud Tool**. This switches the Context Tool Bar to Cloud settings. Depending on your purpose, choose **Blue** for the Fill Color and **None** for **Stroke**. At the appropriate position, hold down the Shift Key and drag.

This is the Default Cloud drawn on the previous page. Have a look at the bubble and note the **12**.

Click on the **Bubbles** Flyout button and move the slider from 12 to 20 bubbles.

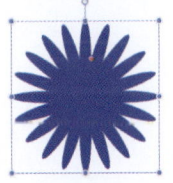

Choose 51% for the **Inner Radius**, noting how the bubble is now longer. The outer radius stays the same, while the inner radius is smaller—like a flower petal.

211

Chapter 8: Using the Drawing Tools (Vector Data)

## 8_21: Using the Pie Tool to Draw

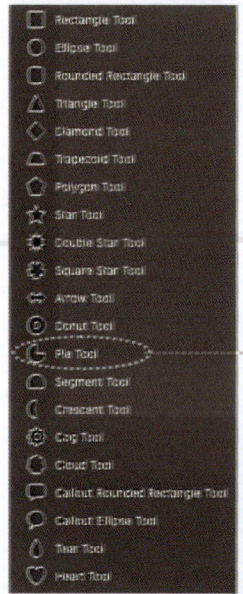

Select the **Pie Tool**. The Context Tool Bar now changes to Pie Tool settings. Depending on the line, choose Blue for the Fill color. For Stroke, adjust settings to **None**. Hold down the Shift key in the desired spot and drag.

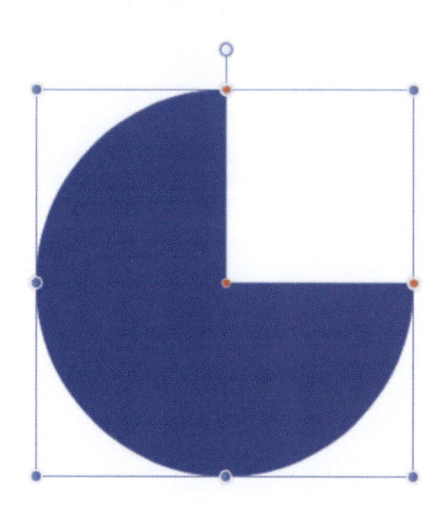

Chapter 8: Using the Drawing Tools (Vector Data)

This is an example of the Default Pie Tool that we drew on the previous page.

Adjust **Hole Radius** to 14%.

Use the Slider to adjust the **Start Angle** to 190°. It should now look like a fan.

Next, adjust the **Total Angle** to 160°.

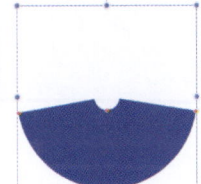

Then **Invert the angle**.

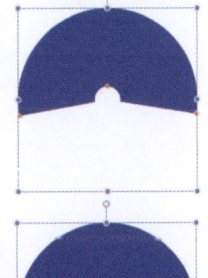

It still doesn't quite look like a fan, does it? Drag **the red points on the right and left** upward to complete it.

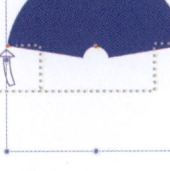

213

## Chapter 8: Using the Drawing Tools (Vector Data)

### 8_22: Using the Segment Tool

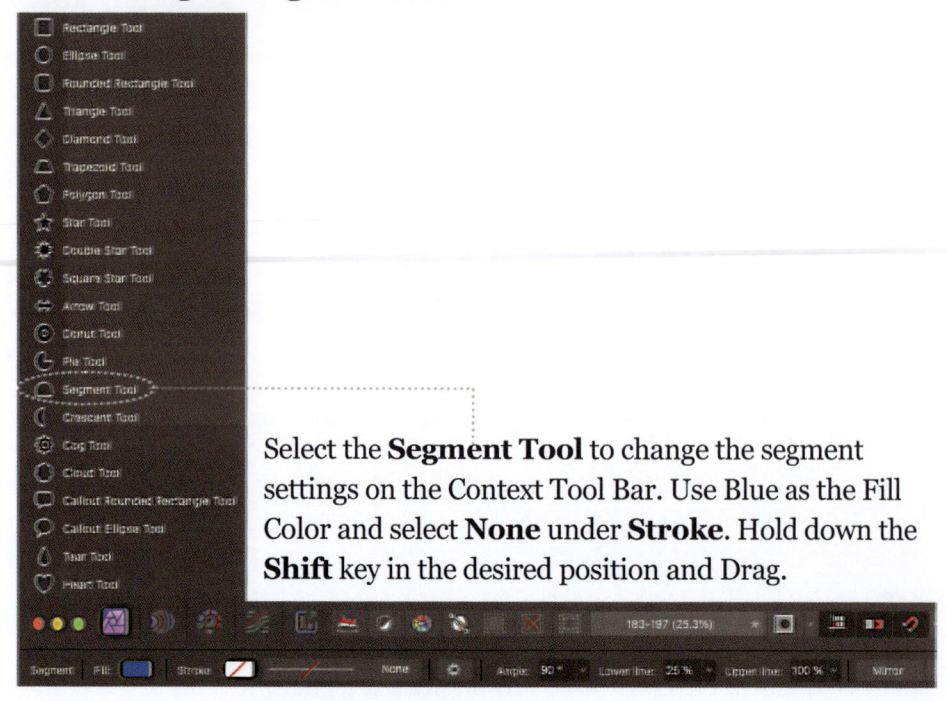

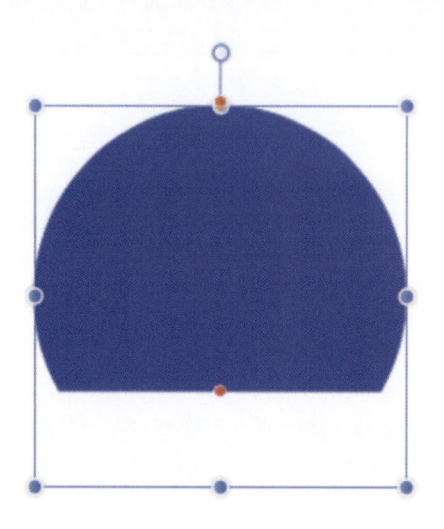

Select the **Segment Tool** to change the segment settings on the Context Tool Bar. Use Blue as the Fill Color and select **None** under **Stroke**. Hold down the **Shift** key in the desired position and Drag.

Chapter 8: Using the Drawing Tools (Vector Data)

This is an example of the Segment Tool on the previous Default page.

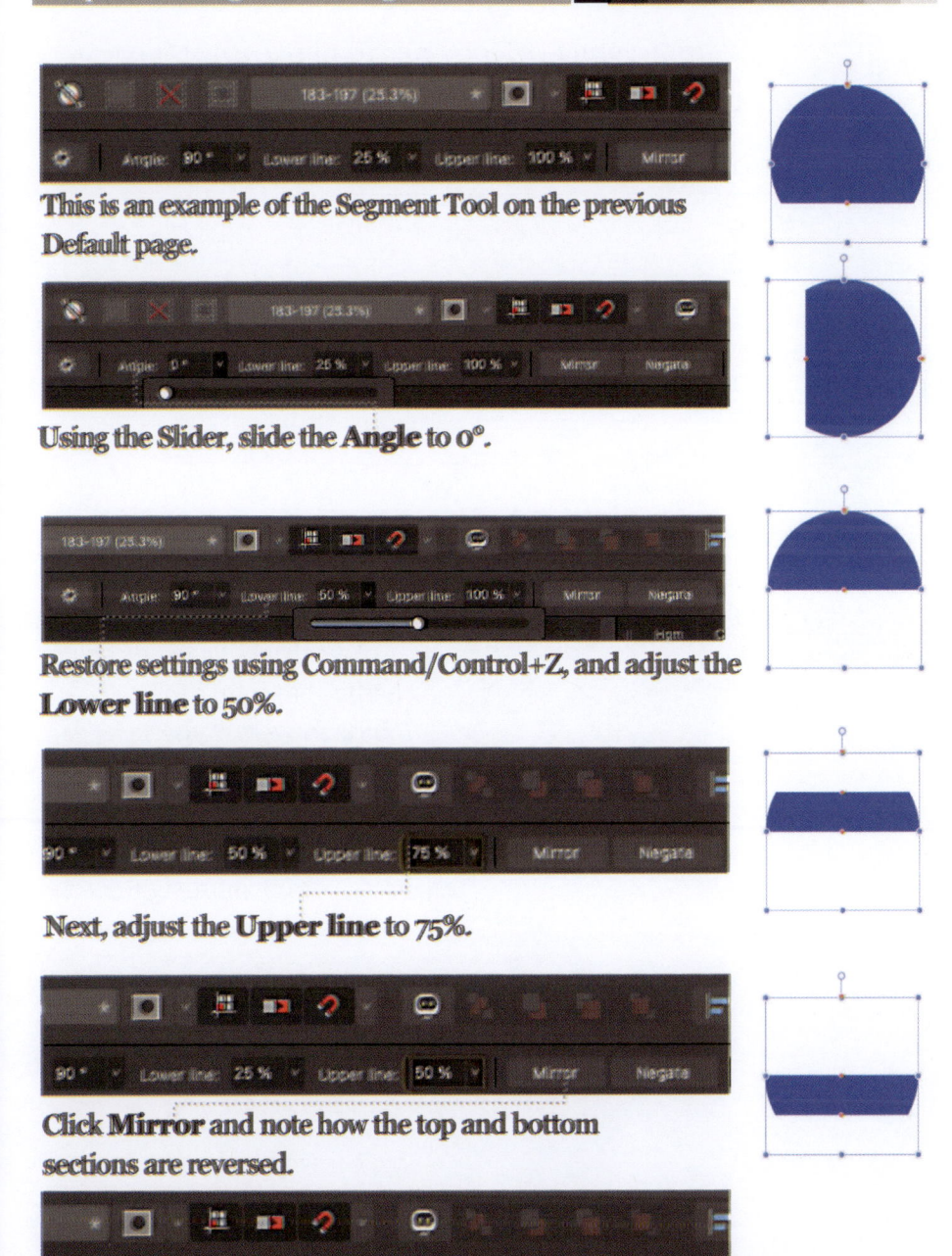

Using the Slider, slide the **Angle** to 0°.

Restore settings using Command/Control+Z, and adjust the **Lower line** to 50%.

Next, adjust the **Upper line** to 75%.

Click **Mirror** and note how the top and bottom sections are reversed.

Lastly, click **Negate** to reverse figure values.

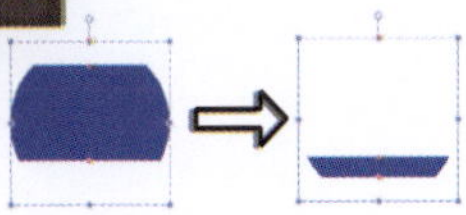

215

## 8_23: Use the Crescent Tool to Draw

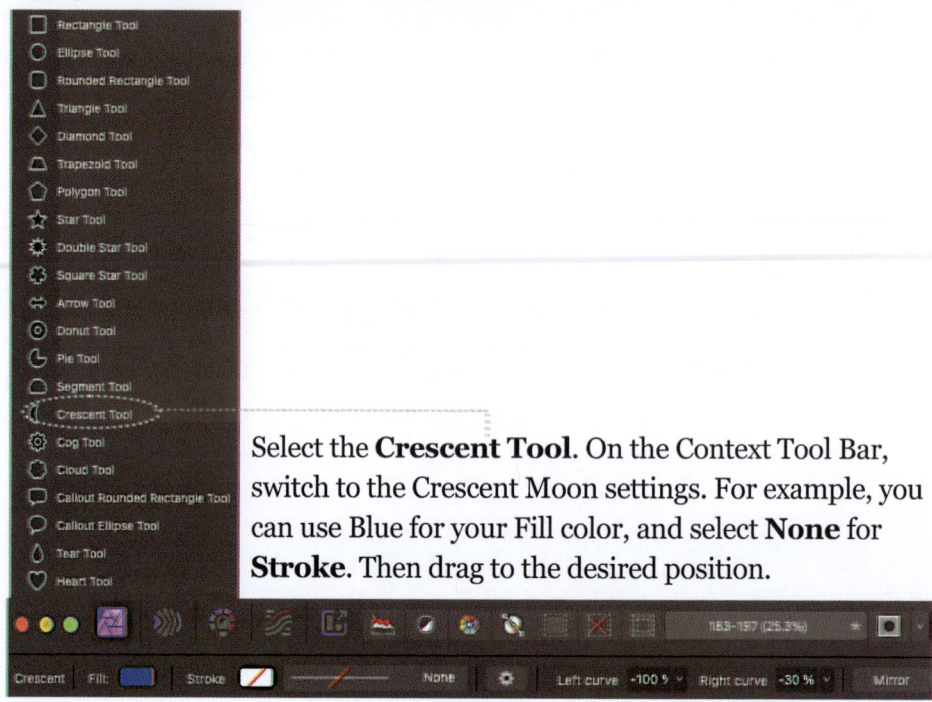

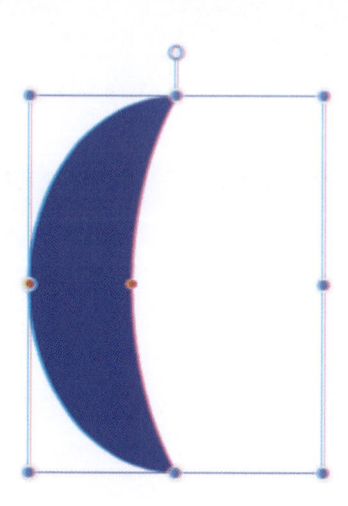

Select the **Crescent Tool**. On the Context Tool Bar, switch to the Crescent Moon settings. For example, you can use Blue for your Fill color, and select **None** for **Stroke**. Then drag to the desired position.

Chapter 8: Using the Drawing Tools (Vector Data)

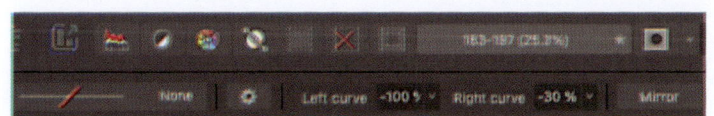

This is an example of how to use the default Crescent Tool drawn on the previous page. Make sure the Left Curve is at -100%, and the Right Curve at -30%.

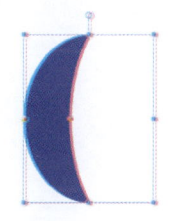

Here we used the Slider to select **-73%** for the **Left Curve**. The curve on the Left has now moved to the inside.

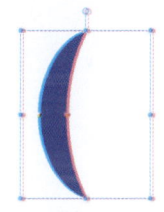

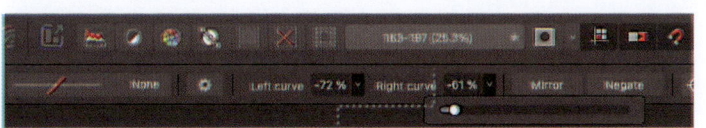

Next, select -60% under **Right Curve**. The Right Curve will move.

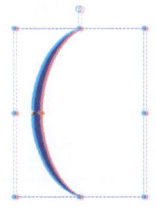

Then, adjust the **Right Curve** to **9%** in the same way.

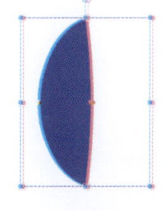

Click **Mirror** to switch the two sides.

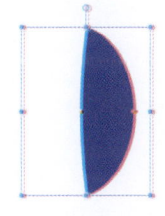

217

## Chapter 8: Using the Drawing Tools (Vector Data)

### 8_24: Use the Cog Tool to Draw

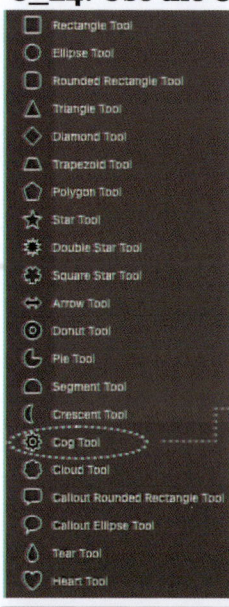

Select the **Cog Tool**. The Context Tool Bar settings are switched to gear settings. Depending on what you'd like to use, use Blue for the Fill color. Under **Stroke** select **None**. Once you are in the right place, hold down the Shift key and Drag.

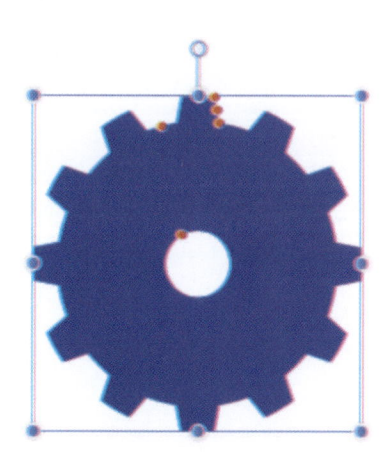

## Chapter 8: Using the Drawing Tools (Vector Data)

The following is an example of how to use the default Cog Tool, which we drew on the previous page. Note the various settings: Teeth, Inner radius, Hole radius, Tooth Size, Notch Size, and Curvature.

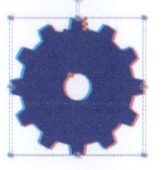

Under **Teeth**, select 16. Click on the Flyout button. The Slider will appear. Select your settings. The number of teeth is now 16 instead of 12.

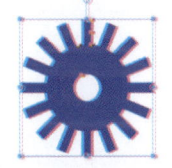

For **Inner Radius**, select 63%. Notice the longer gear teeth. The Outer Radius hasn't changed.

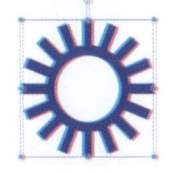

If we make the **Hole Radius** bigger, at 49%, the rounded part of the gear shaft is now larger as well.

Let's make **Tooth Size** smaller. Note how they are more pointed because they are smaller than on the previous page (38%).

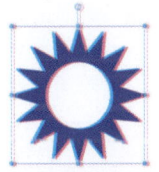

Next, for **Notch Size**, select 0%. This means that the triangular teeth fit perfectly.

Next we determine **Curvature**. Select 100%. Doesn't it look more like a flower than a gear now?

## 8_25: Use the Callout Rounded Rectangle Tool to Draw Balloons

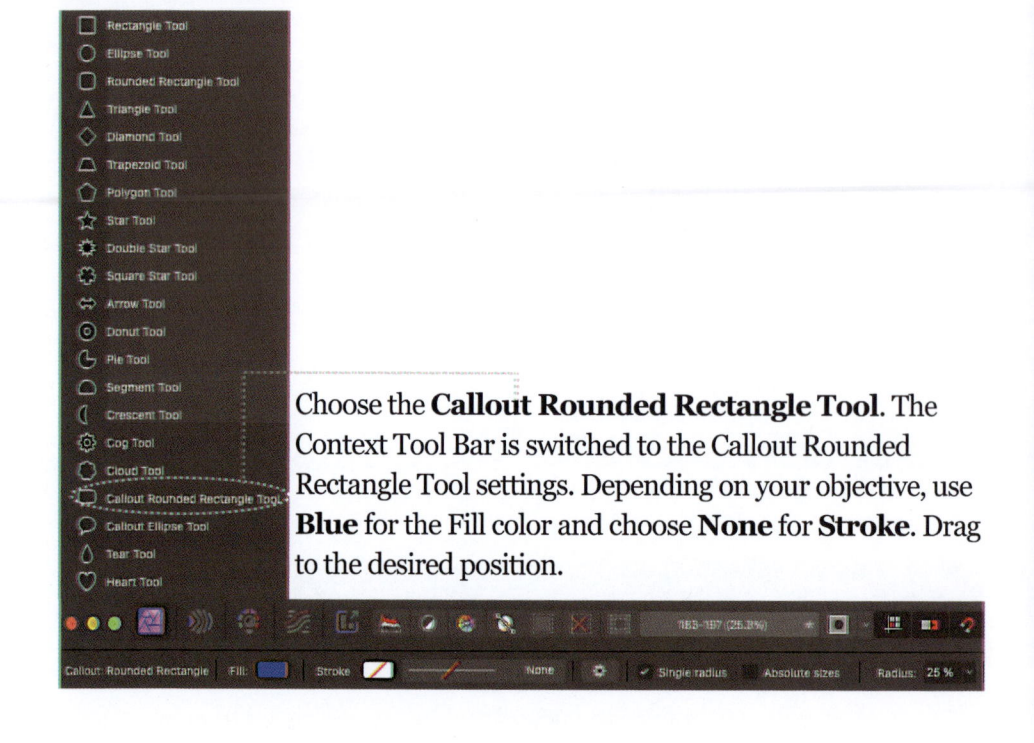

Choose the **Callout Rounded Rectangle Tool**. The Context Tool Bar is switched to the Callout Rounded Rectangle Tool settings. Depending on your objective, use **Blue** for the Fill color and choose **None** for **Stroke**. Drag to the desired position.

# Chapter 8: Using the Drawing Tools (Vector Data)

The following is an example of the default Callout Rounded Rectangle Tool from the previous page.

Adjust the **radius** of the Rounded Rectangle. Click on the Radius default button and move the Slider to 50%.

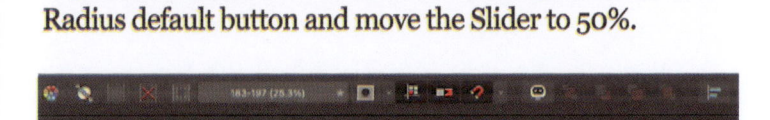

For **Tail Height,** move the slider from 30% to 64%. The tail is now longer and the balloon shorter.

For **Tail End Position**, choose 67%. The tail moves to the right.

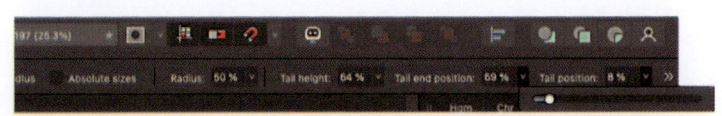

Now choose 9% for **Tail Position**. The tail moves 9% from the left.

Finally, we work with the width of the tail. If you do not see the Tail Width button, click on ">>" to open the settings. Choose 70% for **Tail Width**.

## 8_26: Use the Callout Ellipse Tool to Draw a Balloon

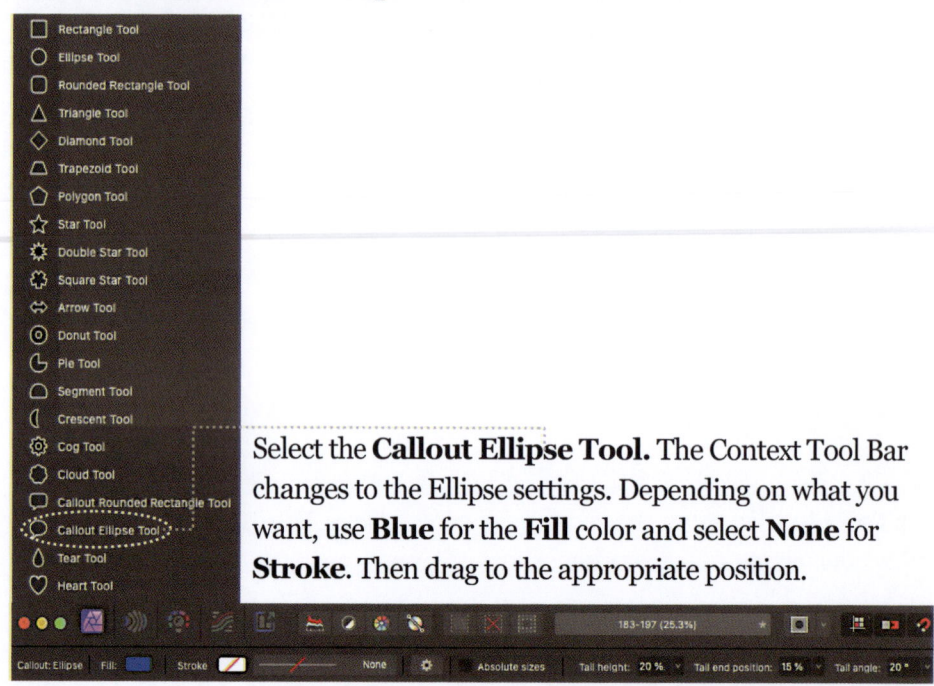

Select the **Callout Ellipse Tool.** The Context Tool Bar changes to the Ellipse settings. Depending on what you want, use **Blue** for the **Fill** color and select **None** for **Stroke**. Then drag to the appropriate position.

Chapter 8: Using the Drawing Tools (Vector Data)

The following is an example of the default Callout Ellipse Tool drawn on the previous page.

For **Tail Height**, adjust the Slider from 20% to 65%. Note how the tail is longer and the balloon is lower.

For the **Tail End Position**, select 100%. Then move the tail to the right.

Let's now work on the **Tail Angle**. Select 86° for the Tail Angle.

223

## Chapter 8: Using the Drawing Tools (Vector Data)

**8_27: Use the Tear Tool to Draw**

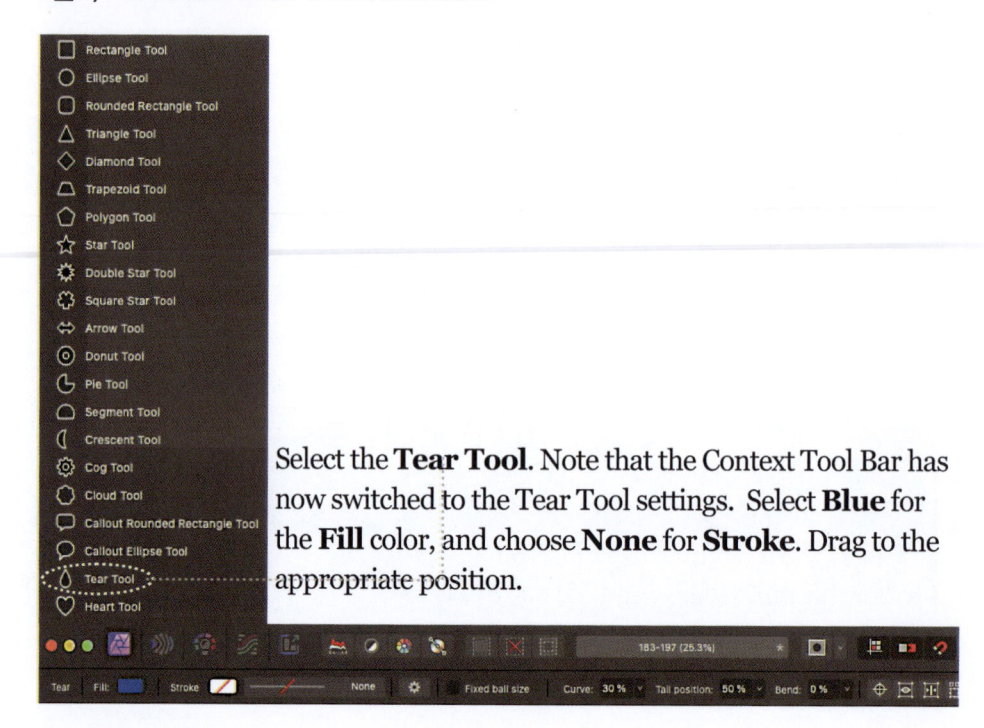

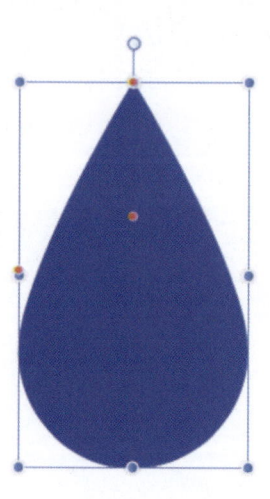

Select the **Tear Tool**. Note that the Context Tool Bar has now switched to the Tear Tool settings. Select **Blue** for the **Fill** color, and choose **None** for **Stroke**. Drag to the appropriate position.

Chapter 8: Using the Drawing Tools (Vector Data)

The following is an example of how to use the default Tear Tool on the previous page.

Slide the **Curve** Slider 30% to **88%**. Make sure the right-left curve has been updated.

Select **81%** for the **Tail Position**. Note how the tail shifts to the right.

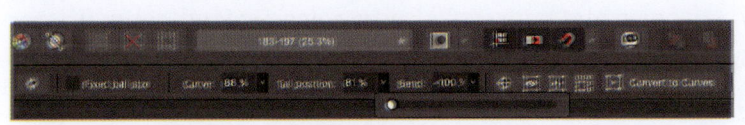

Select **-100%** for the **Tail Bend**.

225

## 8_28: Use the Heart Tool to Draw

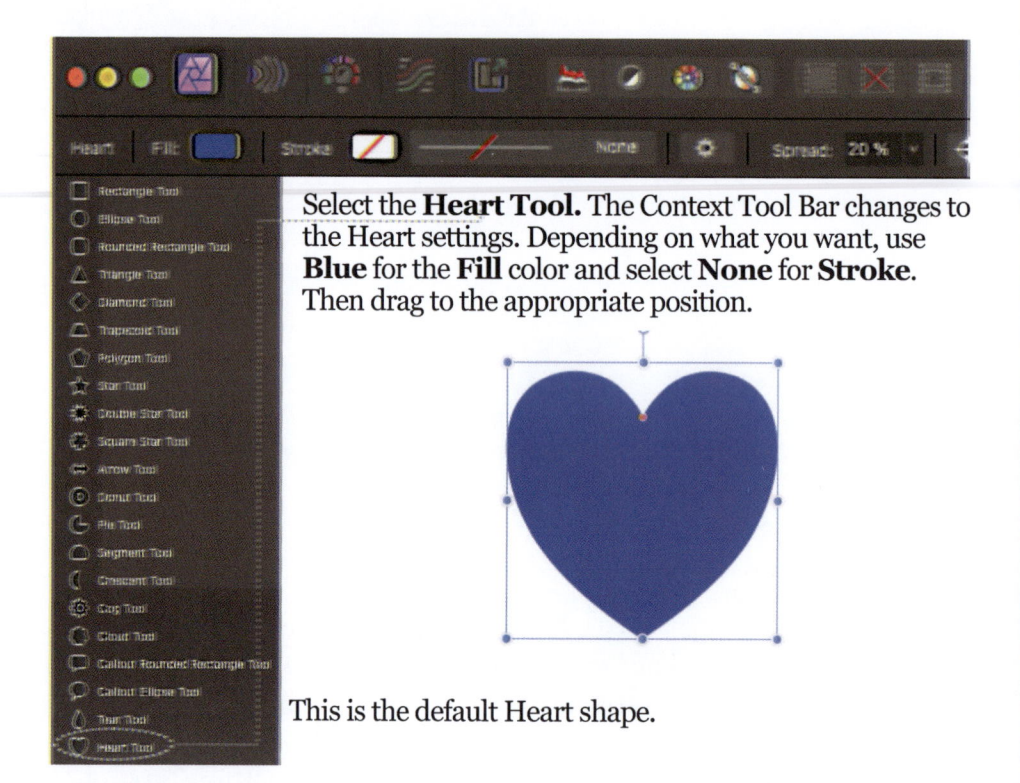

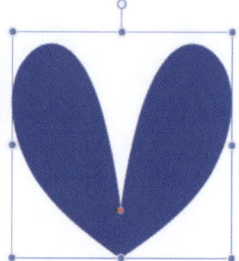

Select the **Heart Tool.** The Context Tool Bar changes to the Heart settings. Depending on what you want, use **Blue** for the **Fill** color and select **None** for **Stroke**. Then drag to the appropriate position.

This is the default Heart shape.

Slide **Spread** from 20% to 79%.

226

# Chapter 8: Using the Drawing Tools (Vector Data)

## 8_29: Line up Multiple Figures

Until now, we've been learning about how to use individual tools. From this Chapter onward, we learn how to create new figures by combining figures of different shapes using the control buttons. Select the **Rectangle Tool** and use **Blue** for the **Fill** color. Select **Red** for **Stroke**. Choose **2pt** for the line thickness. Drag to the desired position.

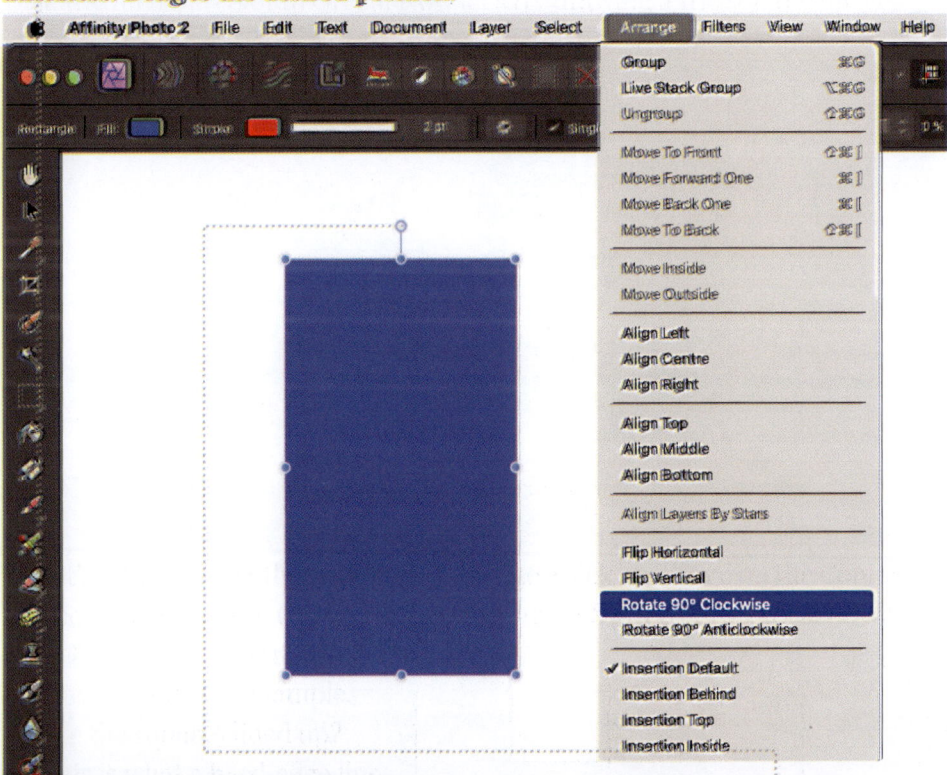

Render the Rectangle vertical. You can rotate using the **Arm Point** directly. Now try controlling from the Menu Bar. To rotate, click **Arrange>Rotate 90° Clockwise**. The same applies to other commands. Check it and then restore settings to **Rotate 90° Anticlockwise**.

Chapter 8: Using the Drawing Tools (Vector Data)

Next, select **Ellipse Tool** from the Tool Menu. Next, hold down the Shift key at the top right of the rectangle drawn above and drag to **create a circle** as below.

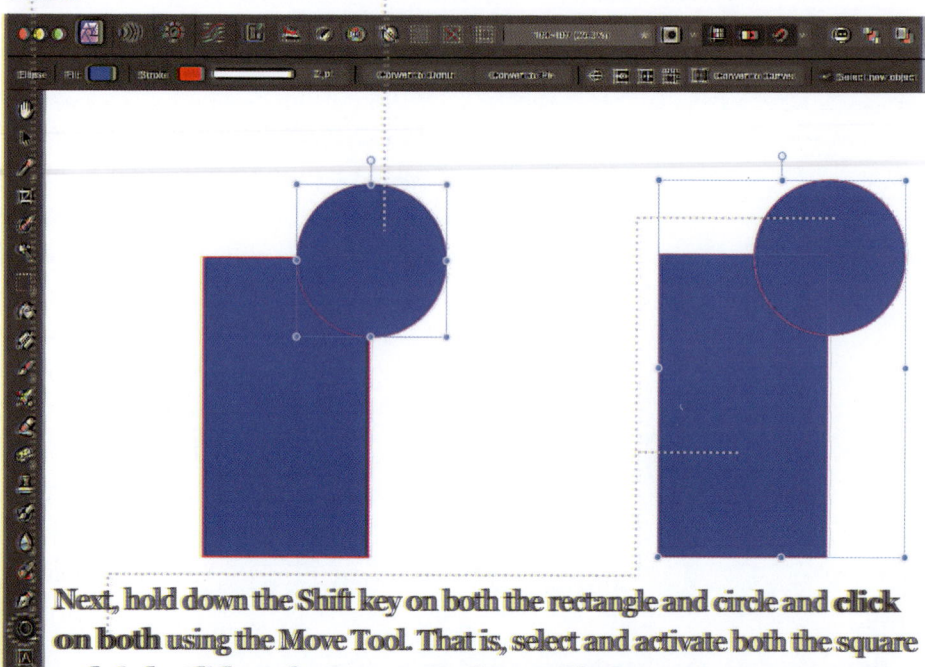

Next, hold down the Shift key on both the rectangle and circle and **click on both** using the Move Tool. That is, select and activate both the square and circle. Click on the Persona Tool Bar>**Alignment** button. You will then see the dropdown menu. Then click the **Align Top** button to align in the vertical direction. The Dropdown Menu appears. The figures should now be top-aligned as follows.

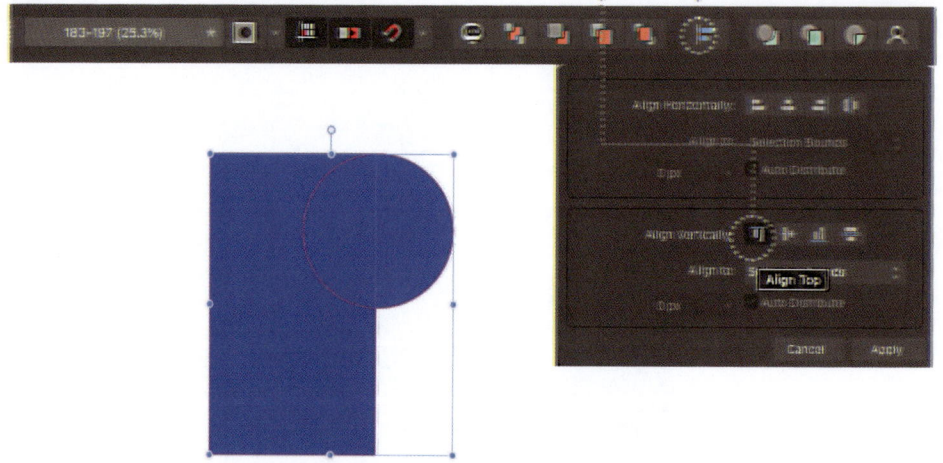

Chapter 8: Using the Drawing Tools (Vector Data)

Click on the margins to De-select. Holding down the Shift Key, and use the Move Tool to select the rectangle and circle. Then, as on the previous page, click the Persona tool Bar>Alignment. Click the **Align Middle** button next to it. The figure should now be centered as below.

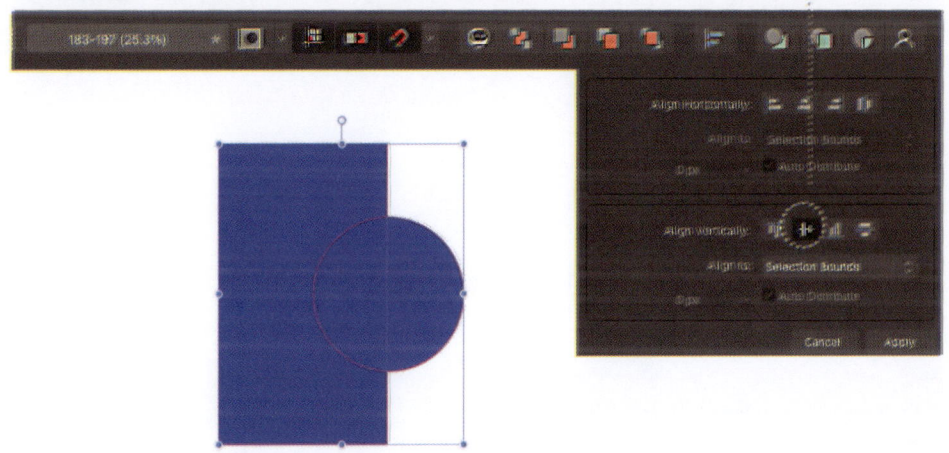

Next, let's align the bottoms of the rectangle and circle. This time we'll do it without using the dropdown menu. Select both the rectangle and circle objects. Click Menu Bar>**Arrange**>**Align Bottom**. How does it look? That was fast, wasn't it?

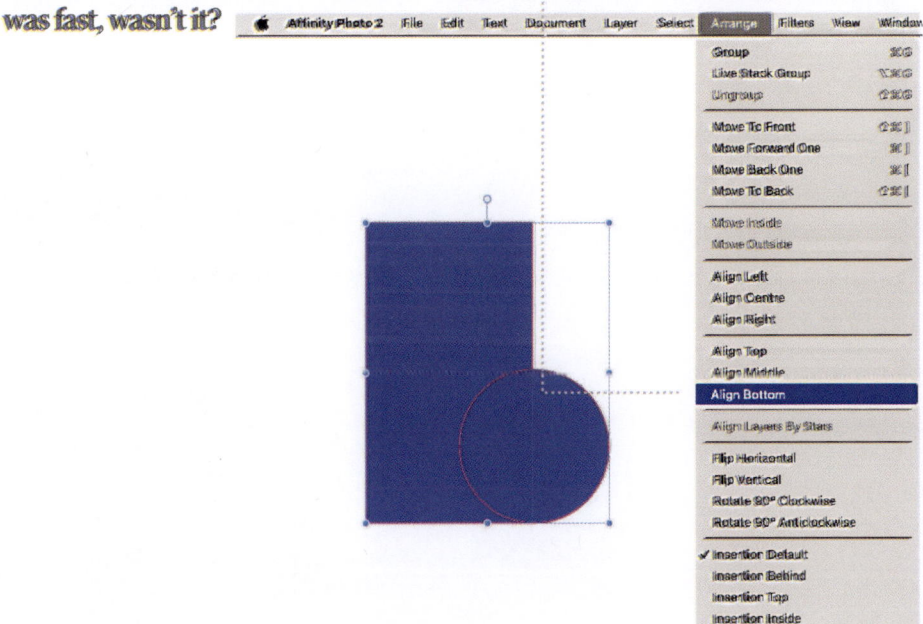

229

Chapter 8: Using the Drawing Tools (Vector Data)

## 8_30: Create a Composite Object

Sometimes we want to combine images. Here, let's make a new object from two different ones.

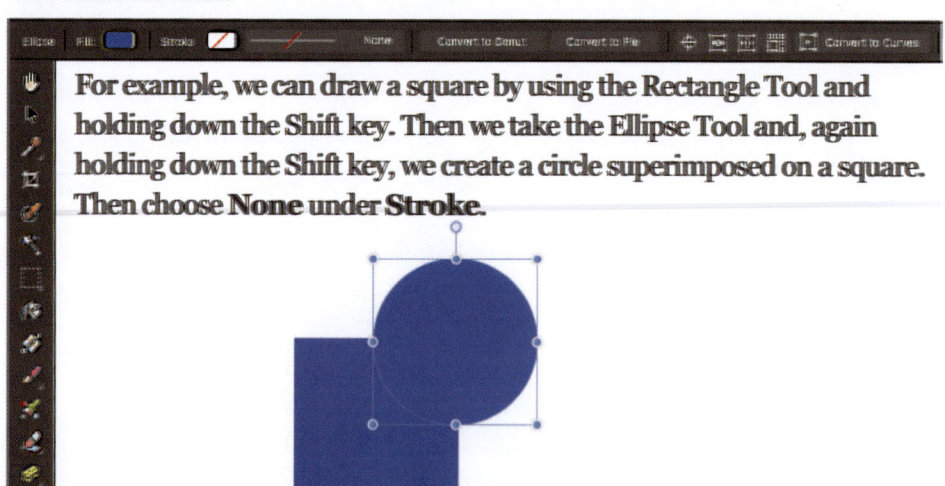

For example, we can draw a square by using the Rectangle Tool and holding down the Shift key. Then we take the Ellipse Tool and, again holding down the Shift key, we create a circle superimposed on a square. Then choose **None** under **Stroke**.

Activate both the rectangle and square holding down the Shift key. Precisely speaking, the circle is superimposed on the square.

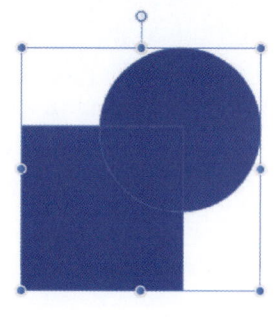

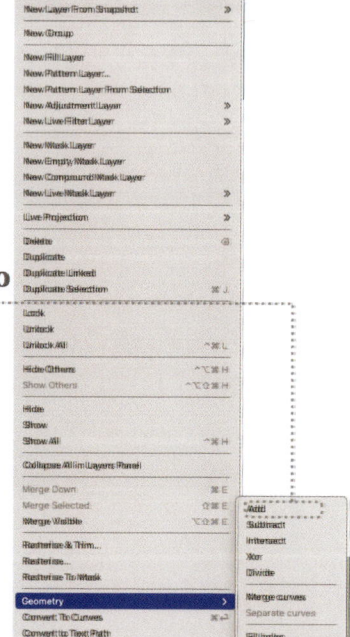

Click Menu Bar>Layer>Geometry>**Add**. The two figures are now one!

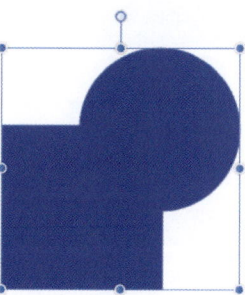

230

## Chapter 8: Using the Drawing Tools (Vector Data)

The Layer>Geometry features has not only an Add feature but also Subtract and other commands. Let's try Subtract. Using Command/Control+Z, restore the rectangle and circle to their original forms. Then click again on Layer>Geometry>**Subtract**. Does it look like the figure below?

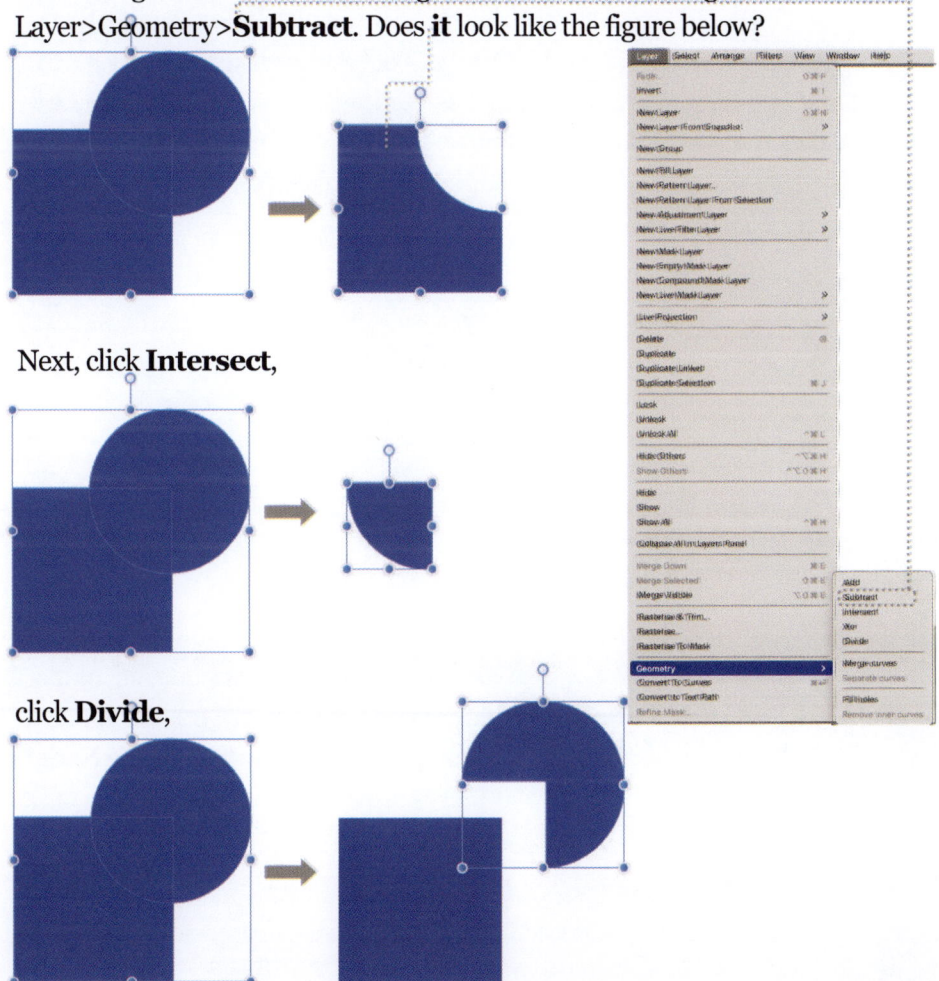

Next, click **Intersect**,

click **Divide**,

and then click **Combine**. How does it look? This is all the geometry we need! This technique can be used for many things, so it's important to remember it!

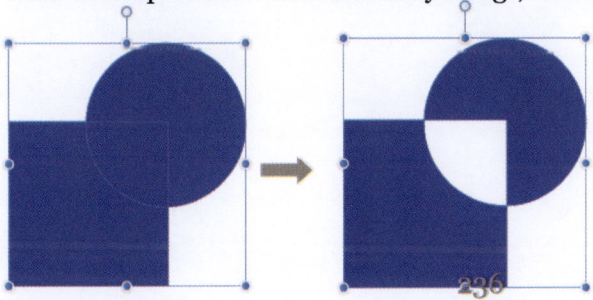

231

Chapter 8: Using the Drawing Tools (Vector Data)

## 8_31: Change the figure to curve

Change the figure drawn with the Tool any way you like. First choose the Rectangle tool. Click on Fill on the Context Tool Bar and switch the color to Gray. Once you have drawn a rectangle as pictured below, find **Convert to Curves** on the lower right of the Context Tool Bar, and click on it.

Click on **Convert to Curves** to change the Context Tool Bar for **use as a Node Tool**. Straight or curved lines are altered using the Node Tool. This is how **Convert to Curves** works. Proceed to the next page once you have determined that the shape is converted to fit **the Node Tool points**.

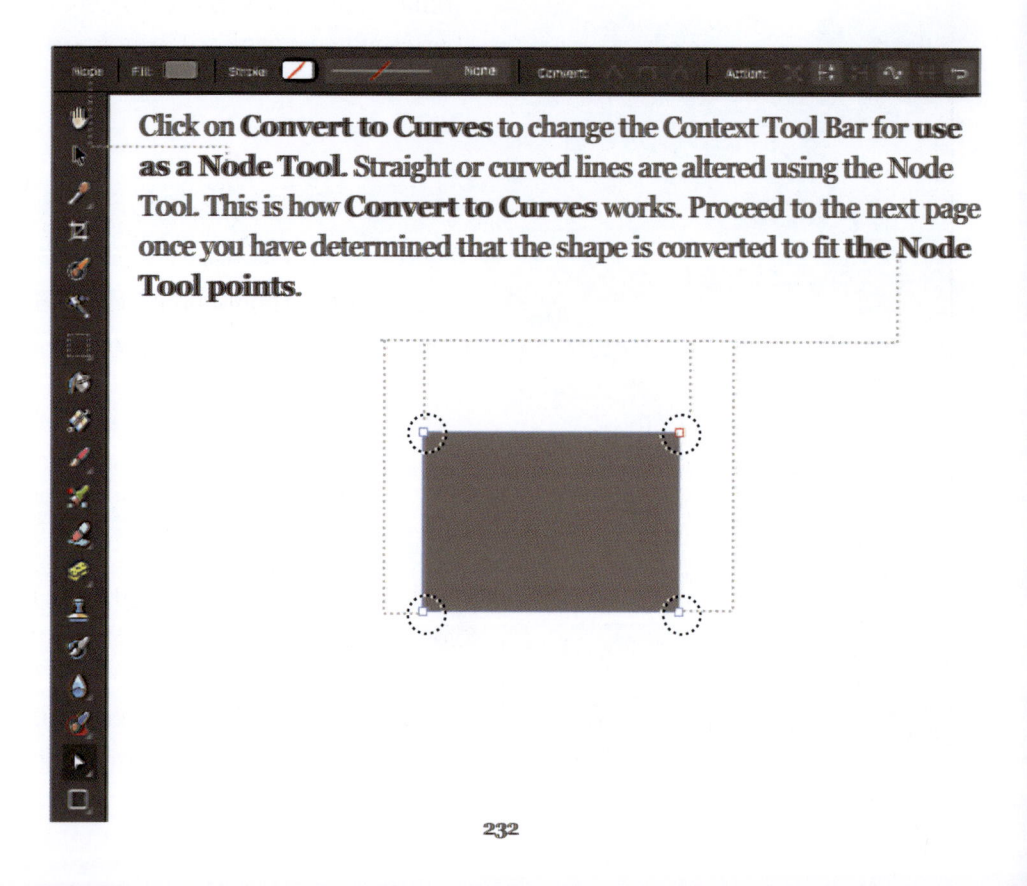

Chapter 8: Using the Drawing Tools (Vector Data)

You should be on the Node Tool since we were using it on the previous page. Click on **the midde of the top line** to add a node. Next, on the Context Tool Bar, click on **Convert>Sharp**. Drag **the node point upward**. The top should now look like a triangular-shaped roof.

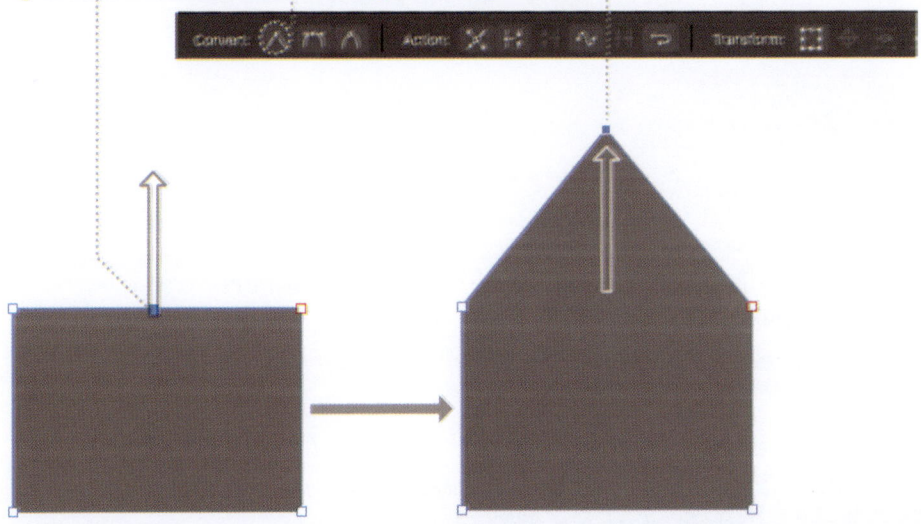

Restore your original work Command/Control+Z, and add Nodes again. On the Context Tool Bar, click **Convert>Smooth**. Then drag up. You should now have a curved line.

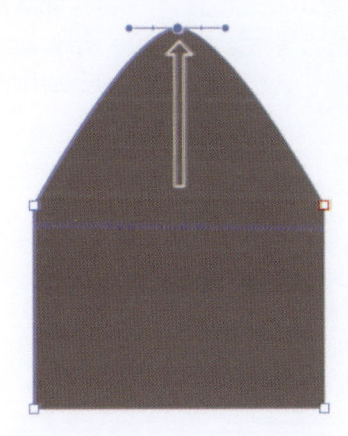

Chapter 8: Using the Drawing Tools (Vector Data)

Stretch **the arm points** right and left to round out the top of the head. Add a node on **the middle of the bottom line** and drag downward.

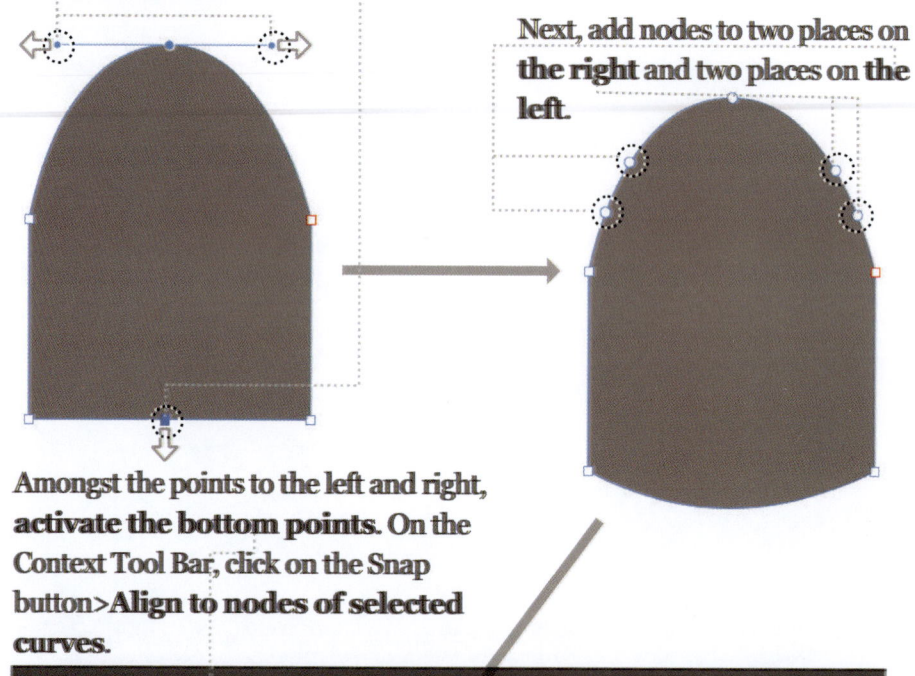

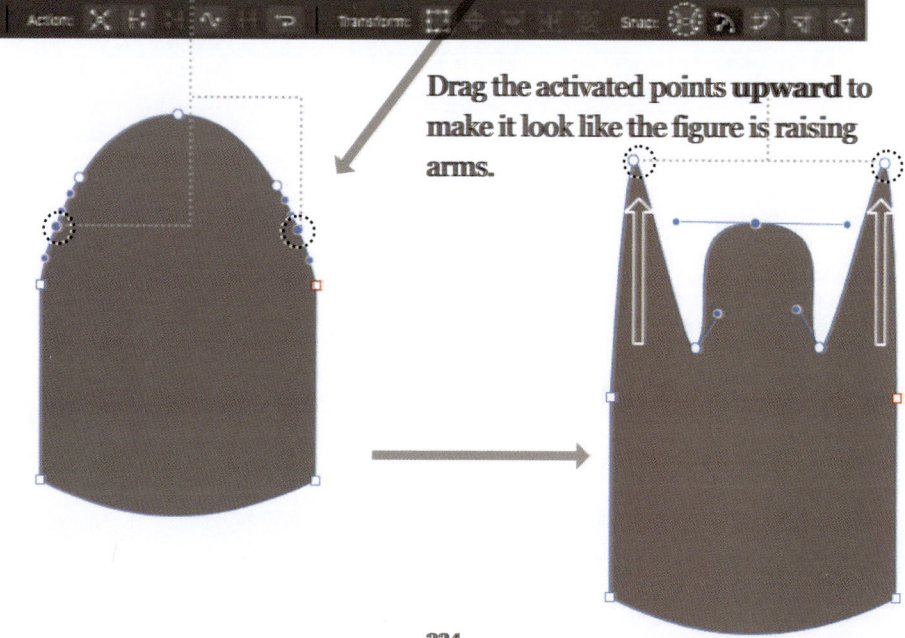

Next, add nodes to two places on **the right** and two places on **the left**.

Amongst the points to the left and right, **activate the bottom points**. On the Context Tool Bar, click on the Snap button>**Align to nodes of selected curves**.

Drag the activated points **upward** to make it look like the figure is raising arms.

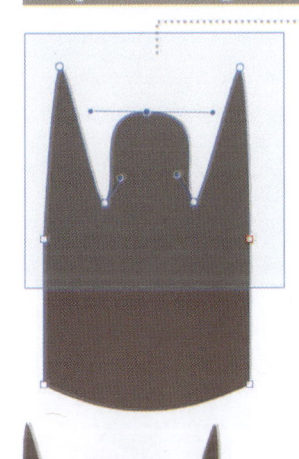

Chapter 8: Using the Drawing Tools (Vector Data)

Drag the node tool of **the top half upward** to activate. Then **drag to the left**.

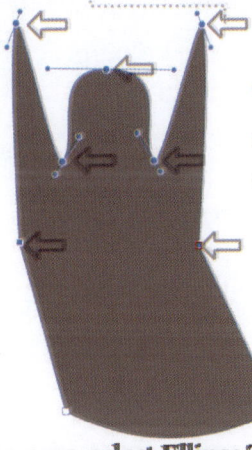

The figure should be slanted as shown as in the example. Next, add the eyes.

For the eyes, select Ellipse Tool to temporarily apply the color red. You now have **a red ellipse**. The ellipse is used to open up a white hole against the gray background. This is the first step.

The image is a synthesis of a background figure and the figure above it. **Click on the background figure**, hold the Shift key down, and **click on the ellipse**—in other words, select both.

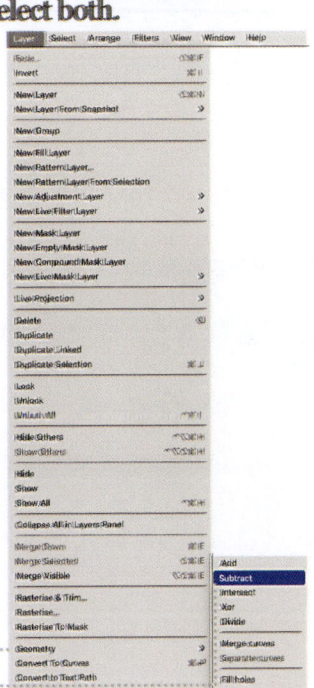

Next, click on Menu Bar>Layer>**Geometry>Subtract**. The red disappears to leave **white** in its place. There should now be a hole in the background. This method is known as **subtractive synthesis**.

235

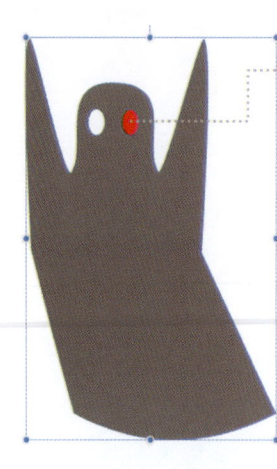

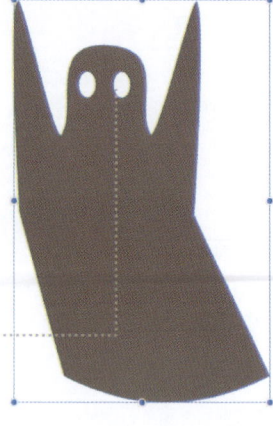

Chapter 8: Using the Drawing Tools (Vector Data)

Now add **the right eye**. Draw the right eye with Ellipse, choose both the background figure and elliptical figure, and click on Menu Bar>Layer>Geometry>**Subtract**. You are now finished with **the right eye**. Next, add the mouth using the Crescent Tool. Once you have drawn it using **Drag**, use the Move Tool to rotate. Then click on Geometry>**Subtract**. You did it! Now let's take this another step further. Switch to the Node Tool, and activate **the points on the bottom right**. Drag to the right to finish. The rectangle has now changed.

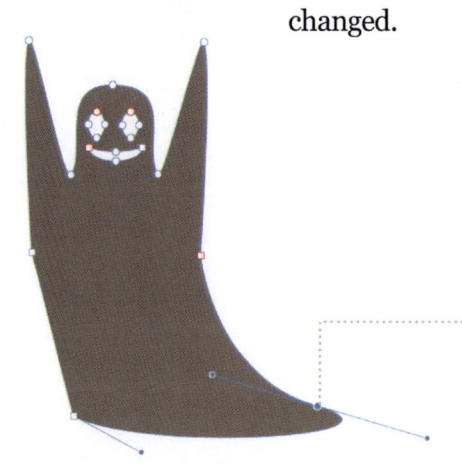

241

236

Chapter 8: Using the Drawing Tools (Vector Data)

## 8_32: Duplicate and Object

When copying an object, Affinity_Photo copies position, size, rotation, etc. Using this feature makes copying more efficient. Let's give it a try! Choose the **Rectangle Tool**, and fill in with **Gray**. Under **Stroke**, select **None**. Drag from the appropriate place on the left end to **draw a long-and-slim rectangle**.

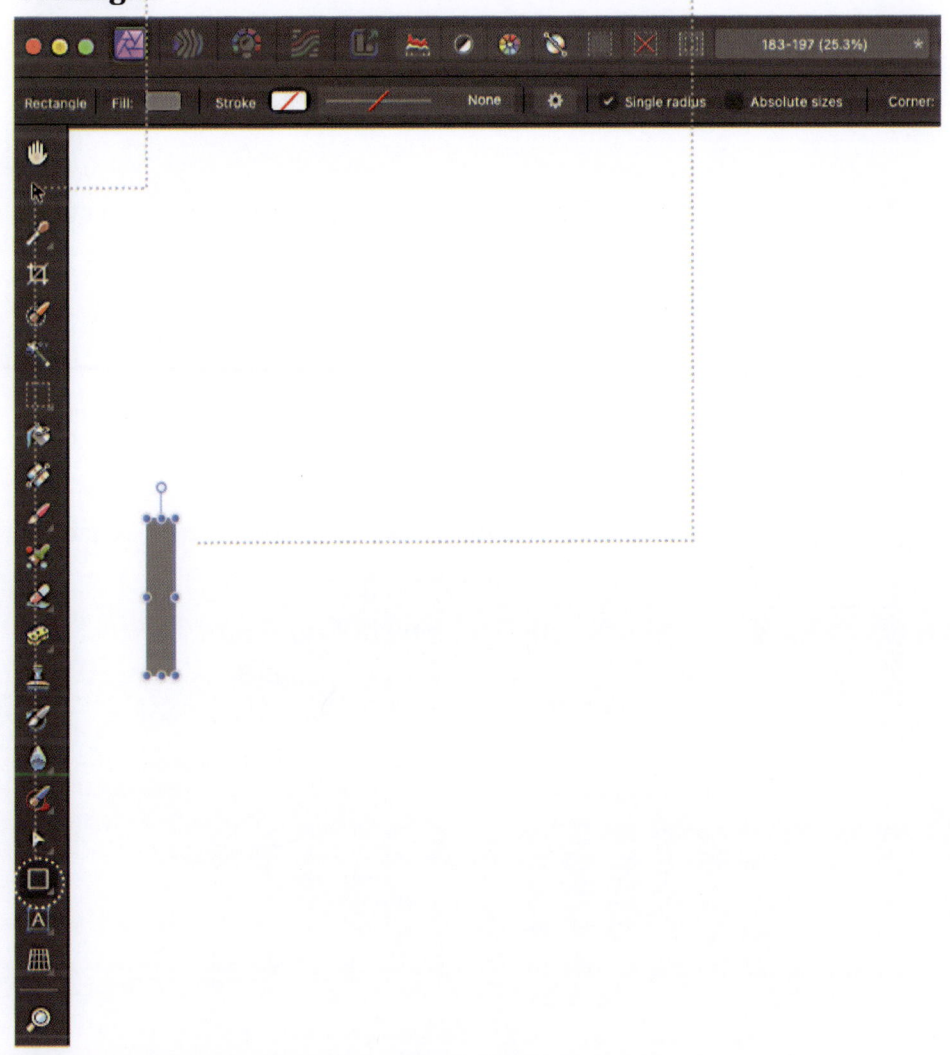

Chapter 8: Using the Drawing Tools (Vector Data)

Check that your rectangle is active (if it is not, click on the object),

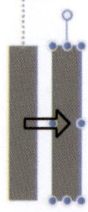

**hold down the Option/Alt key and drag the figure you have drawn to the right**. Distance moved, size, and angle are all retained.

Next, without touching the object, create a shortcut on your keyboard with **Command/Control+J**. You now have a third rectangle. You don't even need to specify where you want it. The program remembers the position interval and pastes it. Affinity Photo is an intelligent program!

For **the fourth one, type in Command/Control+J.** Use Command/Control+J and Command/Control+J to create the following. Note how efficient it is!

Chapter 8: Using the Drawing Tools (Vector Data)

On the preceding page, we learned how we could do a series of copies, noting that the program remembers the distance moved. Now let's add size increase/decrease. Then let's draw a rectangle.

Hold down the Option/Alt key and drag. You've made copies!

**Make the top and bottom margins bigger**, keeping the left and right margins the same. Distance moved, size, and angle are all retained.

**Without touching the object, use the shortcut Command/Control+J** on the keyboard to paste three objects. Make the margins bigger on the top and bottom of the object, keeping it the same on right and left.

Do the same for the fourth object using Command/Control+J.

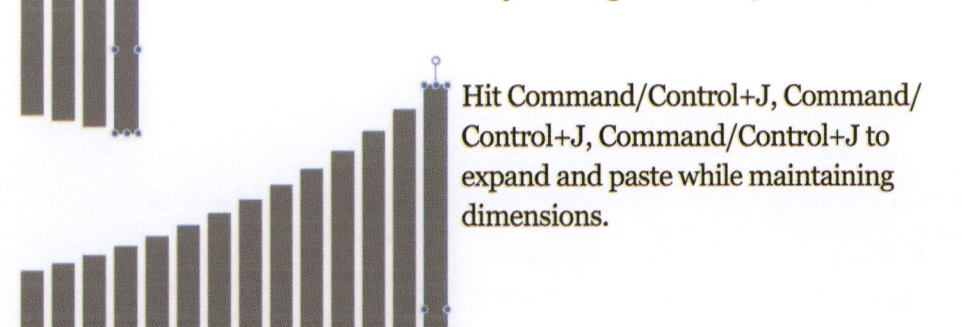

Hit Command/Control+J, Command/Control+J, Command/Control+J to expand and paste while maintaining dimensions.

# Chapter 8: Using the Drawing Tools (Vector Data)

It's time to make a copy! Let's draw another rectangle.

Click on the object Option/Alt and drag.

Next, let's rotate the Object.

Without touching the object, paste using Command/Control+J. Use rotate to copy the third.

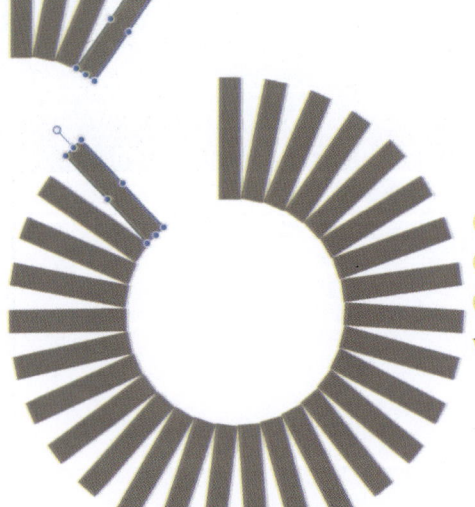

Continue with Command/Control+J, Command/Control+J, Command/Control+J to paste while maintaining the angle.

# Chapter 9: Using the Text Tool

## Chapter 9: Using the Text Tool

**9_1: Inputting text**

Affinity_Photo includes text tools to write in titles and body copy. Click on the Tool Panel>Text Tool **flyout button** to display the Artistic Text Tool and Frame Text Tool. The Artistic Text Tool is used to write single lines of text such as titles and names of buttons. The Frame Text Tool, meanwhile, is used to write longer text such as body copy. Choose the **Artistic Text tool**. The Context Tool Bar settings have now changed to Text Tool settings.

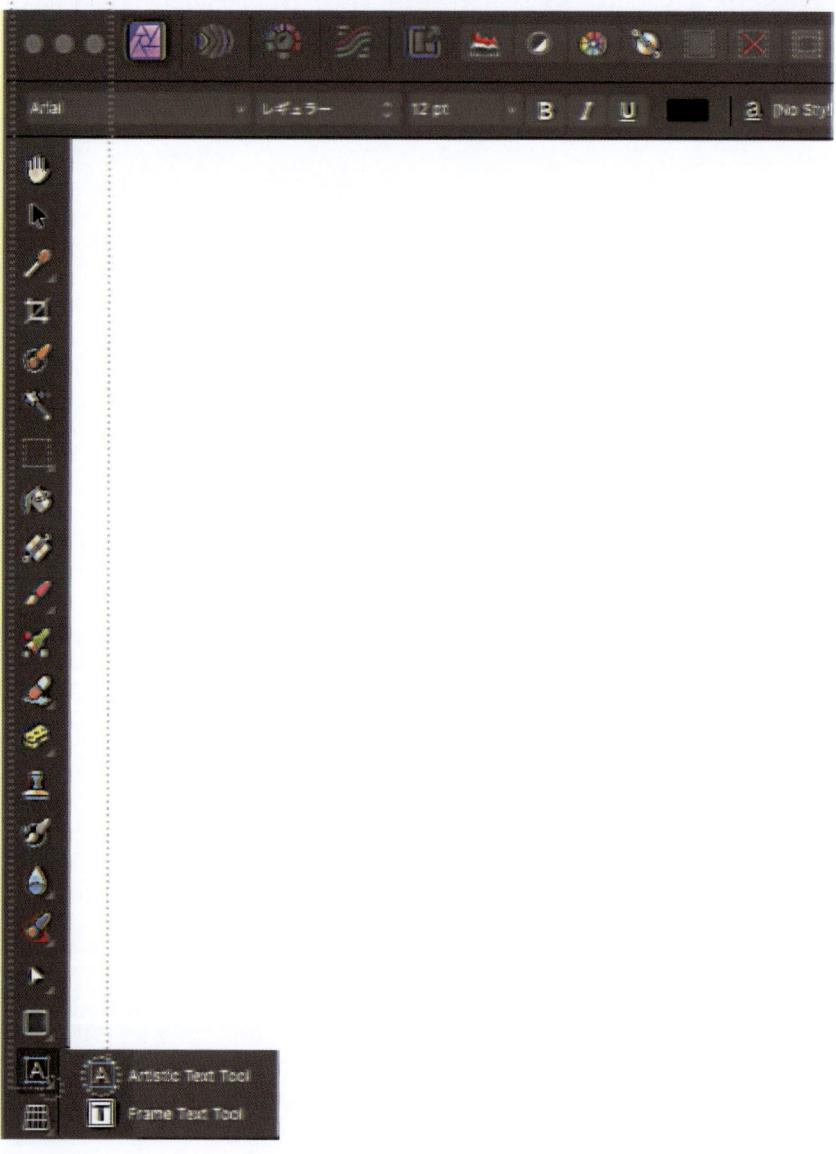

Chapter 9: Using the Text Tool

Let's have a close look at the Context Tool Bar. From the left, click on the **Font Selection button, font size, bold/italic/underline** settings button, **style**, etc. In addition to the Context Tool Bar, the feature can also be used for advanced font settings such as the **Studio Character tab**, Kerning, Tacking, etc., as well as advanced **Paragraph** settings.

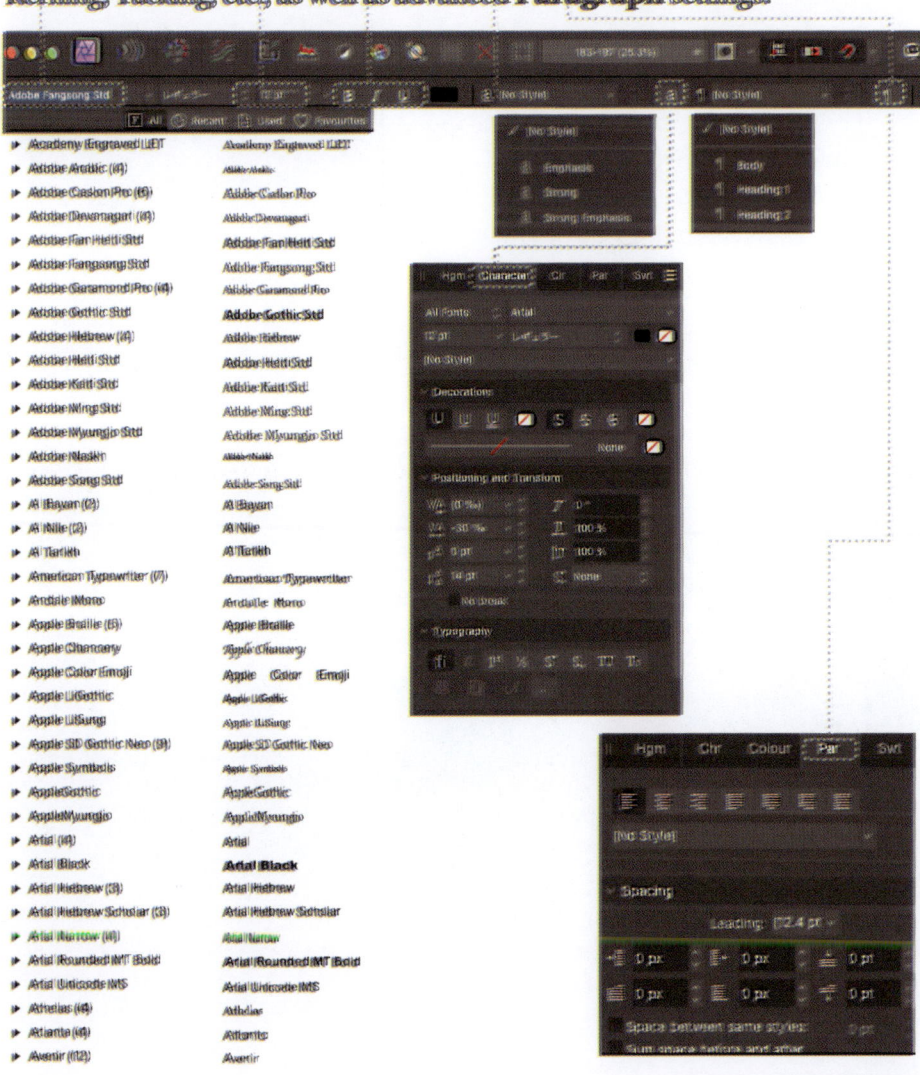

## 9_2: Using the Artistic Text Tool to input text

Check that the Text Tool is on **Artistic Text Tool**, select **Arial** for your font, select **48 pt** for character size, and **B** for bold, Then click on any position. Then type in **Affinity Photo**. It's easy, isn't it?

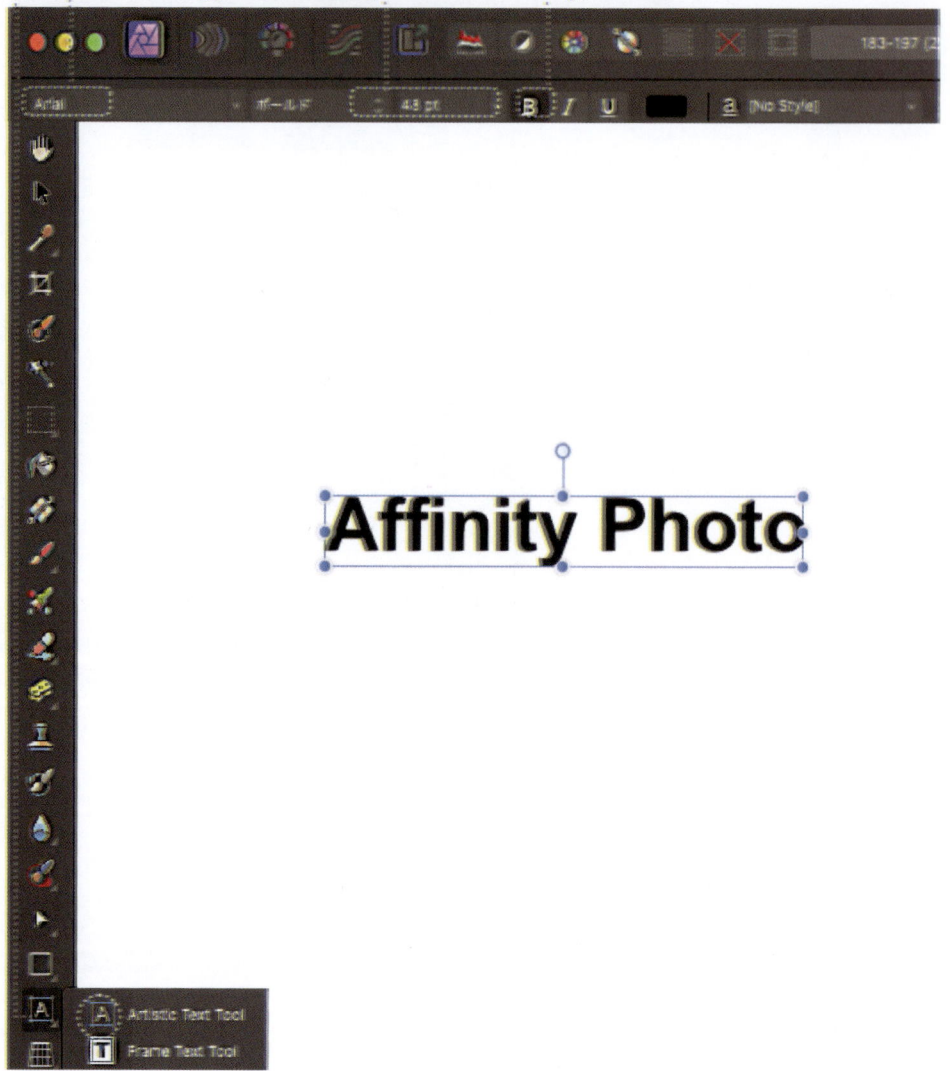

Chapter 9: Using the Text Tool

## 9_3: Use the Frame Text Tool to input the main text

Next, switch the Text Tool to **Frame Text Tool.** Click on the Tool Panel >Text Tool Flyout button, and select **Frame Text Tool.** Choose **Arial** for your font, and set the font size to 12 pt. Drag from left to right on the screen. You should now be ready to input text.

Next, type any long string of text. Pull up on **the bottom anchor points** to widen the margins. After inputting the text, **drag the anchor point on the right** to the left to shrink left-right. The text should wrap automatically in accordance with the frame size. Use the Frame Text Tool to draw boxes easily.

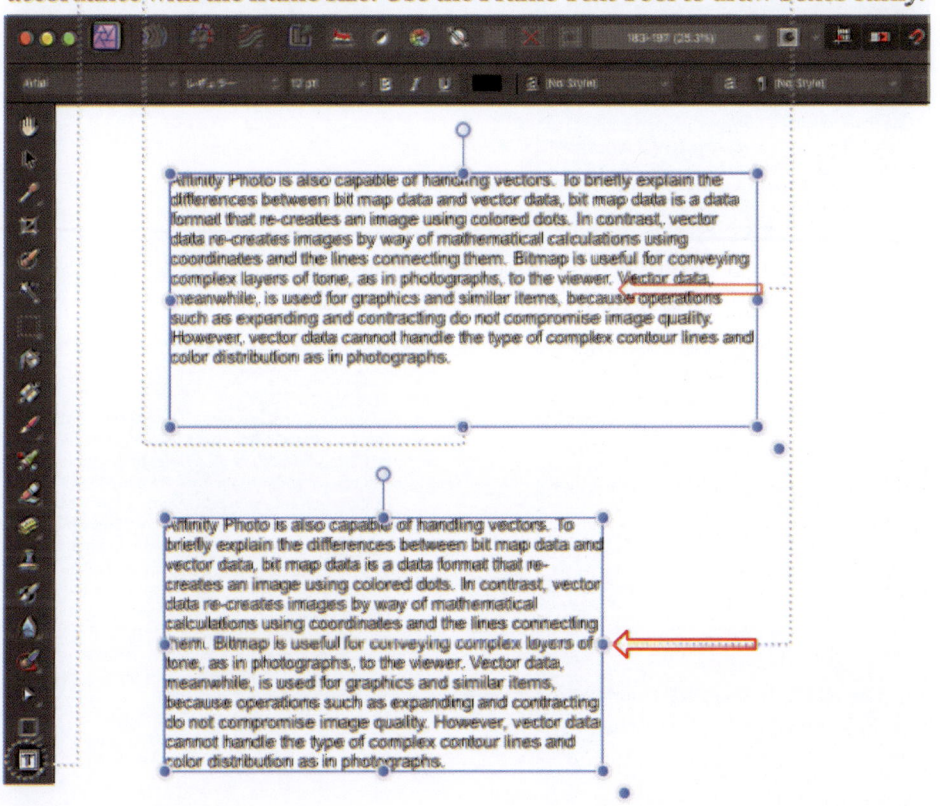

Chapter 9: Using the Text Tool

## 9_4: Beautiful framing: the Tracking feature

Once you are finished framing, let's try changing the characters. Drag the entire text you have input and select. Have you selected the blue fill? The Leading Override on the previous page makes the characters too close together, which can render them difficult to read. Let's spread the characters out somewhat, to **14 pt**. The characters still don't look right, do they? Let's use the Tracking function to fix the problem.

Click on Studio>**Character** to bring up Advanced Settings Panel options such as Tracking and Kerning. Once you have selected the characters you have typed in, set **Tracking** on the Advanced Settings panel to **-30%**. The characteristics should now be lined up in appropriate distance to each other as in the sample at the bottom.

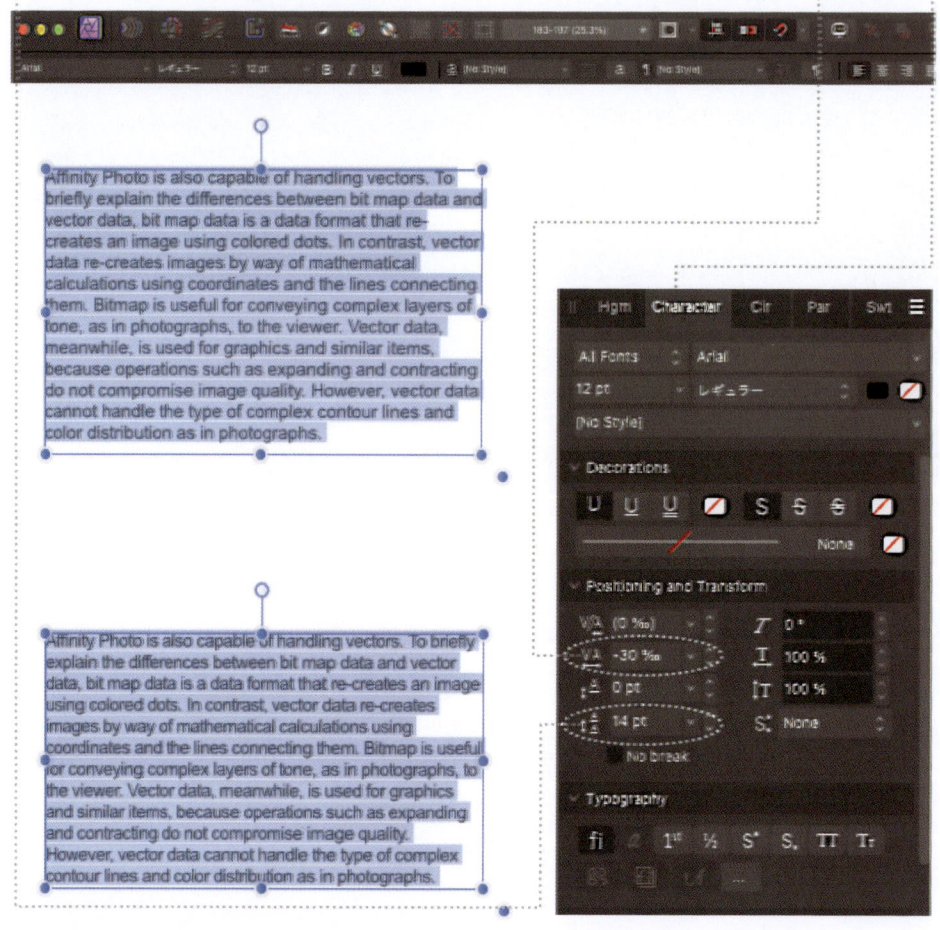

The font may appear slightly different because the sample utilizes built-in fonts for Macintosh (same as below).

Chapter 9: Using the Text Tool

## 9_5: Leading Override between lines

Space between lines is important to Framing, that is striking a balance between visuals and how easy or difficult the text is to read. In sample (A), the font is set to **12pt**, while Leading Override is set to **10 pt**. The text is difficult to read, and it doesn't look good either!

A

(B) shows font size set to **12 pt** and **Leading Override to 14 pt**. With these settings, the text is easy to read, and each line is more distinct.

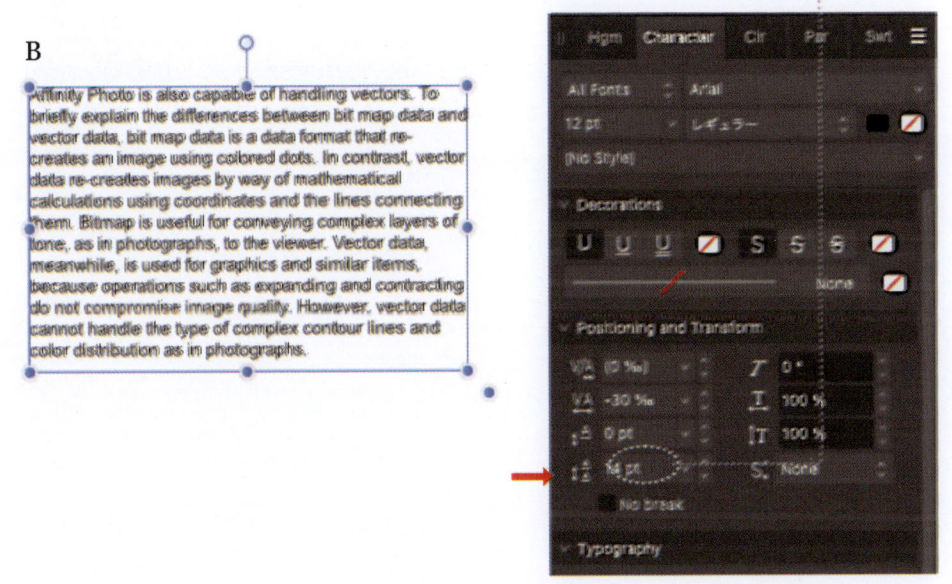

B

Chapter 9: Using the Text Tool

(C) is set to Leading Override 24 pt. The text looks way too long! It's important for the individual to find the optimal space between lines.

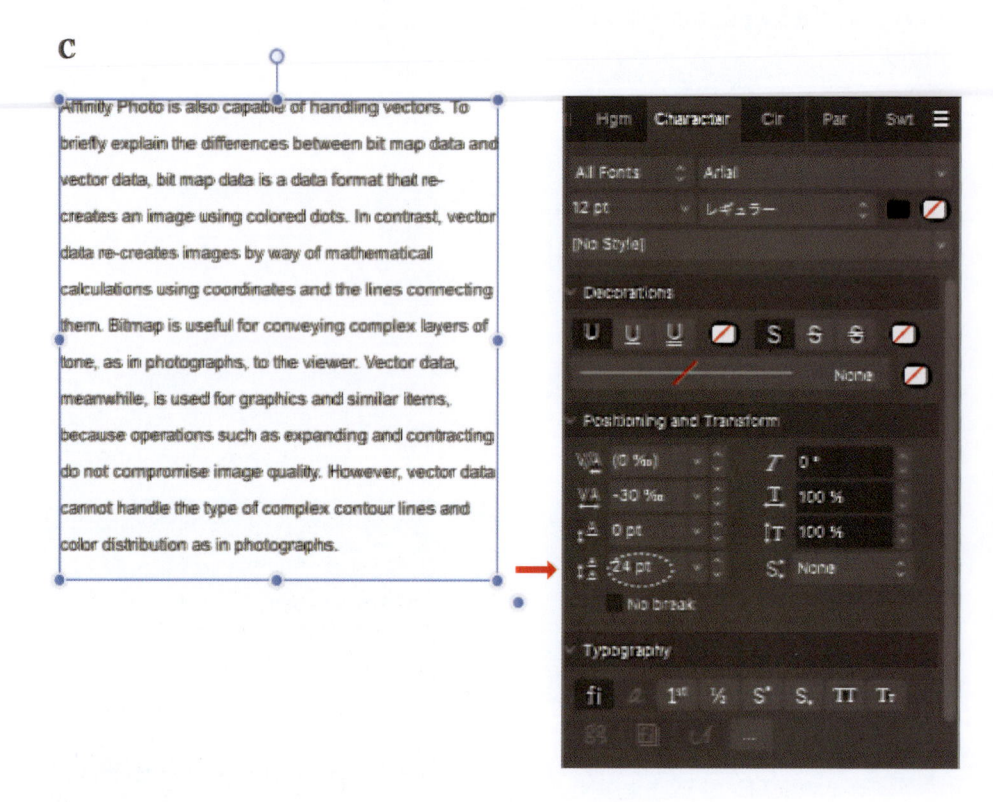

C

## 9_6: Vertical Scale/Horizontal Scale

We have now covered space between characters and between lines. Next, we need to adjust one more thing: the vertical-horizontal ratio of each character. Let's try the Vertical Scale, **adjusting it to 70%**. Each line is emphasized without compromising the look of the font.

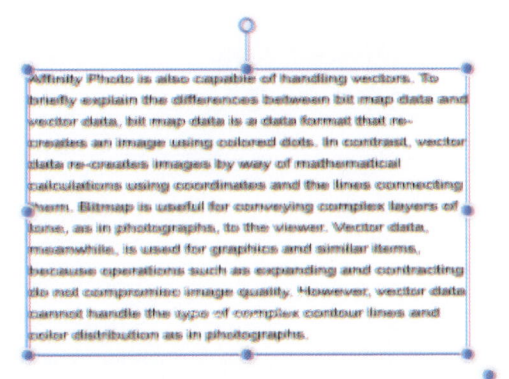

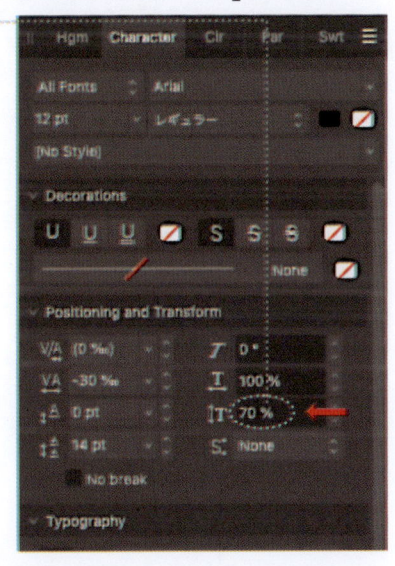

Now let's do the opposite: shrink the right-left and try the Horizontal Scale to expand the top and bottom margins. Adjust the size to 12 pt and **75%**. But this doesn't look good, so let's change the setting some more. Change the font as follows to arrive at your own best framing.

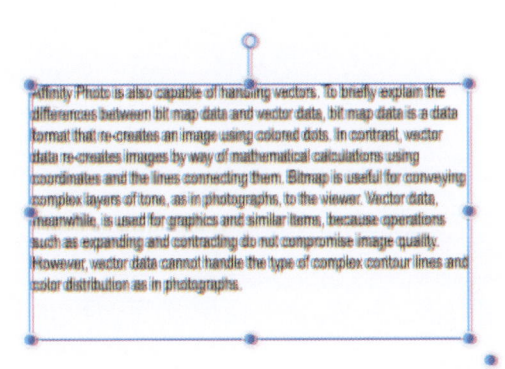

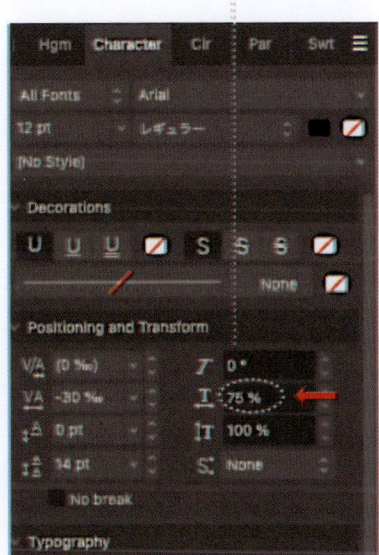

Chapter 9: Using the Text Tool

This concludes our section on Framing. Additional methods include activating all characters with the Move Tool. Display Studio>**Paragraph**, click on **Justified Left**, and frame (find the appropriate number of characters for your frame).

Affinity Photo is also capable of handling vectors. To briefly explain the differences between bit map data and vector data, bit map data is a data format that re-creates an image using colored dots. In contrast, vector data re-creates images by way of mathematical calculations using coordinates and the lines connecting them. Bitmap is useful for conveying complex layers of tone, as in photographs, to the viewer. Vector data, meanwhile, is used for graphics and similar items, because operations such as expanding and contracting do not compromise image quality. However, vector data cannot handle the type of complex contour lines and color distribution as in photographs.

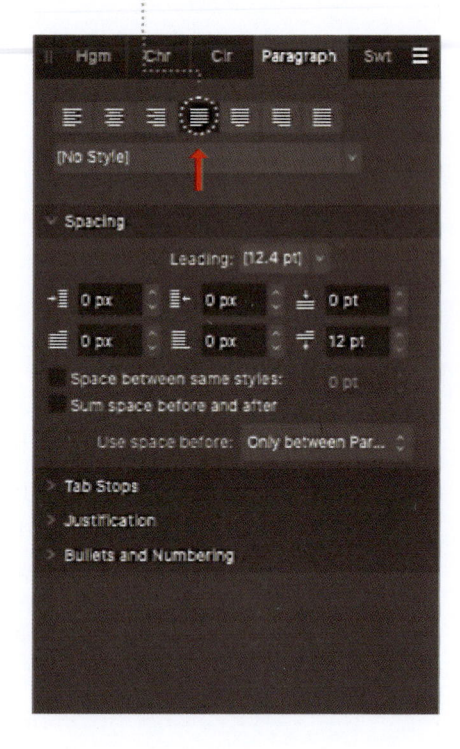

## 9_7: Change the color of the text

Select the entire text and drag, and change the text color to **red**.

Drag the part of the text that you want to change,

and color it **green**.

## 9_8: Text kerning and outlining

Let's now try the kerning and outlining. Switch to the **Artistic Text Tool**, select select the **Arial** font, size **72 pt**, and Fill with black. Then type in Affinity_Photo.

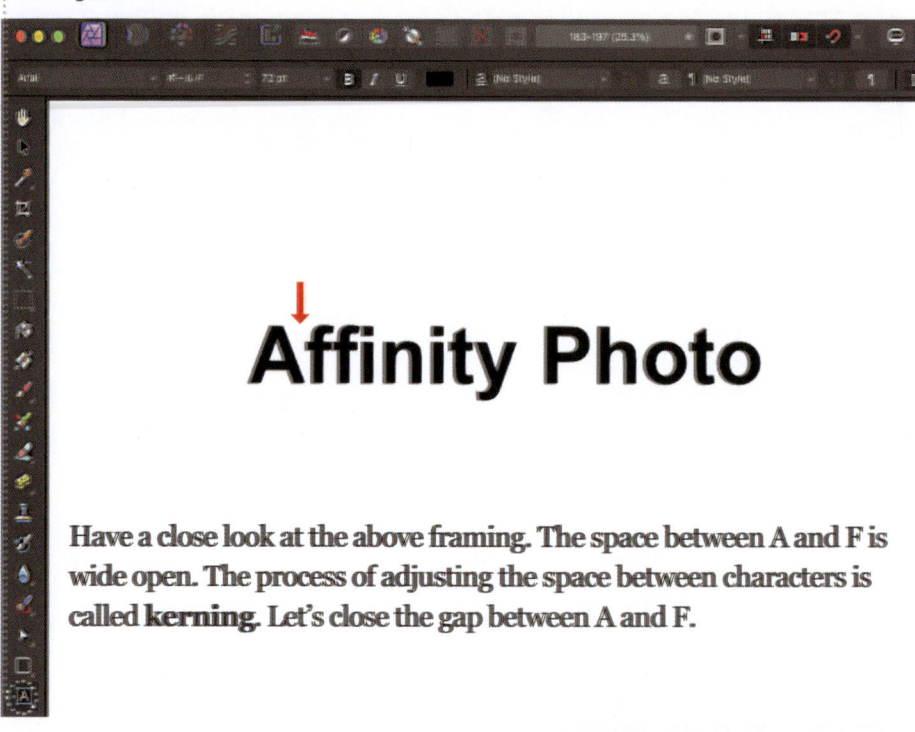

Have a close look at the above framing. The space between A and F is wide open. The process of adjusting the space between characters is called **kerning**. Let's close the gap between A and F.

Use the mouse to click on the area **between A and F** to insert a vertical line. Next, adjust Studio>Character>**Kerning** to **-30%**.

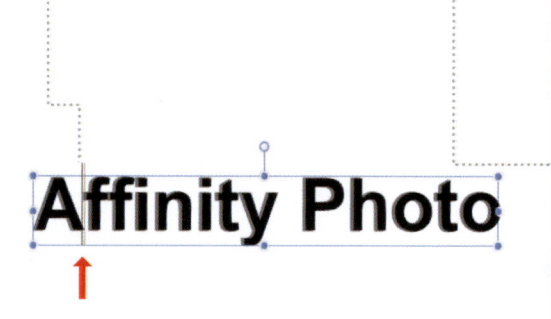

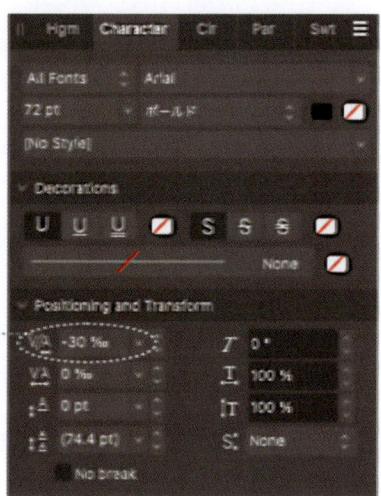

Chapter 9: Using the Text Tool

# Affinity Photo

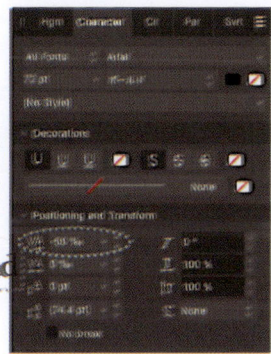

The space **between P and H** is open as well. Close it up by clicking on the area between P and with your mouse. Next, click on Studio>Character>**Kerning** and adjust to **-50%**.

# Affinity Photo

Well, how does it look? The space between each of the characters should now be visually even.

### 9_10:Outlining the text

The characters of your text should now be nicely spaced. Next, let's outline the text. Data on your PC is re-created as font. Here, **outlining** does not refer to internal font data; instead it means switching to figures drawn with lines; i.e. vector data. Shapes can be altered as desired.

Click on the Menu Bar **Layer** to create an Outline, and select **Convert to Curves**.
This completes the action.
Does it look like nothing has happened?
Let's check on it.

# Affinity Photo

253

## Chapter 9: Using the Text Tool

The characters on the previous page have been outlined and Grouped at the same time, which is the reason they do not look any different from each other. The text is Ungrouped in order to check it. Click on the Menu Bar>Arrange>**Ungroup,**

and then click on Studio>**Layer** Tab. Click on the text to make sure the layers are in place. Now the characters are black with black background.

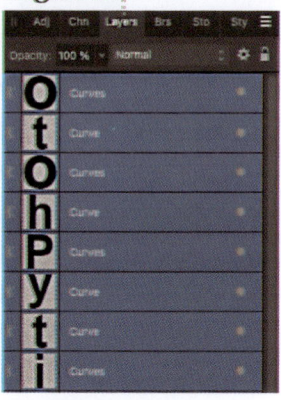

Click on Studio >Colour. **The top layer circle** is black. Activate this part and **click on the small colorless mark**. The characters should now be colorless. The text has now been successfully outlined.

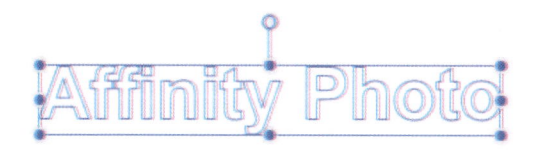

254

Chapter 9: Using the Text Tool

Next, let's outline the characters with black. Click on the line settings and choose **Black.** The figure should appear as follows:

Let's try out some more design features. Activate Affinity_Photo "**A**" with the Move Tool and color it **red**, and color the "**P**" **blue**.

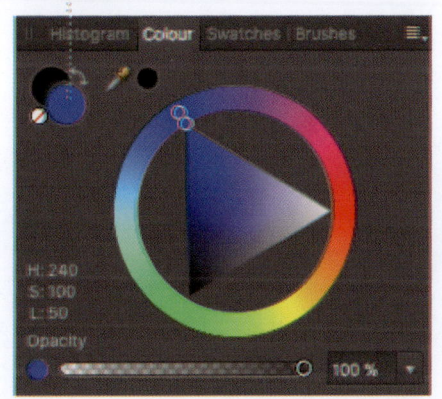

Chapter 9: Using the Text Tool

Now restore the text to a simple black line. Then enlarge A using the Move Tool.

Next, switch to the **Node Tool**, and add **Node Points** to either side of the A. Then click on the Convert>**Smooth** button. **Drag these Node Points right and left.**

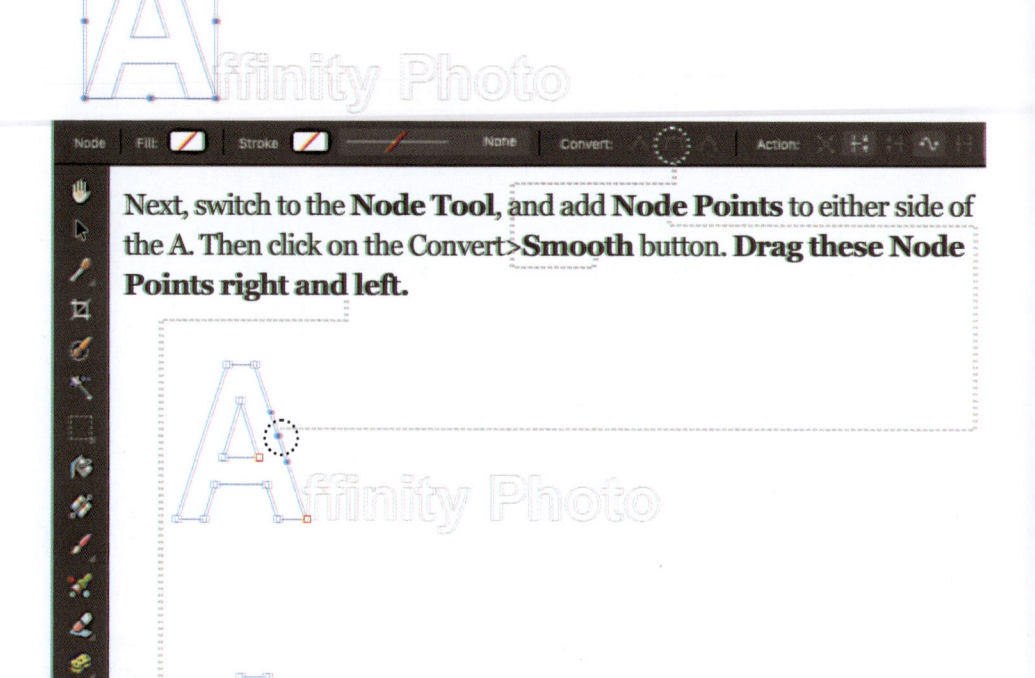

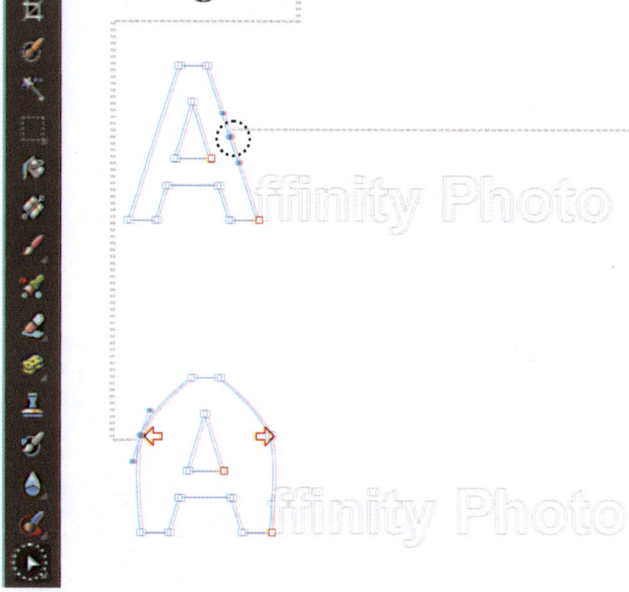

Then paint the now-fat "**A**" **red**.
Outlining the characters allows the user to create designs as desired.

256

# Chapter 10: Effects

Chapter 10: Effects

## 10_1: Understanding filters and how to use them

Affinity Photo is equipped with numerous different types of filters. Live filters are used to keep your original work as it is. Let's have a look at the Filters feature specifically. The materials we need are the greenback leaf and flower photo that we worked on in Chapter 5. If you have a photo that you like in your album, go ahead and use that.

If you don't have a photo to practice on, this author recommends that you download your choice of images from Creative Commons:
Visit the following URL:http://creativecommons.org
You will need two photos. Launch the Internet browser and type in the above URL.

Photo of a leaf:
http://goo.gl/lcaqjD

Photo of a flower:
http://goo.gl/LE1Bcd

Once you have your photos, drag on the first photo (leaf) file and drag directly to the Affinity_Photo icon.

Note: The above address utilizes Google_url_shortener. If the link is broken, search for http://creativecommons.org on the Web.

Chapter 10: Effects

Have you been able to position the leaf photo? To select a filter, click on the Menu Bar>Filters to display the menus. You should see a number of them. The first step is to see what we have to choose from. Let's start with Blur.

**Gaussian Blur**

Click on the Menu Bar> Filters>Blur>**Gaussian Blur**. The bigger the radius, the more prominent the Blur.

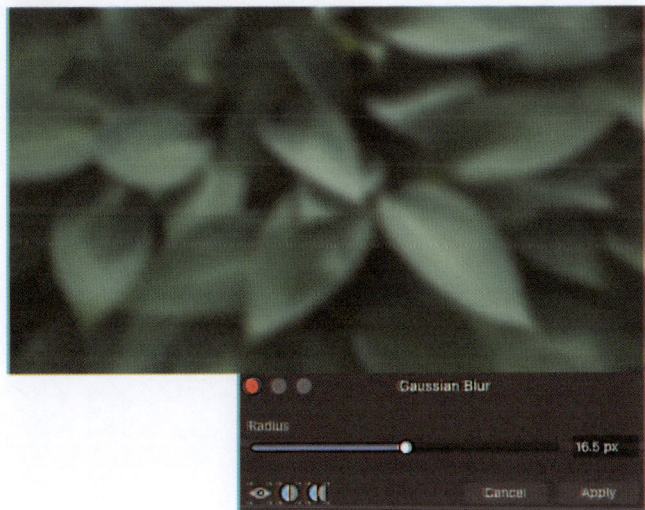

Gaussian Blur
Radius: 14.5px

259

## Using the (Distort)>Ripple filter

Click on the **Menu Bar>Filters>Distort>Ripple** to display the dialog box.

Distort>Ripple
Intensity:123

## Detect Edges

Click on the **Menu Bar>Filters>Detect>Detect Edges**. You can also select Detect Horizontal Edges or Detect Vertical Edges

Detect>**Detect Edges**

Chapter 10: Effects

## Creating a Distort filter with an equation

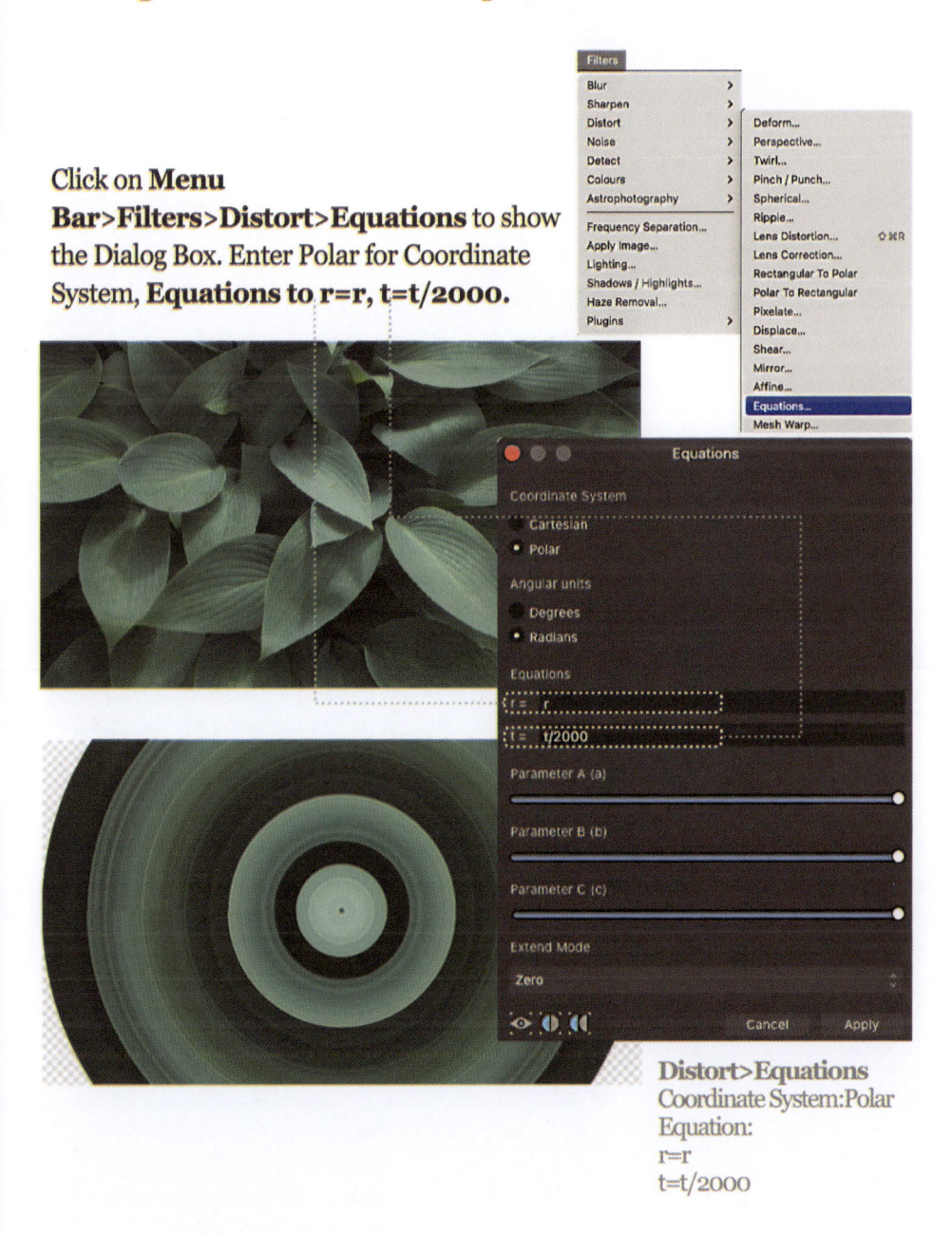

Click on **Menu Bar>Filters>Distort>Equations** to show the Dialog Box. Enter Polar for Coordinate System, **Equations to r=r, t=t/2000.**

**Distort>Equations**
Coordinate System: Polar
Equation:
r=r
t=t/2000

## Chapter 10: Effects

## Use the Colour Filter to switch to Web Safe Colors.

Click on the **Menu Bar>Filters>Colours>Web Safe Dither** to optimize colours for the Web (Dithering).

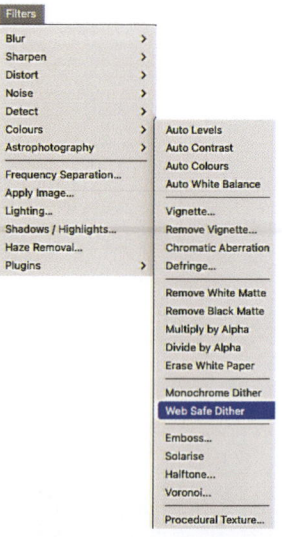

## Use the lighting effects

Affinity Photo has filters designed to simulate different lighting effects such as spotlight, lighting up an area around a certain object, directional lighting, etc. Click on the Menu Bar> Filters>**Lighting** to display the Settings Panel.

**Lighting**
Light:1
Type:Spot

**Spot**:Casts a beam of light focusing on a specific subject of interest, like a flashlight
**Point**:Casts omnidirectional light, like a light bulb.
**Directional**:Casts light directionally, e.g. from the sun.

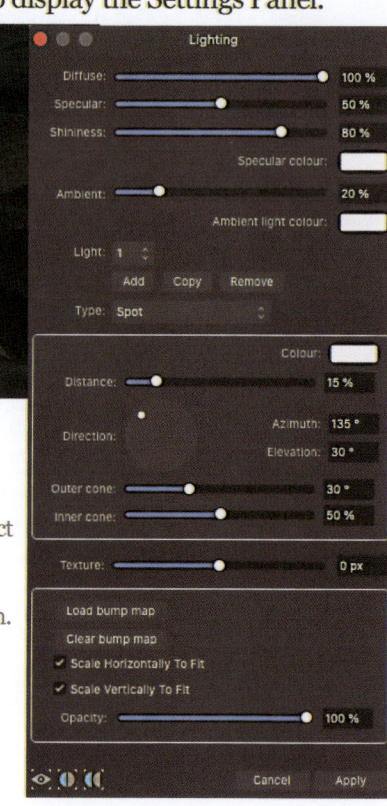

Chapter 10: Effects

## Blending multiple images

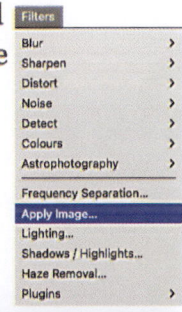

Affinity Photo has a Blending feature where formulas are used to operate Color Channels. Let's give these a try. First, the base image is the photo of the leaf, which we have worked with through the present time. First we restore it to its original form and activate it. Click on Menu Bar >Filters>**Apply Image** to display the Settings Panel. Click on the **Load Source From File** button, and select the Flower photo that we prepared earlier.

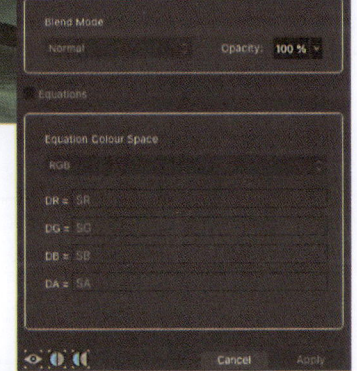

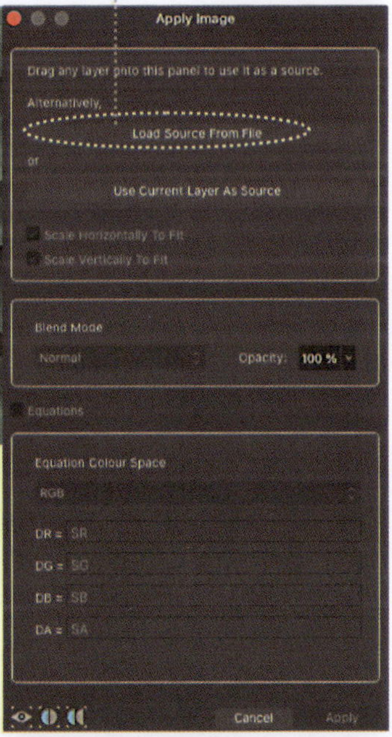

The screen should be the Flower photo. Use this as the Source photo. This image is automatically scaled down to the size of the **leaf** photo. The top and bottom margins of the **flower** photo have been reduced to achieve this. We'll fix this later. Simply leave it as it is for now.

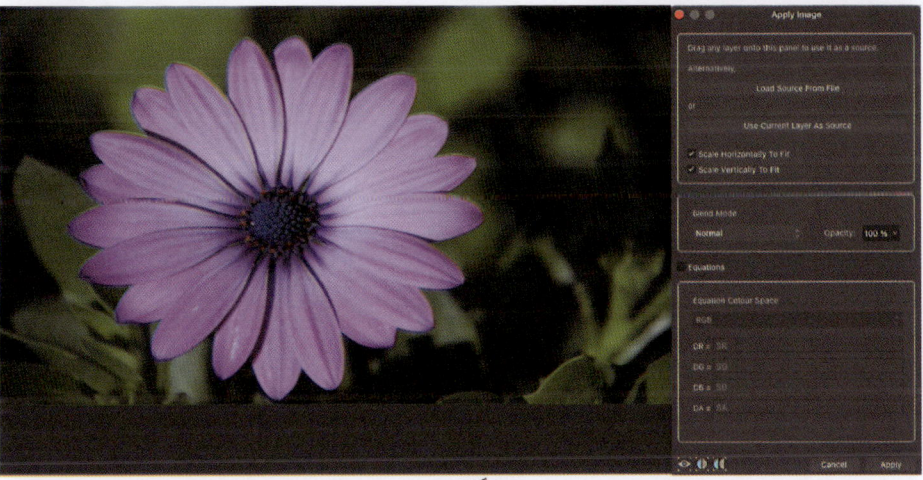

263

Chapter 10: Effects

Adjust **Opacity** to 63% to blend colors. Next, set the Blend Mode to **Linear Light**. The two images should now be blended.

Next, let's try using color channels with equations. For **Equation Colour Space**, enter RGB, **DR=SR+SG, DG=SG, DB=SB, DA=SA**. We have been working with DR or the Red Channel value to change the flower petals red. Refer to the later Chapters for details on Color Channels.

Blend Mode :Linear Light
Opacity:63%
Equation Colour Space:RGB
DR=SR+SG
DG=SG
DB=SB
DA=SA

Chapter 10: Effects

### 10_2: Creating an effect for an object

Let's now see how Affinity_Photo's effect features work. Effects are used not only to enhance shapes but also photographs. If you have a good photo to practice on, use that. If not, you can use the photo of the flower from the previous page. Drag the photo to the Affinity Photo icon, open it, and crop around the flower petals in a rectangular shape using the Cut Tool. Save the photo as a JPEG file and use it to practice effects.

Now go ahead and launch the JPEG file. Adjust the settings on the document with Command/Control+N. Adjust size to A4, horizontal direction, Select **Rounded Rectangle Tool** on the **Tool Panel**, **Fill to Blue, Stroke to None**. Hold down the shift key to draw a rounded rectangle. Then line it up with the photo next to it to make it the same size. Hold down the Shift key and click on both objects to activate them.

# Chapter 10: Effects

## Gaussian Blur: Add blur effect

Let's now move on to the Gaussian blur. Click on the Studio>Layar>**Layar Effects** to display the Effects tab menu. Click on the **Gaussian Blur** flyout button at the top. Adjust Radius to **20 px** and turn the feature On using the checkbox. Notice the blur?

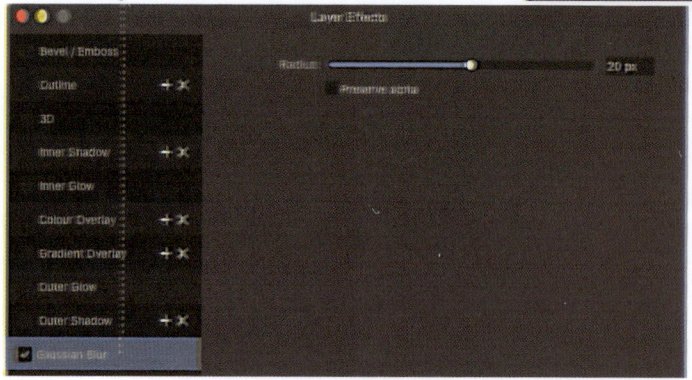

**Radius**: Adjust pixels using the Blur slider.

Chapter 10: Effects

## Outer Shadow: Add a shadow outside the object

Make sure you are on Gaussian Blur, activate the object, click on the Gaussian Blur Flyout button, and close the Gaussian blur settings screen. At the same time, turn **Gaussian Blur off using the check box**. Next, click on the **Outer Shadow** Button below and switch to On. The Effects Settings screen appears.

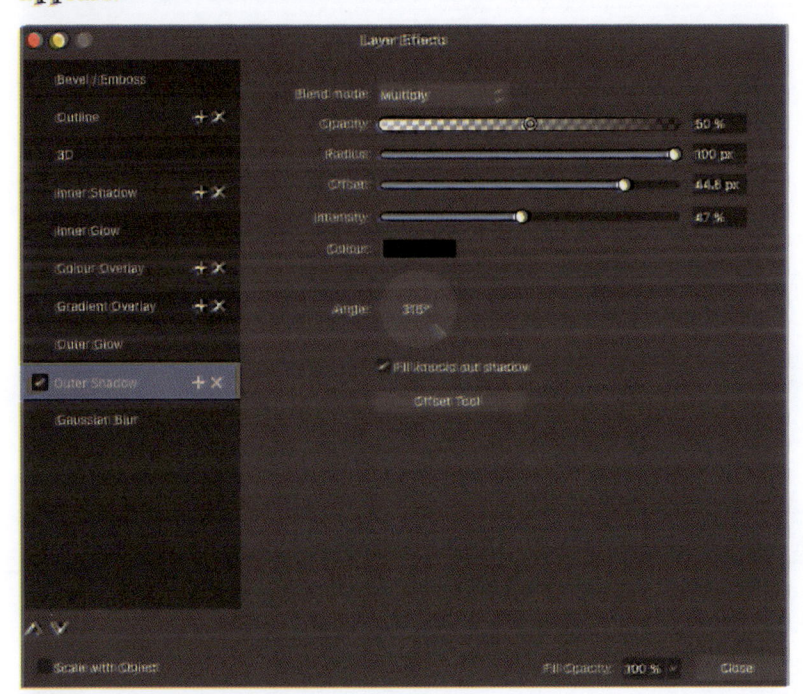

**Blend mode**: Select blend
**Opacity**: Adjust base color opacity (%)
**Radius**: Adjust blur
Offset: Adjust shadow length with pixels
**Intensity:** Adjust intensity(%)
**Color**: Select colour
**Angle**: Adjust angle

Chapter 10: Effects

## Inner Shadow: Add shadow effect to the inside

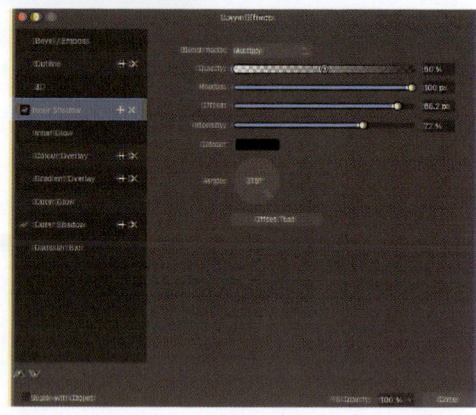

**Blend mode:** Select blend
**Opacity**: Adjust base color opacity (%)
**Radius**: Adjust blur
**Offset**: Adjust shadow length using pixels
**Intensity**: Adjust intensity (%)
**Color:** Select color
**Angle**: Adjust angle

## Outer Glow: Add glow effect to the outside

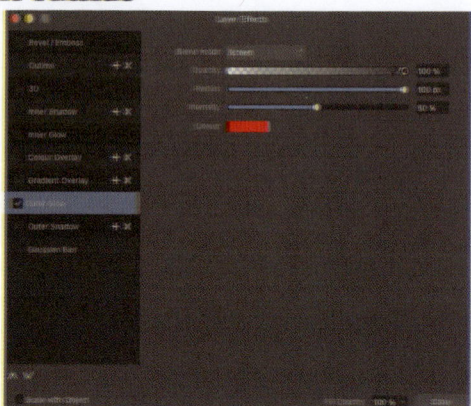

**Blend mode:** Select blend
**Opacity**: Adjust base color opacity (%)
**Radius**: Adjust blur
**Intensity**: Adjust intensity %
Colour: Select colour

Chapter 10: Effects

## Inner Glow: Add glow effect to the inside

**Blend mode:** Select blend
**Opacity:** Set base color opacity (%)
**Radius:** Adjust blur
**Intensity:** Set %
**Color:** Select color
**Centre/Edge:** Set glow effect from center/from edges

## Outline: Visual effect is added to outline

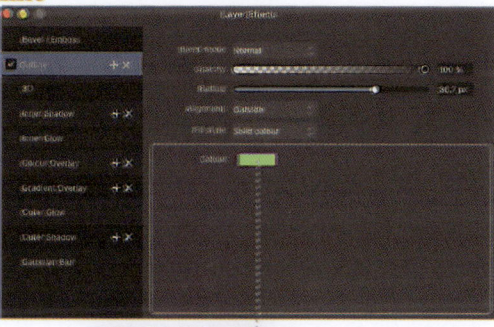

**Blend mode:** Select blend
**Opacity:** Adjust base color opacity (10%)
**Radius:** Adjust blur
**Alignment:** Outside/Center/Inside
**Fill style:** Solid color/Contour/Gradient
**Color:** Select color

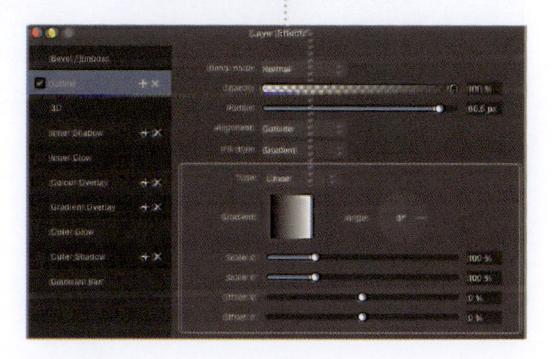

269

# Chapter 10: Effects

## 3D Effect: Add a 3D effect

**Radius**: Adjust blur
**Depth**: Adjust depth (%) (remove blur link with blur feature)
**Soften**: Adjust softness level with px
**Opacity**: Determine base color opacity (%)
**Profile**: Click to set advanced effects/Invert
**Diffuse**: Adjust level of light diffusion
**Specular**: Adjust level of reflected light
**Shininess**: Adjust brightness
**Ambient:** Adjust ambient lighting
**Light source:** Adjust number of light sources
**Direction**: Adjust angle

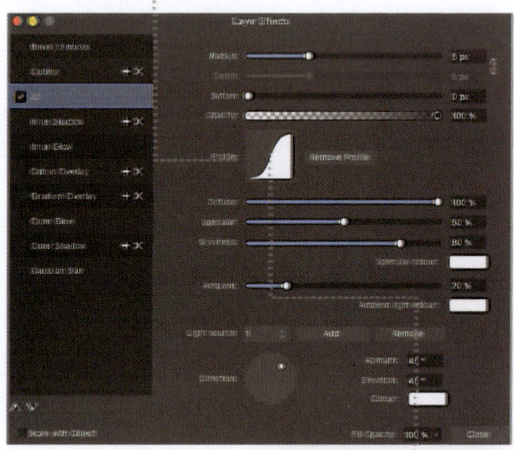

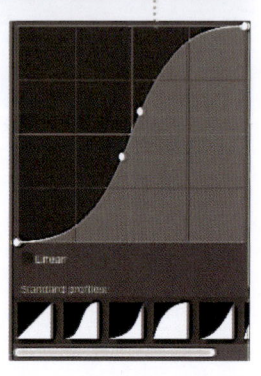

## Bevel/Emboss: Add bevel/emboss effect

**Type**: Select Inner/Outer/Emboss/Pillow effect
**Radius**: Adjust blur
**Depth**: Adjust depth (px) (remove blur link with blur feature)
**Soften**: Adjust softness with px
**Profile**: Click to set advanced effects/Invert
**Direction**: Adjust angle
**Highlight**: Adjust highlight colors
Shadow: Adjust shaded area colors

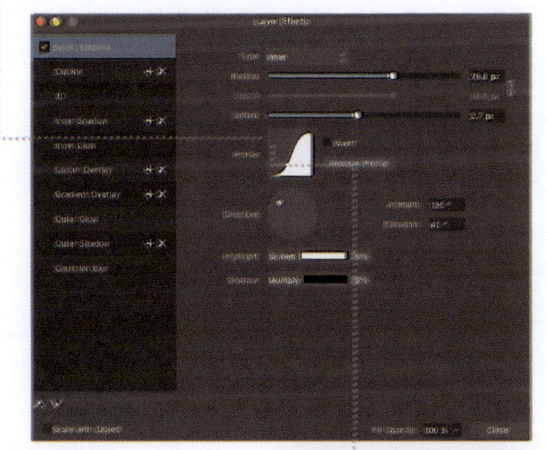

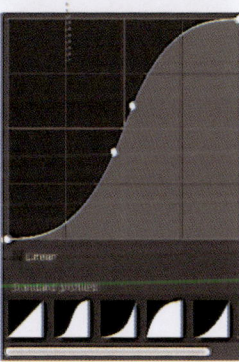

## Chapter 10: Effects

## Colour Overlay: Add an in-layer topcoat effect

**Blend mode:** Select blend
**Opacity:**
Determine base color opacity (%)
**Color:** Choose color

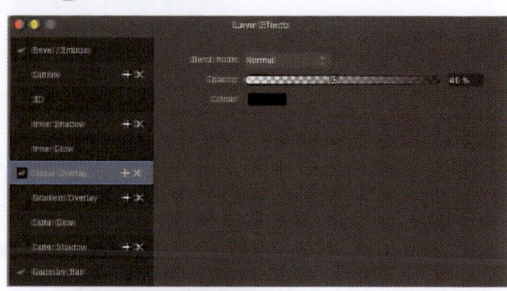

## Gradient Overlay: Add an in-layer topcoat effect

**Blend mode:** Select blend
**Opacity:** Determine base color opacity with (%)
**Type:** Linear/Elliptical/Radial/Conical/Gradient: Advanced gradation settings
**Scale X:**
Adjust lateral direction scale (%)
**Scale Y:**
Adjust vertical direction scale (%)
**Offset X:** Adjust horizontal direction offset (%)
**Offset Y:** Adjust vertical direction offset (%)
**Angle:** Adjust angle

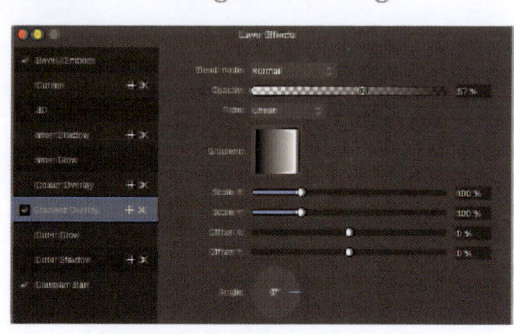

# Chapter 11: The three primary colors/color adjustment

## 11_1: The three primary colors

Affinity_Photo has many powerful features including processing pixel-based images. One of these is color adjustment. To master this feature, it's useful to have knowledge of the three primary colors. Do you remember them?
The three primary colors are Red, Green, and Blue. Mixing these colors gives rise to all colors, and also lightens them due to the energy of light. Mixing the three colors together produces white, a process known as additive color mixing. Palette mixing includes the three colors of yellow, magenta, and cyan. Mix all three to get black. This process is called subtractive color mixing,

PC screens display color by the above additive color mixing process, or RGB model. To adjust color with Affinity_Photo, keep in mind the concept of additive color mixing. The figure on the right shows the familiar three primary colors.

To control color adjustment of images, as we learn in the next chapter, we need to have a consistent grasp on the colors next to Red (R), Green (G), and Blue (B). To help with this, the author has created the circle below, in the order of R(Red), M(Magenta), B(Blue), C(Cyan), G(Green), and Y(Yellow).

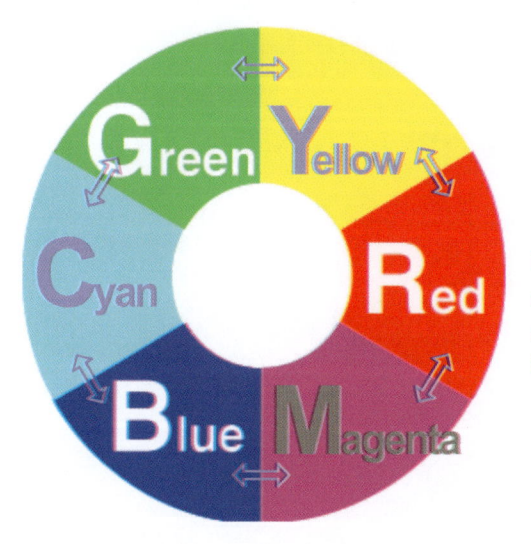

Memorize this order (reverse also acceptable). This is also convenient when we learn to use the slider in the next chapter.

Chapter 11: The three primary colors/color adjustment

## 11_2: Color adjustment

We now have a look at the specifics of color adjustment. The author recommends downloading a sample photo from Creative Commons:
http://creativecommons.org
**http://goo.gl/3591PH**
Launch your Internet browser and enter the URL noted above.
Note: Once you have a photo, drag the file directly to the Affinity_Photo icon.

© liz west

To adjust the color, double click on Photo Persona > Studio > Layers > **Adjustment** to display the menu.

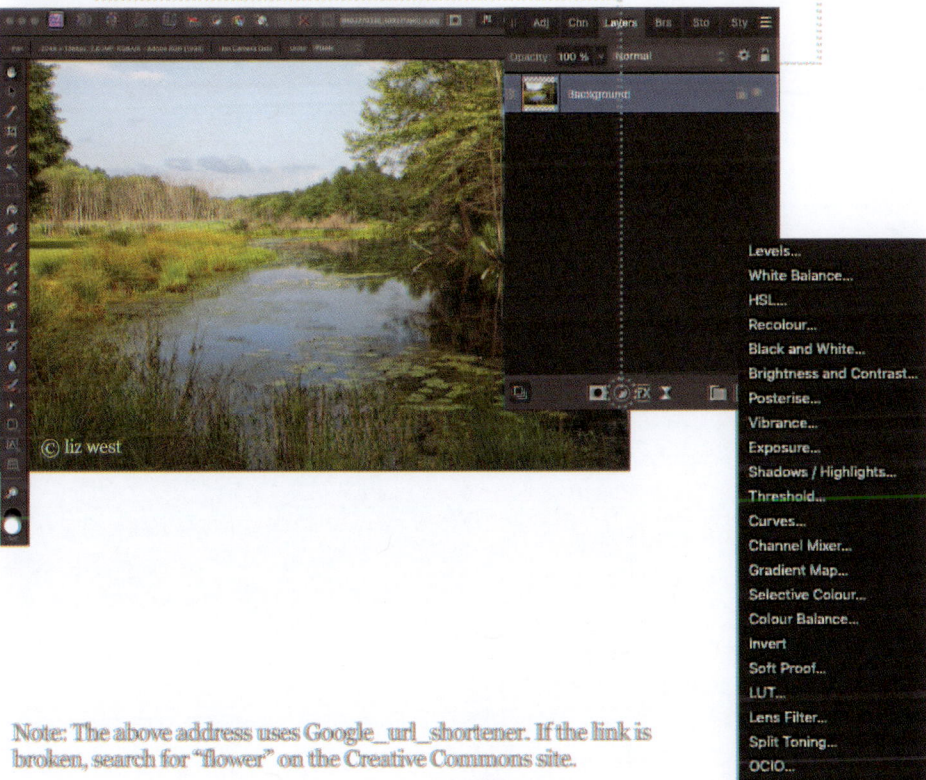

© liz west

Levels...
White Balance...
HSL...
Recolour...
Black and White...
Brightness and Contrast...
Posterise...
Vibrance...
Exposure...
Shadows / Highlights...
Threshold...
Curves...
Channel Mixer...
Gradient Map...
Selective Colour...
Colour Balance...
Invert
Soft Proof...
LUT...
Lens Filter...
Split Toning...
OCIO...
Normals...

Note: The above address uses Google_url_shortener. If the link is broken, search for "flower" on the Creative Commons site.

275

## Adjust Color Levels

Decide on the Black Level, White Level and Gamma to adjust the tone and balance.

**Black Level**: Drag the slider to the right to emphasize the shadow.

**White Level**: Drag the slider to the left to emphasize highlights.

**Gamma**: Drag the slider left and right to redistribute Black and White Levels.

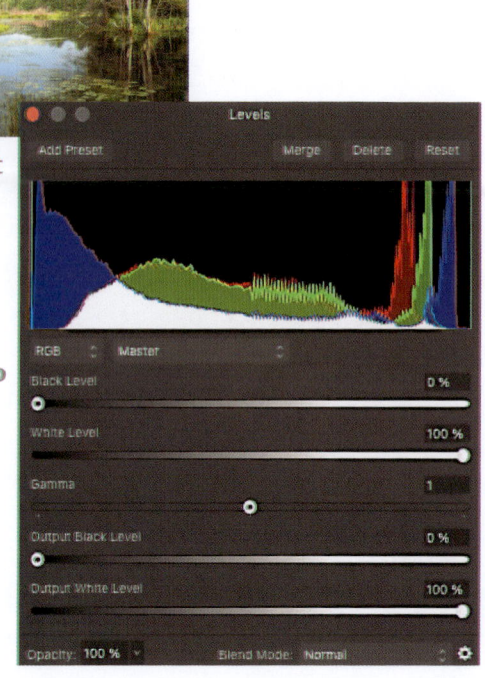

## Adjust White Balance

Use the White Balance to remove unwanted color, increase warmth of the color in the photo, or to add a cooler tone.

**White Balance**—The White Balance controls the warmth/coolness of the photo. **Drag the slider to the left to add a blue tone**. Drag to the right to add a yellow tone.

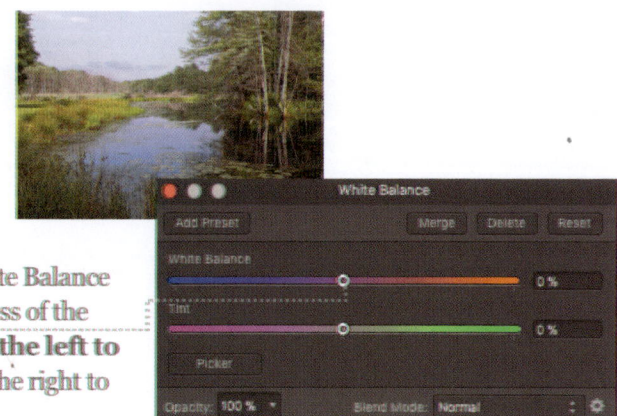

**Tint**—Add magenta or green to the photo.
**Picker**—Click on the near-white part of the photo to sample it. This automatically adjusts the White Balance. Then pick a part of the photo, drag, and sample the average of the colors inside the rectangle.

## HSL adjustment

Adjustments are made to the colors in the photo by changing the HSL (Hue, Saturation, and Luminosity). **HSV** refers to **hue saturation value**.

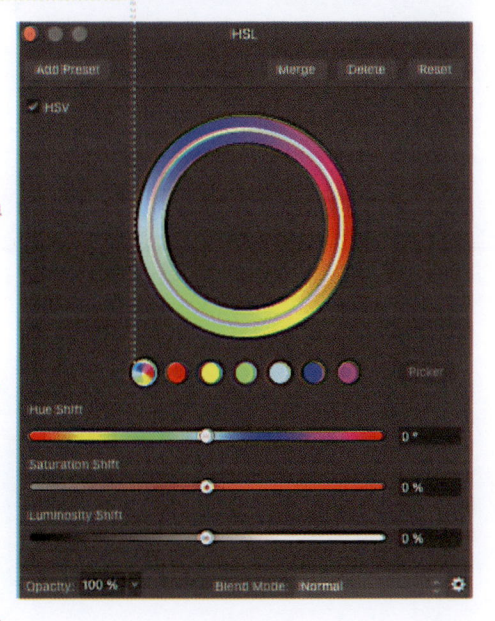

**Master:** Change all colors at once. Click on the different colors to change them.

**HSV:** Insert a check mark to switch from the HSL model to the HSV model. The Saturation Shift and Luminosity Shift features work differently.

**Hue Shift:** Change the hue of the photo. Drag on the slider to change the hue. Slide slightly to the left on the top left sample. Then slide to the right on the sample in the center of the photo.

**Saturation Shift:** Control the color saturation of the photo. Slide to the left to reduce saturation, and to the right to increase it. In the sample on the top right, the slider is all the way to the left.

**Luminosity Shift:** Control the Luminosity of the photo. Slide to the left to darken, and to the right to brighten.

Chapter 11: The three primary colors/color adjustment

## Recolor Adjustment

Recolor adjusting is used to create a monotone with using the full spectrum of color, i.e. monochromatic color photos.

**Hue**—Choose the monochrome color slider. Shift the color in accordance with the spectrum.
**Saturation**—Control the level of color saturation. Move the slider to the left to the left to lower saturation, and to the right to increase it.

**To create a sepia photo**, adjust the **Hue** slide to orange. Move the **Saturation** slider to the left of the center.

## Adjusting Black & White

Black & White tones are added by monochrome conversion as the user adjusts each color.

The sliders control the level of brightness of each color. For example, shifting the red slider to the left darkens the original red. Shifting to the right brightens the color.
**Picker**—This feature detects the predominant color of the spot you clicked. Drag the color to the left to lighten or darken.

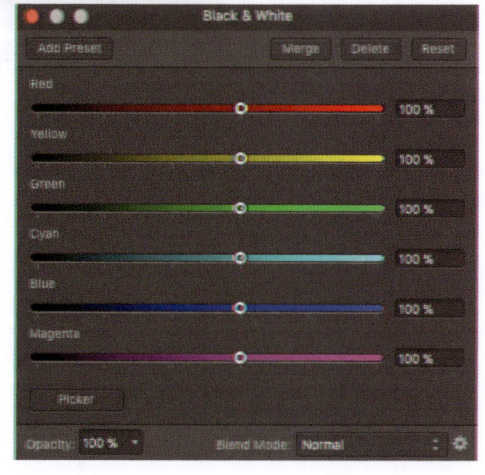

## Brightness/Contrast Adjustment

Brightness and contrast are adjusted to emphasize or de-emphasize shadow and highlights in the photo.

**Brightness**—Slide to the left to darken and to the right to lighten.

**Contrast**—Slide to the left for less contrast and to the right for more contrast.

**Linear**—Unless you insert a check mark, the system reverts to the original level of brightness. With the check, changes are made in relation to Absolute Value.

## Posterise

Use the Posterize feature to change photos to look like illustrations.

**Posterise Levels**—Slide to the left for a rougher look, i.e. the Posterise effect.

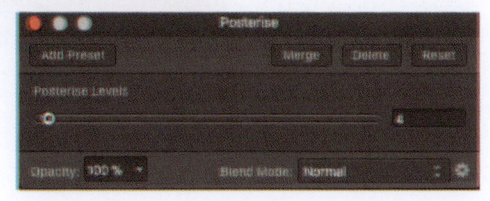

Chapter 11: The three primary colors/color adjustment

## Adjusting Vibrance

Vibrance adjusts the pale color saturation of the photo, helping to maintain natural tone.

**Vibrance**—Move the slider to the left for less saturation, and to the right for more saturation.

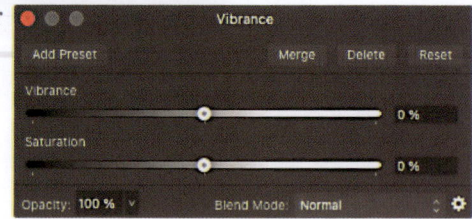

## Exposure Adjustment

Exposure Adjustment corrects for overexposure and underexposure.

**Exposure**—Move the slider to the left to darken (correct overexposure). Move the slider to the right to brighten (correct underexposure).

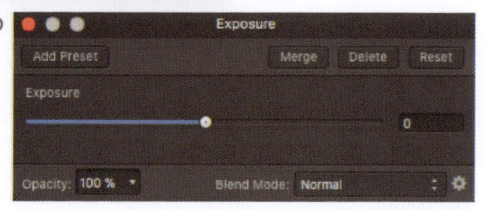

## Adjust Shadows/Highlights

Separately adjust shadow and highlights for impact on these areas rather than the photo as a whole.

**Shadows**—Slide to the left to darken the shadow areas, and to the right to brighten.

**Highlights**—Slide to the left to darken the highlighted areas, and to the left to brighten.

## Threshold Adjustment

Adjust the Threshold to render a multi-colored photo into a duotone (black-and-white) shot. Switch all pixels brighter than the indicated value to white, and all pixels darker than the indicated value to black.

**Threshold**—Use the slider to control the threshold between black and white. Move the slider to the left to switch more pixels to white, and to the right to switch more pixels to black.

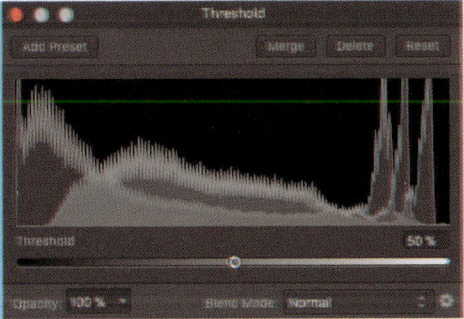

## Adjusting Curves

The process of adjusting the curves is accomplished with the curve controller. The user can intuitively make complex revisions by moving the curve as desired. From the next page onward, check on the specifics of each of the curves as you go along.

©liz west

**Master**: Choose **all RGB channels**, **Red** channel, **Green** channel, **Blue** channel, or **Alpha** channel.

**Make direct changes to curve graph**: Click on the straight line to add a node. Then drag the node to correct image color. Click on the curve to add a node, and click it again to delete it.

**Picker**: Correct color by dragging on the image. The first click adds a node to the curve. Drag on it to change the straight line to a curve (graph).

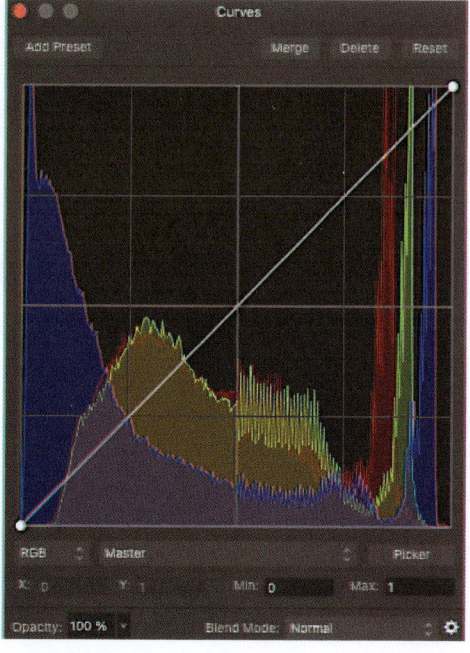

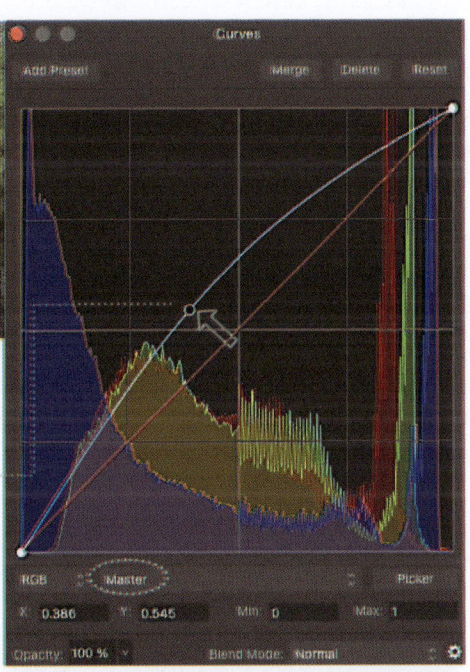

Chapter 11: The three primary colors/color adjustment

**Bell curve :**
Click **Master**, then **Channel**, and drag **the node toward the upper left**. The entire image should be brighter.

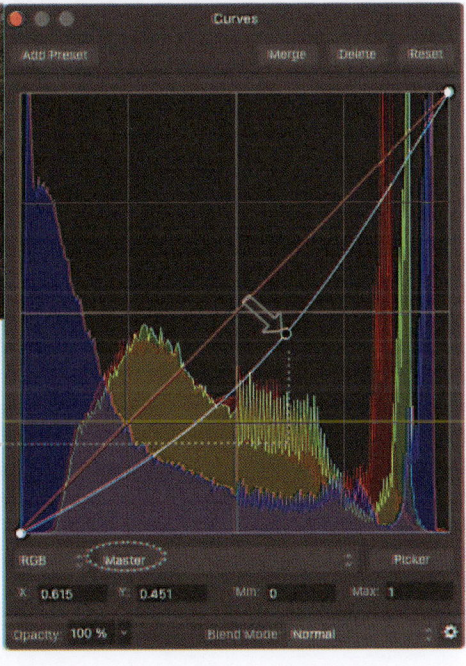

**Valley curve :**
Click **Master**, then **Channel**, and drag the node to **the lower right**. The entire image is darkened.

283

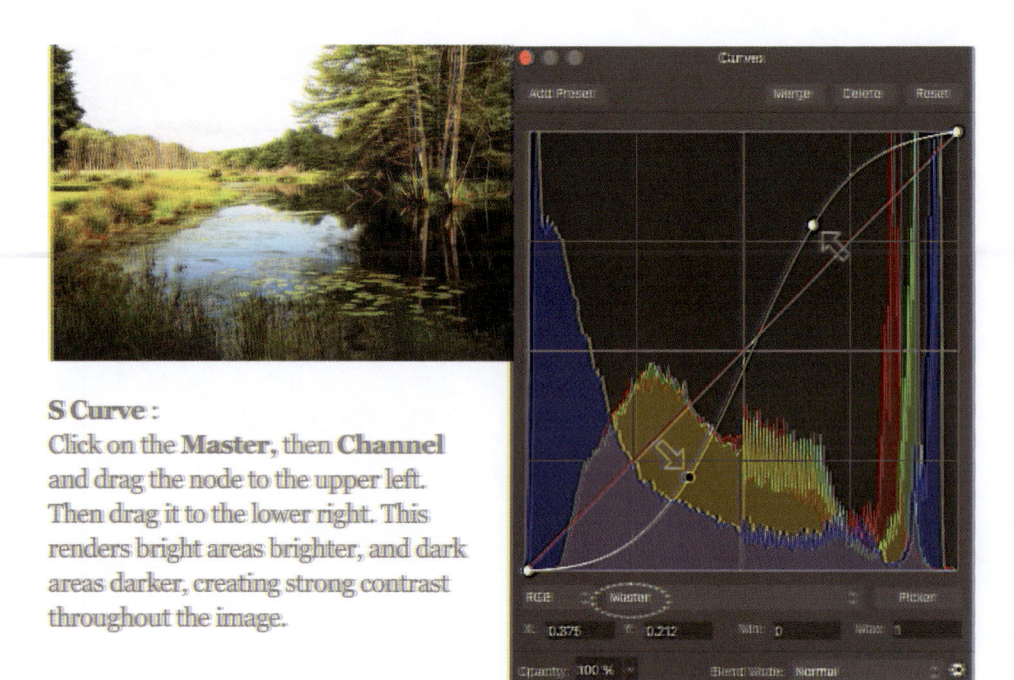

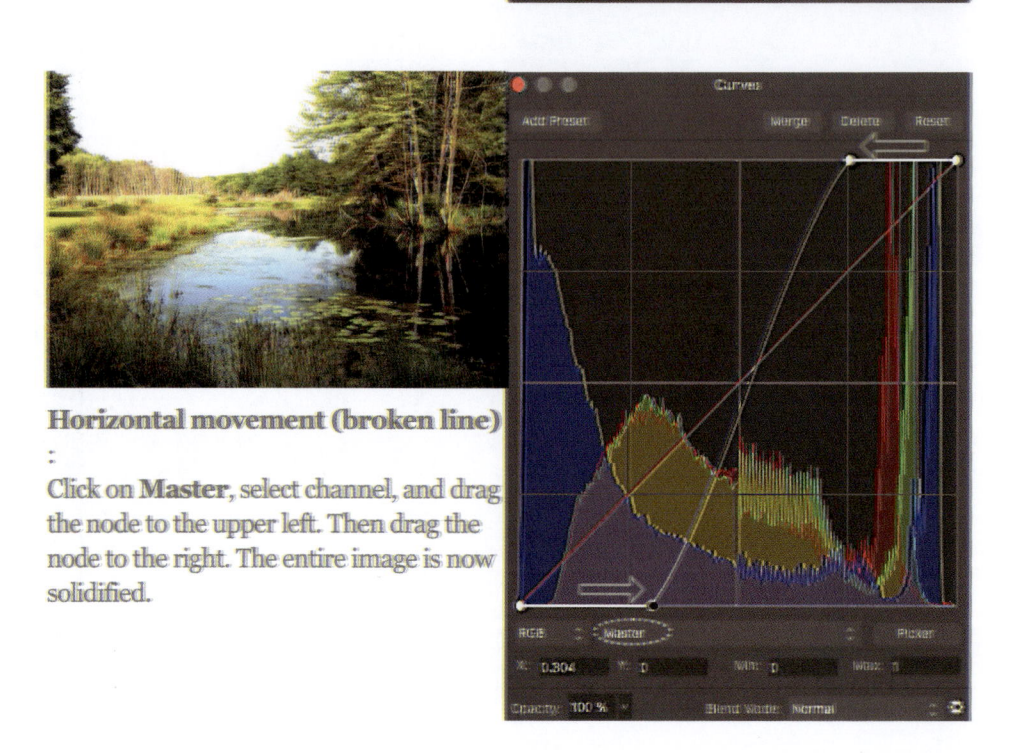

Chapter 11: The three primary colors/color adjustment

**S Curve** :
Click on the **Master**, then **Channel** and drag the node to the upper left. Then drag it to the lower right. This renders bright areas brighter, and dark areas darker, creating strong contrast throughout the image.

**Horizontal movement (broken line)** :
Click on **Master**, select channel, and drag the node to the upper left. Then drag the node to the right. The entire image is now solidified.

284

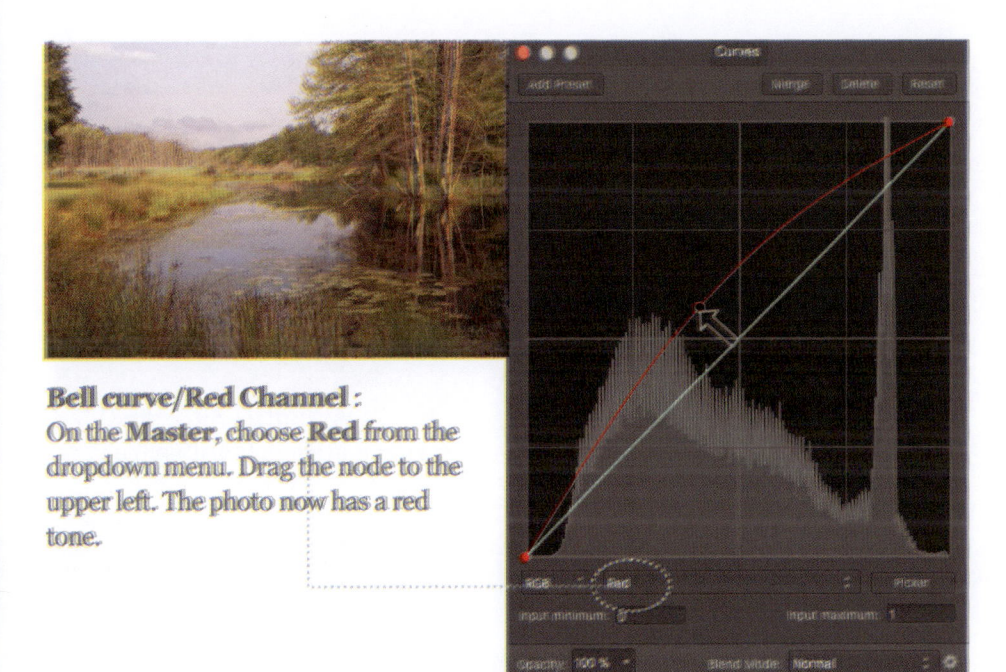

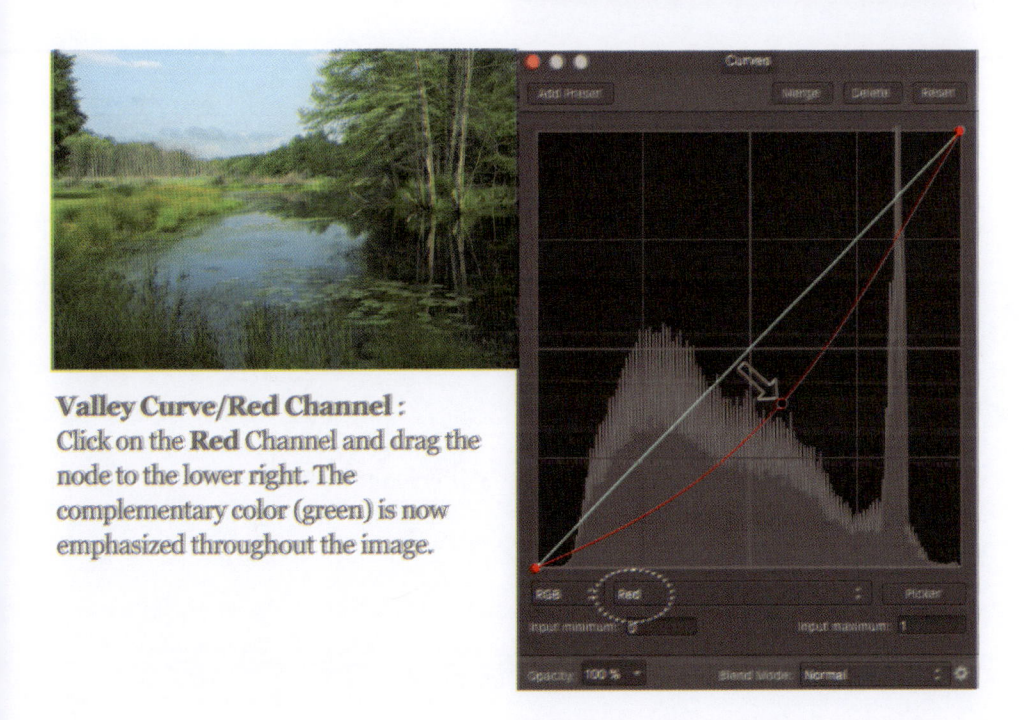

Chapter 11: The three primary colors/color adjustment

**Bell curve/Red Channel** :
On the **Master**, choose **Red** from the dropdown menu. Drag the node to the upper left. The photo now has a red tone.

**Valley Curve/Red Channel** :
Click on the **Red** Channel and drag the node to the lower right. The complementary color (green) is now emphasized throughout the image.

285

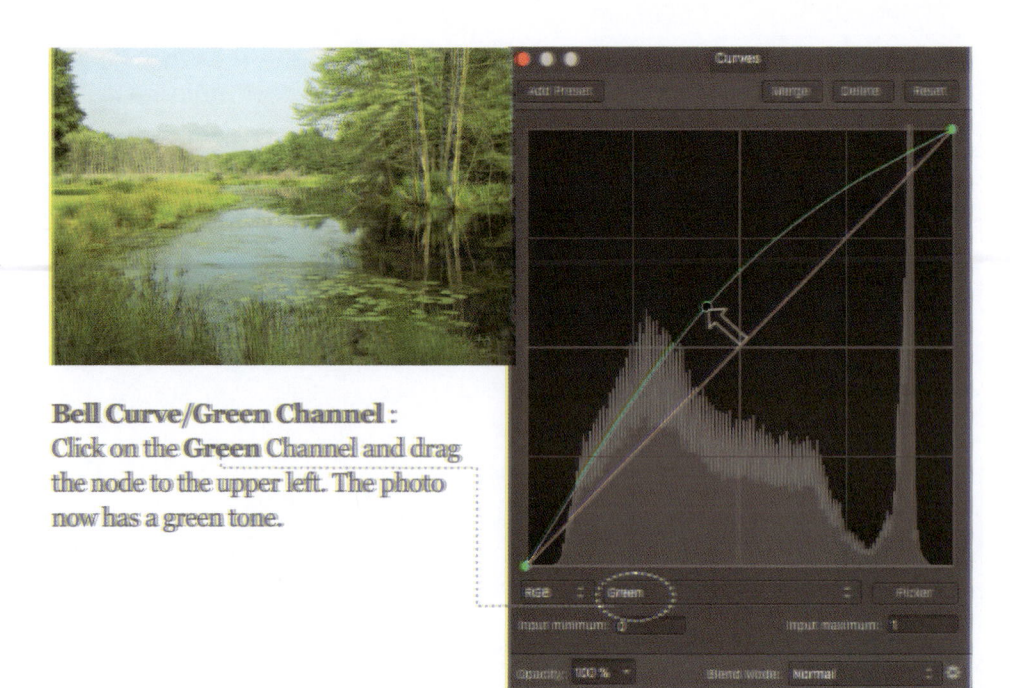

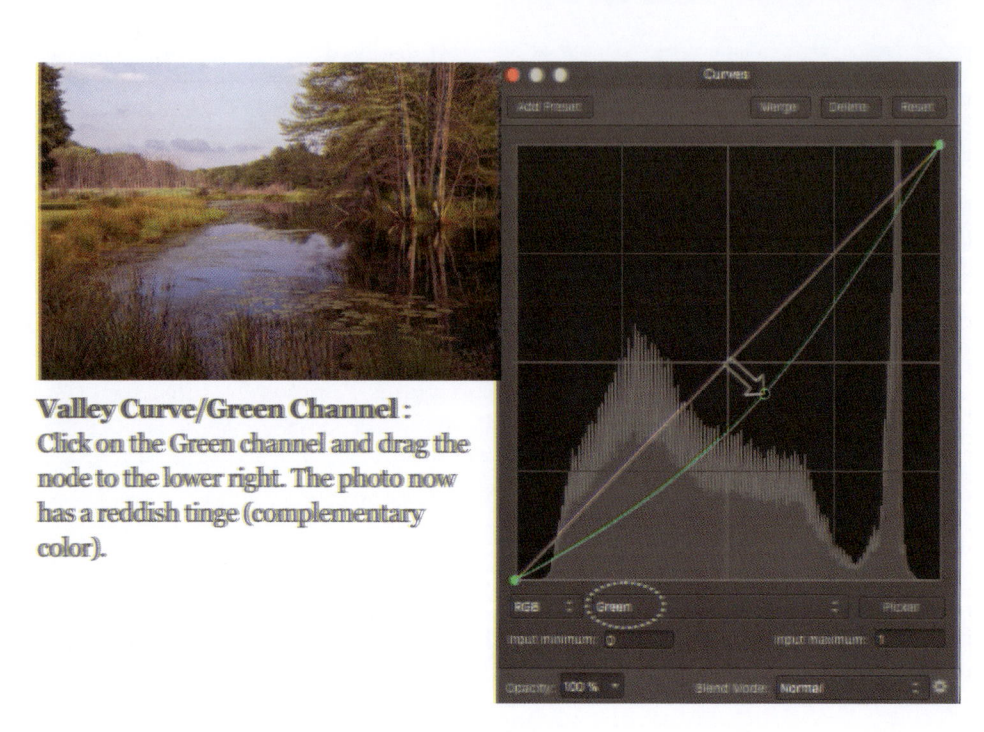

Chapter 11: The three primary colors/color adjustment

**Bell Curve/Green Channel :**
Click on the **Green** Channel and drag the node to the upper left. The photo now has a green tone.

**Valley Curve/Green Channel :**
Click on the Green channel and drag the node to the lower right. The photo now has a reddish tinge (complementary color).

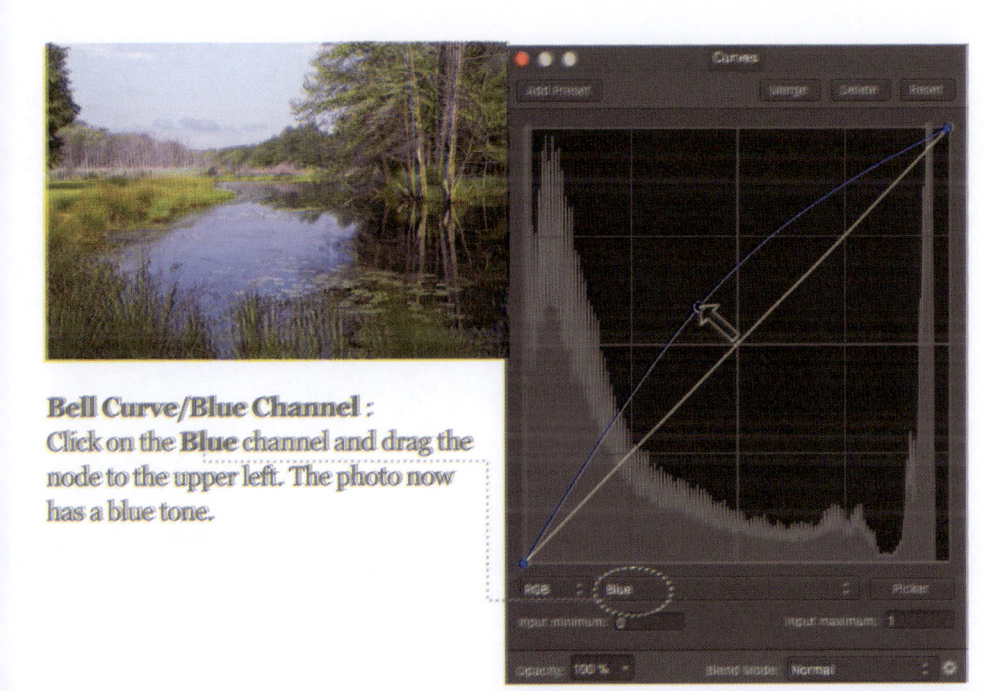

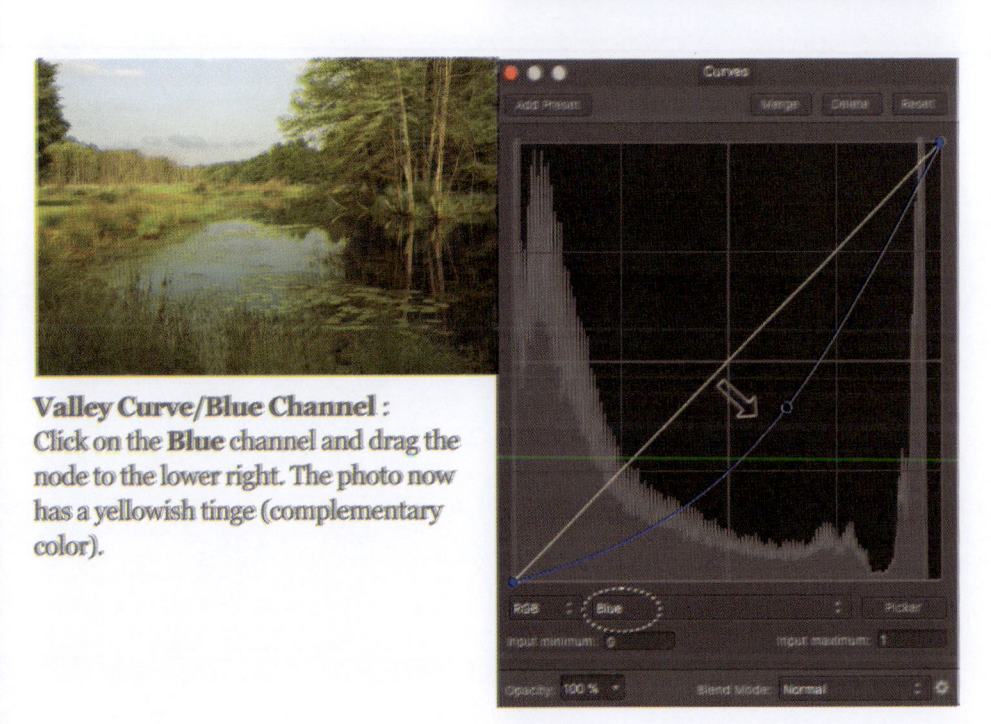

# Chapter 11: The three primary colors/color adjustment

**Bell Curve/Blue Channel :**
Click on the **Blue** channel and drag the node to the upper left. The photo now has a blue tone.

**Valley Curve/Blue Channel :**
Click on the **Blue** channel and drag the node to the lower right. The photo now has a yellowish tinge (complementary color).

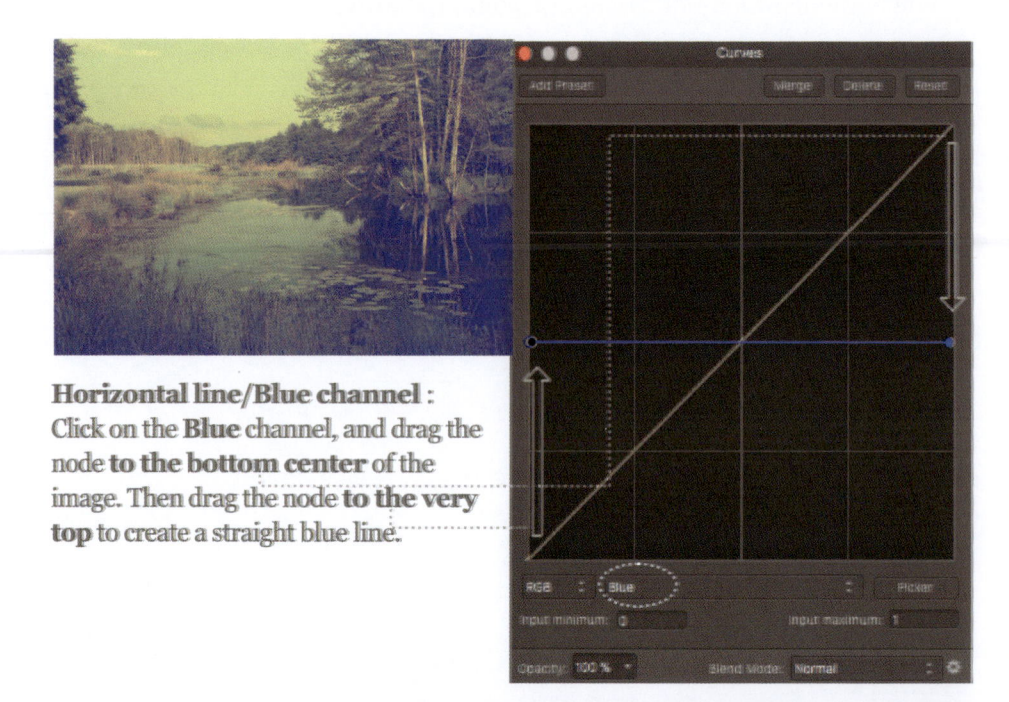

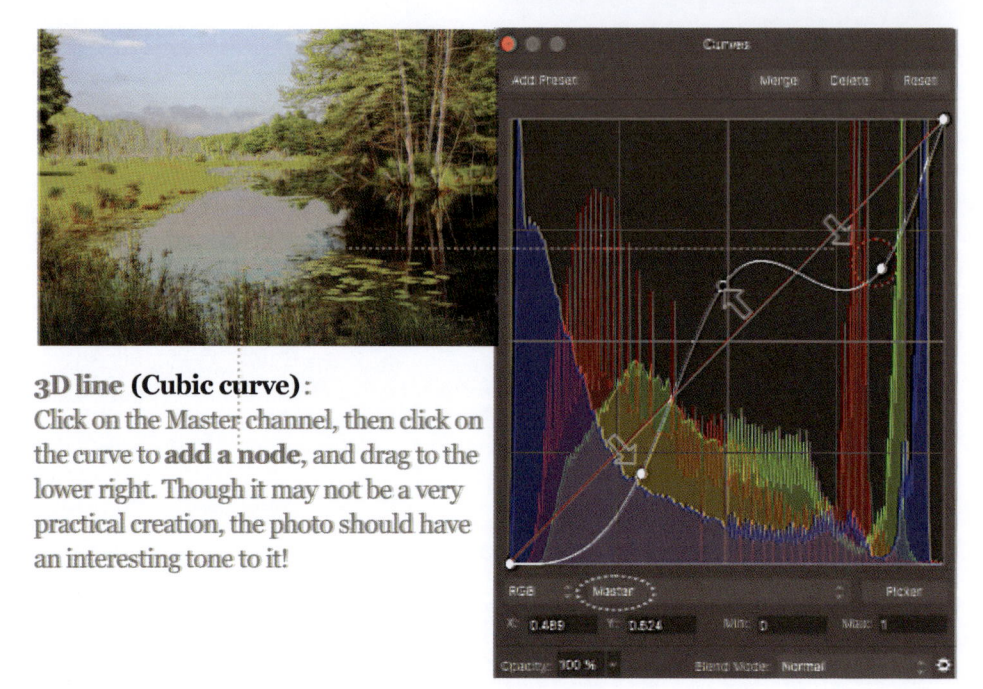

Chapter 11: The three primary colors/color adjustment

**Horizontal line/Blue channel :**
Click on the **Blue** channel, and drag the node **to the bottom center** of the image. Then drag the node **to the very top** to create a straight blue line.

**3D line (Cubic curve) :**
Click on the Master channel, then click on the curve to **add a node**, and drag to the lower right. Though it may not be a very practical creation, the photo should have an interesting tone to it!

## 11_3: The three primary colors (RGB)

The next chapter takes us into an overview of the Channel Mixer. The Channel Mixer is used to make changes to the colors Red, Green, and Blue. To achieve this, it is important to gain an understanding of the RGB color concept. RGB colors are expressed in the RGB 16 chart. The number 0 is the smallest value on the chart (0123456789ABCDEF).
F is the largest value. The six figures are read two at a time. The first two are red, the second two are green, and the last two are blue. For instance, FF0000 is the maximum value for Red, which makes the tone Red. 00FF00 is Green.
Green and Red are stacked on top of each other to create a yellow tone. Try stacking **red FF0000** and **Green 00FF00** (F0000+00FF00=FFFF00). **FFFF00** is yellow. This notation is great!

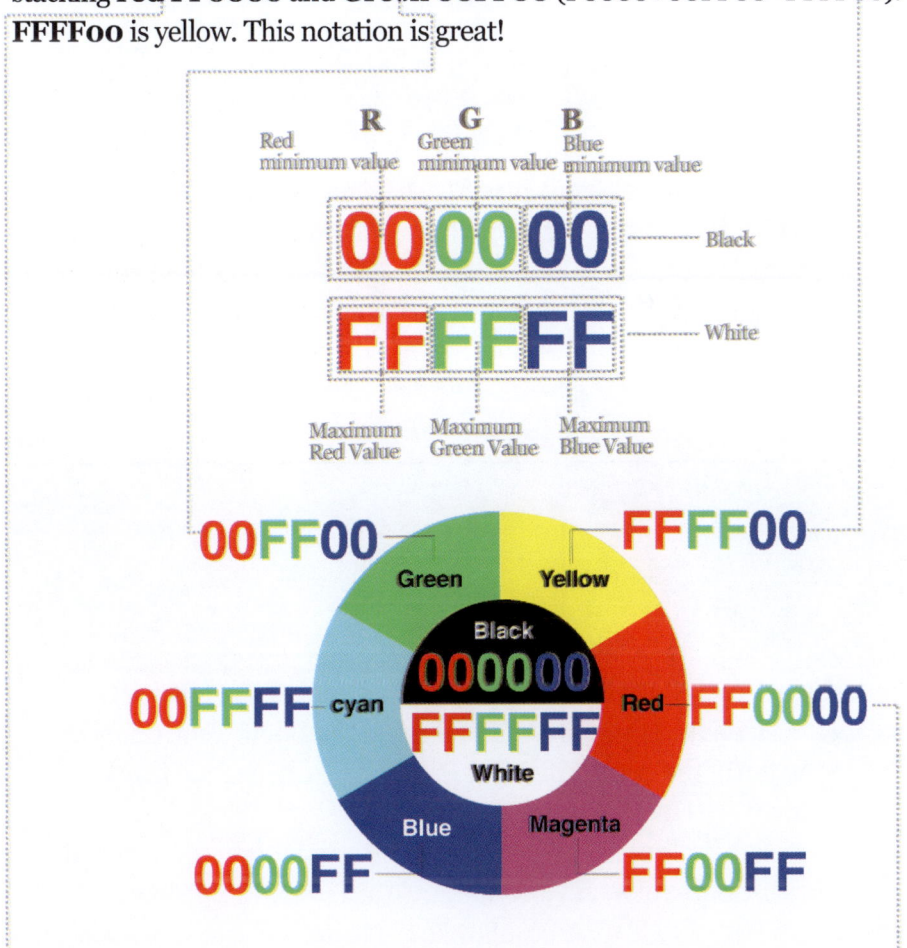

Chapter 11: The three primary colors/color adjustment

## 11_4: Create a color circle to gain an understanding of the Channel Mixer

The computer screen color is made up of three primary colors, as explained on the previous page: Red (R), Green (G), and Blue (B). Mixing these colors creates all colors. Use the Channel Mixer to control the Red Channel, Green Channel, and Blue Channel to control each and created dramatic color changes.

Because the Red, Green, and Blue channels are directly controlled, the process is very different from the more intuitive approach used elsewhere. To directly control the color, the user must have a working understanding of complimentary colors and adjacent colors. The Color Chart helps with this. Let's make a color chart as on the previous page.

Press the Flyout Button to select the Donut Tool from the Tool Panel. On the Tool Panel, click on the Diagram tools, and select the Donut Tool. Choose Yellow on the top of the circle. The left side shows **H:60**, **S:100**, **L:50**, a color space for HSL (Hue, Saturation, Lightness).

The external color circle of Affinity_Photo is set to Saturation of 100% and Lightness to 50% pure color. Click on the circle at **H:60**. This yellow is notated as FFFF00 of RGB16. Adjust Stroke to **None**. Draw a donut once your settings are complete.

Chapter 11: The three primary colors/color adjustment

Are you able to draw a yellow donut? Have a look at the top menu at the top: we have Start angle, End angle, and Total angle. Adjust **Start Angle to 30°** and **End Angle to 90°**. This should automatically adjust Total Angle to 60°.

Next, activate the diagrams with the Move Tool. Copy with Command/Control+C, and paste with Command/Control+V. Click on the **Green part of the circle at H:120,** S:100, and L:50.

Next, adjust the **Start Angle to 90°**, and the **End Angle to 150°**, so that the Total Angle is 60°. The fan shape should now be rotated 60° counter-clockwise at 30°+60°.

291

Chapter 11: The three primary colors/color adjustment

Once the diagram is activated, then Copy-and-Paste. Click on the Sky Blue part of the Color Circle (00FFFF) at positions H:180, S:100, and L:50. Next, adjust the Start angle to 150°, the End angle to 210°, and the Total angle to 60°.

Then Copy-and-Paste as before. Click on the Blue part (0000FF) of the Color Circle in positions H:240, S:100, and L:50. Next, adjust the Start Angle to 210°, End Angle at 270°, and Total Angle at 60°.

Copy-and-Paste again. Click on the Magenta part (FF00FF) of the Color Circle in positions H:300, S:100, and L:50. Next, adjust the Start Angle to 270°, End Angle at 330°, and Total Angle to 60°.

Copy-and-Paste once again. Click on the Magenta part (FF0000) of the Color Circle in positions H:0, S:100, and L:50. Next, enter the Start Angle at 270°, End Angle at 330°, and Total Angle at 60°.

Finally, switch to Text and add text against the Green, Red, and Blue backgrounds. Select All, Menu Bar and Arrange>**Group**.

292

Chapter 11: The three primary colors/color adjustment

## Making Adjustments with the Channel Mixer

Once you're ready, bring up the Channel Mixer Setting page. Click on Studio>Layers > **Adjustment**. The **Channel Mixer** Output Channel is adjusted individually for Red, Green, and Blue. Use the Red, Green, and Blue sliders to adjust the source.

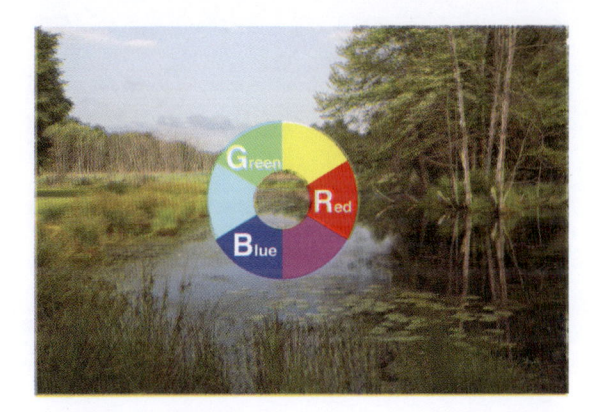

**Output Channel:**
Choose the Color Channel you wish to adjust. Drag the slider to the left to reduce output of the chosen color, and to the right to boost it.
Switch **Alpha** for a Keying/Matte effect.
**Offset:**
Using the Output Channel selected, control the overall impact. Slide to the left to lower the output channel level, and slide to the right to increase it.

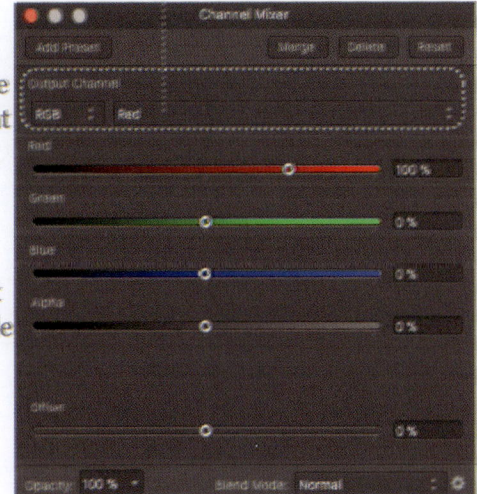

293

Chapter 11: The three primary colors/color adjustment

Try the Red Output Channel.

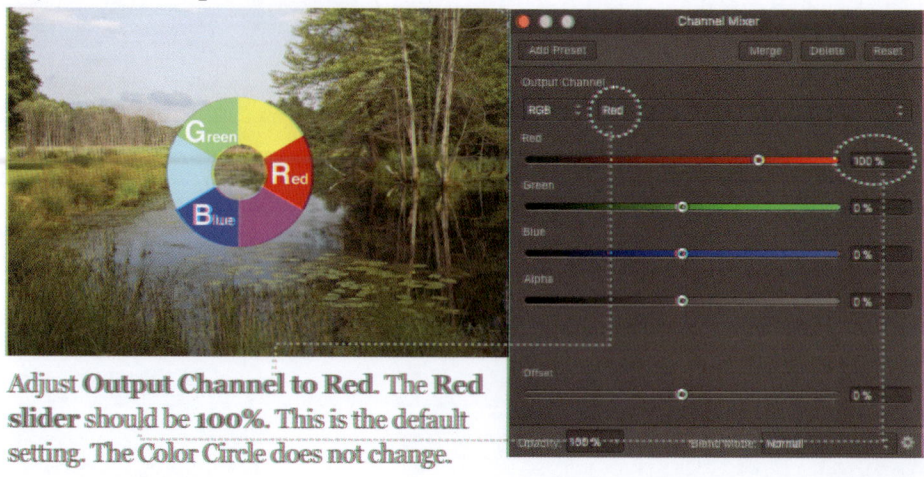

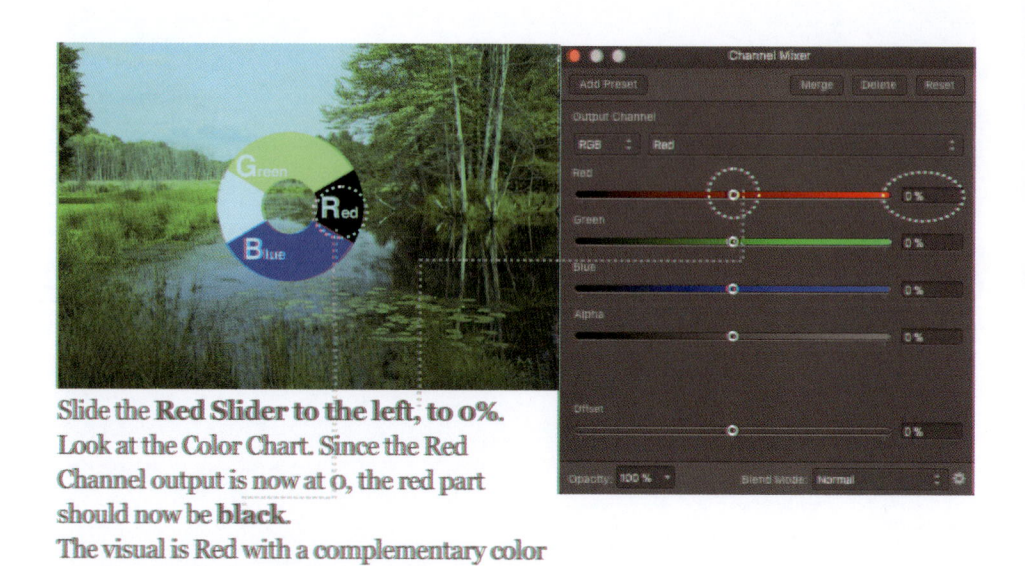

Adjust **Output Channel to Red**. The **Red slider** should be **100%**. This is the default setting. The Color Circle does not change.

Slide the **Red Slider to the left, to 0%**. Look at the Color Chart. Since the Red Channel output is now at 0, the red part should now be **black**.
The visual is Red with a complementary color of cyan. Let's have a look at the RGB16 chart. Red was FF0000. FF is now **00** and the Red part of the Color Circle is black, 000000 on the RGB16 chart.

Chapter 11: The three primary colors/color adjustment

Let's try the Green Output Channel and the Blue Output Channel. Reset the work we did on the previous page and open the Channel mixer.

Adjust the **Output Channel to Green** and slide the Green Slider to **0%**. Have a look at the Color Cart. The Green area should be **Black**.

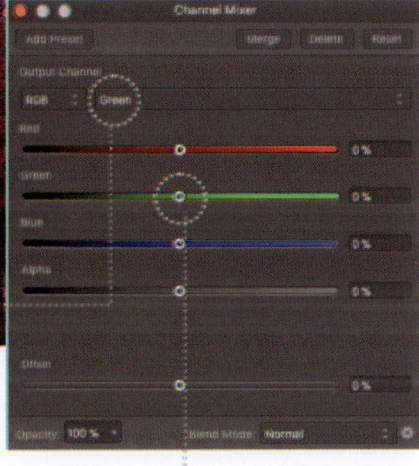

The tone of this photo is Magenta, a complementary color to Green. Adjust the Green (00FF00) value to 00 for a total value of 000000. That makes it Black! Then, adjust the Yellow value (FFFF00) next to it to 00 to arrive at a total value of FF0000. It should now be Red (FF0000).

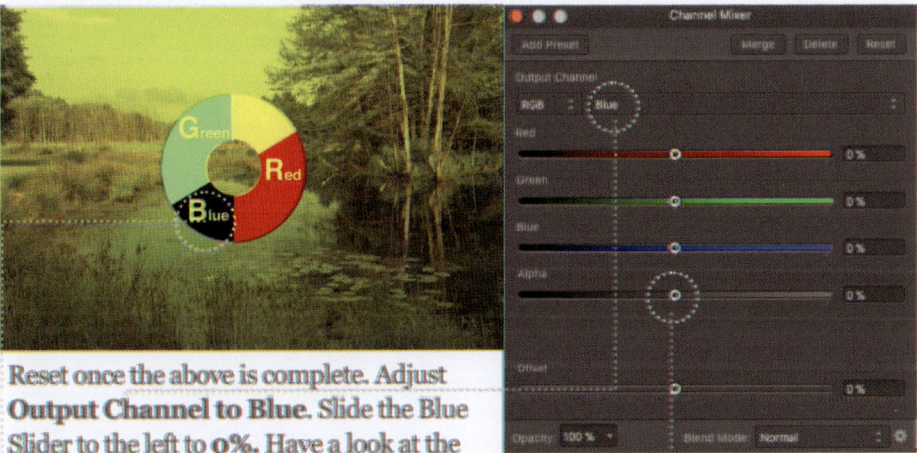

Reset once the above is complete. Adjust **Output Channel to Blue**. Slide the Blue Slider to the left to **0%**. Have a look at the Color Chart. The Blue should now be **Black**. Switching Blue (0000FF) to a Blue Value of 00 yields Black. Reset once this process is complete.

Chapter 11: The three primary colors/color adjustment

Next, let's create a monochrome image with the Channel Mixer. Reset your work on the previous page to display the Channel Mixer again. Leaving the Red Output Channel as is (choose the Default setting, with the Slider at 100%), adjust the settings from the Green Output Channel.

Adjust the **Output Channel to Green**, and then slide the **Green Slider to 0%**. Slide the **Red Slider to the right, to 100%**.

Next, adjust the **Output Channel to Blue**. Move the **Blue Slider to the left, to 0%**. Move the **Red Slider to the Right, to 100%**. Look at the Color Chart. It should now be monochrome. Note that changing the channel produces these kinds of results.

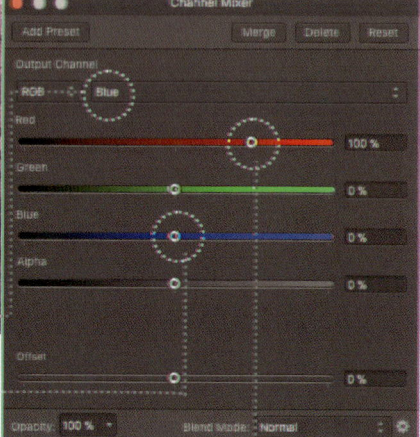

296

## 11_5: Use the Color Channel to change a red car to a yellow car

Next, let's do a review of how to make adjustments with Channel Mixer. Prepare a red object (it can be a flower, car, etc.). If you don't have an image that you can use, this author recommends downloading the same photo as the sample, from Creative Commons:
**http://goo.gl/y32xbz**
Launch your Internet Browser and type in the above in the URL line.

Drag the Affinity_Photo icon that you downloaded and launch. Click on the **Tool Panel > Selection Brush Tool** and click on Add under Mode. Select the car body. Switch to Add/Subtract under Mode and select **the car body/shadow**.

Note: The above address utilizes Google_url_shortener. If the link is broken, search for http://creativecommons.org on the Web. Search "Red Car" or similar.

Chapter 11: The three primary colors/color adjustment

Let's now change a red car to a yellow car. Now let's change the color of the car from red to yellow.

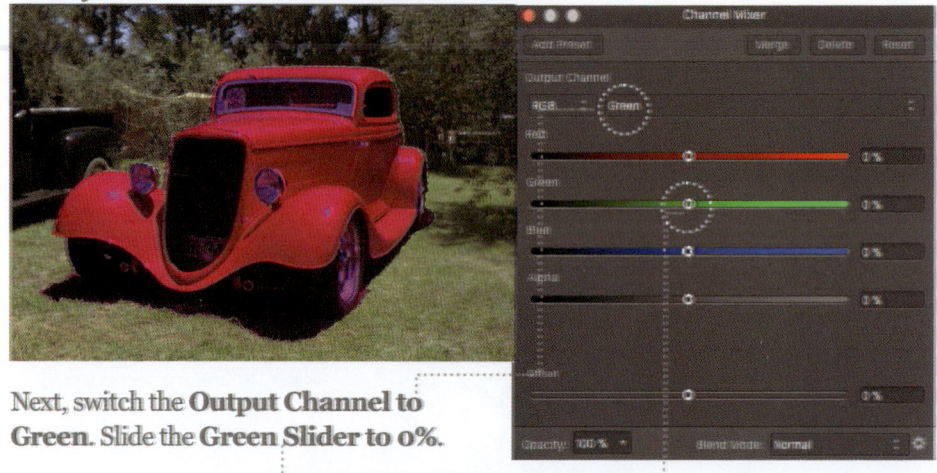

Next, switch the **Output Channel to Green**. Slide the **Green Slider to 0%**.

Keeping the Output Channel Green, slide the **Red Slider to the right, to 100%**. How does it look? Were you able to change the car from Red to Yellow? The Output Channel was on Green. Now slide the Blue slider to 0% to change it to Blue. Slide the Red Slider to 100% to switch the color of the car to Magenta.

Chapter 11: The three primary colors/color adjustment

Now that we have completed our overview of Color Channel, let's go back to the scenic view photos that we were working with earlier.

## Making Adjustments with Gradient Map

Adjusting the Gradient Map means to map the color gradation as indicated by the photograph tone.

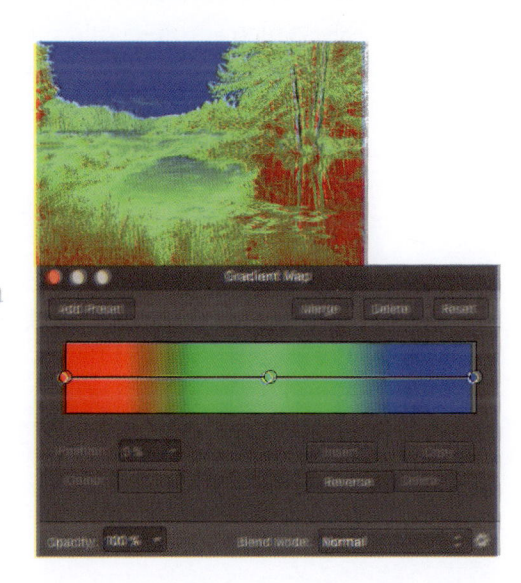

Drag the slider above the Gradation Menu left and right. Choose your colors with the pointers.

## Selective Color Adjustment

Selective Color Adjustment is accomplished using the channels to adjust or emphasize color. Even moving the slider all the way to one extreme or another yields a detailed, soft effect.

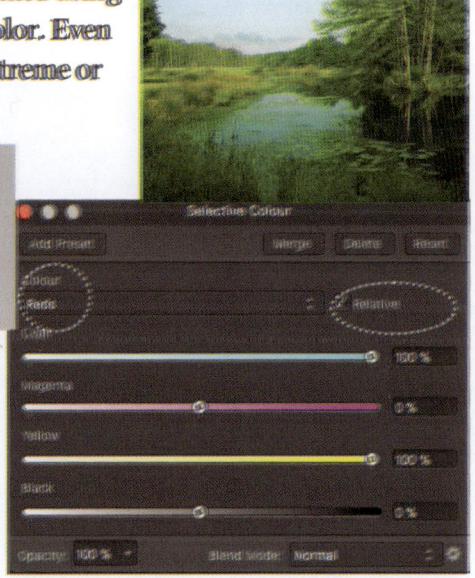

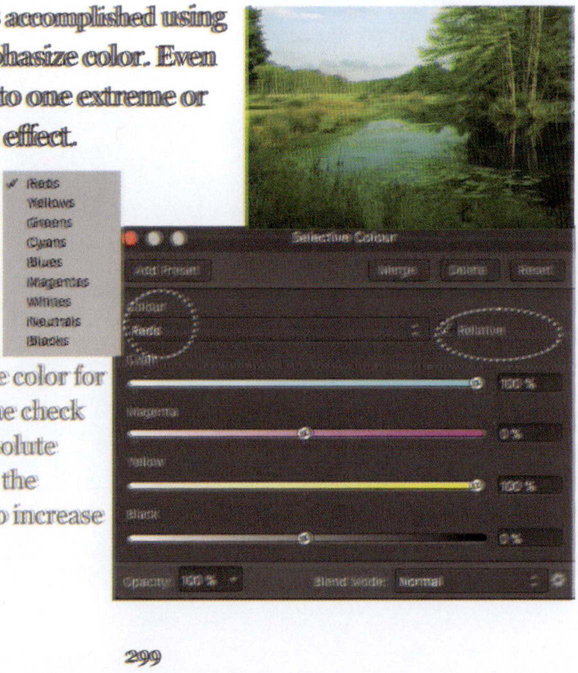

Choose the Color you wish to adjust using the Pop-up Menu.

Check **Relative** to add or reduce color for a more natural effect. Remove the check mark to add or reduce color (absolute value). Slide to the left to reduce the selected Color, and to the right to increase it.

Chapter 11: The three primary colors/color adjustment

## Adjusting the Color Balance
Adjust the Color Balance to change the specified Color Level of the tonal range.

**Tonal Range**—Select tone from Shadows, Midtones, and Highlights.

Shadows
Midtones
Highlights

The Slider controls the specified color balance. Slide toward the color you would like to emphasize.

Check off **Preserve Luminosity** to use the previous luminosity as your baseline. Remove the check to discard the previous luminosity values.

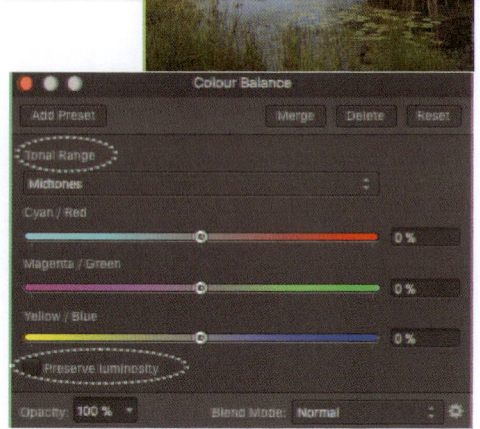

## Invert
Invert the colors to create a negative image.

This setting does not include Control features.

Chapter 11: The three primary colors/color adjustment

## LUT Adjustment

The 3D Lookup Table (LUT), is used to map out color spaces.
Incorporating half-tone blends of the RGB colors, it is used to re-map pixel color values re-map pixel color values onto objects based on the XYZ matrix.

Compatible LUT files are as follows:.3dl, .csp, .cube, and look

## Lens Filter Adjustment

The Lens Filter is an optional color filter.

**Filter Color**: Click and select from the Color Chart.
**Optical Density**: Slide to the right for a more pronounced effect.

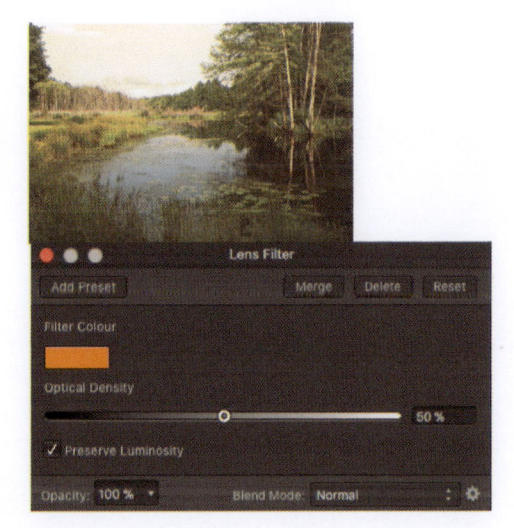

Chapter 11: The three primary colors/color adjustment

## Split Toning Adjustment

The Split Toning feature adjusts the hue and saturation of highlighted areas as well as shadowed areas.

**Highlights Hue**: Slide to select the optimal hue. Values for the photos on the left and right are 0° and 160.7 respectively.

**Highlights Saturation**: Increase saturation by sliding to the right. Values for the photos on the left and right are 0% and 47% respectively.

**Shadows Hue**: Slide to select optimal tone. Values for the left and right photos are 0° and 241.8° respectively.

**Shadows Saturation**: Slide to the right to increase Saturation. Values for the photos on the left and right are 0% and 97% respectively.

**Balance**: Values for the photos on the left and right are 50% and 16% respectively.

# Chapter 12:
# Data export with various formats/configuration/alignment/record macro

# Chapter 12: Data export with various formats/configuration/alignment/record macro

This Chapter covers exporting files other than those made using Affinity_Photo (Export), inserting Affinity_Photo screens (Place), and by boosting efficiency with Macros. Here we also learn how to replicate these functions.

## 12_1: Export in a different format

Use any photo for purposes of practice. This author downloaded one from the Creative Commons site below:
**http://goo.gl/QpSTf8**

Drag the photo of your choice to the Affinity_Photo icon to open.
Click File> **Export**.

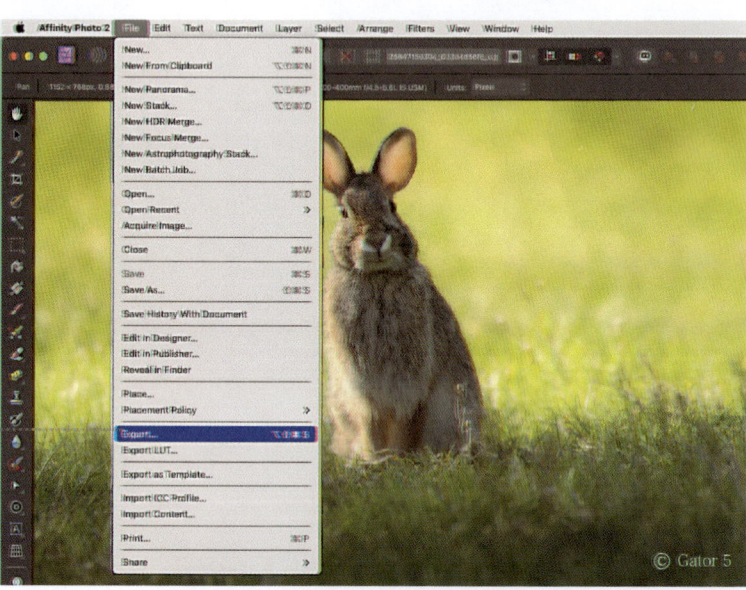

A dialog box showing various formats appears. **Select PNG**. For the size, select about 500 px.
Where the **Lock symbol** on the right is locked, height is adjusted proportionately.
Click Export to save the file under the name of your choice. See subsequent chapters for further details on **Export**.

Chapter 12: Data export with various formats/configuration/alignment/record macro

## 12_2: Place an object on the screen

Were you able to save the exported file? Next, place the file in the Affinity_Photo working area. Click **File** >**New**. On Page Preset, select A4 horizonal.

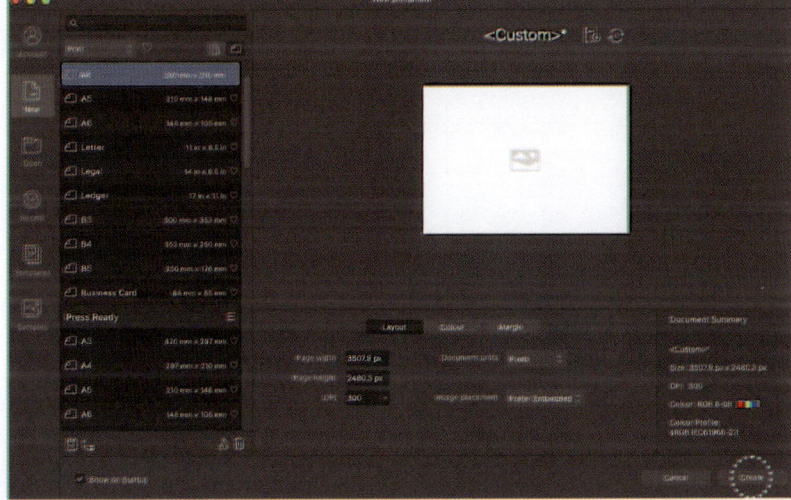

On New Document Dialog Box, click the **Create** button to show the screen. Click **Menu Bar>File>Place**.

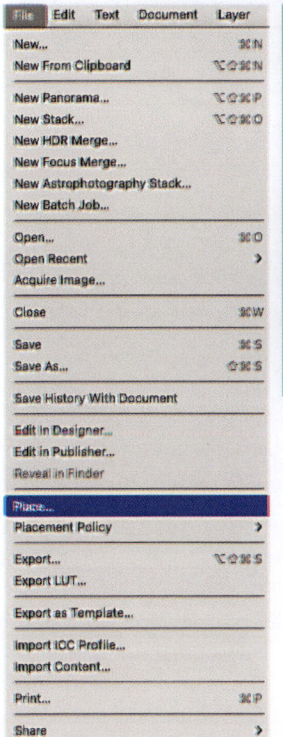

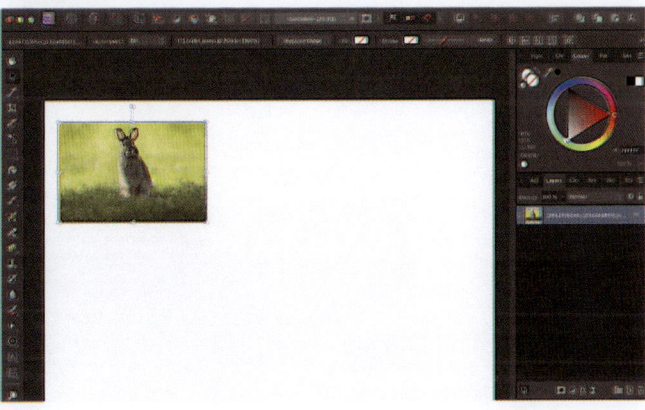

305

Chapter 12: Data export with various formats/configuration/alignment/record macro

## 12_3: Object (layer) Alignment

Click on the object and copy using Command/Control+C. Then paste with Command/Control+V. That is, lay out two objects on your screen. Select both objects using Shift + Move Tool,

and then click on **Persona Tool>Alignment button**. Click through **Alignment Dialog>Align Vertically>Align Middle**, and then click the Done button to align the objects.

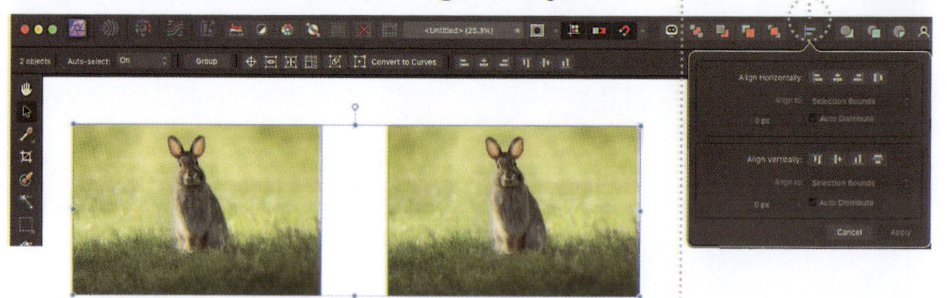

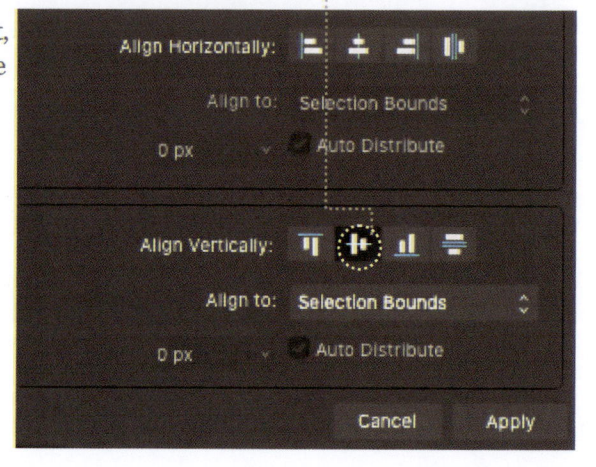

**Align Horizontally**: Align Left, Align Centres, Align Right, Space Horizontally

**Align to**:
- Selection Bounds
- Spread
- Margin
- First Selected
- Last Selected

**Align Vertically**: Align Top, Align Middle, Align Bottom, Space Vertically

**Align to**:
- Selection Bounds
- Spread
- Margin
- First Selected
- Last Selected

306

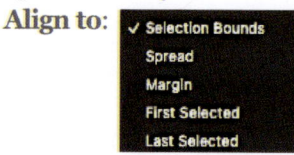

# Chapter 12: Data export with various formats/configuration/alignment/record macro

## 12_4: Record a Macro

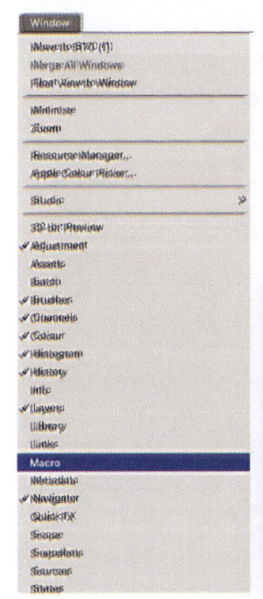

Affinity_Photo has a powerful built-in macro designed to record work flow and automatically implement it. Let's give this a try. On the Menu Bar select **Window > Macro**. It appears on the left-hand **Macro Panel**. **First activate the object** you want to work with: click on the photo of a rabbit on the left.

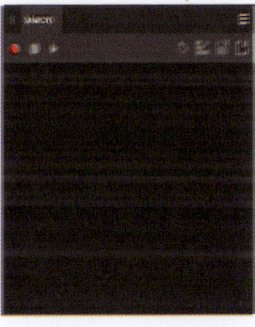

Click on the **Start Recording** button to begin recording.

Start recoding    Stop recoding    Play    Reset    Add To Library    Export    Inport

Click on the **Studio > Effects** tab and select **Gaussian Blur**. Adjust the Radius to 17px. Your macro is now **recorded on the Macro Panel**, on the left.

307

Chapter 12: Data export with various formats/configuration/alignment/record macro

Let's continue here with the recording. Remove the check from Gaussian Blur above. Under Effects, select **Bevel/Emboss**. Bring opacity to 75%, and Radius to 45 px. Note that **each piece of information** is recorded. **Remove the check mark** on any items you do not want to record. To finish, press **Stop Recording**.

To continue recording your macro, click on the "Start recording" button again. Click on the "Play" icon to preview the macro. To change parameters of past operations, click on **the category settings icon**.

### Saving a Macro

Click on the **Add to Library** button, type in **a name** for the macro you would like to record, and click OK. The screen will change to the library panel, showing **your saved macros under Default**. If you want to perform another similar operation, click on the relevant object and select.

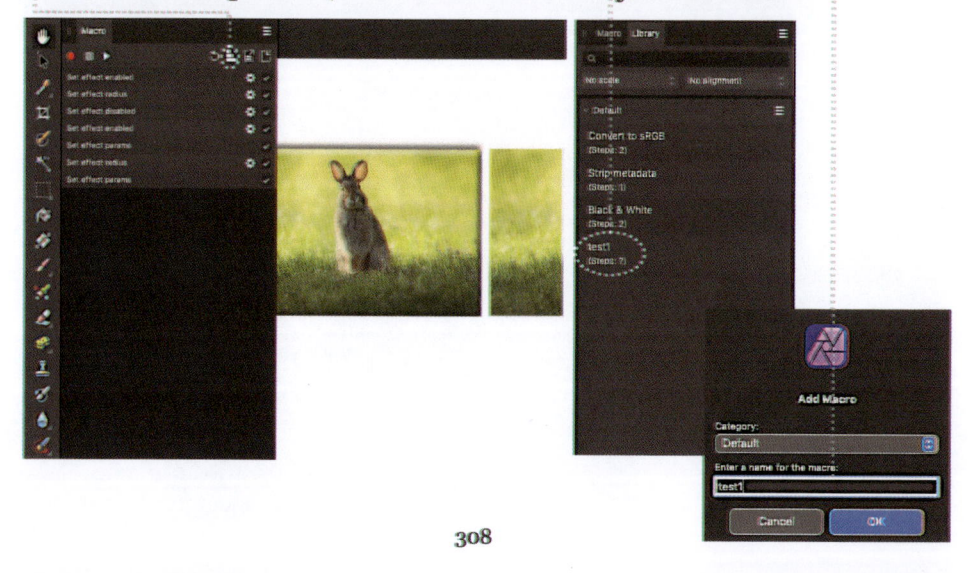

308

Chapter 12: Data export with various formats/configuration/alignment/record macro

**Duplicate a Macro Recording**

To repeat the same procedure, activate a new object. Click on the desired Library **list**. How did it go? Note how the process was duplicated in an instant.

**Export/Import Macros**

Use the **Macro Panel** to Export a Macro. Click on the **Export button**, add a file name (.afmacro), and save. To **Import**, click on **Browse** and **Open** to display the **Library**.

Chapter 12: Data export with various formats/configuration/alignment/record macro

## 12_5: Exporting with batch jobs /Batch processing of raw data

The Batch Job feature can be used to export multiple files and raw data processing.

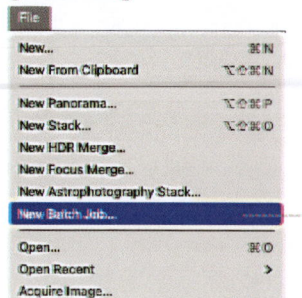

Select **File>New Batch Job** to show the pulldown menu. Click **Sources>Add** to select all the files you want for your **Batch Job**. Click **Open** to insert to Source.

To **Output**, save in the original place or check off a different place to save it, specify the file, decide on the **output file format**, choose **Macros**, and click on **OK** to finish. Finally, check the folder to make sure it's in there. Amazing, isn't it?

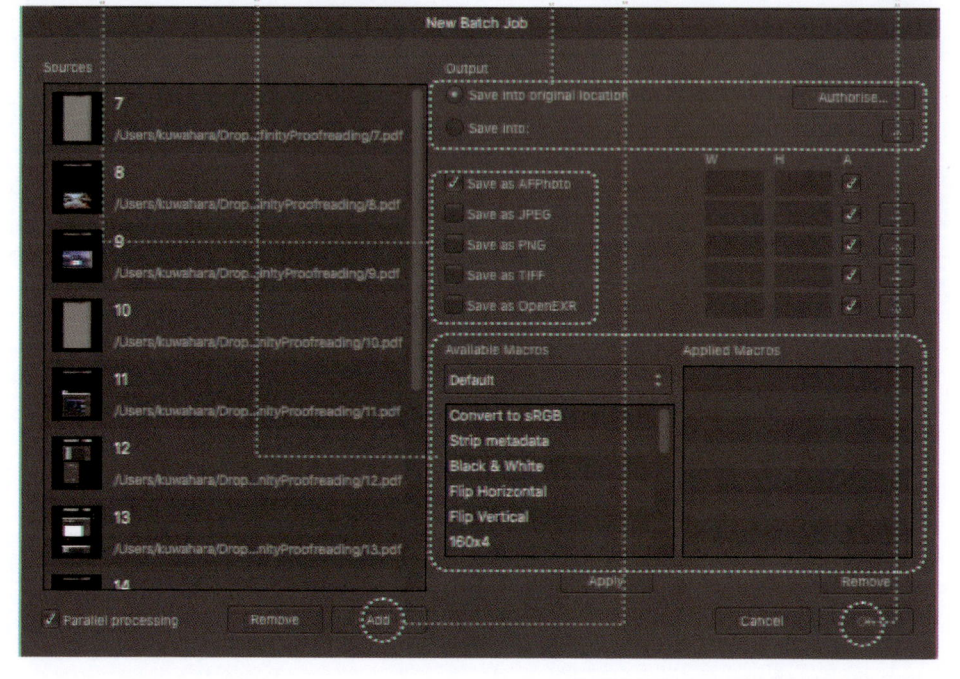

310

# Chapter 13: Raw data processing

Chapter 13: Raw data processing

Open raw data directly using the Affinity_Photo Develop Persona digital camera. Use this feature to process images yourself. The majority of importable raw data images are supported. For updated information, check the Affinity_Photo site:
https://affinity.serif.com/ (Supported Develop (RAW) Cameras)

### 13_1: Opening raw data images

To open raw data images, click **Menu Bar>Fail>Open**. Select a digital camera or SD card raw data file connected to your PC and click **Open**. **Develop Persona** is used to read raw image data for processing,

Note: For raw image data samples, use data taken with your own digital camera.

Data Persona analyzes and pre-processes data so that it can be edited. To undo pre-processing raw data, use the Develop Assistant. Let's give this a try on the next page.

Chapter 13: Raw data processing

### 13_2: The Develop Assistant Feature

Your raw image data is now ready. It was opened by Default last time, which means **Enable Assistant** is active. RAW Engine (Serif_Labs) for raw data processing is already happening in 16 bit or 32 bit output format, automatic Tone curve, etc.

To change your initial settings, select RAW Engine and RAW output format, and choose either 16 bit, or 32 bit for higher resolution, followed by Tone curve, Exposure bias, etc., as well as mapping (GPS data) location data.

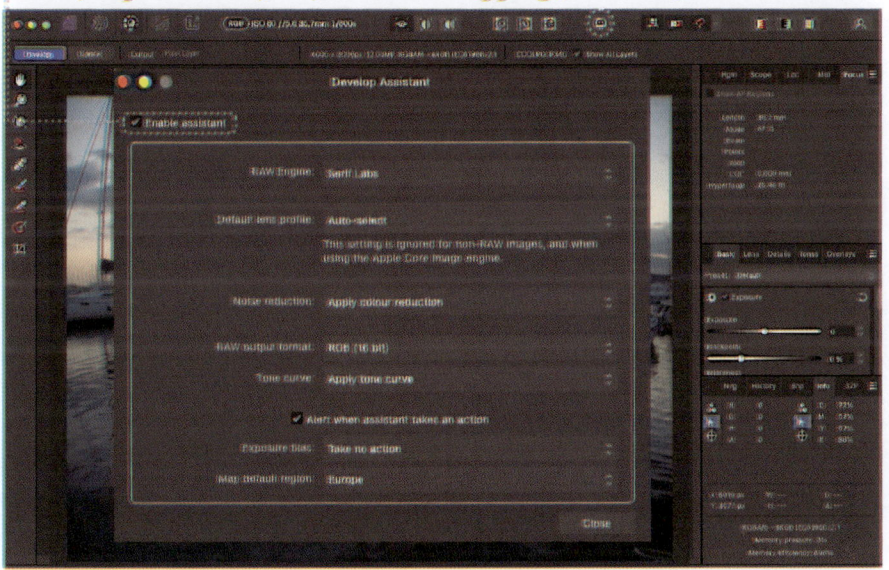

### 13_3: Use the Split display for raw data processing, comparing as you go along.

To adjust Raw image data, it's extremely convenient if you're able to compare as you proceed. Affinity Photo has this feature. **Click Split** on the Personal Menu Bar> **None/Split/Mirror**.

Chapter 13: Raw data processing

## 13_4: Adjusting Raw Data Exposure

Now adjust exposure. For exposure, click on **Studio** > **Basic** > **Exposure**, adjust **Exposure** overall, and change **Blackpoint/Brightness**.

The image on the right is created with the Default setting, while the image on the left has been adjusted. Slide the **Exposure** to the Right.

Adjust Exposure and **Blackpoint**

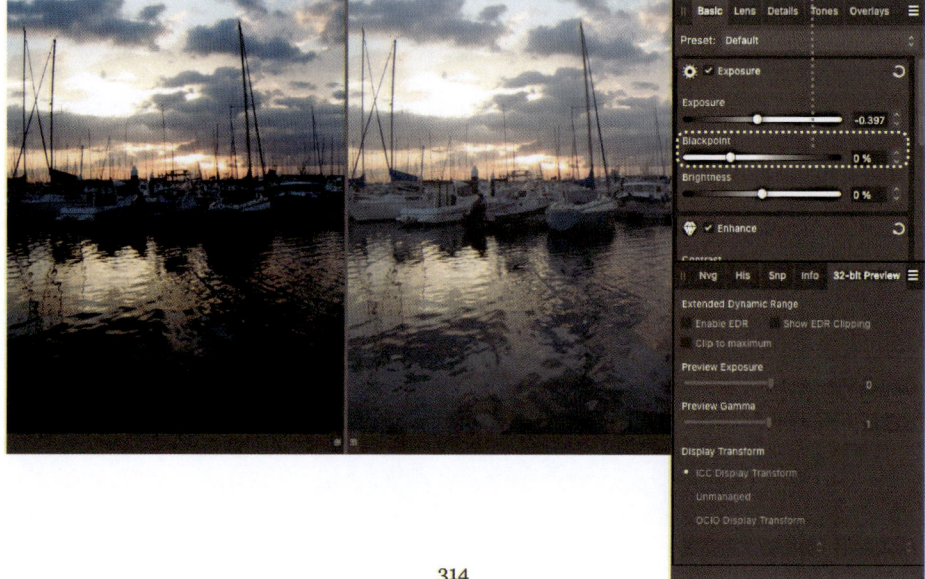

314

Chapter 13: Raw data processing

## 13_5: Check Clipping

Where the Exposure level is incorrect or where the capacity of the display is surpassed, the shadow and highlights may be clipped such that half-tone details are lost. These are called Clippings. Affinity_Photo Develop Persona has a feature to display these. On the Persona Tool Bar, click **Clipping**.

Click **Show Clipped Highlights** on the left to show all highlights.

Click on **Show Clipped Shadows** to show the clipped shadows in blue.

Click on the **Show Clipped Tones** on the left to infuse the image with a yellow tone.

315

Chapter 13: Raw data processing

## 13_6: Adjusting Enhance/White Balance/Shadows & Highlights

Besides Exposure, use **the Studio>Basic Panel** to **adjust Enhance**, **White Balance, Shadows & Highlights**, and **Color Management** of **Profiles**.

**Enhance**: Adjust using Contrast, Clarity, Saturation, etc.

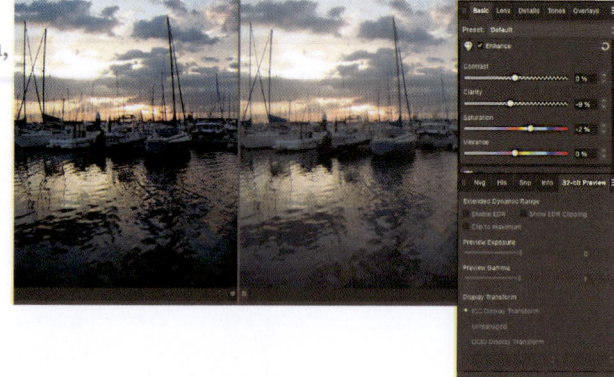

**White Balance**: Adjust Temperature. The Default settings maintain the settings in place at the time the photo was taken.

**Shadows & Highlights**: Adjust shadows and highlights

## 13_7: Develop Persona Overlays Feature

The Overlays feature is similar to the Photo Persona Mask feature. To work with only part of the image, you will need to block off the desired area. Use the brush to paint it a translucent red temporarily. Color is adjusted for the selected area only. Let's give it a try.

Select the **Studio > Overlays panel**, followed by the **Brush Overlay** or Overlay Paint Tool, and adjust the desired part of the raw image. If you paint over too much of the image, use the Overlay Erase Tool on the Tool Panel to fix it.

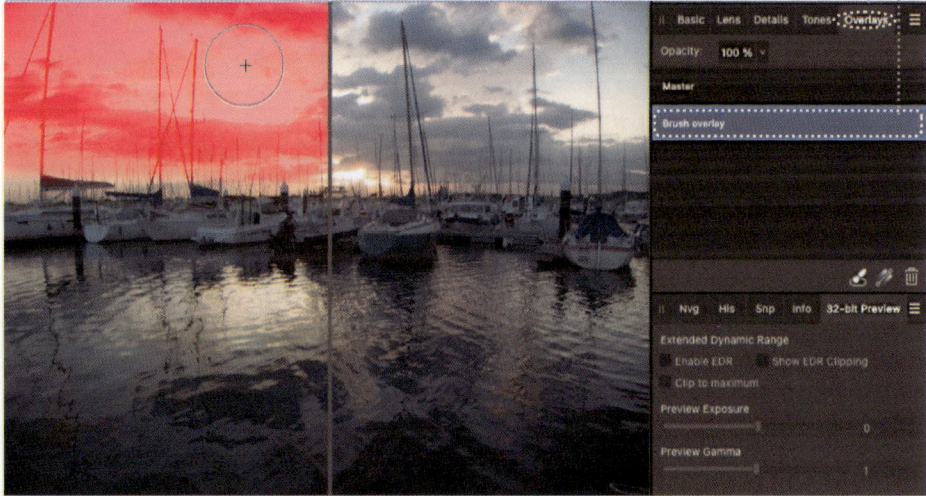

Click the **Basic tab** and slide **Saturation** under **Enhance** all the way to the left. The sky, which we'd covered in a red mask, should now be **monotone**. This tool is used to temporarily cover areas of an image that you don't want to be affected by Overlay.

Chapter 13: Raw data processing

## 13_8: Lens Panel
This feature corrects Lens distortion, specifically Distortion Horizontal, Distortion Vertical, and Distortion Angle.

**Left**: Emphasize Lens > Distortion
**Right**: Default

## 13_9: Details Panel
The Details Panel corrects Detail Refinement, Noise Reduction, and Noise Addition.

**Left**: Details > Noise Addition
**Right**: Default

## 13_10: Other panels
**Location**: Determine location in relation to a camera without a GPS.

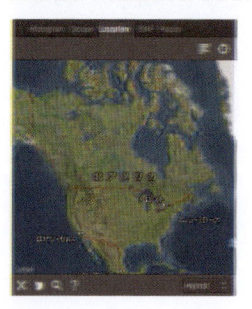

**Focus**: Focus Data

318

Chapter 13: Raw data processing

## 13_11: Synchronizing settings applied in Display mode

We've been making our corrections with the Default settings to the right, with the screen split in two. Let's now synchronize. You'll see how easy it is! Click on **Personal Tool >Sync Before** button, noting how the image is updated. To undo, click on **Sync After** and switch the front and back using **Swap**.

Once you have synchronized the front, click on **Context Tool Bar>Develop** to finish.

# Chapter 14: 32-bit HDR editing/Tone mapping/32-bit OpenEXR

# Chapter 14: 32bitHDR editing/Tone mapping/32bitOpenEXR

# Chapter 14: 32-bit HDR editing/Tone mapping/32-bit OpenEXR

The dynamic range of the light and shadow of the natural world is said to have a contrast ratio of 1,000,000, which is the reason why digital cameras are incapable of capturing the entire range. Instead, the images taken by these cameras take compressed images. For computer monitor displays, 24-bit Color (approximately 1,6770,7216 tones) is sufficient.

This is the familiar JPG format 24-bit Color, called the low dynamic range. However 24-bit color is not sufficient for image synthesis. Here we require data with a broader tone, i.e. 32-bit Color (high dynamic range image) data. Affinity_Photo has editing features for 32-bit HDR.

## 14_1: Creating a 32-bit HDR formatted image

Next we generate 32-bit HDR by combining multiple images of different exposures. Let's get some raw data images together, each of the same subject but with a different exposure. If you do not have a good photo to use, download this author's from the following site: **http://goo.gl/poq163**
Right-click on the image, click Rename and **Save**, and **download**.

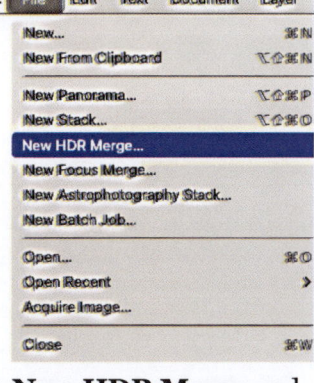

Click on File>**New HDR Merge** and open the Dialog box. Click on **Add** and add **more images**. Check Off on Tone map HDR Image and click **OK**.

# Chapter 14: 32-bit HDR editing/Tone mapping/32-bit OpenEXR

Clik OK to synthesize 32-bit HDR editing image like the one as follows:

The above reflects multiple image data gleaned from different exposures, inserted in the previous page. The displayable dynamic range consists of 256 tonal values. The 32-bit-HDR surpasses this range of tones. Image processing limited to 256 displayable tones is called **Tone Mapping**. Since here we are unable to display all tones, tone mapping is essential.

Click on **Personal Tool Bar>Tone Mapping Persona** to switch to the **Tone Mapping** screen. This will automatically start Tone Mapping. Samples of displayable tones will appear on the left. Click **Default/Natural**, followed by **Apply**. This brings us back to Photo Persona.

Chapter 14: 32-bit HDR editing/Tone mapping/32-bit OpenEXR

## 14_2: Use Tone Mapping on a High Dynamic Range Image (HDR)

To get more of a sense of **Tone Mapping**, switch to the Tone **Mapping Persona** and give it a try. Drag a raw data photo (taken with your digital camera) to the Affinity_Photo icon.
Launch **Develop Persona** since we are working with raw data. Click Develop and switch to Photo Persona. (For JPEG images, launch Photo Persona).

Now click on **Tone Mapping Persona**. Well, what do you think? You're now able to use **Tone Mapping**! That was easy, wasn't it? You've now mapped to recreate a 256-tone display.

## Chapter 14: 32-bit HDR editing/Tone mapping/32-bit OpenEXR

**Tone Mapping contains a number of pre-settings. Let's have a look.**

Default/Natural

Default/Detailed

Crazy/Cruel And Unusual

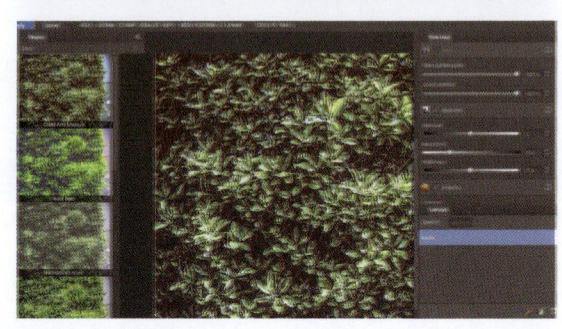

**Tone Compression**:
Control degree of mapping.
**Local Contrast**: Turn up to adjust clarity of the image.
**Exposure**: Increase or decrease overall exposure:
**Blackpoint**: Adjust black clipping settings.
**Brightness**: Controls half-tone brightness.
**Contrast**: Control image contrast.
**Saturation**: Increase or decrease overall color intensity.
**Vibrance**: Increase or decrease color intensity without color tone mapping.
**White Balance**: Adjust Color Temperature and control Tint.
**Detail Refinement**: Control sharpness.
**Curves**: Control tone with the Curve Graph.

# Chapter 14: 32-bit HDR editing/Tone mapping/32-bit OpenEXR

## 14_3: 32-bit OpenEXR Import/Export

Affinity_Photo fully supports Import and Export of the 32-bit OpenEXR. First, drag a suitable raw data photo to the Affinity_Photo icon. This will launch the Develop Persona. After development, switch to Photo Persona. (Note that the photo need not be raw data, in which case you would simply launch Photo Persona).

Once the image displays, click **Menu Bar**>File >**Export** to show the **Export dialog**. Select **EXR**. Under **OpenEXR 32_bit Linear(layered)**, click **More**. Make any desired changes to settings in the **Advanced Dialog box**, or click **Close**. Go back to the Export Dialog box, click **Export**, give the file a name, and save it to finish. Import the same way as you normally open a file.

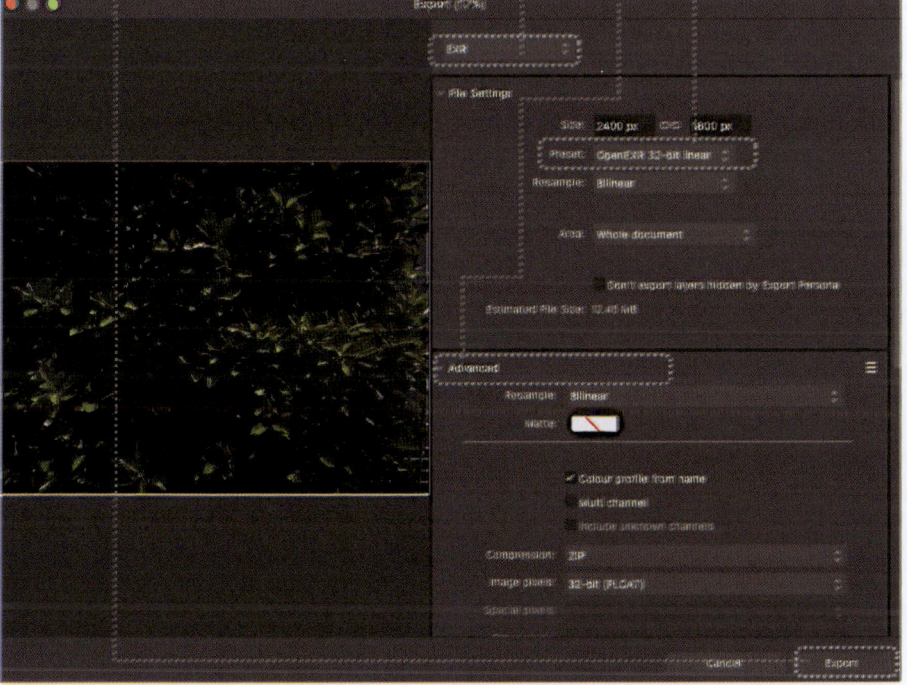

# Chapter 15:
Image Stacking/Focus Merge/Panorama/Equirectangular Projection

## 15_1: Imaging Stacking Feature

This feature is used to blend images of the same scenes or similar subjects. Our objective is to blend images taken at different levels of exposure for a more dynamic range, reducing noise as well as eliminating unnecessary objects, for example a bird that momentarily entered into the frame.

**Exposure Composition with Stacking**

Get together some images of the same subject, but of different exposures. Use a tripod to fix the camera in place to take images. To achieve the desired dynamic range, take a number of pictures, changing the exposure as you go along. If you do not have any sample images, download one from the author's site. Type the following in the URL line: **http://goo.gl/poq163**

Once you have collected some images, click **Menu Bar>File>New Stack**. Click **Add** under Dialog and insert all of the images in the folder. They should now be in your Stack List. Click on the **OK** button.

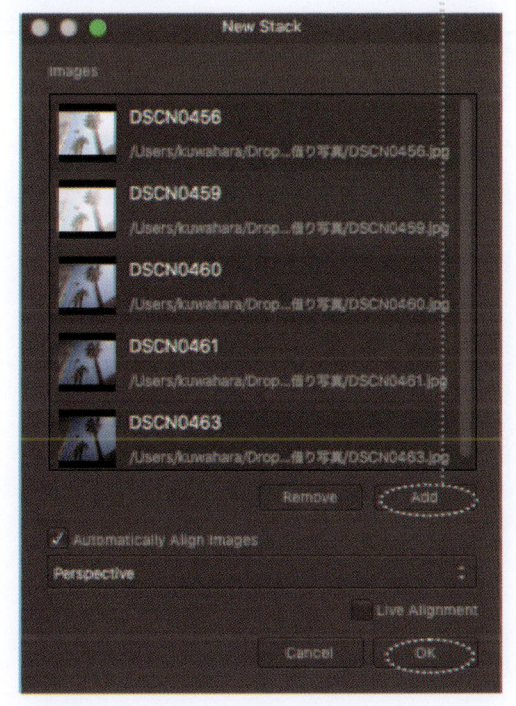

Chapter 15: Image Stacking/Focus Merge/Panorama/Equirectangular Projection

Click on **Studio>Layers Panel>Live Stack Group** layer. You should now see the Mean, Median, Maximum, Minimum, etc. layers.

Mean    Median    Maximum    Minimum

Range    Mid-Range    Total    Standard Deviation

That's it! Once you've ascertained these, select **Median**, with slightly reduced noise. Note that Exposure Composition differs from HDR composition and tone mapping. Decide on noise reduction by comparing **Mean**, **Median**, etc.

Chapter 15: Image Stacking/Focus Merge/Panorama/Equirectangular Projection

## 15_2: Use Focus Merge to create focused images both near and far

By synthesizing different images of the same subject with the focus at different distances, we create an image where the focus is sharp, both near and far. Images are taken with a tripod, and exposure settings are all the same. Take a number of photos, changing only the focus. If you do not have any images, download sample images from the author's site below. **http://goo.gl/poq163**

Here we have a series of photos: **one focused on the bottle cap,** another **focused on the center,** and another **focused on the label.** Let's put them together to create a photo where the entire image is in focus. Click **Menu Bar > File > New Focus Merge,** and insert the photo above the Dialog Box using Add. Click **OK** to begin merging.

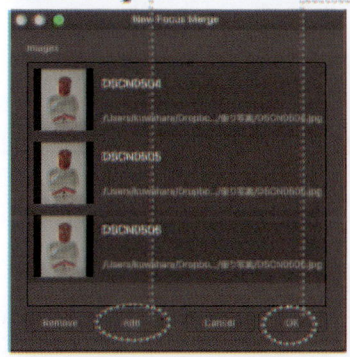

We now have **a merged image** where all parts are in perfect focus.

Here we used a curve to help adjust the color.

Chapter 15: Image Stacking/Focus Merge/Panorama/Equirectangular Projection

## 15_3: Creating a Panorama Photo

Panorama photos are created using a specialized tool. First we need a photo to work with. We can also use a tripod. Using a fast shutter speed, take the different parts with the same exposure. Here the author used an image of waves moving in the ocean, but you actually get better results if your subject is not moving.

Download a sample photo from the following: **http://goo.gl/poq163**

Once you have gathered together the materials you need, click **Menu Bar > File > New Panorama**. With the Dialog Box open, Click **Add** to insert the image. Click **Stitch Panorama** to **Preview**. If everything is as you want it, click **OK**.

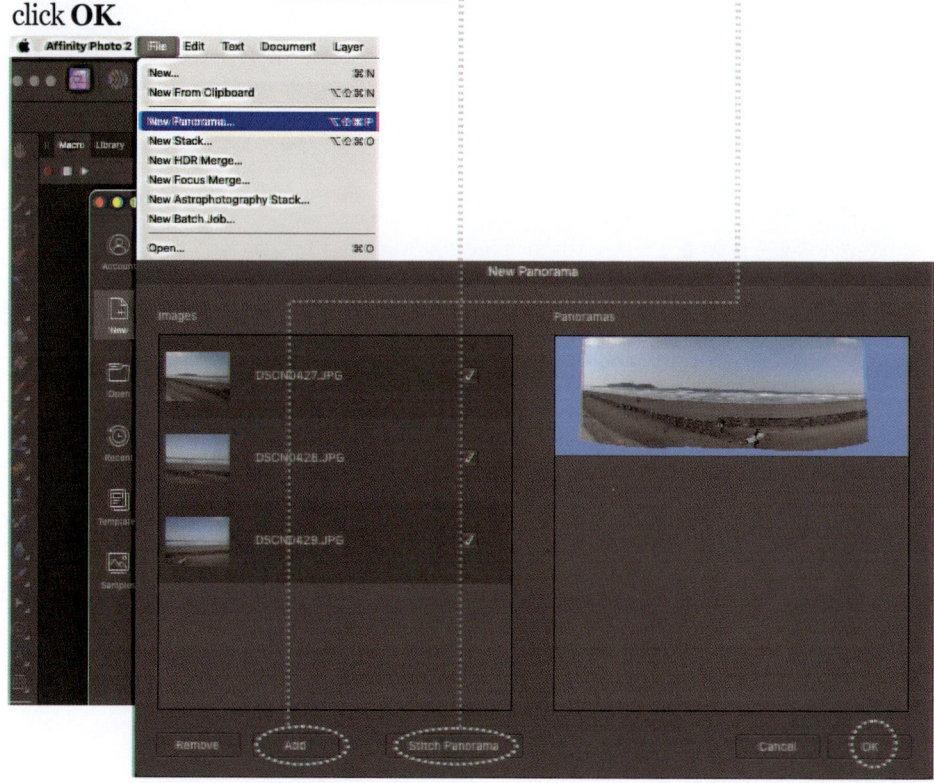

Chapter 15: Image Stacking/Focus Merge/Panorama/Equirectangular Projection

Well, what do you think? Did it take a little time? But wait...there's something strange about this picture. There are **two surfers** right in the middle! But really there's only one surfer. This happened because the photographer was trying to get a series of pictures—and the timing between images was slightly off.

So, let's make it one surfer instead of two! Click Persona Menu Bar > **Inpaint Missing Areas** and use Inpainting. Activate the image in the middle using the Move Tool. Click **Tool Panel** > **Add To Source Image Mask Tool** on the left to fill in **the surfer** that appears larger, in the front.

Use the Move Tool and click outside the area you were just working with. How does it look? We now have just one surfer.

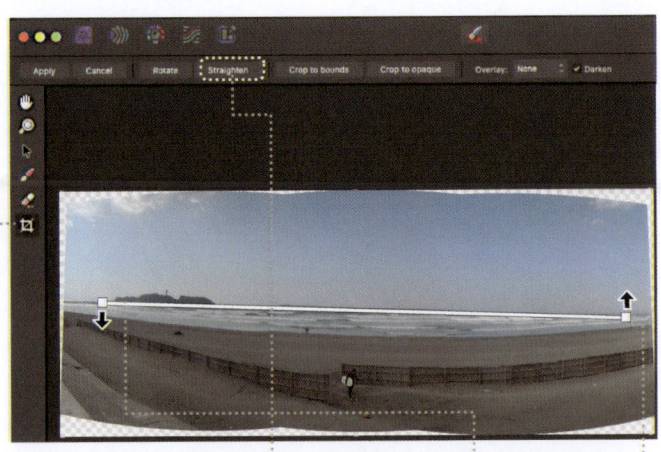

Chapter 15: Image Stacking/Focus Merge/Panorama/Equirectangular Projection

Now there's only one surfer. Note how the horizontal line is sloping. Select **Tool Panel>Crop Tool, Context Tool Bar>Straighten. Drag the horizontal line** on the image from left to right. **Using the mouse, move the cursor upward** to straighten the horizontal line.

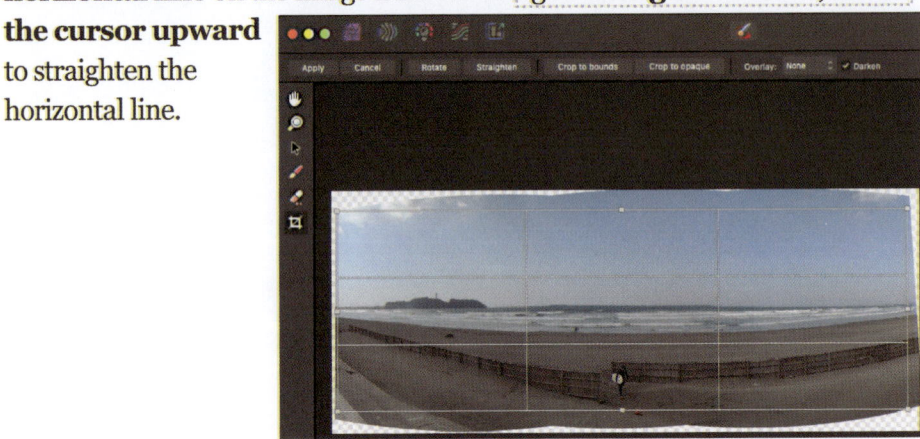

Crop the four corners to finish.

Chapter 15: Image Stacking/Focus Merge/Panorama/Equirectangular Projection

## 15_4: Equirectangular (Panorama) Live Projection Mapping

Affinity_Photo uses Live Projection mapping to edit Equirectangular(360x180) files. Equirectangular images require a dedicated application or camera. The author downloaded a free image from the Pixexid link below:https://pixexid.com
This site is run based on an inspiring idea: anyone can utilize the site provided they simply follow the rules. Simply launch your Internet browser and type in the following in the URL line.
**https://pixexid.com/search/360-panoramic**

Drag the downloaded photo to the Affinity_Photo icon and launch. You should now see a photo like the one above. With equirectangular data, the top and bottom of a spherical object are compressed to form a plane surface—which can mean that the top and bottom look distorted. Let's now try Live Projection mapping.

Chapter 15: Image Stacking/Focus Merge/Panorama/Equirectangular Projection

Click **Menu Bar**> **Layer** > **Live Projection** > **Equirectangular Projection**. How does it look? The top and bottom have been revised to for a live image. Drag on the image with your mouse.

GO 360° around the image to get a full view. How did it turn out?

**15_5: Edit Live Projection**

Stop at any angle and edit with live projection. Select **Layer**>**Live Projection**>**Edit Live Projection**.

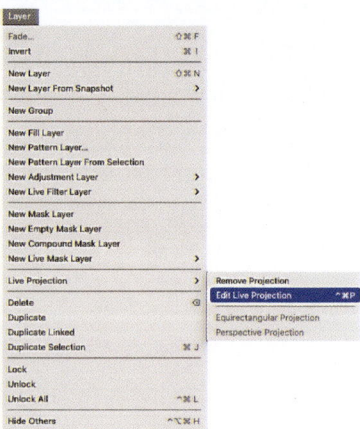

334

## Chapter 15: Image Stacking/Focus Merge/Panorama/Equirectangular Projection

Let's add a neon sign somewhere in the panorama image. Check that the screen is ready for editing, switch to the **Artistic Text Tool,** and input the following settings:

Font: Santa_Fe_LET, Size: 64pt, Fill Color: Cream, **Affinity Photo**.

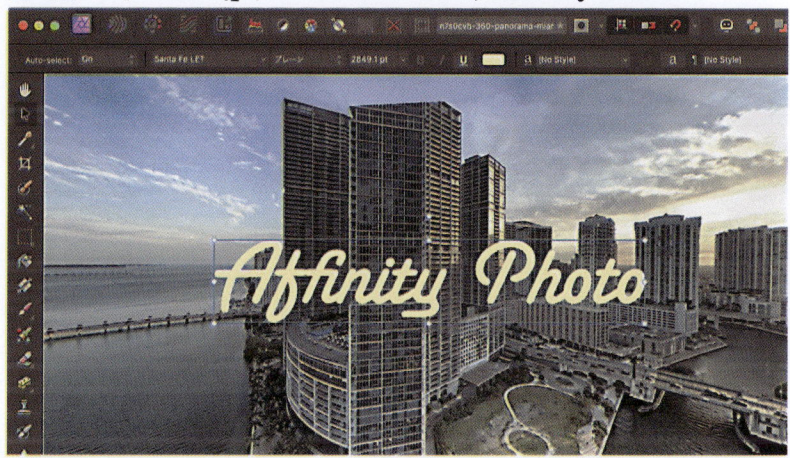

Next, click **Studio** > **Effects**. Check that the text is activated, switch on **Outer Glow**, and input the following settings for Outer **Glow** and **Inner Glow**.

**Outer Glow**
Blend mode: Screen  Radius: 47Pt
Intensity: 54%    Color: Red

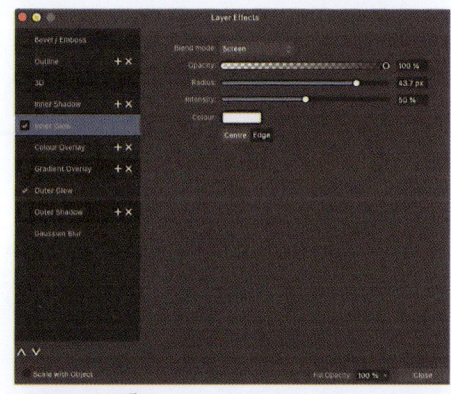

**Inner Glow**
Blend mode: Normal Radius: 26.7Pt
Intensity: 45% Color: White/Centre

Does it now look like the image on the right?

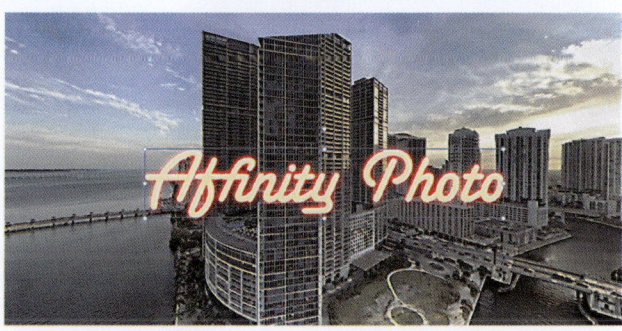

335

## Chapter 15: Image Stacking/Focus Merge/Panorama/Equirectangular Projection

Once you have input the text, then merge the layers. Click **Layer>Merge Down**. You're done!

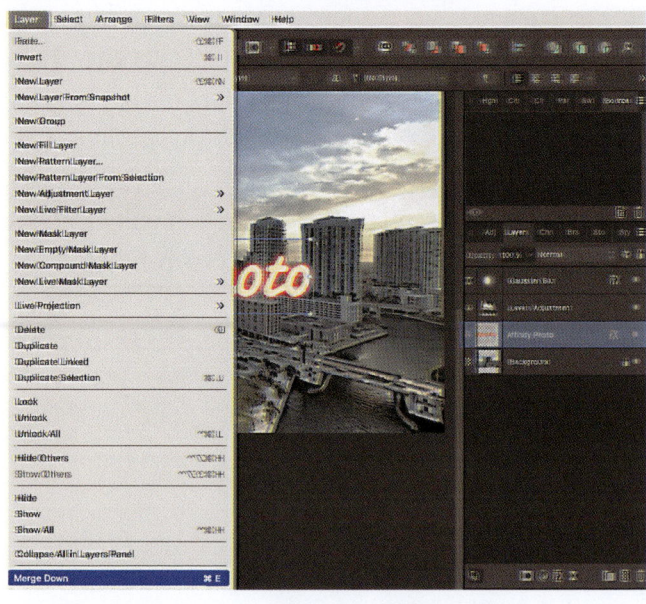

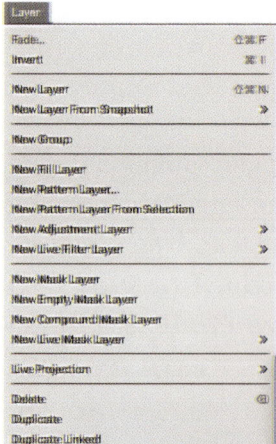

Check that the text is now part of the panorama image. After inserting the text, the screen temporarily moves from Live Projection View. To go back to Live Projection, click **Layer>Live Projection>Edit Live Projection**. This takes you back to global settings. The neon sign should also be panoramic now.

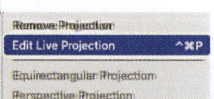

336

# Chapter 16:
# Create a Slice/Compatible Formats and Export/Configuration

Chapter 16: Create a Slice/Compatible Formats and Export/Configuration

## 16_1: Creating a Slice and Exporting

The Slice Export feature, where part of an image is isolated and exported, is essential to everyday Web design. In Affinity_Photo, the slice export feature is a distinct Export Persona.

We need a sample photo for learning purposes. The author recommends downloading a free image from Creative Commons:
http://creativecommons.org

There are lots of great photos to choose from here. Note the rules of the Creative Commons website and download the sample photo shown here:
**http://goo.gl/EFZHrg**
Launch your Internet browser and type the above in the URL line.

Drag the Affinity_Photo icon that you downloaded and launch. We have to first get a few things ready before we learn about exporting our Slice. Select the flower on the left half and click **Tool Panel>Selection Brush Tool**. Click **Context Tool Bar>Mode**, followed by **Add**. Adjust the Width to 47 px and select **the flower to the left**. If you selected a larger area than you wanted to, click **Subtract** under **Mode** to fix it. Were you able to select the flower on the left?

Note: The above address uses Google_url_shortener. If the link is broken, search for "Flower" or similar on the Creative Commons website:http://creativecommons.org

338

# Chapter 16: Create a Slice/Compatible Formats and Export/Configuration

Click **Studio>Adjustment** on the right to open the **Adjustment** menu. On the Menu, select **Channel Mixer** to open Settings. On the **Output Channel**, select **Red** and **slide to 75%**. When the flowers turn blue as in the sample, you're done.

Let's now change the color of the flower on the **Channel Mixer** on the right. Once you have selected the blue flower, click > **Deselect** on the **Persona Tool Bar**. Check that the layers on the image are activated and, as above click **Studio > Adjustment > Channel Mixer**. Next, instead of selecting the flower petals, adjust all layers on the image.

Select **Red** on **the Output Channel**. **Slide Red to the right**, to 153% and **Green to the left,** to -51%. Has the flower on the right turned pink? The Channel Mixer offers dramatic control over specific colors. Refer to the **Channel Mixer** chapter for details.

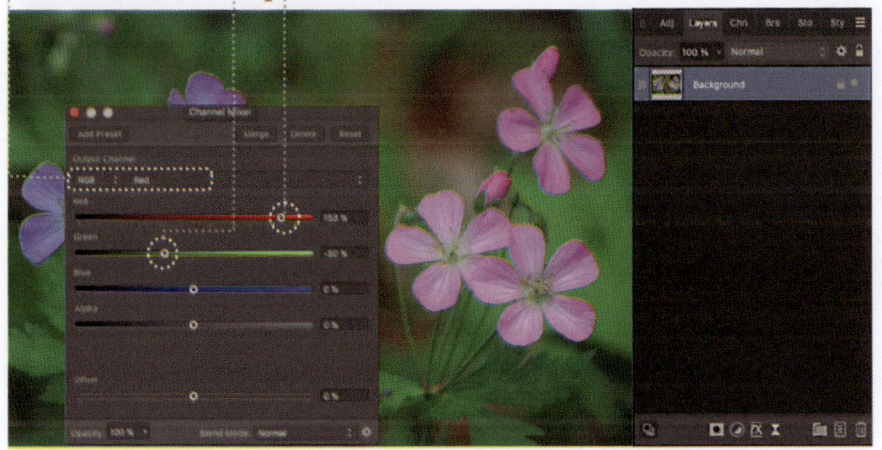

Chapter 16: Create a Slice/Compatible Formats and Export/Configuration

Now that we have fully prepared for Exporting the Slice, click on **Persona Tool Bar** > **Export Persona**. Once the **Tool Panel** is switched, select **Slice Tool** at the very top.

Using the **Slice Tool**, **drag the blue flowers** until the slice is surrounded. Next, add pink flowers around the slice. Under **Studio** on the right, click **Export Options** Click Export Options. Under Preset, select **PNG**.

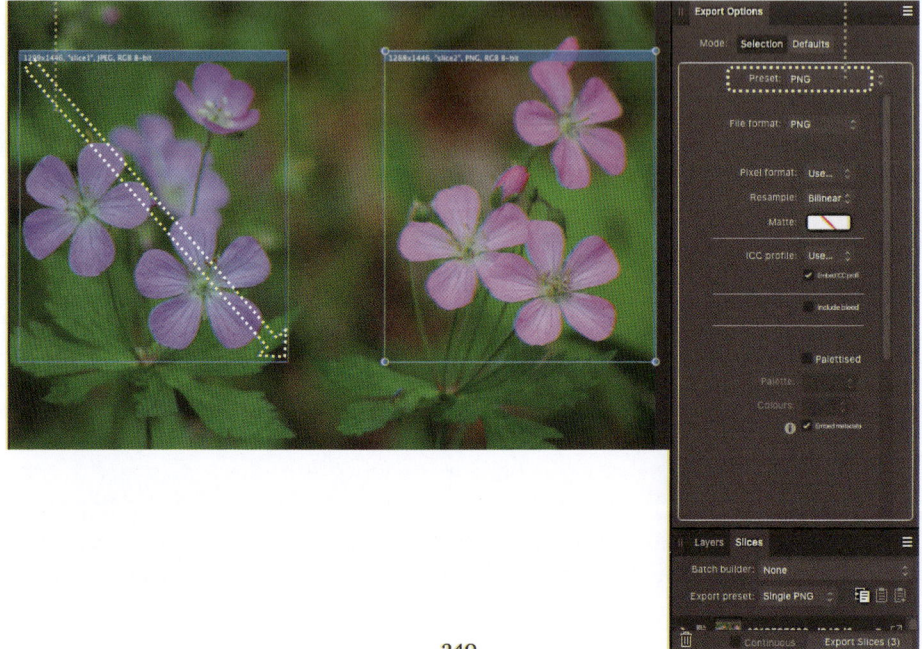

340

Chapter 16: Create a Slice/Compatible Formats and Export/Configuration

## 16_2: Slice Selection Tool

Click **Export Persona > Tool Panel > Slice Selection Tool**, and activate the two slices. This tool is a dedicated **Export Persona Tool**. Next, click **Studio > Slice** tab. Check Slice 1 and Slice 2. Click **Export Slices** and save the file. Have a look at the **Saved** folder to confirm. You've now saved slice 1.png and slice 2.png.

Slice 2.png    slice 1.png

To the right is the Preset dropdown menu. Affinity_Photo is equipped with a wide variety of formats. See subsequent sections regarding export formats.

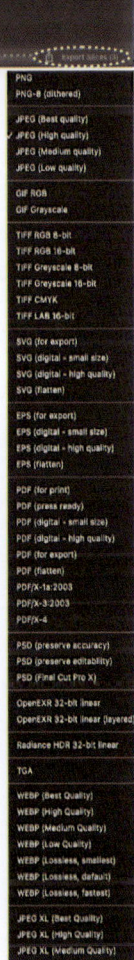

341

Chapter 16: Create a Slice/Compatible Formats and Export/Configuration

## 16_3: Affinity_Photo Export Format

Affinity_Photo is capable of exporting images in a variety of different formats. Click **Menu Bar** > **File** > **Export** to open the Dropdown Menu.

**PNG**

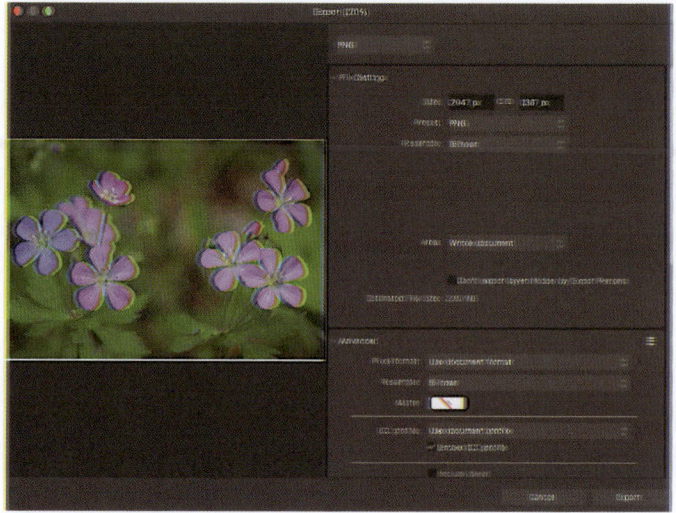

PNG was developed as a format designed for Web images. Under **Preset**, select 256-color PNG-8 (Dithered) and PNG, which can be saved in full color.

**JPEG**

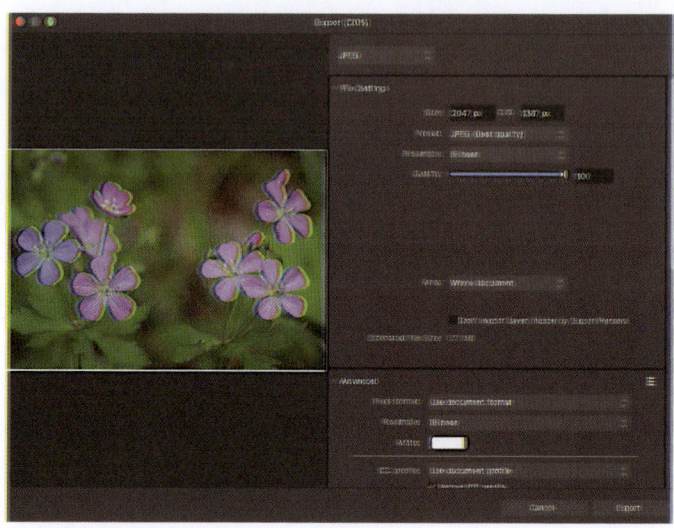

Because it can be used for full color images and also because of its high compression ratio, the JPEG format is broadly utilized with digital cameras. With this format, however, the higher the compression ratio, the lower the image quality. Preset offers four selections: JPEG (Best quality), JPEG (High quality), JPEG( Medium quality), and JPEG (Low quality). Use the slider to adjust the compression ratio.

## GIF

An extremely **low data** capacity format, the GIF offers up to 256 colors. Use **Preset** to select Color GIF RGB and Gray Tone GIF Grayscale.

## TIFF

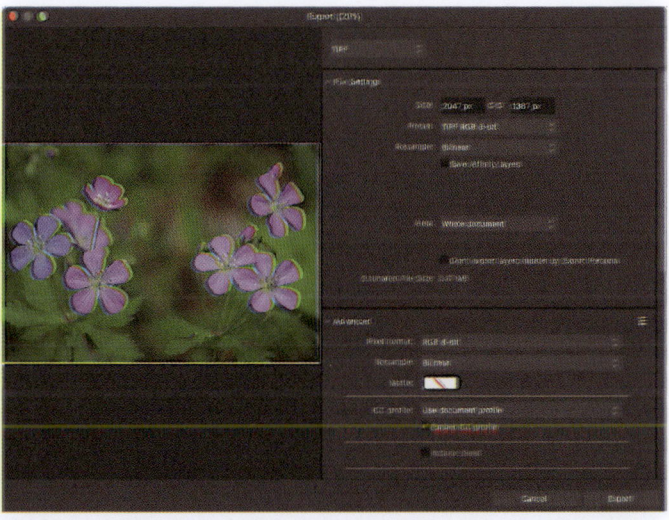

TIFF is a high-capacity file format. Basically it is not used on the Web. Use **Preset** to select TIFF RGB 8-bit, TIFF RGB 16-bit, TIFF Greyscale 8-bit, TIFF Greyscale 16-bit, TIFF CMYK, or TIFF LAB 16-bit.

# Chapter 16: Create a Slice/Compatible Formats and Export/Configuration

**PSD**

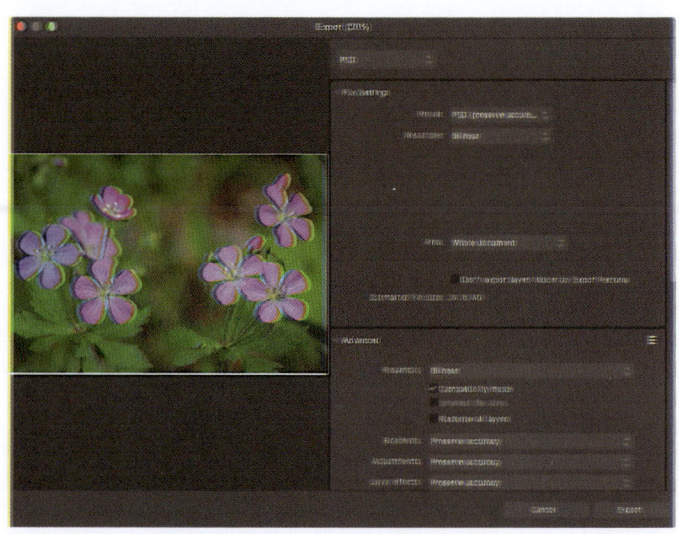

PSD is a general-purpose format used with Photoshop. Under Preset, select PSD (Preserve Accuracy), PSD (Preserve editability), or PSD (Final Cat Pro X).

**PDF**

PDF is a file format used to save images and store images as you would a printed piece of paper. Under Preset, select PDF (for print), PDF (Press ready), PDF (digital-small), PDF (digital-high quality), PDF (flatten), and for printable versions: PDF/X-1a:2003, PDF/X-3:2003, PDF/X-4. Multiple layers are saved from the bottom up.

## SVG

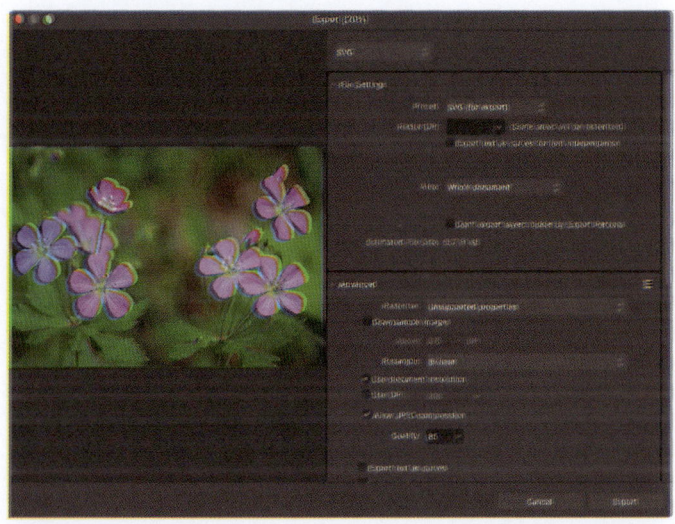

SVG is a Vector Data format, written in XML. It's a general-use format that can be saved using Illustrator. Under Preset, select SVG (for export), SVG (for print), SVG (for web), or SVG (flatten).

## EPS

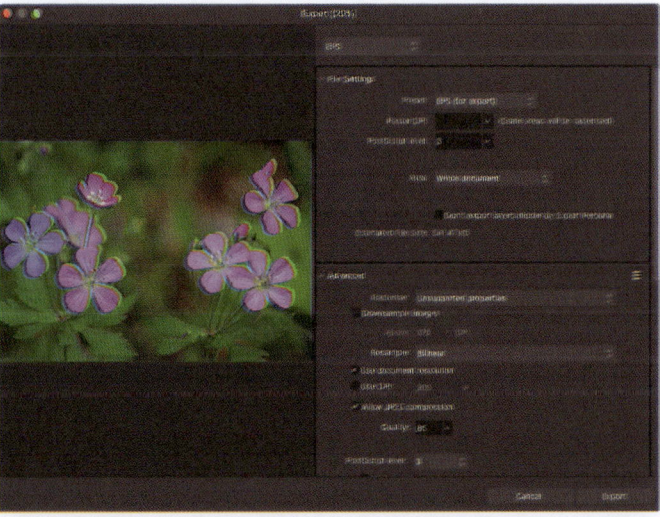

EPS is a general-use format capable of storing Vector Data and Bitmap Data. Under Preset, select EPS (for export), EPS (for print, EPS (for web), or EPS (flatten) to save.

**EXR**

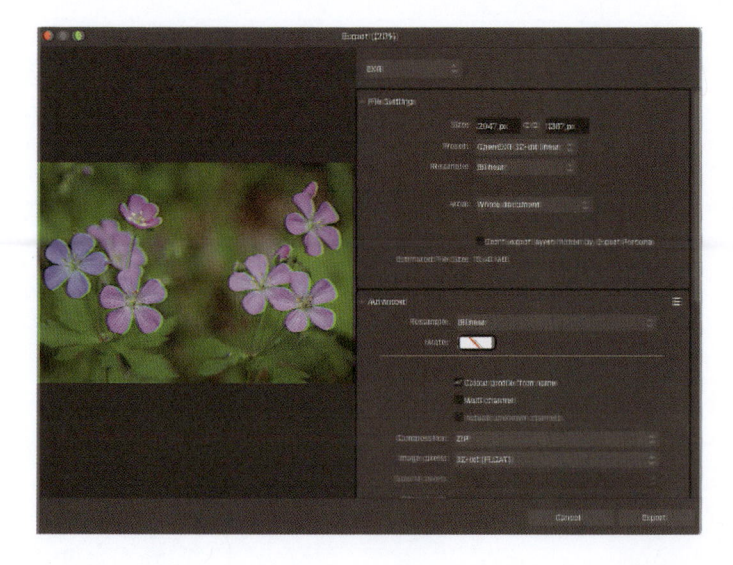

EXR, called **OpenEXR**, is a format capable of storing color data of 24 bits or higher. Under Preset, select Open EXR 32-bit linear or Open EXR 32-bit linear (layered) to save.

**HDR**

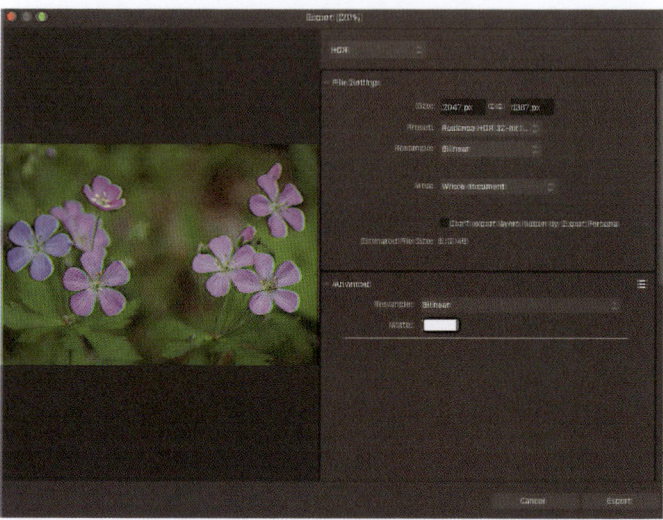

HDR, like EXR, is a format used to store 24-bit or higher color data. Until the subsequent Open EXR was released, this format was the only High Dynamic Range image format. Select the preset Radiance HDR-32 bit liner (Default).

## 16_4: Importing to Affinity Photo

Affinity_Photo can import the following file formats.

## File type Open

| |
|---|
| Adobe Illustrator(AI) |
| Adobe Freehand(10 and MX) |
| Adobe PhotoShop(PSD) |
| Adobe PhotoShop(PSB) |
| DNG |
| EPS |
| GIF |
| HEIF |
| JPEG |
| J2K JP2 |
| JPEG-XR/JXR(WDP/HDP) |
| PDF |
| PNG |
| RAW |
| SVG |
| TGA |
| TIFF |
| WEBP |
| OpenEXR |
| Radiance HDR |
| FITS |

Affinity is a register trademark of Serif(Europe)_Ltd.
"Illustrator" and "Photoshop" are registered trademarks of Adobe Systems Incorporated in the U.S. and other countries.

Profile of Leslie Higley:

Leslie C. Higley graduated from the American University School of International Service in Washington D.C. with a B.A. in Economics and International Relations and a minor in Asian Studies/Japanese Language. Having resided in Japan for a total of two decades, Leslie has worked as a Japanese-English translator and interpreter for 25 years, translating a wide array of subject matter ranging from Buddhist texts to business presentations, new products and technologies, fashion magazines, tourism campaign materials, and executive speeches for high-profile corporations such as Toyota and Panasonic. During this time she has collaborated with the top American copywriters working in Tokyo for leading companies. She passed the highest level (Level I) of the Japanese Proficiency Test, an internationally recognized certification, in 1997.


Profile of Akira Kuwahara:

President and computer programmer/designer
Akira Kuwahara worked for an extensive period of time as Art Director and Interactive Producer at HAKUHODO Inc., one of Japan's premier advertising agencies. Upon retiring from HAKUHODO, he launched GAME-INDEX.net Co., Ltd., a company specializing in interactive business models, application software, etc., specifically targeted for advertising promotion and campaigns. He has received numerous awards for his creative advertising and digital work.


The Affinity Photo Instant Professional
Compatible with Mac and Windows
February 2023
1st Edition
Authors: Akira Kuwahara and Leslie Higley
Binding and Design: Akira Kuwahara
Publisher: Akira Kuwahara, GAME-INDEX.net Co., Ltd.

Reproduction of this book, in whole or in part, without prior permission is strictly prohibited. Any said reproduction is considered a copyright infringement, except where required by law.
All efforts have been made on the part of the authors to ensure that this volume contains no mistakes. However, please note that the authors and publisher take no responsibility whatsoever for any damages incurred as a result of using this book.

Printed in Great Britain
by Amazon